More Acclaim for *We Were Soldiers Once . . . and Young*

"Between experiencing combat and reading it lies a vast chasm. But this book makes you almost smell it."

—*Wall Street Journal*

"It's not just a war story, it's a love story . . . war at its most terrible and glorious, exemplary heroism, desperate sacrifice, relentless suffering. Powerfully written and superbly researched."

—*Chicago Tribune*

"Heroes stride across the pages. A revelation. There are stories here that freeze the blood. . . . The men who fought at Ia Drang could have no finer memorial than this one."

—*New York Time Book Review*

"An epic story that minces not a word in its relentlessly honest rendering. It will stun those whose knowledge of war has been shaped mainly by military briefings staged by the brass far to the rear and well out of harm's way."

—*Pacific Stars and Stripes*

"If you want to know what it was really like to go to Vietnam as a young American . . . and find yourself caught in ferocious, remorseless combat with an enemy as courageous and idealistic as you were, then you must read this book. . . . A minute-by-minute, hour-by-hour account of the opening battle of the war that reads with the mesmerizing swiftness of combat. Hal Moore and Joe Galloway have captured the terror and exhilaration, the comradeship and self-sacrifice, the brutality and compassion that are the dark heart of war."

—Neil Sheehan

"Did you ever wonder where *the* classic book of battle of the Vietnam War was? Here it is, and finally—a book about Vietnam that is not ideology but tragic heroism of the highest caliber, a book that makes us understand not politics but life."

—Georgie Anne Geyer

"A remarkable book."

—Lewis Puller, Jr.

"The best contribution yet to the growing collection of literature that attempts to understand the Vietnam War."

—*Atlanta Journal-Constitution*

Lt. Gen. Harold G. Moore, USA (Ret.) and Joseph L. Galloway

■ HarperPerennial
A Division of HarperCollins*Publishers*

WE WERE SOLDIERS ONCE . . . AND YOUNG

IA DRANG: THE BATTLE THAT CHANGED THE WAR IN VIETNAM

Grateful acknowledgment is made to the following for permission to reprint previously published material:

ARMOR MAGAZINE: Excerpt from "Company B" by Major Walter B. Tully, Jr., from the September/October 1967 issue of *Armor* magazine. Reprinted by permission of *Armor* magazine.

HOUGHTON MIFFLIN COMPANY AND DEAN BRELIS: Excerpt from *The Face of South Vietnam* by Dean Brelis and Jill Krementz. Text copyright © 1967 by Dean Brelis. Reprinted by permission of Houghton Mifflin Company and Dean Brelis.

ST. MARTIN'S PRESS: Excerpt from *Pleiku: The Dawn of Helicopter Warfare in Vietnam* by J. D. Coleman. Copyright © 1989 by J. D. Coleman. Reprinted by permission.

Title page and part title photos: Peter Arnett/AP/Wide World Photos; U.S. Army photo; Joseph L. Galloway; Rick Merron/AP/Wide World Photos; Linda L. Creighton.

A hardcover edition of this book was published in 1992 by Random House, Inc. It is here reprinted by arrangement with Random House, Inc.

HarperCollins books may be purchased for educational, business, or sales promotional use. For information please write: Special Markets Department, HarperCollins Publishers, Inc., 10 East 53rd Street, New York, NY 10022.

First HarperPerennial edition published 1993.

Library of Congress Cataloging-in-Publication Data
Moore, Harold G., 1922–
    We were soldiers once . . . and young : Ia Drang, the battle that changed
    the war in Vietnam / Harold G. Moore and Joseph L. Galloway.
    — 1st HarperPerennial ed.
        p. cm.
    Originally published : New York : Random House, 1992.
    Includes bibliographical references and index.
    ISBN 0-06-097576-8 (paper)
    1. Ia Drang Valley (Vietnam), Battle of, 1965.   I. Title.
DS557.8.I18M663   1993
959.704′342—dc20   93-15836

93 94 95 96 97 CC / CW 10 9 8 7 6 5 4 3 2 1

Dedicated to the memory of these brave soldiers who gave their lives for their country and for the men who fought beside them in the Pleiku campaign in October and November 1965:

1st Battalion, 7th Cavalry

Headquarters Company

THOMAS C. METSKER
Indianapolis, Indiana

WILLIAM B. MITCHELL
Chester, Pennsylvania

CALVIN BOUKNIGHT
Washington, D.C.

Alpha Company

JACK E. GELL
Montmorenci, South Carolina

ROBERT E. TAFT
Highland Park, Illinois

BILLY R. ELLIOTT
Heavener, Oklahoma

RAMON BERNARD
Mayagüez, Puerto Rico

TRAVIS O. POSS
Brook Park, Ohio

ALEXANDER WILLIAMS
Jacksonville, Florida

RAFAEL A. BERLANGA
New York, New York

ALBERT WITCHER
Pittsylvania, Virginia

JOHN F. BRENNAN
Braddock, Pennsylvania

GAIL L. DAVIS
Nottinghill, Missouri

ROBERT L. MOORE
Montgomery, Alabama

Bravo Company

HENRY T. HERRICK
Laguna Beach, California

CARL L. PALMER
Pelham, Georgia

WILBUR CURRY, JR.
Buffalo, New York

ROBERT L. STOKES
Salt Lake City, Utah

BERNARD BIRENBAUM
New York, New York

JOHNNIE L. BOSWELL
Eatonton, Georgia

DOMINIC A. DE ANGELIS
Cambria Heights, New York

ROBERT M. HILL
Starkville, Mississippi

DONALD B. RODDY
Ann Arbor, Michigan

PAUL E. HURDLE
Washington, D.C.

JAMES R. HINES
Chicago, Illinois

RICHARD C. CLARK
Kankakee, Illinois

Charlie Company

JOHN L. GEOGHEGAN
Redding, Connecticut

NEIL A. KROGER
Oak Park, Illinois

THOMAS J. BARRETT, JR.
Many, Louisiana

ANTONIO BERNARD-ROBLES
New York, New York

SIDNEY COHEN
Camden, New Jersey

ABRAHAM L. FIELDS
Spring Lake, North Carolina

JEREMIAH JIVENS
Savannah, Georgia

ROY LOCKHART
Vallejo, California

PARIS D. DUSCH
Carrollton, Kentucky

CARL E. HARRIS
Rock Hill, South Carolina

CHARLES E. HERRINGTON
Texas City, Texas

HERMON R. HOSTUTTLER
Terra Alta, West Virginia

JAMES D. SMITH
Altoona, Alabama

REGINALD A. WATKINS
Charlotte, North Carolina

NATHANIEL BYRD
Jacksonville, Florida

LEON C. CHASE, JR.
St. Augustine, Florida

ROBERT A. DAVIS
Oxford, Pennsylvania

RONALD D. FERGUSON
San Francisco, California

GEORGE FOXE
Rocky Mount, North Carolina

EARL C. GRAHAM
Charleston, South Carolina

BOBBY JOE HAMES
Blacksburg, South Carolina

DONALD L. HARRISON
Rockport, Indiana

DOUGLAS H. LEACH
Atlanta, Georgia

ROBERT L. LEWIS
Hopewell, Virginia

DONNELL PHILLIPS
Smithville, Texas

EDDIE L. POUGH
Columbus, Georgia

ALBERT W. SONNIER
Baytown, Texas

THOMAS E. TUCKER
Richton, Mississippi

WILLIAM T. VICTORY
Weirwood, Virginia

IVORY WARD, JR.
St. Louis, Missouri

DAVID J. CARNEVALE
Woodside, California

RALPH W. CARTWRIGHT
Virginia Beach, Virginia

CHARLES H. COLLIER
Mount Pleasant, Texas

WILLIE F. GODBOLDT
Jacksonville, Florida

JOHN E. HIGMAN
Bellingham, Washington

SAMUEL L. MCDONALD
Harrisburg, Pennsylvania

LEONARD W. SRAL
Hastings, Pennsylvania

RICHARD TESTA
New York, New York

LUTHER V. GILREATH
Surgoinsville, Tennessee

RICHARD B. BRADLEY
Wampsville, New York

FRED D. WITCHET
Houston, Texas

THOMAS C. PIZZINO
Hopedale, Ohio

Delta Company

GILBERT NICKLAS
Niagara Falls, New York

ROBERT GOMEZ
Los Angeles, California

HILARIO DE LA PAZ, JR.
Houston, Texas

2nd Battalion, 7th Cavalry

Headquarters Company

THOMAS E. BURLILE
London, Ohio

HAROLD D. MCCARN
Lexington, North Carolina

CHARLES W. BASS
Winterset, Iowa

MELVIN W. GUNTER
Vincent, Alabama

CHARLES W. STOREY
Birmingham, Alabama

FRED H. JENKINS
Frogmore, South Carolina

CHARLES T. MOORE, JR.
Columbus, Ohio

DONALD C. PETERSON
Chicago, Illinois

CHARLIE ANDERS
Leckie, West Virginia

CHARLES A. COLLINS
Holly Springs, North Carolina

GERALD A. KOSAKOWSKI
Lincoln Park, Michigan

DAVID L. MENDOZA
Cleveland, Ohio

WILLIAM A. PLEASANT
Jersey City, New Jersey

ELWOOD W. DAVIS, JR.
Salineville, Ohio

JAMES E. HOLDEN
Millsboro, Delaware

ALPHA R. JACKSON
Houston, Texas

KENNETH C. BOLICH
Auburn, Pennsylvania

Alpha Company

WILLIAM A. FERRELL
Stanton, Tennessee

JAMES L. FISHER
Dallas, Texas

LEROY IRELAND
Athens, Georgia

MEGDELIO
CARABALLO-GARCIA
Yauco, Puerto Rico

RONALD R. MARTIN
Erie, Pennsylvania

GLENN E. MCCAMMON
Woodsfield, Ohio

PAUL E. TOLBERT
Williams, Indiana

LAVINE J. BANKS
New Orleans, Louisiana

GERALD B. EVANS
Junction City, Kansas

THOMAS JAMES
Jamaica, New York

WILBERT H. JOHNSON
Morgantown, West Virginia

ROGER A. STONE
Parish, Alabama

NEOPOLIS WIGFALL
Fruitland, Maryland

OSCAR BARKER, JR.
Matter, Georgia

ROLLIE L. BOLDEN
Albany, Oregon

BARRY T. BURNITE
Springfield, Pennsylvania

CHARLES E. COX
Lexington, Alabama

JERRY A. HIEMER
Memphis, Tennessee

RAMON KUILAN-OLIVERAS
Bayamon, Puerto Rico

MICHAEL MILLER
Peru, Indiana

ROBERT S. SHRIVER, JR.
Eugene, Oregon

MIGUEL D. VERA-DURAN
San Sebastian, Puerto Rico

GORDON P. YOUNG
Drakes Branch, Virginia

JIMMIE W. BARTON
Onaka, South Dakota

DENNIS W. BLACK
Laotto, Indiana

THOMAS G. BRANDES
Silver Lake, Wisconsin

WILLIAM R. BURTON, JR.
Orange, New Jersey

DANNY E. CARLTON
Greenfield, Tennessee

TOMMY A. DOAK
Cincinnati, Ohio

OTIS J. HAMPTON
New York, New York

HENRY T. LUNA
Fresno, California

JULIO MORALES-GONZALES
Aguada, Puerto Rico

GUY L. SCHAEFFER
Deptford, New Jersey

JOHN A. SHAW
Rising Fawn, Georgia

Bravo Company

CHARLES V. MCMANUS
Woodland, Alabama

ELIAS ALVAREZ-BUZO
Ponce, Puerto Rico

EDDIE BROWN, JR.
Macon, Georgia

RICHARD T. YOUNG
Hildebran, North Carolina

Charlie Company

EARL D. AULL
New Orleans, Louisiana

RONALD A. MILLER
Wichita Falls, Texas

HARRY F. JEDRZEJEWSKI
Pittsburgh, Pennsylvania

CLARENCE V. BEVERHOUDT
St. Thomas, Virgin Islands

DONALD C. CORNETT
Lake Charles, Louisiana

ROGER T. NELSON
Barrett, Minnesota

RICHARD D. OTT
Baltimore, Maryland

CECIL W. KITTLE, JR.
Huttonsville, West Virginia

ARTHUR R. MOODY III
St. Petersburg, Florida

AUGUSTIN C. PAREDEZ
Big Spring, Texas

GEORGE A. WILSON
Cartersville, Georgia

CHARLES T. STEINER
Cardiff, Maryland

KENNETH E. R. BURCH
Samson, Alabama

JORDEN D. FORRESTER
Tulsa, Oklahoma

PHILIP HOWELL
Parrot, Virginia

CARL M. HUME
Fresno, California

DEAN A. JACKSON
Morning Sun, Iowa

JAMES C. JACKSON
Oil Springs, Kentucky

JOSEPH S. LA FASO
Garfield, New Jersey

GARRETT F. LEE
Chicago, Illinois

GEORGE S. MCHELLON
Atlanta, Georgia

DARRELL W. SANDERS
Wayne, West Virginia

ROBERT POSIUS
Detroit, Michigan

RICHARD P. SAWICKI
Grand Island, Nebraska

HAROLD SCOTT
New York, New York

FINIS R. STUDDARD
Steele, Alabama

DAVID M. VANCELLETTE
Oxford, Massachusetts

ROBERT E. WALDVOGEL
St. Paul, Minnesota

BRIAN F. CARLQUIST
Draper, Utah

RUBEN G. CHAVEZ
Robstown, Texas

BUREN R. DAVIS
Muskogee, Oklahoma

ROBERT L. DAVIS
Providence, Kentucky

JOSEPH R. HILLARD
Bay City, Texas

WAYNE T. LUNDELL
Silver Spring, Maryland

ROBERT MORENO
Los Angeles, California

SHERMAN E. OTIS
Mobile, Alabama

LOUIS D. RICHARDSON
Biloxi, Mississippi

ROY L. RYSE, JR.
Inglewood, California

ROGER A. SIMRAU
Gladwin, Michigan

MICHAEL T. SMITH
New York, New York

GEORGE J. STEPHENS
Camden, New Jersey

ERNEST E. TAYLOR
Kaycee, Wyoming

BOBBY C. VINSON
Jackson, Tennessee

MACK A. WARE
Bessemer, Alabama

RONALD H. CHITTUM
Vinton, Virginia

DAVID W. MICHAEL
Oelwein, Iowa

FRANK J. NOSTADT, JR.
Philadelphia, Pennsylvania

Delta Company

MARTIN C. KNAPP
Wheeling, West Virginia

OSVALDO AMODIAS
Miami, Florida

BERNARD CREED
Medford, Massachusetts

JAMES W. ERVIN
Gilroy, California

PALMER B. MILES
Columbus, Georgia

LLOYD J. MONSEWICZ
Jacksonville, Florida

EARTHELL TYLER
Columbia, South Carolina

ISMAEL J. PAREDES
Jersey City, New Jersey

SNYDER P. BEMBRY
Unadilla, Georgia

RALPH W. BROWN
Benton, Pennsylvania

DONALD E. CRANE
Stillwater, Pennsylvania

JAMES R. DRAGOTI
New York, New York

CHARLES L. ELLER
Warrensville, North Carolina

FREDERICK C. HERIAUD
Oswego, Illinois

REYNALDO C. HERNANDEZ
Tulare, California

DUNCAN F. KRUEGER
West Allis, Wisconsin

JACK D. LYNN
Hillard, Ohio

ROGER E. MERCK
Salem, South Carolina

HOWARD G. RILEY
Philadelphia, Pennsylvania

JOHN SCHLECHT III
New York, New York

MATTHEWS SHELTON
Cincinnati, Ohio

EDWARD L. SIMMONS
LaFayette, Georgia

GARY D. SMITH
Knoxville, Tennessee

JOHN H. WOODY
Suches, Georgia

JOSEPH M. WORKMAN
Peoria, Illinois

LESTER R. BECKER
Harvard, Illinois

1st Battalion, 5th Cavalry

Alpha Company

LARRY L. HESS
Gettysburg, Pennsylvania

CLAYTON G. ROGERS
Bridgeport, Alabama

NORMAN W. SOLTOW
Chicago, Illinois

JAMES O. VAUGHAN
Baltimore, Maryland

ROBERT G. WRIGHT
Youngstown, Ohio

RONNIE T. MATHIS
Atlanta, Georgia

HENRY F. SMITH
Albemarle, North Carolina

JOHN R. ACKERMAN
Gary, Indiana

FRANCISCO CONCEPCION, JR.
Kilauea, Hawaii

RALPH H. ERNST
St. Louis, Missouri

JIMMY HARRIS
Beattyville, Kentucky

ROBERT L. HIRST
Allentown, Pennsylvania

MARVIN SCHALIPP, JR.
Leavenworth, Kansas

JERELL L. GRAYSON
Duke, Missouri

VINCENT LOCATELLI
Santa Cruz, California

JESSE N. RODRIGUEZ
Houston, Texas

EUGENE C. SCOTT
St. Louis, Missouri

Bravo Company

MACK C. COX
Tampa, Florida

DALE F. HUDSON
Poplar Bluff, Missouri

JIMMY F. BOREN
Cadiz, Kentucky

Charlie Company

OSCAR E. COOPER
Bel Air, Maryland

Delta Company

WILLIAM J. LINDSEY
Augusta, Georgia

2nd Battalion, 5th Cavalry

Charlie Company

RICHARD D. BRODA
Portsmouth, Virginia

2nd Battalion, 19th Artillery

C Battery

EDWARD JOUJON-ROCHE
Bakersfield, California

1st Battalion, 21st Artillery

A Battery

FLOYD L. REED, JR.
Heth, Arkansas

HARLEY D. BECKWORTH
Baxley, Georgia

B Battery

SIDNEY C. M. SMITH
Manhasset, New York

MELVIN F. FORT
Memphis, Tennessee

JOSEPH P. MARA
Belwood, Illinois

C Battery

TIMOTHY M. BLAKE
Charleston, West Virginia

227th Assault Helicopter Battalion

Delta Company

HAROLD E. WILKINS
Vale, North Carolina

229th Assault Helicopter Battalion

Bravo Company

VIRGIL KIRKLAND, JR.
Chattanooga, Tennessee

JAMES W. MAYES
Mill Hall, Pennsylvania

RALPH A. COPELAND
Minot, North Dakota

Charlie Company

HERMAN L. JEFFERSON, JR.
New Orleans, Louisiana

8th Engineer Battalion

RUSSELL E. HAMMOND
Pittsburgh, Pennsylvania

ARLEN C. TUTTLE
Fort Campbell, Kentucky

HOOVER MORRIS
Lufkin, Texas

SCOTT O. HENRY
Commodore, Pennsylvania

JIMMY D. NAKAYAMA
Rigby, Idaho

United States Air Force

1st Air Commando Squadron

PAUL T. MCCLELLAN, JR.
West Stayton, Oregon

1st Squadron, 9th Cavalry

Headquarters Troop

CHARLES R. DAVIS, JR.
Cincinnati, Ohio

Alpha Troop

JAMES HOOVER
Kingston, Ohio

ALTON E. BAKER
Salinas, California

JESUS R. BERMUDEZ
Mendota, California

Bravo Troop

DANIEL D. HARDEN
Memphis, Tennessee

Charlie Troop

JAMES R. PARRETT
Columbia City, Indiana

FLORENDO B. PASCUAL
Honolulu, Hawaii

BENEDICTO P. BAYRON
Waianae, Hawaii

BILLY J. TALLEY
McCrory, Arkansas

JAMES L. RILEY
Vienna, West Virginia

BILLY M. KNIGHT
Ganado, Arizona

Delta Troop

THOMAS D. DUNCAN
Attalla, Alabama

1st Battalion, 8th Cavalry

Alpha Company

SAMUEL BESS
Sanford, North Carolina

TOMMIE KEETON
Huntsville, Tennessee

THEOPHILOS ORPHANOS
New York, New York

GARY W. PLATT
Boulder, Colorado

Delta Company

GUNDER P. GUNDERSON
Walhalla, North Dakota

RICHARD E. GEORGE
San Diego, California

2nd Battalion, 8th Cavalry

Headquarters Company

JAMES L. ALLEN
Beaumont, Texas

RICHARD A. NOELKE
Fontana, California

Alpha Company

DENNIS L. LONG
Chicago, Illinois

JAMES H. JARZENSKI
Cochranton, Pennsylvania

ALAN L. BARNETT
Astoria, Oregon

CARL S. DANIELS
New Orleans, Louisiana

RONALD H. LUKE
Miami, Florida

FRED MOORE, JR.
Sharpsville, Indiana

Bravo Company

CHARLES W. ROSE
Wye Mills, Maryland

GEZA TEGLAS
Washington, D.C.

FELIX D. KING, JR.
Florence, Alabama

RALPH N. SMITH
Morganton, North Carolina

WILLIAM A. SULLIVAN
Fayetteville, North Carolina

RUDOLPH RODRIGUEZ
Lindsay, California

CLYDE R. HERMAN
Roanoke, Virginia

EARL G. PHILLIPS
War, West Virginia

JAMES J. CRAFTON
Philadelphia, Pennsylvania

Charlie Company

MORRIS E. WHEELER
Philadelphia, Pennsylvania

JAMES W. BARKSDALE
St. Petersburg, Florida

MILES H. LOPER, JR.
Fort Knox, Kentucky

VARIS SAVAGE, JR.
Nashville, Tennessee

LEWIS SHERROD
Washington, D.C.

DENNIS LICHOTA
Detroit, Michigan

TIMOTHY B. JOHNSON
Milwaukee, Wisconsin

JOHN K. KEAO III
Los Angeles, California

JUSTIN M. LYNCH
Fort Bragg, North Carolina

THOMAS H. MAYNARD
El Monte, California

JOSEPH P. MINNOCK
Cranford, New Jersey

JAMES MOONEY
Selma, Alabama

ANTHONY E. PENDOLA
Peoria, Illinois

WILLIE C. PICKETT
Pensacola, Florida

PHILLIP K. REA
Chicago, Illinois

DANIEL SANTOS-TRUJILLO
Loiza, Puerto Rico

ALVIN C. SLIGH
Greensboro, North Carolina

Delta Company

RICHARD A. COFFEY
Los Angeles, California

EDDIE L. HILL, JR.
Mobile, Alabama

WRIGHT B. HAMILL
Albany, Oregon

1st Battalion, 12th Cavalry

Alpha Company

NEIL R. HANS
Muncy, Pennsylvania

Delta Company

RALPH W. ONANA
Los Angeles, California

RODNEY C. HARRIS
Jacksonville, Florida

JAMES V. POTTKOTTER
New Weston, Ohio

2nd Battalion, 12th Cavalry

Headquarters Company

ROBERT A. TILLQUIST
New Haven, Connecticut

Alpha Company

CARRIER PIERRE
New York, New York

Bravo Company

CHARLES C. COX
High Point, North Carolina

WALTER B. OLIVER
Newark, Ohio

LARIS WHITE, JR.
Bonifay, Florida

RONALD J. LOERLEIN
Pittsburgh, Pennsylvania

Headquarters, 3rd Brigade

DAVE MAYES, JR.
Jonesville, Louisiana

CONTENTS

A section of photographs follows page 224.

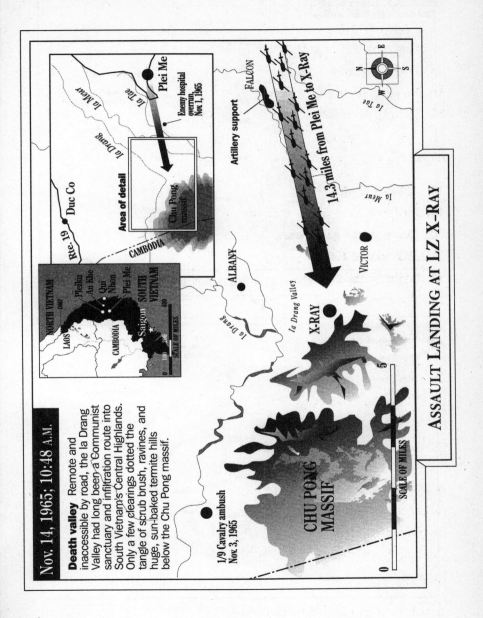

ASSAULT LANDING AT LZ X-RAY

Nov. 14, 1965; 10:48 A.M.

Death valley Remote and inaccessible by road, the Ia Drang Valley had long been a Communist sanctuary and infiltration route into South Vietnam's Central Highlands. Only a few clearings dotted the tangle of scrub brush, ravines, and huge, sun-baked termite hills below the Chu Pong massif.

Area of detail

Plei Me

Enemy hospital overrun, Nov. 1, 1965

Ia Tae

Ia Meur

Ia Drang

Duc Co

Rte. 19

CAMBODIA

Chu Pong massif

FALCON

Artillery support

14.3 miles from Plei Me to X-Ray

Ia Tae

Ia Meur

VICTOR

ALBANY

Ia Drang

Ia Drang Valley

X-RAY

CHU PONG MASSIF

1/9 Cavalry ambush
Nov. 3, 1965

SCALE OF MILES
0   5

N E S W

NORTH VIETNAM
DMZ
LAOS
Pleiku
An Khe
Qui Nhon
Plei Me
SOUTH VIETNAM
Saigon
CAMBODIA
SCALE OF MILES
0   100   200   300   400

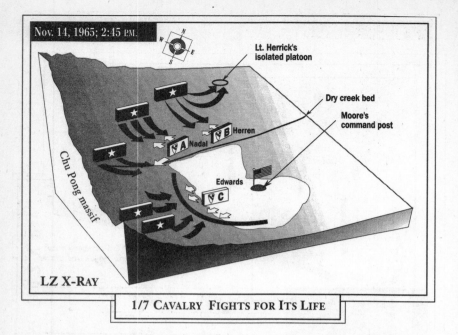

N
W · E
S

Lt. Herrick's
isolated platoon

Dry creek bed

Moore's
command post

Chu Pong massif

A Nadal

B Herren

Edwards

C

LZ X-RAY

1/7 CAVALRY FIGHTS FOR ITS LIFE

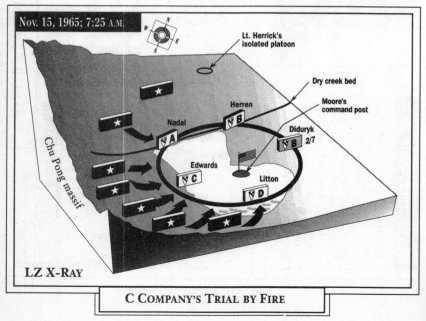

Nov. 15, 1965; 7:25 A.M.

N
W · E
S

Lt. Herrick's
isolated platoon

Dry creek bed

Moore's
command post

Chu Pong massif

Nadal

A

Herren

B

Diduryk 2/7

B

Edwards

C

Litton

D

LZ X-RAY

C COMPANY'S TRIAL BY FIRE

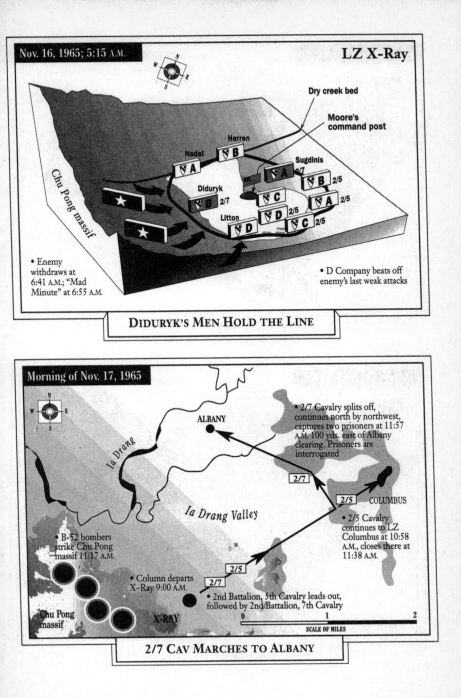

Nov. 16, 1965; 5:15 A.M.

LZ X-Ray

Dry creek bed

Moore's command post

Chu Pong massif

Herren **B**

Nadal **A**

Sugdinis **A** 2/7

B 2/5

Diduryk **B** 2/7

C

A 2/5

Litton **D**

D 2/5

C 2/5

• Enemy withdraws at 6:41 A.M.; "Mad Minute" at 6:55 A.M.

• D Company beats off enemy's last weak attacks

DIDURYK'S MEN HOLD THE LINE

Morning of Nov. 17, 1965

ALBANY

Ia Drang

Ia Drang Valley

• 2/7 Cavalry splits off, continues north by northwest, captures two prisoners at 11:57 A.M. 100 yds. east of Albany clearing. Prisoners are interrogated

2/7

2/5 COLUMBUS

• 2/5 Cavalry continues to LZ Columbus at 10:58 A.M., closes there at 11:38 A.M.

• B-52 bombers strike Chu Pong massif 11:17 A.M.

2/5

2/7

• Column departs X-Ray 9:00 A.M.

• 2nd Battalion, 5th Cavalry leads out, followed by 2nd Battalion, 7th Cavalry

Chu Pong massif

X-RAY

0   1   2

SCALE OF MILES

2/7 CAV MARCHES TO ALBANY

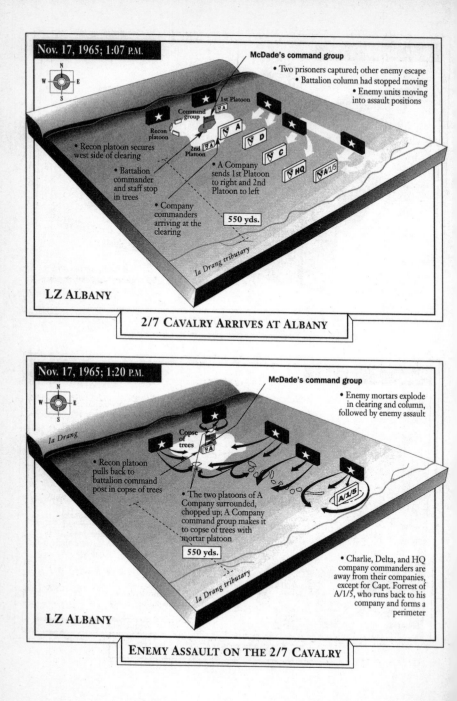

Nov. 17, 1965; 1:07 P.M.

N W S E

McDade's command group

- Two prisoners captured; other enemy escape
- Battalion column had stopped moving
- Enemy units moving into assault positions

1st Platoon
Command group
Recon platoon
2nd Platoon

- Recon platoon secures west side of clearing
- Battalion commander and staff stop in trees
- Company commanders arriving at the clearing

- A Company sends 1st Platoon to right and 2nd Platoon to left

550 yds.

Ia Drang tributary

LZ ALBANY

2/7 CAVALRY ARRIVES AT ALBANY

Nov. 17, 1965; 1:20 P.M.

N W S E

McDade's command group

- Enemy mortars explode in clearing and column, followed by enemy assault

Ia Drang

Copse of trees

- Recon platoon pulls back to battalion command post in copse of trees

- The two platoons of A Company surrounded, chopped up; A Company command group makes it to copse of trees with mortar platoon

550 yds.

A/1/5

- Charlie, Delta, and HQ company commanders are away from their companies, except for Capt. Forrest of A/1/5, who runs back to his company and forms a perimeter

Ia Drang tributary

LZ ALBANY

ENEMY ASSAULT ON THE 2/7 CAVALRY

PROLOGUE

In thy faint slumbers I by thee have watch'd
And heard thee murmur tales of iron wars . . .

—Shakespeare, *Henry IV, Part One,* Act II, Scene 3

This story is about time and memories. The time was 1965, a different kind of year, a watershed year when one era was ending in America and another was beginning. We felt it then, in the many ways our lives changed so suddenly, so dramatically, and looking back on it from a quarter-century gone we are left in no doubt. It was the year America decided to directly intervene in the Byzantine affairs of obscure and distant Vietnam. It was the year we went to war. In the broad, traditional sense, that "we" who went to war was all of us, all Americans, though in truth at that time the larger majority had little knowledge of, less interest in, and no great concern with what was beginning so far away.

So this story is about the smaller, more tightly focused "we" of that sentence: the first American combat troops, who boarded World War II–era troopships, sailed to that little-known place, and fought the first major battle of a conflict that would drag on for ten long years and come as near to destroying America as it did to destroying Vietnam.

The Ia Drang campaign was to the Vietnam War what the terrible Spanish Civil War of the 1930s was to World War II: a dress rehearsal; the place where new tactics, techniques, and weapons were tested, perfected, and validated. In the Ia Drang, both sides claimed victory and both sides drew lessons, some of them dangerously deceptive, which echoed and resonated throughout the decade of bloody fighting and bitter sacrifice that was to come.

This is about what we did, what we saw, what we suffered in a thirty-four-day campaign in the Ia Drang Valley of the Central Highlands of South Vietnam in November 1965, when we were young and confident and patriotic and our countrymen knew little and cared less about our sacrifices.

Another war story, you say? Not exactly, for on the more important levels this is a love story, told in our own words and by our own actions. We were the children of the 1950s and we went where we were sent because we loved our country. We were draftees, most of us, but we were proud of the opportunity to serve that country just as our fathers had served in World War II and our older brothers in Korea. We were members of an elite, experimental combat division trained in the new art of airmobile warfare at the behest of President John F. Kennedy.

Just before we shipped out to Vietnam the Army handed us the colors of the historic 1st Cavalry Division and we all proudly sewed on the big yellow-and-black shoulder patches with the horsehead silhouette. We went to war because our country asked us to go, because our new President, Lyndon B. Johnson, ordered us to go, but more importantly because we saw it as our duty to go. That is one kind of love.

Another and far more transcendent love came to us unbidden on the battlefields, as it does on every battlefield in every war man has ever fought. We discovered in that depressing, hellish place, where death was our constant companion, that we loved each other. We killed for each other, we died for each other, and we wept for each other. And in time we came to love each other as brothers. In battle our world shrank to the man on our left and the man on our right and the enemy all around. We held each other's lives in our hands and we learned to share our fears, our hopes, our dreams as readily as we shared what little else good came our way.

We were the children of the 1950s and John F. Kennedy's young stalwarts of the early 1960s. He told the world that Americans would "pay any price, bear any burden, meet any hardship" in the defense of freedom. We were the down payment on that costly contract, but the man who signed it was not there when we fulfilled his promise. John F. Kennedy waited for us on a hill in Arlington National Cemetery, and in time we came by the thousands to fill those slopes with our white marble markers and to ask on the murmur of the wind if that was truly the future he had envisioned for us.

Among us were old veterans, grizzled sergeants who had fought in Europe and the Pacific in World War II and had survived the frozen hell of Korea, and now were about to add another star to their Combat Infantryman's Badge. There were regular-army enlistees, young men from America's small towns whose fathers told them they would learn discipline and become real men in the Army. There were other young men who chose the Army over an equal term in prison. Alternative sentencing, the judges call it now. But the majority were draftees, nineteen- and twenty-year-old boys summoned from all across America by their local Selective Service Boards to do their two years in green. The PFCs soldiered for $99.37 a month; the sergeants first class for $343.50 a month.

Leading us were the sons of West Point and the young ROTC lieutenants from Rutgers and The Citadel and, yes, even Yale University, who had heard Kennedy's call and answered it. There were also the young enlisted men and NCOs who passed through Officer Candidate School and emerged newly minted officers and gentlemen. All laughed nervously when confronted with the cold statistics that measured a second lieutenant's combat life expectancy in minutes and seconds, not hours. Our second lieutenants were paid $241.20 per month.

The class of 1965 came out of the old America, a nation that disappeared forever in the smoke that billowed off the jungle battlegrounds where we fought and bled. The country that sent us off to war was not there to welcome us home. It no longer existed. We answered the call of one President who was now dead; we followed the orders of another who would be hounded from office, and haunted, by the war he mismanaged so badly.

Many of our countrymen came to hate the war we fought. Those who hated it the most—the professionally sensitive—were not, in the end, sensitive enough to differentiate between the war and the soldiers who had been ordered to fight it. They hated us as well, and we went to ground in the cross fire, as we had learned in the jungles.

In time our battles were forgotten, our sacrifices were discounted, and both our sanity and our suitability for life in polite American society were publicly questioned. Our young-old faces, chiseled and gaunt from the fever and the heat and the sleepless nights, now stare back at us, lost and damned strangers, frozen in yellowing snapshots packed away in cardboard boxes with our medals and ribbons.

We rebuilt our lives, found jobs or professions, married, raised families, and waited patiently for America to come to its senses. As the years passed we searched each other out and found that the half-remembered pride of service was shared by those who had shared everything else with us. With them, and only with them, could we talk about what had really happened over there—what we had seen, what we had done, what we had survived.

We knew what Vietnam had been like, and how we looked and acted and talked and smelled. No one in America did. Hollywood got it wrong every damned time, whetting twisted political knives on the bones of our dead brothers.

So once, just this once: This is how it all began, what it was really like, what it meant to us, and what we meant to each other. It was no movie. When it was over the dead did not get up and dust themselves off and walk away. The wounded did not wash away the red and go on with life, unhurt. Those who were, miraculously, unscratched were by no means untouched. Not one of us left Vietnam the same young man he was when he arrived.

This story, then, is our testament, and our tribute to 234 young Americans who died beside us during four days in Landing Zone X-Ray and Landing Zone Albany in the Valley of Death, 1965.

That is more Americans than were killed in any regiment, North or South, at the Battle of Gettysburg, and far more than were killed in combat in the entire Persian Gulf War. Seventy more of our comrades died in the Ia Drang in desperate skirmishes before and after the big battles at X-Ray and Albany. All the names, 305 of them including one Air Force pilot, are engraved on the third panel to the right of the apex, Panel 3-East, of the Vietnam Veterans Memorial in Washington, D.C., and on our hearts. This is also the story of the suffering of families whose lives were forever shattered by the death of a father, a son, a husband, a brother in that Valley.

While those who have never known war may fail to see the logic, this story also stands as tribute to the hundreds of young men of the 320th, 33rd, and 66th Regiments of the People's Army of Vietnam who died by our hand in that place. They, too, fought and died bravely. They were a worthy enemy. We who killed them pray that their bones were recovered from that wild, desolate place where we left them, and taken home for decent and honorable burial.

This is our story and theirs. For we were soldiers once, and young.

GOING TO WAR

HEAT OF BATTLE

> You cannot choose your battlefield,
> God does that for you;
> But you can plant a standard
> Where a standard never flew.
>
> —Stephen Crane, "The Colors"

The small bloody hole in the ground that was Captain Bob Edwards's Charlie Company command post was crowded with men. Sergeant Hermon R. Hostuttler, twenty-five, from Terra Alta, West Virginia, lay crumpled in the red dirt, dead from an AK-47 round through his throat. Specialist 4 Ernest E. Paolone of Chicago, the radio operator, crouched low, bleeding from a shrapnel wound in his left forearm. Sergeant James P. Castleberry, the artillery forward observer, and his radio operator, PFC Ervin L. Brown, Jr., hunkered down beside Paolone. Captain Edwards had a bullet hole in his left shoulder and armpit, and was slumped in a contorted sitting position, unable to move and losing blood. He was holding his radio handset to his ear with his one good arm. A North Vietnamese machine gunner atop a huge termite hill no more than thirty feet away had them all in his sights.

"We lay there watching bullets kick dirt off the small parapet around the edge of the hole," Edwards recalls. "I didn't know how badly I had been hurt, only that I couldn't stand up, couldn't do very much. The two platoon leaders I had radio contact with, Lieutenant William W. Franklin on my right and Lieutenant James L. Lane on Franklin's right, continued to report receiving fire, but had not been penetrated. I knew that my other two platoons were in bad shape and the enemy had penetrated to within hand-grenade range of my command post."

The furious assault by more than five hundred North Vietnamese regulars had slammed directly into two of Captain Edwards's platoons, a thin line of fifty Cavalry troopers who were all that stood between the enemy and my battalion command post, situated in a clump of trees in Landing Zone X-Ray, Ia Drang Valley, in the Central Highlands of South Vietnam, early on November 15, 1965.

America had drifted slowly but inexorably into war in this far-off place. Until now the dying, on our side at least, had been by ones and twos during the "adviser era" just ended, then by fours and fives as the U.S. Marines took the field earlier this year. Now the dying had begun in earnest, in wholesale lots, here in this eerie forested valley beneath the 2,401-foot-high crest of the Chu Pong massif, which wandered ten miles back into Cambodia. The newly arrived 1st Cavalry Division (Airmobile) had already interfered with and changed North Vietnamese brigadier general Chu Huy Man's audacious plans to seize the Central Highlands. Now his goal was to draw the Americans into battle—to learn how they fought and teach his men how to kill them.

One understrength battalion had the temerity to land by helicopter right in the heart of General Man's base camp, a historic sanctuary so far from any road that neither the French nor the South Vietnamese army had ever risked penetrating it in the preceding twenty years. My battalion, the 450-man 1st Battalion, 7th Cavalry of the U.S. Army, had come looking for trouble in the Ia Drang; we had found all we wanted and more. Two regiments of regulars of the People's Army of Vietnam (PAVN)—more than two thousand men—were resting and regrouping in their sanctuary near here and preparing to resume combat operations, when we dropped in on them the day before. General Man's commanders reacted with speed and fury, and now we were fighting for our lives.

One of Captain Edwards's men, Specialist 4 Arthur Viera, remembers every second of Charlie Company's agony that morning. "The gunfire was very loud. We were getting overrun on the right side. The lieutenant [Neil A. Kroger, twenty-four, a native of Oak Park, Illinois] came up in the open in all this. I thought that was pretty good. He yelled at me. I got up to hear him. He hollered at me to help cover the left sector."

Viera adds, "I ran over to him and by the time I got there he was dead. He had lasted a half-hour. I knelt beside him, took off his dog tags, and put them in my shirt pocket. I went back to firing my M-79 grenade launcher and got shot in my right elbow. The M-79 went flying and I was knocked down and fell back over the lieutenant. I had my .45 and fired it with my left hand. Then I got hit in the neck and the bullet went right through. Now I couldn't talk or make a sound.

"I got up and tried to take charge, and was shot a third time. That one blew up my right leg and put me down. It went in my leg above the ankle, traveled up, came back out, then went into my groin and ended up in my back, close to my spine. Just then two stick grenades blew up right over me and tore up both my legs. I reached down with my left hand and touched grenade fragments on my left leg and it felt like I had touched a red-hot poker. My hand just sizzled."

When Bob Edwards was hit he radioed for his executive officer, Lieutenant John Arrington, a twenty-three-year-old South Carolinian who was over at the battalion command post rounding up supplies, to come forward and take command of Charlie Company. Edwards says, "Arrington made it to my command post and, after a few moments of talking to me while lying down at the edge of the foxhole, was also hit and wounded. He was worried that he had been hurt pretty bad and told me to be sure and tell his wife that he loved her. I thought: 'Doesn't he know I'm badly wounded, too?' He was hit in the arm and the bullet passed into his chest and grazed a lung. He was in pain, suffering silently. He also caught some shrapnel from an M-79 that the North Vietnamese had apparently captured and were firing into the trees above us."

Now the North Vietnamese were closing in on Lieutenant John Lance (Jack) Geoghegan's 2nd Platoon. They were already inter-mingled with the few survivors of Lieutenant Kroger's 1st Platoon and were maneuvering toward Bob Edwards's foxhole. Clinton S. Poley, twenty-three, six feet three inches tall, and the son of an Ackley, Iowa, dirt farmer, was assistant gunner on one of Lieuten-ant Geoghegan's M-60 machine guns. The gunner was Specialist 4 James C. Comer, a native of Seagrove, North Carolina.

Poley says, "When I got up something hit me real hard on the back of my neck, knocked my head forward and my helmet fell off in the foxhole. I thought a guy had snuck up behind me and hit me with the butt of a weapon, it was such a blow. Wasn't anybody there; it was a bullet from the side or rear. I put my bandage on it and the helmet helped hold it on. I got up and looked again and there were four of them with carbines, off to our right front. I told Comer to aim more to the right. After that I heard a scream and I thought it was Lieutenant Geoghegan."

It wasn't. By now, Lieutenant Jack Geoghegan was already dead. His platoon sergeant, Robert Jemison, Jr., saw him go down trying to help a wounded man. "Willie Godboldt was twenty yards to my right. He was wounded, started hollering: 'Somebody help me!' I yelled: 'I'll go get him!' Lieutenant Geoghegan yelled back: 'No, I will.' He moved out of his position in the foxhole to help Godboldt and was shot." Just five days past his twenty-fourth birthday, John Lance Geoghegan of Pelham, New York, the only child of proud and doting parents, husband of Barbara and father of six-month-old Camille, lay dead, shot through the head and back, in the tall grass and red dirt of the Ia Drang Valley. PFC Willie F. Godboldt of Jacksonville, Florida, also twenty-four years old, died before help ever reached him.

Sergeant Jemison, who helped fight off five Chinese divisions at Chipyong-ni in the Korean War, now took a single bullet through his stomach but kept on fighting. Twenty minutes later the order came down for every platoon to throw a colored smoke grenade to mark friendly positions for the artillery and air strikes. Jemison got up to throw one and was hit again, this time knocked down by a bullet that struck him in the left shoulder. He got up, more slowly now, and went back to firing his M-16. Jemison fought on until he was hit a third time: "It was an automatic weapon. It hit me in my right arm and tore my weapon all to pieces. All that was left was the plastic stock. Another bullet cut off the metal clamp on my chin strip and knocked off my helmet. It hit so hard I thought my neck was broke. I was thrown to the ground. I got up and there was nothing left. No weapon, no grenades, no nothing."

James Comer and Clinton Poley, thirty feet to Jemison's left, had been firing their M-60 machine gun for almost an hour, an eternity. "A stick-handled potato-masher grenade landed in front of the hole. Comer hollered, 'Get down!' and kicked it away a little bit with his foot. It went off. By then we were close to being out of ammo and the gun had jammed. In that cloud of smoke and dust we started to our left, trying to find other 2nd Platoon positions. That's when I got hit in the chest and I hit the ground pretty hard."

Poley adds, "I got up and then got shot in my hip, and went down again. Comer and I lost contact with each other in the long grass. We'd already lost our ammo bearer [PFC Charles H. Collier from Mount Pleasant, Texas], who had been killed the day before. He was only eighteen and had been in Vietnam just a few days. I managed to run about twenty yards at a time for three times and finally came to part of the mortar platoon. A sergeant had two guys help me across a clearing to the battalion command post by the large anthill. The battalion doctor, a captain, gave me first aid."

Meantime, Specialist Viera was witness to scenes of horror: "The enemy was all over, at least a couple of hundred of them walking around for three or four minutes; it seemed like three or four hours. They were shooting and machine-gunning our wounded and laughing and giggling. I knew they'd kill me if they saw I was alive. When they got near, I played dead. I kept my eyes open and stared at a small tree. I knew that dead men had their eyes open."

Viera continues, "Then one of the North Vietnamese came up, looked at me, then kicked me, and I flopped over. I guess he thought I was dead. There was blood running out of my mouth, my arm, my legs. He took my watch and my .45 pistol and walked on. I watched them strip off all our weapons; then they left, back where they came from. I remember the artillery, the bombs, the napalm everywhere, real close around me. It shook the ground underneath me. But it was coming in on the North Vietnamese soldiers, too."

All this, and much more, took place between 6:50 A.M. and 7:40 A.M. on November 15, 1965. The agonies of Charlie Company occurred over 140 yards of the line. But men were fighting and dying on three sides of our thinly held American perimeter. In the center, I held the lives of all these men in my hands. The badly wounded Captain Bob Edwards was now on the radio, asking for reinforcements. The only reserve I had was the reconnaissance platoon, twenty-two men. Was the attack on Charlie Company the main enemy threat? Delta Company and the combined mortar position were also under attack now. Reluctantly, I told Captain Edwards that his company would have to fight on alone for the time being.

The din of battle was unbelievable. Rifles and machine guns and mortars and grenades rattled, banged, and boomed. Two batteries of 105mm howitzers, twelve big guns located on another landing zone five miles distant, were firing nonstop, their shells exploding no more than fifty yards outside the ring of shallow foxholes.

Beside me in the battalion command post, the Air Force forward air controller, Lieutenant Charlie W. Hastings, twenty-six, from La Mesa, New Mexico, radioed a special code word, "Broken Arrow," meaning "American unit in danger of being overrun," and within a short period of time every available fighter-bomber in South Vietnam was stacked overhead at thousand-foot intervals from seven thousand feet to thirty-five thousand feet, waiting its turn to deliver bombs and napalm to the battlefield.

Among my sergeants there were three-war men—men who parachuted into Normandy on D day and had survived the war in Korea—and those old veterans were shocked by the savagery and hellish noise of this battle. Choking clouds of smoke and dust obscured the killing ground. We were dry-mouthed and our bowels churned with fear, and still the enemy came on in waves.

2

THE ROOTS
OF CONFLICT

> There never was a time when, in my opinion, some way could
> not be found to prevent the drawing of the sword.
>
> —General Ulysses S. Grant

One month of maneuver, attack, retreat, bait, trap, ambush, and
bloody butchery in the Ia Drang Valley in the fall of 1965 was the
Vietnam War's true dawn—a time when two opposing armies took
the measure of each other. The North Vietnamese commanders had
a deep-rooted fear that the lessons they had learned fighting and
defeating the French a decade earlier had been outmoded by the
high-tech weaponry and revolutionary airmobile helicopter tactics
that the Americans were trying out on them.

The North Vietnamese wanted their foot soldiers to taste the sting
of those weapons and find ways to neutralize them. Their orders
were to draw the newly arrived Americans into battle and search for
the flaws in their thinking that would allow a Third World army of
peasant soldiers who traveled by foot and fought at the distant end
of a two-month-long supply line of porters not only to survive and
persevere, but ultimately to prevail in the war—which was, for
them, entering a new phase.

The 1st Cavalry Division (Airmobile) was born of President John F. Kennedy's determination that the U.S. Army, which for a decade had focused exclusively on training and arming itself to fight World War III on the plains of Europe, prepare to fight a series of small, dirty wars on the world's frontiers. Toward that end Kennedy gave the U.S. Special Forces their head—and a distinctive green beret to wear. The Special Forces were good at what they did, counterguerrilla warfare, but clearly they were not the force needed to deal with battalions and regiments of regular soldiers in the Communist armies of liberation. For that matter, neither were the regular infantry divisions of the U.S. Army—hidebound, road-bound, and focused on war in Germany. Something new and totally different had to be created to meet the challenge of the jungles of Indochina.

What would that something be? No one was absolutely certain, but a coterie of young colonels and brigadier generals hiding out in the bowels of the Army's research-and-development division in the Pentagon had an idea, a dream, and they had been tinkering with it for years.

In the summer of 1957, Lieutenant General James M. Gavin, who won early fame and swift promotion with the 82nd Airborne Division in World War II, was chief of research and development for the Army. He had a vision of a new fighting force, something that he described in a seminal article as "Cavalry—And I Don't Mean Horses." His vision centered on the helicopter, that ungainly bumblebee, which made a very limited combat debut in Korea, principally hauling wounded to the rear two at a time.

Jim Gavin's dream was that someday bigger, faster, and better helicopters would carry the infantry into battle, forever freeing it of the tyranny of terrain and permitting war to proceed at a pace considerably faster than that of a man walking. The helicopter, Gavin believed, held the possibility of making the battlefield truly a three-dimensional nightmare for an enemy commander.

Gavin's dream was enthusiastically shared by Brigadier General Hamilton W. Howze, chief of Army Aviation, and other pioneers like Colonel John Norton, Colonel George P. (Phip) Seneff, Colonel John J. (Jack) Tolson, Colonel Bob Williams, and Colonel Harry

W. O. Kinnard. World War II had proved there were shortcomings and limitations in the practice of airborne warfare; but airmobile warfare could address most, if not all, of those limitations.

By mid-1962, Defense Secretary Robert S. McNamara, pursuing President Kennedy's vision, seized on the airmobility idea. McNamara ordered the Army to determine if the new UH-1 Huey helicopter, the big CH-47 Chinook transport helicopter, and their sisters in rotary-wing aviation made sense on the battlefield of the future.

An Airmobility Concept Board was created and, in short order, the 11th Air Assault Division (Test) was born at Fort Benning, Georgia, in February 1963. Its commander was Brigadier General Harry Kinnard. The 10th Air Transport Brigade (Test) was activated under the command of Colonel Delbert Bristol, and the Aviation Group (Test) was created under the command of Colonel Phip Seneff. To assess it all was the Test/Evaluation/Control Group, under Brigadier General Bob Williams. These units would encounter no bureaucratic resistance or red tape at Fort Benning: The new assistant commandant there was Brigadier General John Norton. Talk about stacking the deck!

The 11th Air Assault Test began at the bottom and built upward, starting with only three thousand men for individual airmobility training and testing in platoon-size and company-size elements. By June of 1964, the Army added two more brigades of infantry, plus artillery and support units, and began training and testing battalion, brigade, and division tactics.

At that time, America had not yet recovered from the shock of President Kennedy's assassination and was only beginning to measure the man who had succeeded him, Lyndon B. Johnson. Johnson was passing the first wave of Great Society legislation, which would restructure America, and that was his main agenda. But the trouble in South Vietnam would not go away and could not be safely ignored in an election year.

The country he called "Veet-Nam" was already beginning to gnaw at Lyndon Baines Johnson's innards. It was not the place Johnson would have chosen to make a stand against the Communists. In 1954, when the French were trembling on the brink of disastrous defeat at Dien Bien Phu, and President Eisenhower's advisers debated the pros and cons of American intervention in Indochina—intervention possibly even including a nuclear strike—then Senator Lyndon Johnson stood up strongly against that folly, arguing against any war on the Asian mainland. Johnson was proud of that.

Johnson had, however, inherited John F. Kennedy's hyperactive foreign policy as well as Kennedy's principal advisers, the men he derisively nicknamed the "You-Harvards." In Kennedy's thousand days the nation had gone through the Bay of Pigs debacle, the Berlin Wall crisis, the Cuban missile crisis, and the crisis over the tiny, and largely inconsequential, kingdom of Laos. Days before Kennedy fell to an assassin's bullet, Ngo Dinh Diem, the autocratic ruler of South Vietnam, was deposed and murdered in a coup d'état that was at least sanctioned, if not sponsored, by Washington.

Kennedy's successor, new to the job and moving into an election year, could not afford to be seen as soft on communism. President Johnson was approving a slow but steady buildup in the number of American advisers in South Vietnam.

Now, in the summer of 1964, important decisions were also being made in Hanoi, the capital of Communist North Vietnam. In the defense establishment and the ruling councils of the Communist party a group of Young Turks pressed the case for escalating the war so as to liberate the southern half of the country. They argued that simply to continue providing guns and ammunition and encouragement for the Viet Cong guerrillas was not enough: The time had come to intervene on the battlefields of the south with regiments and divisions of North Vietnamese People's Army regulars.

These better-armed, trained, and motivated soldiers should infiltrate South Vietnam, they argued, and launch hammer blows against the weak and unmotivated South Vietnamese army. In short order, they would liberate all of the land and people south of the 17th Parallel. Senior General Vo Nguyen Giap vigorously opposed the suggested escalation as hasty and premature, and urged that the guerrilla-war phase, which was proving ever more successful, be continued.

President Ho Chi Minh came down on the side of escalation and the army high command drew up a daring plan for the dry-season campaign of 1965. Three regular army regiments would be brought up to strength, trained and equipped, and sent south along the Ho Chi Minh Trail through Laos and Cambodia to launch a stunning autumn offensive that would begin in the remote Central Highlands and perhaps end in Saigon.

Hanoi's planners envisioned a classic campaign to crush the Army of the Republic of Vietnam (ARVN), starting in October 1965, after the monsoon rains ended in the mountains and plateaus of Pleiku province. They would lay siege to the American Special Forces camp at Plei Me with its twelve American advisers and four hundred–plus Montagnard mercenaries.

That attack, in turn, would draw an ARVN relief column of troops and tanks out of Pleiku and down Route 14, thence southwest on the one-lane dirt track called Provincial Route 5—where a regiment of People's Army troops would be waiting in a carefully prepared ambush. Once the ARVN relief forces were destroyed and Plei Me camp crushed, the victorious North Vietnamese army regiments would then take Pleiku city and the way would be clear to advance along Route 19 toward Qui Nhon and the South China Sea. Whoever controls Route 19 controls the Central Highlands, and whoever controls the Highlands controls Vietnam. By early 1966, the North Vietnamese commanders were certain, South Vietnam would be cut in two and trembling on the verge of surrender.

The North Vietnamese preparations were well under way by the fall of 1964, while Lyndon B. Johnson campaigned across America promising that "American boys will not be sent to do what Asian boys ought to be doing for themselves." That fall the 11th Air Assault Test Division conducted a crucial two-month test in the Carolinas. The theory of helicopter warfare was proved to the satisfaction of the U.S. Army in the largest field exercises since World War II. Now the Pentagon began the process of incorporating the Air Assault Division into the regular ranks of the Army.

As the new airmobile division moved toward becoming a reality, the situation in the theater of its most likely employment—what Lyndon Johnson called "that damned little pissant country," Vietnam—deteriorated by the day, both politically and militarily. Saigon's generals took turns staging coups d'état and being the strongman of the month, while the Viet Cong guerrillas expanded their control of the rice-growing Mekong Delta and reached north into the rubber country.

So long as he was presenting himself as the reasonable, peaceful alternative to the hawkish Republican challenger, Senator Barry Goldwater, Johnson resisted the recommendations of his advisers for a massive escalation of the American military presence. Once he had beaten Goldwater and was President in his own right, Lyndon Johnson was certain, he could cut a deal in the best Texas tradition with the Vietnamese Communists.

Already frustrated by a series of terrorist incidents aimed at Americans in Vietnam, Johnson exploded when, on the night of February 6, 1965, Viet Cong sappers mortared and mined the U.S. advisers' compound and air base at Pleiku in the Central Highlands. Eight Americans were killed and more than one hundred wounded. "I've had enough of this," Johnson told his National Security Council.

In retaliation, within hours carrier-based Navy jets struck the first targets inside North Vietnam. By March 2, Operation Rolling Thunder, a systematic and continuing program of air strikes against the North, had begun. While the Navy warplanes safely came and went from aircraft carriers at sea, the U.S. Air Force jets based at Da Nang were clearly vulnerable to enemy retaliation.

When General William C. Westmoreland, the American commander in Vietnam, asked for U.S. Marines to guard the air base, he got them. On March 8, a battalion of Marines splashed ashore on China Beach. On April 1, President Johnson approved General Westmoreland's request for two more Marine battalions, plus 20,000 logistics troops. He also agreed with General Westmoreland that the Marines should not be limited to strictly defensive duties; now they would fan out and begin killing Viet Cong. For the first time since the Korean War, American combat troops were now deployed for action on the Asian mainland.

In a major speech on April 7, the President urged that the North Vietnamese negotiate a reasonable settlement, and offered them a piece of a huge Mekong River economic-development project that Washington would finance. Hanoi replied that there could be no negotiations while American planes were bombing North Vietnam.

By April 15, the White House was entertaining Westmoreland's request for the dispatch of an additional 40,000 American troops to South Vietnam to raise the ante. In mid-June, Westmoreland urgently asked that the number of U.S. troops in the pipeline be doubled. He now wanted approval of a force of 180,000 men, most of them American, some of them South Korean, by the end of 1965. And the general was projecting that he would need at least an additional 100,000 or more in 1966.

President Johnson was inclined to give Westmoreland what he wanted, but he was also determined that this war would be fought without unduly distressing the American public. Surely so rich and powerful a nation could afford both a brushfire war and his Great Society programs.

Johnson decided, against the advice of his military chiefs, that the American escalation in South Vietnam be conducted on the cheap: There would be no mobilization of reserve and National Guard units; no declaration of a state of emergency that would permit the Army to extend for the duration the enlistments of the best-trained and most experienced soldiers. Instead, the war would be fed by stripping the Army divisions in Europe and the continental United States of their best personnel and matériel, while a river of new draftees, 20,000 of them each month, flowed in to do the shooting and the dying.

With the U.S. Marines beginning combat operations in the northern part of South Vietnam, and the newly arrived 173rd Airborne Brigade now operating in the central part of the country, Hanoi's military planners were forced to take a new look at the winter-spring campaign planned for Pleiku province. Senior General Chu Huy Man, who commanded the campaign, says that in June 1965, the

People's Army high command decided to postpone the audacious plan to seize the Central Highlands and attack down Route 19 to the coast.

"That plan was postponed for ten years," General Man says. "It was completed in 1975." The new plan would follow the opening sequence of the original: The People's Army forces would lay siege to Plei Me Special Forces Camp, ambush the inevitable South Vietnamese relief column when it ventured out of Pleiku city, and then wait for American combat troops to be thrown into the battle to save the South Vietnamese.

"We wanted to lure the tiger out of the mountain," General Man says, adding: "We would attack the ARVN—but we would be ready to fight the Americans." Major General Hoang Phuong, now chief of the Institute of Military History in Hanoi and a veteran of the Ia Drang battles, recalls: "Headquarters decided we had to prepare very carefully to fight the Americans. Our problem was that we had never fought Americans before and we had no experience fighting them. We knew how to fight the French. We wanted to draw American units into contact for purposes of learning how to fight them. We wanted any American combat troops; we didn't care which ones."

The Americans that Man and Phuong would meet in due course had not yet left the United States in June of 1965, but they smelled something in the wind. In early May 1965, commanders of the 11th Air Assault Division began receiving informational copies of the after-action reports of the 173rd Airborne Brigade's battles and operations in Vietnam. By late May, battalion, brigade, and division commanders and staff were reporting to heavily guarded classrooms at the Infantry School in Fort Benning, Georgia, for top-secret map exercises. The maps the games were played on covered the Central Highlands of South Vietnam.

By mid-June the Pentagon ordered the division commanders to begin an intensive eight-week combat-readiness program that focused on deployment to South Vietnam. Secretary of Defense McNamara announced on June 16 that the Army had been authorized an airmobile division as part of its sixteen-division force.

In early July, the Pentagon announced that the 11th Air Assault (Test) Division would be renamed the 1st Cavalry Division (Airmobile) and that it would take over the colors of that historic division that had distinguished itself in combat in the Korean War and in the Pacific theater in World War II—not to mention horse-cavalry skirmishes with bandits along the Mexican border in Texas and New Mexico in the early 1920s.

In a televised address to the nation on the morning of July 28, 1965, President Johnson described the worsening situation in South Vietnam and declared: "I have today ordered the Airmobile Division to Vietnam."

On that day, convinced that the President's escalation without a declaration of emergency was an act of madness, General Harold K. Johnson, Chief of Staff of the U.S. Army, drove to the White House with the intention of resigning in protest. He had already taken the four silver stars off each shoulder of his summer uniform. As his car approached the White House gates, General Johnson faltered in his resolve; he convinced himself that he could do more by staying and working inside the system than by resigning in protest. The general ordered his driver to turn around and take him back to the Pentagon. This decision haunted Johnny Johnson all the rest of his life.

In South Vietnam, the 320th Regiment of the People's Army of Vietnam was midway through a two-month-long siege of Duc Co Special Forces Camp in the Central Highlands. A young Army major, H. Norman Schwarzkopf, West Point class of 1956, was adviser to the South Vietnamese Airborne battalion that was hip deep in the fighting at Duc Co. A quarter-century later, General Norm Schwarzkopf would date the birth of his famous hot temper to those days, when he begged and pleaded on the radio for someone to evacuate his wounded South Vietnamese soldiers, while American helicopters fluttered by without stopping.

That week, the 33rd People's Army Regiment left Quang Ninh province in North Vietnam on the two-month march down the Ho Chi Minh Trail through Laos and Cambodia to South Vietnam. Brigadier General Chu Huy Man was already in the South overseeing Viet Cong operations against the U.S. Marines in the Da Nang–

Chu Lai region, but he had orders to return to the Western Highlands to establish the B-3 Front, a flexible and expandable headquarters charged with tactical and administrative control over both the People's Army and Viet Cong units operating in the Highlands. Man's new assignment was to prepare a warm welcome for the Americans in Pleiku province.

The first leg of the new, high-tech Airmobile division's journey to the war zone would be decidedly low-tech. Beginning in August, the 1st Cavalry would ride to war in a mini-fleet of World War II–era troopships, and their helicopters would sail to South Vietnam aboard a flotilla of four aging aircraft carriers.

The cavalry troopers launched into a flurry of packing equipment, getting their shots, writing wills, getting last-minute dental and health problems cleared up, resettling their wives and kids off-post, and taking short leaves if they could be spared. In early August an advance party of 1,100 officers and men flew to Vietnam to begin preparing a new home for the division at An Khe, a sleepy hill town halfway up Route 19 between Qui Nhon on the coast and Pleiku in the mountains.

One of the battalions preparing to ship out was mine. My name is Harold G. Moore, Jr., but "Hal" will do just fine. In 1957, as a young major fresh out of the Command and General Staff College at Fort Leavenworth and assigned to the Pentagon office of the chief of research and development, I was in on the birth of the concept of airmobility. I was the one-man airborne branch in the Air Mobility Division for two and a half years. In that job I worked for Lieutenant General Jim Gavin, Colonel John Norton, Colonel Phip Seneff, and Colonel Bob Williams.

I had already worked for Harry W. O. Kinnard when he was a lieutenant colonel heading the Airborne Test Section at Fort Bragg in 1948. As a twenty-six-year-old first lieutenant, I volunteered to test experimental parachutes for Kinnard. It was a certainty that Kinnard would always remember me: On my first jump a new steerable parachute I was testing hung up on the tail of the C-46 aircraft, and I was dragged, twisting and trailing behind the plane, at 110 miles per hour, 1,500 feet above the drop zone. The tangled mess finally broke free a few minutes later, and my reserve chute got me to ground safely. When I reported in to Kinnard all he said was: "Hello, Lucky."

While I was pulling a three-year tour of NATO duty in Norway in the early 1960s, I heard rumors that the Kennedy administration was taking a hard new look at the airmobility concept. In August of 1963, I finished the NATO tour and began a year of schooling at the Naval War College in Newport, Rhode Island. I had been a lieutenant colonel for four years and was fighting for battalion command on my next assignment.

By then the Army had created the 11th Air Assault Test Division, with Major General Harry Kinnard commanding. I wrote my old boss a letter asking for an infantry battalion in his new division. (In those days a division commander could select brigade and battalion commanders simply by asking for them by name. Since the mid-1970s, such commanders are chosen by Army selection boards on a competitive basis.) In April 1964, as I was finishing the War College, the Pentagon informed me that Kinnard had requested that I be assigned to command the 2nd Battalion, 23rd Infantry, which had been detached from the 2nd Infantry Division and assigned to the 11th Air Assault Test.

On Saturday, June 27, I arrived at Fort Benning, Georgia. It had been arranged that I would take the five-day battalion-commander refresher course before actually taking command. But any thoughts of a refresher went out the door when Colonel Thomas W. (Tim) Brown, the 3rd Brigade commander and my new boss, arrived and told me to turn my course books back in. "You take command of your battalion at nine A.M. Monday and we are going out on a three-day field exercise right after." He gave me the phone number of Captain Gregory (Matt) Dillon, the battalion S-3, or operations officer. Dillon told me that the barracks and headquarters were on Kelly Hill, five miles out on the reservation from the main post at Benning. My wife and five children were staying with her parents in nearby Auburn, Alabama, until we got quarters on the post.

On Monday, June 29, as scheduled, I took command of my battalion. I was forty-two years old, a West Point graduate of the class of 1945, with nineteen years' commissioned service, including a fourteen-month combat tour in Korea. In a brief talk to the troops afterward I told them that this was a good battalion but it would get better. "I will do my best," I said. "I expect the same from each of you."

Even before taking command, I had a long talk with the most important man in any battalion: the sergeant major. Basil L. Plumley, forty-four years old and a six-foot-two-inch bear of a man, hailed from West Virginia. The men sometimes called him Old Iron Jaw, but never in his hearing.

Plumley was a two-war man and wore master parachutist wings with five combat-jump stars. He was what the young Airborne types call a four-jump bastard: Plumley had survived all four combat jumps of the 82nd Airborne Division in World War II: Sicily and Salerno in 1943, and then in 1944, D day at Normandy, and Market-Garden in the Netherlands. For that matter, he also made one combat parachute jump in the Korean War, with the 187th Airborne Infantry Regiment. He ended World War II a buck sergeant and was promoted to sergeant major in 1961.

The sergeant major was a no-bullshit guy who believed, as I did, in tough training, tough discipline, and tough physical conditioning. To this day there are veterans of the battalion who are convinced that God may look like Sergeant Major Basil Plumley, but He isn't nearly as tough as the sergeant major on sins small or large. Privately, I thanked my lucky stars that I had inherited such a treasure. I told Sergeant Major Plumley that he had unrestricted access to me at any time, on any subject he wished to raise.

After the ceremony the company commanders and battalion staff got a look at their new boss and a word on my standards. They were fairly simple: Only first-place trophies will be displayed, accepted, or presented in this battalion. Second place in our line of work is defeat of the unit on the battlefield, and death for the individual in combat. No fat troops or officers. Decision-making will be decentralized: Push the power down. It pays off in wartime. Loyalty flows down as well. I check up on everything. I am available day or night to talk with any officer of this battalion. Finally, the sergeant major works only for me and takes orders only from me. He is my right-hand man.

Personal descriptions of the key players in the 11th Air Assault Division, and in my battalion that year, will be useful to the reader. These men appear and reappear throughout this story.

Major General Harry W. O. Kinnard, division commanding general. Harry Kinnard, a native Texan, was forty-nine years old that year. He was West Point, class of 1939, and Airborne qualified in 1942. Kinnard was one of the shooting stars of the 101st Airborne in World War II. He was Brigadier General Tony McAuliffe's operations officer, G-3, at the Battle of Bastogne in the Bulge, and the man who suggested that General McAuliffe specifically respond to a German surrender demand with one historic word: "Nuts!" Kinnard became a full colonel at age twenty-nine.

Brigadier General Richard T. Knowles, assistant division commander. Dick Knowles was forty-five; a Chicago native, he held an ROTC commission from the University of Illinois. Knowles served in Europe in World War II in a tank destroyer group. In Korea he made the Inchon landing with an Army artillery battalion attached to the 1st Marine Division. Later, in North Korea, he earned the Silver Star leading a counterattack that routed seventy-five North Koreans who had penetrated his battalion perimeter. He originally came to the 11th Air Assault as a colonel commanding the division artillery. When Knowles was promoted to brigadier general he shifted to assistant division commander for operations, and in this capacity he spent most of his time in the field supervising the training and operations of the division. Knowles was slender, six feet three inches tall, and enthusiastic; he always arrived with a pocketful of good cigars.

Colonel Thomas W. Brown, 3rd Brigade commander. Tim Brown was forty-four years old and six feet one inch tall; he was West Point class of January 1943, a native New Yorker and another World War II paratrooper who had served with the 11th and 13th Airborne divisions. He and I were students together at the Infantry School Advanced Course in 1951–1952, and we served together in the 7th Infantry Division in the Korean War. In 1952–1953 he was a battalion commander in the 32nd Infantry Regiment, while I commanded two companies and was operations officer of the 17th Infantry Regiment. Brown was quiet, cool, incisive, and perfectionistic. In the true Kinnard mode, he gave his battalion commanders guidance, then gave them the freedom to run their units. He had commanded the brigade since early 1963 and participated in the early development of airmobile doctrine, tactics, and techniques.

The officers of my new battalion were the usual great Army mix of men who had come to their jobs from West Point, ROTC, Officer Candidate School, and military schools like The Citadel. Most of the young second lieutenants had come in through OCS and college ROTC programs. There were three rifle companies in the battalion—Alpha, Bravo, and Charlie companies—each at full strength supposed to have six officers and 164 enlisted men. They were my maneuver elements.

Each rifle company had three rifle platoons plus one platoon of three 81mm mortar squads for fire support. Each rifle platoon, in turn, had three rifle squads plus a weapons squad of two M-60 machine guns for fire support.

In addition, the battalion had a combat support company, Delta Company, consisting of a reconnaissance platoon, a mortar platoon, and an antitank platoon. We converted the unneeded antitank platoon into a machine-gun platoon for Vietnam duty. Delta Company was authorized five officers and 118 enlisted men.

The Battalion Headquarters and Headquarters Company (HHC) was authorized fourteen officers, a warrant officer, and 119 enlisted men. HHC comprised command, staff, communications, medical, transportation and maintenance, and supply personnel. The medical platoon in HHC included the battalion surgeon, a captain, and a Medical Service Corps lieutenant in charge of operations. They ran the battalion aid station in garrison and in the field, and supplied each of the platoons in the other companies with medical-aid men—those conscientious and courageous medics who were invariably called Doc.

Some of the battalion officers:

Captain Gregory P. (Matt) Dillon, operations officer. Matt, the thirty-two-year-old son of a World War I Navy chief petty officer, was a native New Yorker who was married and had two children. He was commissioned out of ROTC at the University of Alabama where he was a dash man on the track team. He had twice commanded companies, including B Company of this battalion. He was blessed with a clear head and a quick mind and he was a "people person." The battalion "3," or operations officer, in any unit is the commander's alter ego, the detail man who turns concepts into plans and then pulls together all the many pieces of a complicated military operation. Matt Dillon was my "3" for two years in both battalion and brigade command and he was simply superb.

Captain Gordon P. (Rosie) Rozanski, the commander of Headquarters Company. Later, in Vietnam, he would serve as battalion supply officer, or S-4. Rosie, twenty-six years old, hailed from Elysian, Minnesota, and was commissioned out of OCS. He was a bachelor who was cheerful, blunt, unflappable. He was responsible for selecting and securing battalion headquarters in the field; for feeding the officers and men in the headquarters and support sections; and for maintaining and securing a huge inventory of weapons and communications and electrical gear.

Captain John D. Herren, the commander of Bravo Company. Herren, a pipe-smoking twenty-nine-year-old bachelor, was an Army brat—his father was an Army lieutenant general—and a graduate of West Point, class of 1958. He was calm, thoughtful, friendly, and steady: No one ever saw John Herren get flustered.

Captain Robert H. (Bob) Edwards, the commander of Charlie Company. Bob was twenty-seven years old, married, a native of New Jersey. He was a Distinguished Military Graduate of the ROTC program at Lafayette College in 1960. Slender, five feet nine inches tall, Edwards was very bright and very quiet; he spoke briefly and to the point. He was exceptionally competent and so were the men and officers he commanded in Charlie Company.

Captain Ramon A. (Tony) Nadal, the commander of Alpha Company. Nadal originally came to the battalion as its S-2, or intelligence officer. He was twenty-nine years old, a West Point classmate of John Herren, and the son of an Army colonel. Tony's father, a native of Puerto Rico, had been an Army specialist in Central and South American affairs, and Tony grew up in that part of the world. He was married and had one child. In the last days before we shipped out to Vietnam, Tony Nadal turned up at my headquarters pleading for a company command. He had a year of combat duty in Vietnam, commanding a Special Forces A Team, and he wanted to go back. He had been assigned to Korea and was on leave in Oklahoma when a friend in Army personnel heard that the 1st Air Cav was shipping out to Vietnam. Nadal got in the family car and drove halfway across the country. At Fort Benning the division personnel types told Tony he could have a job as brigade communications officer. He made a desperate two-day trip through the division searching for a troop command job. I liked what I saw and heard, so I told him that though I couldn't give him a company right away I would take him on as battalion intelligence officer. On the ship, Tony's books on Vietnam, which filled a big box, were required reading, and he taught classes on the terrain and the enemy we would face.

Captain Louis R. (Ray) Lefebvre, the commander of Delta Company. Like Tony Nadal, Ray Lefebvre came to me hunting a troop-command job, and was assigned as an assistant operations officer before he got his company. Lefebvre, a thirty-two-year-old native of Bonners Ferry, Idaho, was married and had four children. Commissioned out of ROTC at Gonzaga University, Ray had also served a previous tour in Vietnam (1963–1964), and was fluent in Vietnamese. Because of his language capability he was slotted for a civil-affairs staff job at division headquarters. Ray came to me pleading for a job that would get him out of headquarters and into the field with troops. "Something is going to happen and I want to be in on it," he said. I told him that if he took the battalion air-operations job in the S-3 shop under Matt Dillon he would eventually get a company. He did.

Air Force First Lieutenant Charlie W. Hastings, twenty-six, an ROTC graduate of the University of Northern Colorado and a trained F-4 pilot, was assigned to us as the battalion forward air controller six weeks before we sailed for Vietnam. Charlie took a lot of good-natured kidding from the Army ground-pounders, but he gave as good as he got. He marched with us, learned the ways of the cavalry, and swiftly demonstrated his competence with an M-16 rifle.

The real strength of my battalion was in its sergeants, most of them combat veterans who had served in the battalion for three to five years. Typical of the senior noncoms was Sergeant First Class Larry M. Gilreath, a Korean War veteran out of Anderson County, South Carolina. He was platoon sergeant of the 1st Platoon, Bravo Company, and had been with the battalion since 1961. During that time he trained more new second-lieutenant platoon leaders than he had fingers on his hands. Lieutenants came and went; Gilreath was forever. He was stability and continuity; he knew every man in his platoon and knew that man's strengths and weaknesses. There was someone just like him in virtually every platoon in the battalion.

Once I had taken command, my goal was to create the absolute best air assault infantry battalion in the world, and the proudest. Every man in the battalion had to know and believe he was an important part of that best. We trained and tested. Senior military officials from throughout the U.S. Army and allied forces were frequent visitors to Fort Benning; the word had gone out that something new, different, and deadly in the art of warfare was being created here. Hundreds of helicopters were handed over to us, and the air crews and the infantry became a tight team as we flew on operations in the forests and swamps of Georgia and the Carolinas.

If this system could be made to work, the soldier's time would be spent fighting, not walking or waiting for a truck or wondering whether supplies would ever find him. Like the knight on a chessboard, we could now attack the flanks and rear of the enemy in a matter of minutes. The helicopter would add a 110-mile-an-hour fast-forward capability to ground warfare.

During those fourteen months before we sailed for Vietnam, we spent most of our time in the field, practicing assault landings from helicopters, and the incredibly complex coordination of artillery, tactical air support, and aerial rocket artillery with the all-important flow of helicopters into and out of the battle zone. Commanders had to learn to see terrain differently, to add a constant scan for landing zones (LZs) and pickup zones (PZs) to all the other features they had to keep in mind. We practiced rapid loading and unloading of men and matériel to reduce the helicopter's window of vulnerability. Total flexibility was the watchword in planning and attitude.

There was one bit of sobering reality that I insisted be introduced at every level in this training: We would declare a platoon leader dead and let his sergeant take over and carry out the mission. Or declare a sergeant dead and have one of his PFCs take over running the squad. We were training for war, and leaders are killed in battle. I wanted every man trained for and capable of taking over the job of the man above him.

The 11th Air Assault's graduation ceremony was the final test program, Air Assault II, conducted in the Carolinas during October and November of 1964. Some 35,000 soldiers were involved; the 11th Air Assault Division was pitted against the "aggressor" forces, the 82nd Airborne Division. Hundreds of VIPs from Washington popped in and out to see helicopter warfare in action; their presence lent weight to a first round of rumors that we were being trained for duty in Vietnam.

Ironically, late one night in the battalion command post we listened in on the new PRC-25 field radio to an American forward air controller directing an air strike in Vietnam. We could hear the rattle of gunfire and the explosions of the bombs twelve thousand miles away on a freak bounce of radio waves that briefly brought the real war to the pine barrens of South Carolina where we were playing war games.

For much of this time my battalion was at, or near, its full authorized strength of thirty-seven commissioned officers, one warrant officer, and 729 enlisted men. That changed in the spring of 1965, when we lost eight of our fifteen platoon-leader lieutenants. Most were reserve officers who had completed their commitments and were released from active duty; others were transferred or reassigned elsewhere. Between April and July we also lost by discharge or reassignment our intelligence officer, surgeon, personnel officer, air operations officer, supply officer, assistant medical officer, chaplain, and two company commanders.

In early June we were assigned six brand-new second lieutenants. We plugged them into the vacant rifle-platoon leader slots and gave them seven weeks of "get rich quick" on-the-job training in airmobile–air assault tactics. But in early August, shortly before we deployed, all six were yanked out of the battalion to stay at Fort Benning and attend the six-month Infantry Officers Basic Course: Someone had discovered an Army policy that new lieutenants could not be sent into combat before attending. The policy may be sound, but the net result was that the battalion and the troops in the ranks were whipsawed by unnecessary leadership changes.

Each rifle company got three new rifle-platoon leaders, except Alpha, which got two. Each rifle company had a mortar platoon, but we had no officers to lead them. Delta Company had a new recon-platoon leader, Lieutenant John Arrington, and a new mortar-platoon leader, First Lieutenant Raul E. Taboada-Requera.

There was precious little time to jam fourteen months' worth of airmobile training into the new lieutenants' heads. We did our best and so did they. When they reported in, I called them all in, together with their platoon sergeants, and told them we were heading for war and time was short. I issued two orders: One, platoon sergeants will teach their new platoon leaders everything they can about airmobility, small-unit tactics, the men in the ranks, and the leadership those men deserve. Two, the new lieutenants will keep their mouths shut except to ask questions, and will listen to and remember everything the platoon sergeant tells them.

In early July the Pentagon announced that the 11th Air Assault Division (Test) had served its purpose; now it would become the 1st Cavalry Division (Airmobile). Colonel Brown, with an eye to military heritage and tradition, immediately asked that his two battalions be given the historic colors of the 7th U.S. Cavalry. My battalion was reborn as the 1st Battalion, 7th Cavalry. Our sister battalion became the 2nd Battalion, 7th Cavalry.

In the days when Lieutenant Colonel George Armstrong Custer commanded the 7th Cavalry the regiment adopted a rowdy Irish drinking song, "Garry Owen," as its marching tune. The words "Garry Owen" made their way onto the regimental crest, and the officers and men of the regiment customarily accompanied each exchange of salutes with a hearty "Garry Owen, sir!" We picked up the tradition with the 7th Cavalry colors, and the troops accepted it all with enthusiasm.

The officers and pilots of Lieutenant Colonel John B. Stockton's highly spirited 3rd Squadron of the 17th Cavalry now became the 1st Squadron, 9th Cavalry—and had already absorbed the very essence of cavalry esprit. They wore big cavalry mustaches and black Stetson hats, and they carried their papers in leather saddle-bags, despite everything that more conservative elements in the division command could do to stop them. Stockton and his men even smuggled their mascot, Maggie the Mule, to Vietnam in spite of a strict no-pets-allowed order intended to ensure that the mule stayed home.

Unfortunately, my battalion and every other in the division now began to suffer the consequences of President Johnson's refusal to declare a state of emergency and extend the active-duty tours of draftees and reserve officers. The order came down: Any soldier who had sixty days or less left to serve on his enlistment as of the date of deployment, August 16, must be left behind.

We were sick at heart. We were being shipped off to war sadly understrength, and crippled by the loss of almost a hundred troopers in my battalion alone. The very men who would be the most useful in combat—those who had trained longest in the new techniques of helicopter warfare—were by this order taken away from us. It made no sense then; it makes no sense now.

Our last night at Fort Benning was Friday, August 13, 1965. I came home early, around seven P.M., in time for dinner with my wife, Julie, and our five children, who ranged in age from thirteen down to three. I told all of them I would be leaving early the next morning, long before they awoke, and I would be going to the war in Vietnam. Later, I sat on the sofa reading aloud to my daughter, Cecile, six. She looked up at one point and asked: "Daddy, what's a war?" I tried my best to explain, but her look of bewilderment only grew.

My alarm clock was set for 1:30 A.M., and by 3:30 A.M. the battalion had loaded aboard chartered buses bound for the port of Charleston, South Carolina, where the transport ship USNS *Maurice Rose* waited at dockside. We sailed from Charleston on Monday, August 16, and it took the better part of a month for the "Ramblin' Rose" to transit the Panama Canal and cross the Pacific to South Vietnam. On that same date, August 16, the last elements of the 66th Regiment of the People's Army left their base in Thanh Hoa, North Vietnam. It would take them nearly two months to cover five hundred miles on foot along the Ho Chi Minh Trail to our meeting place in the Ia Drang Valley.

The *Rose* dropped anchor in the port of Qui Nhon, in central South Vietnam, in mid-September, and we were welcomed ashore by our advance party. With the help of the 101st Airborne a huge area of scrub jungle just north of the town of An Khe had been secured. An Khe, forty-two miles west of Qui Nhon on Route 19, would be the base camp of the 1st Cavalry Division—just as soon as we cleared the jungle and built that camp. It was precisely what General Harry Kinnard had vigorously opposed for his airmobile troops: a fort in the middle of Indian country.

Kinnard lobbied hard in Washington, Saigon, and Bangkok for his new division to be based inside Thailand, in its own sanctuary. From there it could launch combat operations inside South Vietnam and onto the North Vietnamese lines of communication inside Cambodia and Laos. The negative responses General Kinnard's request elicited weren't even polite. His division would now have to build, garrison, and guard a base camp, and that would reduce the number of troops available to actively pursue and destroy the enemy.

As our Chinook transport helicopters ferried the battalion into An Khe we passed over a small airstrip with a beat-up old three-story yellow building at the northwest end. On the boat coming over I had reread Bernard Fall's *Street Without Joy* and I recognized that airstrip as the departure point for the French army's Group Mobile 100 on June 24, 1954, as it headed west on Route 19 and straight into the historic Viet Minh ambush that helped seal the fate of French colonial rule in Indochina.

We stepped off the choppers into a tangle of trees, weeds, and brush, in the middle of what would become our airfield, the Golf Course. Brigadier General John M. Wright, assistant division commander, had decreed that the airfield for the 1st Cav's 450-plus helicopters and fixed-wing aircraft would have to be "smooth as a golf course." He wanted no bulldozers scraping the land bare to become a mud hole in the monsoons and a red dust storm in dry season.

The men of the division and some two thousand Vietnamese laborers cleared the site by hand, with machetes and axes, and General Wright had his instant Golf Course. They also built a heavily fortified twelve-mile-long and hundred-yard-wide defense perimeter, called the Barrier Line, around the base. We lived rough: pup tents, C-rations, and showers only when it rained. The battalions took turns manning the picket line of outposts well out from the barrier and running patrols to keep the Viet Cong off guard. My battalion lost two men by drowning on patrol crossings of the Song Ba river during that first month.

In the first days there were a few light probes by the local guerrillas, and nervous troopers shot up a lot of green trees before fire discipline was restored. Alas, one casualty of a nervous sentry was Colonel Stockton's beloved cavalry mascot, Maggie the Mule, who was gunned down by one of my Charlie Company men as she wandered the perimeter on a dark night.

Sergeant Major Plumley reported the death of Maggie to me: "She was challenged and didn't know the password." Plumley added that he would "properly dispose" of the slain mule. He had Maggie's body winched aboard the division chow truck as it made its morning rounds delivering rations to the battalions. Maggie was dropped off with the C-rations at the truck's next stop: Colonel Stockton's 1st Squadron, 9th Cavalry. An efficient but hardly diplomatic solution: Maggie's death and subsequent delivery on the chow truck caused some bad blood between the battalions.

Once each day every man of us, under close supervision, choked down a bitter, dime-size yellow malaria pill. It was an automatic Article 15 offense—one subject to nonjudicial punishment—to be caught sleeping outside one's mosquito net, no matter how hot it was. Even so, we began losing men to malaria within two or three weeks. Within six weeks fifty-six troopers from my battalion alone had been evacuated to hospitals, suffering serious cases of malaria. The problem was a particularly virulent falciparum strain of the disease, prevalent in the Central Highlands; it was resistant to the antimalarial drugs available to us at that time.

The drain on battalion manpower due to expiring enlistments also continued. At the end of September my battalion had 679 officers and men against an authorized strength of 767. Four sergeants and seventeen enlisted men rotated home in October. In November, six sergeants and 132 men of the battalion were scheduled to leave.

In October we received two officer replacements and two or three NCOs via the "Infusion Program," which transferred to us men already serving in Vietnam in other units, who presumably would be more knowledgeable of the country and the enemy. One of those officers was Captain Thomas C. Metsker, a muscular six-foot-tall Special Forces officer who was a 1961 graduate of The Citadel, where he was a four-year letter man on the track team. Metsker, a Foreign Service brat who had grown up in Japan and Korea, was an impressive young officer.

Tony Nadal now took command of Alpha Company; I made Metsker the battalion intelligence officer and put him high on my list for command of a company. He often joined me on my five-mile morning runs around the internal camp perimeter.

The other new arrival was First Lieutenant William J. Lyons, twenty-five years old, a Californian and a 1962 Ripon College graduate. Like Metsker, Lyons was qualified as a paratrooper and a Ranger; he came to us from an adviser slot with the 41st ARVN Ranger Battalion. He was fluent in Vietnamese. I assigned him to be Bob Edwards's executive officer in Charlie Company. In the late afternoon of November 4, Lyons and Sergeant Roy Hitt, a thirty-three-year-old Alabama native, were killed in the head-on collision of two Huey helicopters while delivering mail and chow to Charlie Company out on the picket line.

Our battalion conducted two sweep operations in the vicinity of the An Khe base during this period; we suffered a few wounded (by snipers) and captured a huge Viet Cong flag.

In late October the 1st Cavalry Division's 1st Brigade moved up to Camp Holloway at Pleiku and began pursuing enemy forces involved in the attack on Plei Me Special Forces Camp and the attempted ambush of a South Vietnamese relief column.

Colonel Stockton and his helicopter scout–gunship teams quickly got on the trail of the retreating North Vietnamese. On November 1, one of the cavalry teams spotted a dozen or so enemy troops eight miles west of Plei Me. They were fired on, and fled. Minutes later more enemy were spotted. Stockton put riflemen on the ground and within minutes they captured the 33rd People's Army Regiment's field hospital. Fifteen enemy were killed and forty-four others, including patients and hospital staff, were captured, along with tons of medical supplies, rice, documents, and weapons. The North Vietnamese counterattacked that afternoon; the fight had been going on for hours before the 2nd Battalion, 12th Cavalry arrived to reinforce Stockton. There were eleven Americans killed and fifty-one wounded, with enemy casualties estimated at 250.

On that same day, November 1, the lead elements of the 66th People's Army Regiment began crossing into South Vietnam from Cambodia, moving along the Ia (River) Drang. Among the documents captured in the hospital fight was an enemy map of the Ia Drang Valley showing trails used by the North Vietnamese. On November 3, General Dick Knowles directed Colonel Stockton to begin a reconnaissance in force on a specific trail running along the Ia Drang two miles inside the border.

Stockton moved his operations base to the Duc Co Special Forces Camp and, concerned that the 1st Brigade had moved so slowly in getting infantry reinforcements to come to his assistance during the hospital fight, prevailed on Knowles to shift Captain Theodore S. Danielsen's Alpha Company, 1st Battalion, 8th Cavalry to Duc Co as well.

That night Stockton set three platoon-size ambushes, one along the Ia Drang trail, the others a mile or so north. The southernmost platoon watched as a reinforced North Vietnamese company approached their ambush on the trail 2.2 miles inside the Vietnam border. The North Vietnamese stopped for a rest break just 120 yards short of the ambush site and then, shortly after nine P.M., resumed the march eastward.

The Americans let the lead elements pass through, but when the heavy-weapons company clattered into the kill zone, the Americans touched off their eight claymore mines, each spewing hundreds of steel ball bearings in a semicircle of death, and poured a storm of rifle and machine-gun fire into those who survived the mine blasts. Captain Charles S. Knowlen then ordered all his ambush parties back to the patrol-base clearing and within half an hour came under heavy attack by a large force of very angry North Vietnamese. When his men radioed that they were in danger of being overrun, Colonel Stockton ordered Captain Danielsen's company helicoptered in as reinforcements.

The move saved the day, but it also cooked Stockton's goose: General Knowles said he had ordered Stockton to obtain his explicit permission before committing Ted Danielsen's Alpha Company troops to action. The incident ended with Stockton being transferred to a staff job in Saigon, and the division losing one of its most controversial and successful battalion commanders.

Whatever else ensued, division headquarters did not at that time move to exploit the success of Stockton's ambush and pursue the considerable number of enemy reinforcements who had just arrived off the Ho Chi Minh Trail. Instead, on November 6 orders were issued for the 1st Brigade to return to An Khe and for the 3rd Brigade to take the field in Pleiku province, effective November 10.

The 3rd Brigade battalions, under Colonel Tim Brown, were my 1st Battalion, 7th Cavalry; Lieutenant Colonel Robert McDade's 2nd Battalion, 7th Cavalry; and Lieutenant Colonel Robert Tully's 2nd Battalion, 5th Cavalry. McDade, a Korean War veteran, had been the division personnel officer (G-1) for nearly two years and had been given command of our sister battalion in late October.

On November 9, Colonel Brown and I went to the division's forward command post in Pleiku for a briefing on the battlefield situation. The intelligence map hanging on the wall had a large red star on the Chu Pong massif above the Ia Drang Valley, west of Plei Me. I asked one of the briefers what significance that star had, and he replied: "Enemy base camp." The next day my battalion was flown from An Khe to brigade field headquarters in the Catecka Tea Plantation, where Colonel Brown's staff briefed us and gave me my mission: to conduct an air assault five miles *east* of Plei Me, and find and kill the enemy. I was surprised and puzzled. All the 1st Brigade contact with the enemy had been *west* of Plei Me, yet they were ordering us to beat the bushes in a different direction. Then there was that big red star on the intelligence map, which indicated that the biggest target of all was way out west.

3

BOOTS AND SADDLES

Come on, boys, and grab your sabers
Come on, boys, and ride with me.
Give the cry of "Garry Owen,"
Make your place in history.
— author unknown, Vietnam 1965

Before our air assault on the target area, Captain Matt Dillon and I flew a brief, high-altitude helicopter recon mission, selecting landing zones and forming the operation plan. During the flight we spotted a small Jarai Montagnard village, and I made a note to warn the troops that there were civilians, either friendly or at least neutral, in the area. And I decided to forgo using artillery or tactical air-prep fires before landing. Most of the clearings in that area were Montagnard slash-and-burn farm fields. Bad enough we had to land helicopters and men to trample through their pitiful yam and cassava patches; we didn't need to plow them up with the heavy stuff or cause civilian casualties.

We shuttled the battalion in on sixteen Huey troop-transport choppers, called slicks to differentiate them from the rocket- and machine gun–carrying Huey gunships. Plumley and I landed with the first elements of Captain Tony Nadal's Alpha Company. There was no resistance, but the clearing was occupied—by half a dozen Montagnard men and women, all bare to the waist and busy cutting brush. They disappeared swiftly into the heavy jungle. I was glad we had skipped the prep fires.

For the next two and a half days we ran small-unit patrols throughout the area. UPI reporter Joe Galloway, a twenty-three-year-old native of Refugio, Texas, marched with us. Earlier, Joe had wangled a helicopter ride into the Plei Me Special Forces Camp while it was under siege and, because of the shortage of fighters, found himself assigned to man a .30-caliber light machine gun. When he hooked up with us, he carried on his shoulder an M-16 rifle, which the Special Forces commander, Major Charles Beckwith, had handed him when the Plei Me fight was over. Galloway told Beckwith that, strictly speaking, under the Geneva Convention he was "a civilian noncombatant." Beckwith's response: "No such thing in these mountains, boy. Take the rifle."

Galloway remembers: "My first time out with Hal Moore's 1st Battalion, 7th Cavalry was a hellish walk in the sun to a remote Montagnard mountain village. We got into a patch of brush and wait-a-minute vines so thick and thorny that every step had to be carved out with machetes. We covered maybe three hundred yards in four hours, and forded a fast-running, chest-deep mountain stream just as darkness fell, then huddled in our ponchos, wet and freezing, all night long.

"At first light I pinched off a small piece of C-4 plastic explosive from the emergency supply in my pack and used it to boil up a canteen cup of water for coffee. If you lit C-4 very carefully you could be drinking hot coffee in maybe thirty seconds; if you were careless it blew your arm off. Over a first cigarette I watched Moore's men. First, they shaved. Shaved? Up here? I was amazed. Then the colonel himself, blond, jut-jawed, and very intense, a son of Bardstown, Kentucky, and West Point, walked by on his morning rounds with Sergeant Major Plumley. Moore looked me over and said: 'We all shave in my outfit—reporters included.' My steaming coffee water went for a wash and a shave, and I gained a measure of respect for the man."

That day we came to a Montagnard village, deep in the mountains. A toothless old man emerged from the longhouse, fumbling with the buttons on a tattered old French army tunic and proudly waving a small French tricolor flag, certain that the comrades of his younger days had at last returned. I'm not certain that the situation and our nationality were ever explained to his satisfaction.

Our medics treated the sick and injured, while Tom Metsker and an interpreter sought information on any enemy in the area. They drew a blank on possible enemy, but the medics turned up one young boy with a badly burned arm, who needed hospital treatment. The village leader and the boy's father finally agreed to his evacuation. The medics called in an American helicopter to carry out the child, who had been wounded by fire from another American helicopter.

The boy and his father, carrying a jug of water, a large chunk of raw meat wrapped in green leaves, and a crossbow, climbed aboard quivering with fright. They had crossed from the fifteenth century to the twentieth in a matter of minutes. Galloway, watching and photographing the scene, thought to himself: "Nothing is simple in this war; maybe it never is in any war."

We continued patrolling south and east, finding nothing and growing more frustrated by the hour.

Turns out we weren't the only ones who were frustrated. General Dick Knowles was decidedly unhappy with the lack of results. Says Knowles: "Conventional wisdom indicated that the enemy had drifted into an area southeast of Pleiku and we were directed to conduct operations there. Shortly after the operation started, Major General Stanley (Swede) Larsen, the Corps commander, visited us and asked how things were going. I told him we had no contact to speak of and didn't expect any. Whereupon Larsen asked, 'Why are you conducting operations there?' My response: 'That's what your order in writing directed us to do.' The general answered that our primary mission was: Find the enemy and go after him."

Knowles knew what to do with that kind of guidance. In the late afternoon of November 12, he flew south from Pleiku in his command helicopter looking for Colonel Tim Brown, who was with me in the field. He climbed out of the chopper, cigar in hand, and asked how it was going. Brown, who seldom wasted words, replied: "Dry hole, sir." Knowles turned to me: What do you think? "Nothing here, General; we're just wearing out the troops." He turned back to Brown: "Tim, what do you think about heading west—a long jump into the Ia Drang Valley?" Brown said that would be better than here: "From what I remember, your G-2 said something about a base camp out there."

Knowles gave us the go sign. Later he would say that he gave that order "based on strong instincts and flimsy intelligence." In minutes Knowles and Brown boarded their helicopters and were gone. I told my staff to do a map study of the Ia Drang Valley and begin planning an operation. I had no doubt that my battalion would be chosen to mount the attack into the Ia Drang. To date Brown had given the 1st Battalion, 7th Cavalry every job in which there was a possibility of contact with the enemy. The 2nd Battalion, 7th Cavalry, his other battalion, had a new commander and staff and Brown was trying to break them in gently.

Knowles, Brown, and I were comfortable with each other. We had worked together closely for the last eighteen months. They knew their stuff on airmobility and helicopter warfare, and I had gone to school on them. They knew they could count on me, and I knew they would provide all the support I needed, sometimes even before I knew I needed it. General Harry Kinnard had fostered that kind of leadership in the 1st Cavalry Division. Kinnard came out of the great Airborne school of thought that authority has to be pushed down to the man on the spot, because you never know where leaders will land when units jump out of airplanes. What was true for parachute operations was likewise true for fast-moving airmobile combat units leapfrogging across difficult terrain.

Early on Saturday, November 13, Colonel Brown shifted my battalion to new areas south and southwest of Plei Me, where we again conducted patrols from widely scattered company bases. We set up the battalion command post in an old French fort just outside the fence of the Plei Me Special Forces Camp. The American Special Forces often located their camps on the sites of old French army posts, strategically situated on Communist infiltration routes.

The enemy had not changed, nor had the need to keep track of his movements. In almost every case the French had chosen well, locating these eyes-and-ears posts so that they covered the most logical enemy routes through these rugged mountains. But for the French army, and for their American successors as well, these patrol bases were remote and isolated, far from help, which was tied to bad roads. They were tempting targets, often attacked and sometimes overwhelmed and overrun.

Each leg of this triangular fort was a heavily overgrown six- to eight-foot-high wall of dirt about ninety yards long. Long years of disuse, and the annual monsoon rains, had crumbled the firing positions, the steps, and the walls themselves. The adjacent Special Forces camp, also triangular, didn't look all that much better. During the late-October siege, Plei Me camp had been attacked by mortars, sappers, and a storm of machine-gun and small-arms fire, and the few flimsy, tin-roofed structures that the enemy hadn't blown up had been beaten up by big pallets of supplies that U.S. Air Force transport planes had dropped in by parachute.

That afternoon Colonel Brown ordered me to send a rifle company back to Catecka Tea Plantation to help secure the defense perimeter around his 3rd Brigade command post for the night. Captain John Herren's Bravo Company drew that assignment. The night before, at 11:23 P.M., an estimated two companies of Viet Cong guerrillas had attacked the brigade headquarters and nearby aviation-fuel storage and engineer facilities. The attack was beaten off in an hour, but seven Americans were killed and twenty-three were wounded. Six enemy dead, clad in black pajamas, were found.

Not a quarter-mile through the tea bushes from Brown's tents stood a lovely white colonial mansion. The French plantation manager lived there, and if you strolled the road you caught glimpses of young women in bikinis taking the sun beside the swimming pool. The mansion had been neither mortared nor attacked the night before. Army intelligence said the French owners paid the Viet Cong a million piasters a year in protection money and paid the Saigon government three million piasters a year in taxes. The plantation billed the U.S. government $50 for each tea bush and $250 for each rubber tree damaged by combat operations. Just one more incongruity.

That afternoon, Saturday, November 13, Joe Galloway hitched a lift from Pleiku out to Catecka to Brown's headquarters. He says: "Two French correspondents who had ridden out with me wangled an invitation to spend the night with their countryman in the mansion. I dug a foxhole under one of those $50 tea bushes out on the perimeter around brigade headquarters with Bravo Company. Dug it deep, set out some spare magazines for the rifle, and settled in to celebrate my twenty-fourth birthday with a can of C-ration peaches and another can of pound cake. The word was that Hal Moore's battalion would launch deep into the bush the next morning."

Galloway had the word and the word was right. He may have gotten it before I did. At about four P.M. Captain Tony Nadal and his Alpha Company troopers were out patrolling when they came on the clear waters of the small Glae River. Nadal approved a request for small parties of his men, under guard, to take turns bathing and washing up. "I was going back with First Sergeant [Arthur J.] Newton and a couple of other guys when I heard rockets firing," Nadal remembers. "We ran back and found our own helicopters had dumped a bunch of rockets on us in two strafing runs. I got on the radio screaming: 'Get this goddamn thing away from me!' "

Sergeant Major Plumley and I flew to the scene and met with Nadal and Major Roger (Black Bart) Bartholomew, commander of the aerial rocket artillery helicopter company, who had flown in to investigate. It seems that a unit of our sister battalion—2nd Battalion, 7th Cavalry—had screwed up the map coordinates when calling for fire support. Four of Nadal's men were wounded and carried out by medical evacuation choppers.

Not long after, Colonel Brown flew in, checked on the situation with Alpha Company, and then called me aside. "Hal, I'm moving your battalion west tomorrow morning," he said, unfolding his map. "Here is your area of operations—north of Chu Pong in the Ia Drang Valley. Your mission is the same one you have now: Find and kill the enemy." He rapidly outlined the scope of the operation and the resources he could spare: sixteen UH-1D Hueys to move my troops, two 105mm howitzer batteries within range to support us, and at least two days on the ground patrolling.

He added that Alpha Company of the 229th Assault Helicopter Battalion would provide the helicopters; the 229th's A Company commander, Major Bruce Crandall, was on the way now. "One more thing, Hal. In that area be sure your companies are close enough for mutual support." After he left, I alerted Captain Nadal to what was coming and flew back to the old French fort. On the way, I jotted notes on what needed to be done and radioed Matt Dillon, my operations officer, telling him to put out a warning order to the other company commanders and support units and get the staff together. We had a lot to do and not much time to do it in.

Bruce Crandall, thirty-four years old, was an All-American college baseball star out of Olympia, Washington. He used the distinctive radio call sign "Ancient Serpent 6," which readily lent itself to profane permutations. Crandall was already there with Captain Mickey Parrish, the helicopter liaison officer, who would stay with us throughout the operation to coordinate helicopter movements. This was standard operating procedure in the 1st Cavalry Division: detailed planning and coordination between the helicopter lift company and the infantry.

We had not yet been in any battalion-size fight in Vietnam, and Bruce Crandall's helicopter pilots were likewise unblooded. All of us were soon to be put to the test. Crandall was my kind of guy: good at what he did, straight-talking, and dead honest. He knew his people were good—he personally saw to that—and he expected the same high standards of everyone he worked with. It didn't hurt that Ancient Serpent 6, or "Old Snake" or "Snakeshit 6," as everyone called him, was one of the funniest men alive. His pilots and air and ground crews proudly reflected Old Snake's attitudes and professionalism, and Crandall loved them.

"We had sixteen aircraft flying out of twenty assigned to the unit," Crandall says. "What we lacked in combat experience we made up for in flying time. Our junior pilot had about seven hundred hours in helicopters and was instrument-rated. Most were dual-rated [trained to fly] fixed-wing [aircraft] and helicopters, and every one of the leaders was dual instrument-rated. Most of us had been in the battalion through air-assault training, and our company flew with the expeditionary force sent to the Dominican Republic in mid-1965."

Crandall continues: "On November thirteenth I sat in on a briefing by Colonel Moore. We went through some discussion as to how we could carry out the attack, artillery sites, tactical air support and so forth, and set up a reconnaissance flight for early the next morning. Moore expected us, the aviation element, to be present during planning and briefing and to be a part of his staff. This attitude was shared by his staff and his commanders. As a team we proved that the whole was even better than the sum of the parts."

Captain Paul Patton Winkel, whose great-grandfather rode with William Tecumseh Sherman, was a Bravo Company 229th platoon leader attached to Bruce Crandall's task force for the Ia Drang operation. He talks about what went into the making of that first generation of airmobile aviators: "We trained from July, 1964, until our arrival in Vietnam with the 1st Cavalry in precision flying—four aircraft in V formation at 80 to 120 knots barely above treetop level, flowing with the contour lines of the ground. Radio work, navigation, foul-weather flying. Timing, timing, always timing. Crossing the release point at a critical second. Coordinating with gunships, artillery, infantry. Practice, practice, practice. On the ground with the troops, high overhead, reconnaissance, reporting. This all paid off. Many of us are alive today because we learned our lessons well."

By now the word had gone out to Tony Nadal and Bob Edwards to pull their men in from the bush and assemble them in the largest clearings available in their areas for helicopter pickup the next morning. Both companies were operating about six miles south of Plei Me. John Herren's Bravo Company was already assembled at brigade headquarters.

My staff and I and the liaison officers talked about the hundred and one details that have to be analyzed in a combat operational plan: the terrain; possible landing zones in that rough scrub-and-jungle region; weather forecasts; the enemy; manpower strength in each of our companies; logistics, supporting firepower; and helicopter lift capabilities.

Bruce Crandall's lift ships, the sixteen Hueys, would arrive at Plei Me fort by 9:30 A.M. Five big Chinook helicopters would arrive even earlier than that to sling a battery of six 105mm howitzers beneath them and take them to Falcon, where they would join another battery of six guns already in place. I ordered an early-morning recon flight, of two Huey slicks and two gunships, over the Ia Drang Valley. Matt Dillon; Bruce Crandall; John Herren; the artillery battery commander, Captain Don Davis; the Cavalry Scout section leader, Captain Rickard; the fire support coordinator, Captain Jerry Whiteside; the forward air controller, Lieutenant Charlie Hastings; and I would fly the mission.

"Since Bravo Company is already in one location and will be brought back early, it will be the assault company," I told the gathering. "Plan for a twenty-minute artillery prep followed by thirty seconds of aerial rocket artillery, then thirty seconds by the gunships. Bravo Company will land right after the gunship run. I will go in with Bravo in the lead assault ship. Tell the commanders to have their men carry the maximum load of ammunition, one C-ration and two canteens per man. That's it for now. Questions?" There were none.

It was eight P.M. and things were buzzing in the command post (CP), which consisted of four small tents, each about ten feet in diameter—one for the battalion surgeon and aid station; one for S-2 and S-3 (intelligence and operations); one for S-1 and S-4 (personnel and logistics); and one for the headquarters company commander. The rest of us slept on the ground, rolled up in our ponchos. Chow in the field was almost always C-rations—cans of ham and lima beans, or spaghetti and meatballs, or beans and franks, zipped open with the little P-38 can openers we all wore on the dog-tag chains around our necks.

Sergeant Major Plumley and I ate and then walked around the inner perimeter of the old French fort, occasionally climbing the dirt berms to peer out into the darkness. Headquarters was guarded by the recon platoon and the machine-gun platoon from Delta Company. We stopped and talked with some of the troopers on the perimeter. It was a quiet night, the bird calls and the croaking of the geckos mingling with the muted hissing of the kerosene camp lanterns that lighted the scene inside the blacked-out tents.

I thought again of the French soldiers who had built and guarded this crumbling post on the frontiers of a now-dead colonial empire. Some things change, but not the rhythms of military life. How different a scene would it have been for a French commander preparing to launch an operation fifteen years earlier?

My thoughts turned to tomorrow's operation. I felt strongly that the enemy had been using the Ia Drang Valley as a jumping-off point for the attacks on Plei Me and likely had returned there to regroup and treat their wounded. The Ia Drang had plenty of water for drinking and for cooking rice. Best of all, for the PAVN, was its location on the border with Cambodia. The Vietnamese Communists came and went across that border at will; we were prohibited from crossing it.

I knew that the 1st Cavalry's 1st Brigade, the Plei Me garrison, the division's helicopter cavalry squadron, and our heavy air and artillery fire support must have taken a heavy toll on them over the last three weeks. The intelligence people were telling me their best guess: possibly one battalion at the base of the Chu Pong massif two miles northwest of the area we were aiming for; possibly enemy very near a clearing we were considering for the assault landing zone; and a possible secret base a half-mile east of our target area. If even one of those possibles was an *actual,* we would get a violent response.

How ready was my battalion for combat? We had never maneuvered in combat as an entire battalion, although all three rifle companies had been in minor scrapes. Most of the men had never even seen an enemy soldier, dead or alive. We had killed fewer than ten men, black-pajama guerrillas, in the get-acquainted patrols and small operations since our arrival in An Khe.

The four line companies had twenty of their authorized twenty-three officers, but the enlisted ranks had been badly whittled down by expiring enlistments, malaria cases, and requirements for base-camp guards and workers back in An Khe. Alpha Company had 115 men, 49 fewer than authorized. Bravo Company, at 114 men, was 50 short. Charlie Company had 106 men, down by 58. And the weapons company, Delta, had only 76 men, 42 fewer than authorized. Headquarters Company was also understrength, and I had been forced to draw it down further by sending men out to fill crucial medical and communications vacancies in the line companies.

I didn't like being short-handed, but things had been no different in the Korean War and somehow we made do. You just suck it up and do it, and we would do it the same way in the Ia Drang. The officers and NCOs would do what they could to take up the slack, just as we had done in Korea.

I could only hope that the enemy had been hurt badly in the earlier fighting and was, likewise, short of men. At least I could rely on strong fire support to help stack the deck. The weather forecast—clear sunny days and moonlit nights—practically guaranteed air support, and two batteries of twelve 105mm howitzers would be dedicated entirely to our use.

But my main concern focused on the fact that we would have only sixteen Huey slicks to ferry the battalion into the assault area, an average fifteen-mile one-way flight from the various pickup points. What that meant was that fewer than eighty men—not even one full company—would hit the landing zone in the first wave, and would be the only troops on the ground until the helicopters returned to Plei Me, loaded another eighty, and returned. Later lifts would carry more men—ninety to one hundred—as they burned off fuel and grew lighter in weight.

It was a thirty-minute round trip and at the expected rate it would take more than four hours to get all of my men on the ground. The Hueys would also have to divert to refuel during this process, costing even more time; and if the landing zone was hot and any of the sixteen helicopters were shot up and dropped out, that, too, would immediately impact on the timetable.

I ran an endless string of "what if's" through my mind that night as I leaned against the earthen wall of the old French fort. Time so spent is never wasted; if even one "what if" comes to pass a commander will be a few precious seconds ahead of the game. My worst-case scenario was a hot LZ—a fight beginning during or just after our assault landing—and I certainly had to assume the enemy would be able to provide it. In any assault into an enemy-held area—whether it's a beachhead or a paratroop drop zone, and whether you have to cross a major river or, as in our case, land in the base area—the hairiest time is that tenuous period before your troops get firmly established and organized, and move out. This is when you are most vulnerable.

I ran through what I could do to influence the action if the worst came to pass. First, I would personally land on the first helicopter, piloted by Bruce Crandall. That would permit me a final low-level look at the landing zone and surrounding terrain, and with Crandall in the front seat and me in the back we could work out, on the spot, any last-minute diversion to an alternate landing zone, if necessary, and fix any other problems with the lift.

In the American Civil War it was a matter of principle that a good officer rode his horse as little as possible. There were sound reasons for this. If you are riding and your soldiers are marching, how can you judge how tired they are, how thirsty, how heavy their packs weigh on their shoulders?

I applied the same philosophy in Vietnam, where every battalion commander had his own command-and-control helicopter. Some commanders used their helicopter as their personal mount. I never believed in that. You had to get on the ground with your troops to see and hear what was happening. You have to soak up firsthand information for your instincts to operate accurately. Besides, it's too easy to be crisp, cool, and detached at 1,500 feet; too easy to demand the impossible of your troops; too easy to make mistakes that are fatal only to those souls far below in the mud, the blood, and the confusion.

With me in that first ship would be Sergeant Major Plumley; Captain Tom Metsker; my radio operator, Specialist Bob Ouellette; and our interpreter, Mr. Nik, a Montagnard.

The second aspect of my plan to deal with any problems at the landing zone was as follows. I would put my fire support team overhead, in the battalion-command helicopter with Matt Dillon coordinating. From 2,500 feet overhead Dillon would have radio contact with 3rd Brigade Headquarters, with the battalion rear command post at Plei Me, and with all the company pickup zones. He could monitor all that was said over the battalion command network. Jerry Whiteside would direct the artillery and the rocket gunships. Charlie Hastings would deal with the Air Force fire support. And Mickey Parrish would deal with Bruce Crandall and the helicopter people.

Third, I had to maximize the impact of the eighty men who would be on the ground alone during the first critical half-hour. Standard operating procedure in the new science of airmobile warfare dictated that the lead elements scatter out over 360 degrees and secure the entire perimeter. Not this time. I had been thinking about a new technique that seemed tailor-made for this situation. Bravo Company would assemble in a central location in the landing zone as a reserve and strike force. Four seven-man squads would be sent out in different directions to check out the perimeter and surrounding area. If one of those squads encountered enemy forces I could then shift the rest of the company in that direction and carry the fight to the enemy well off the landing zone.

Around 10:30 P.M. Plumley and I walked back to the operations tent to check on preparations. Everything was going fine. Plumley suggested we get some sleep, saying it might be a long while before we got another chance. We walked back to where we had left our packs, got out our ponchos, rolled up in them on the ground— weapons close at hand—and went to sleep.

4

THE LAND AND
THE ENEMY

> He who controls the Central Highlands controls South Vietnam.
>
> —Vietnamese military maxim

The Central Highlands is a beautiful region; from the heavily populated coastal areas with their white, sandy beaches and flat rice paddies bounded by dikes, it climbs into the rougher, stream-cut foothills and finally on into the two-thousand- to three-thousand-foot-high mountains of the interior, where the French built their coffee and tea plantations. In 1965 the Highlands were the domain of the Green Berets, the U.S. Special Forces. But before the military men and before the French this was the homeland of the many different tribes of Montagnards, or mountain people, each tribe with its own dialect and territory, living a life little changed since the Bronze Age, when they were driven out of southern China to settle the mountain ranges of Indochina, the Malay archipelago and even some of the Indonesian islands.

They practiced slash-and-burn agriculture, creating small clearings in the thick jungle, tilling and cultivating corn and cassava and yams in the thin mountain soil until, in three or four years, it was exhausted, and then moving on. The Montagnards live communally in thatch-roofed longhouses built on stilts. They had always steered clear of the lowland Vietnamese, who called them savages and treated them with contempt and harshness. The hatred was returned in kind, and the Montagnards willingly soldiered against the Vietnamese, first for the French and then for the Americans. They were brave, loyal, and deadly mercenaries who were highly effective soldiers in their home territory.

The principal communications and supply route across the Highlands is the fabled Colonial Route 19, which runs from the port of Qui Nhon west to Pleiku, the largest city of the Highlands, and on into Cambodia. The 1st Cavalry Division base camp at An Khe was halfway between Qui Nhon and Pleiku, about forty miles from each of those key cities.

Shortly after we arrived in Vietnam, Sergeant Major Plumley and I took a jeep and a shotgun guard and drove ten miles west of An Khe on Route 19, into no-man's-land, to the PK 15 marker post. There, the Viet Minh had destroyed most of the French Group Mobile 100 in a deadly ambush eleven years earlier. We walked the battleground, where a bullet-pocked six-foot-high stone obelisk declares in French and Vietnamese: "Here on June 24, 1954, soldiers of France and Vietnam died for their countries." In my hand was Bernard Fall's *Street Without Joy,* which describes the battle. Plumley and I walked the battleground for two hours. Bone fragments, parts of weapons and vehicles, web gear and shell fragments and casings still littered the ground. From that visit I took away one lesson: Death is the price you pay for underestimating this tenacious enemy.

North of Route 19 and west of the spectacular Mang Yang Pass, the land is hilly and mountainous, with some primary jungle and occasional broad plateaus. The few secondary roads are unpaved, and impassable in the monsoon season. In the Laos–Cambodia–South Vietnam tri-border region there are dense triple-canopy rain forests where the sun never penetrates, the soil is always wet, and tangles of wait-a-minute vines wait for the walker. South of Pleiku and Route 19, north of Ban Me Thuot and west of the Plei Me Special Forces Camp is scrub jungle with stunted hardwood, criss-crossed only by rushing mountain streams, animal trails, and Montagnard paths.

The dominant terrain feature is the Chu Pong massif, rising to just over 2,400 feet, a jumble of mountains, valleys, ravines, and ridges that runs westward for more than fifteen miles, the last five of them inside Cambodia. North to south the massif measures between ten and thirteen miles. The limestone heights of the Chu Pong are full of springs, streams and caves. Along the massif's north side runs the Ia Drang. (*Ia* means "river" in one of the Highlands dialects.) The Ia Drang is born of the marriage of two smaller streams near the Catecka Tea Plantation on Colonial Route 14 between Pleiku and Plei Me camp. By the time it reaches the Chu Pong area it is swift and deep, and during the monsoon it is a raging torrent. It flows to the west, on into Cambodia, where eventually it empties into the Mekong River and returns to Vietnam far south in the delta.

The soldiers commanded by Brigadier General Chu Huy Man had been training for more than eighteen months. When they joined the People's Army, each recruit was issued two khaki shirts, two pairs of khaki trousers, a sewing kit, and a pair of "Ho Chi Minh" sandals cut from used truck tires. Those uniforms were expected to last for five years. Basic training lasted thirteen weeks, six days a week, 6:00 A.M. to 9:15 P.M. The instructors emphasized weapons and tactics, the hows of warfare, while the political commissars had time set aside each day to lecture on the whys of this war. The recruits were reminded constantly that their fathers had beaten the French colonialists; now it was their duty to defeat the American imperialists. They were imbued with Ho Chi Minh's dictum: "Nothing is more precious than freedom and independence."

After basic training, some were selected for six months of NCO school and would emerge as new corporals. For the rest, advanced infantry training included familiarization with all weapons, the use of explosives, ambush tactics, reconnaissance tactics, adjusting mortar fire, and patrol tactics. In June of 1964, Man's soldiers moved up into the mountains of North Vietnam, terrain similar to that in the Western Highlands of South Vietnam. Here physical conditioning was emphasized; they scaled steep slopes while wearing rucksacks loaded with fifty to sixty pounds of rocks. Their advanced training now also focused on the art of camouflage. They got rudimentary instruction in anti-aircraft defenses: Fire on full automatic straight in front of the aircraft's line of flight, so that the helicopter or airplane will fly into a wall of bullets.

When the time came for them to begin the arduous two-month journey down the Ho Chi Minh Trail through Laos, General Man's regiments broke down into battalions for security purposes, each moving separately and at least three days ahead of the next. Each soldier carried four pounds of rice—seven days' rations—plus another eight pounds of foodstuffs that were expected to last him the whole trip: two pounds of salt; two pounds of wheat flour; and four pounds of salt pork. One man in every squad carried the aluminum cookpot that the squad's rice would be boiled in. Each man also carried fifty antimalaria pills, one for each day on the trail, and a hundred vitamin B_1 tabs to be taken at the rate of three per week. Despite the pills, virtually every man who walked the trail contracted malaria and, on average, three or four soldiers of each 160-man company would die on the journey. Malaria, diarrhea, accidents, poisonous snakes, and American air raids all took their toll.

Along the route the men passed construction crews; many of the workers were young girls, who were employed by the thousands in improving the network of trails and the campsites that were situated every nine miles along the route. Each camp, which could shelter a company of troops, consisted of a series of crude bamboo huts dispersed along a half-mile of trail to make a smaller target for the warplanes. Each man carried a light canvas hammock to string up in the huts at night. Each also carried a long rectangular piece of green plastic for a makeshift poncho. The nights on the trail were cold, the days comfortable. Man's soldiers marched nine miles each day, the distance between the rest camps where they spent each night. Every fourth day they stayed in camp, taking the day off to rest up, wash their clothes, and tend to minor medical problems.

Porters pushed bicycles, modified with one long pole tied to the frame and rising three feet above the saddle and another long steering pole tied to the left handlebar. Bundles containing more than 350 pounds of rice or ammunition or medical supplies were strapped and tied to the bicycle frame and the tall pole. The porter walked alongside and pushed the load, steering the contraption with the pole tied to the handlebar. No-tech, primitive, ridiculously simple, yes; but it delivered the goods. Packhorses also worked the trail.

Besides his food and medicine, each soldier carried his weapon and a basic load of ammunition. The weapons were those the men had trained with all those months on the firing ranges, a jumble of East Bloc surplus from the factories of the Soviet Union, China, Czechoslovakia, and Albania. Among them were the Kalashnikov AK-47 assault rifle, a superb infantry weapon; the SKS Siminov semi-automatic carbine with folding bayonet; the Degtyarev automatic rifle; the Maxim heavy machine gun; 60mm, 82mm, and 120mm mortars; the 12.7mm anti-aircraft machine gun; the wooden-handled potato-masher type hand grenade; and a Chinese-made 9mm automatic pistol for the officers.

People's Army soldiers, young and old, were inveterate diarists. Almost every man carried a small notebook, which he filled with copied love poems, the lyrics of popular songs, and his own writings. The men yearned for home and family. The notebook and two or three small snapshots of a sweetheart or wife and children were carried wrapped inside plastic.

Now, in late September, as the American cavalrymen were hacking their new base camp out of the jungle near An Khe, one of General Man's regiments, the 320th, was already in South Vietnam; a second, the 33rd, had just reached the Cambodian–South Vietnamese border; and a third, the 66th, still had battalions strung out along the trail. The terrain where they would operate for the next two months, from Plei Me camp west to the Cambodian border, is largely a rolling savanna of four- to five-foot-high elephant grass wooded with scrub trees, not unlike the American scrub oak, and some other varieties that are taller and thicker, especially along the creek and stream beds. There are no roads, and only a few trails, in the interior of this region.

The land is drained from northeast to southwest by two small rivers, the Ia Meur on the west and the Ia Tae to the east. Although the topographical maps we carried were sprinkled with twenty or so black dots marking Montagnard villages, we saw no villages or Montagnards out there.

The Vietnamese People's Army historian, Major General Hoang Phuong, who as a lieutenant colonel was sent to the Ia Drang Valley in the fall of 1965 to study the battles and write an after-action report for the high command, says: "When we received the news that the 1st Air Cavalry had come to Vietnam, the commanders of our divisions in the South were very nervous, very worried by what they were hearing about this strong, mobile unit so well equipped with helicopters. The liberation forces moved mainly by foot, were poorly equipped. Our hospital and food services were not so good. How can we fight and win against the cavalry?"

Major General Phuong adds: "In September of 1965, when you landed at An Khe, our commanders in the Central Highlands studied how to cope. We foresaw that the coming battle would be very fierce. First, we evacuated the population and prepared training camps. We improved our positions, dug shelters, and prepared caches of food and underground hospitals. We knew that sooner or later you would attack our zones, and we tried to prepare positions that would neutralize you. We knew that it would not be enough just to make propaganda saying that we were winning. We had to study how to fight the Americans."

Phuong continues: "On October nineteenth we started our attack on Plei Me at 11:50 P.M. We attacked from three directions. This was the 33rd Regiment. They had rehearsed the attack. When we encircled Plei Me the ARVN sent one regiment as a relief force. On October twenty-third, at one P.M., the first reinforcements reached our ambush position. Our 320th Regiment had set up the ambush. The battle took place along four kilometers of Provincial Route 5. The enemy made many air strikes, bombing our positions fiercely. The fighting continued until October twenty-fifth. We destroyed the first group of Saigon forces, but other ARVN occupied the high ground and kept fighting. We could not destroy the entire relief column. There were too many of them who survived. Our 320th Regiment suffered heavy losses to air strikes and at five P.M. October twenty-fifth we ordered the withdrawal of our troops from the battle area, including the forces surrounding Plei Me. They were ordered to withdraw rapidly and be prepared to fight against Americans. That was the end of Phase I of the campaign.

"The two regiments involved in this battle were recently arrived from the North, and they did not have much knowledge of this area. The commanders of these two regiments were also new. During the French war they had been company commanders. The commander of the 320th Regiment was Major Ma Van Minh. The commander of the 66th Regiment was Lieutenant Colonel La Ngoc Chau. On October twenty-eighth the Americans dropped some troops in the rear of our base. At that time the headquarters of General Chu Huy Man, B-3 Front, was at Plei Bong Klo.

"We opened Phase II of the campaign from October twenty-ninth to November ninth. At that time our troops were in great disorder. We had many difficulties. You dropped troops close to our headquarters and very close to our units. Our units were broken up, dispersed, and then the Americans dropped into Plei The near the Cambodian border on November third. You destroyed many caches and supplies of food, as well as our hospital. We lost weapons, war matériel, supplies, and our communications. When we withdrew you dropped troops to cut off our units. We lost communications with the retreating units. During these ten days you caused much distress and disorder. Our soldiers did not have time to rest and regroup. When we withdrew to our base here [Chu Pong], we had to send soldiers far away to carry rice and foodstuffs back for their units. Normally it took one day to go there, one day to come back—two days round trip. We lacked communications equipment. We had very few radios and those we had were in very bad condition. Your attacks were very effective. We tried to take advantage of the terrain and avoid contact and casualties. General Man's headquarters were now in Plei The. He had moved close to the border, to the south of Chu Pong."

Lieutenant General Nguyen Huu An, now commandant of the Vietnamese army's Senior Military Academy, was a senior lieutenant colonel and the deputy commander of the B-3 Front in the fall of 1965. From an advance command post near the ambush site, he directed the failed ambush against the South Vietnamese relief force bound for Plei Me camp. During the withdrawal he had pulled his command post back to a position on the slopes of the Chu Pong massif.

For decades the senior commanders of the North Vietnamese army have been shadowy, mysterious figures who often fought under noms de guerre. Not much was known of their background and history; even the secret files of the Central Intelligence Agency and Defense Intelligence Agency held little information. An's biography is that of a soldier with more than forty-five years on active duty, much of it spent in the field in Vietnam's two great wars:

"I was born in 1926 in Hanoi. My father was a technician at Bach Mai airport. He was involved in the anti-French movement since 1937 and was put into prison by the French in 1939. So I got this infection from my father and it was a passion for me from a young age. When our Autumn Revolution succeeded in 1945, I joined the army. My first tour was as an enlisted soldier. After that, I was assigned to a school training squad leaders. I also applied for political school and became a company commissar. But I asked to change my job back to military commander. So I have been through all levels in the army: corporal, sergeant, company commander, battalion commander. I became deputy commander and then commander of a regiment at Dien Bien Phu. My regiment fought on [the French strongpoint] Eliane I, right on top of the shelter of the French commander, General [Christian de la Croix de] Castries. When the French war was over, I became a staff officer, then a division commander. I commanded four different divisions—the 35th Division, the 1st Division, and the 308th Division, a very famous division with a proud history. I took my current position as commandant of the Senior Military Academy four years ago. Before that I commanded the military academy, which trains regimental commanders. I have three children. My daughter is a major and she is married to a major. My second son is an engineer. My other son is a marine construction designer. I have three grandchildren, all girls. My wife was a teacher of chemistry, but [is] now retired."

Of the Ia Drang campaign, An says, "When we attacked Plei Me camp, in Phase I, we encircled the position in order to destroy the reinforcements. Our purpose was to draw the Saigon ARVN column into coming out to reinforce. We had a strong force, but no intention of liberating territory. We wanted to destroy enemy forces. As we launched this campaign, we learned that American troops had landed in Vietnam. We believed that in Phase I if we attacked Plei Me, the ARVN will come and we will ambush their reinforcements. In Phase II, we believed that the Americans would come and we would attack them. We had learned that the Americans could drop troops far behind us. So in Phase III, we would be ready to attack Americans in our rear areas. We sent an advance command post to be near the ambush, staffed by myself, deputy B-3 commander, and Lieutenant Colonel Duc Vu Hiep, deputy political commissar of B-3 Front, who is now also a lieutenant general. We had a very small group escorting us, maybe forty people total. Some intelligence officers and operations officers on staff. It was a very small, very mobile command group."

Senior General Chu Huy Man, former chief political commissar of the People's Army and until recently a member of the Communist Party Central Committee, is now near eighty years of age. He retired from the army only in 1990. His rank of senior general, the highest in the Vietnamese army, is equivalent to the rank of five-star general in the American army; only five men, including Vo Nguyen Giap, have ever achieved it. Man's personal story: "I joined the revolutionary movement in 1930, just after the Indochina Communist Party was formed. I was imprisoned in Kontum by the French. In 1945, during the Autumn Revolution, I joined the army and became a regimental commander. I commanded a number of regiments and was involved in most of the campaigns of the French war. During Dien Bien Phu, I was political commissar of the 316th Division column. General Nguyen Huu An was one of my regimental commanders in the Dien Bien Phu attack. I moved to South Vietnam in 1964. I was at first stationed in the delta of central Vietnam, then moved to the Central Highlands in 1965."

General Man says the arrival of the first American combat troops in South Vietnam, especially the 1st Cavalry Division, forced a major change in plans for the fall–winter offensive as early as June of 1965. "We used our new plan to lure the tiger out of the mountain. First we attack Plei Me, then the ARVN reinforcements come into our ambush. Then, I was confident, the Americans will use their helicopters to land in our rear, land in the Ia Drang area. It was our intention to draw the Americans out of An Khe. We did not have any plans to liberate the land; only to destroy troops." Man says he employed five battalions in Phase I—one reinforced battalion to besiege Plei Me camp and four to prepare the Route 5 ambush— while a sixth battalion remained in reserve. "We didn't have enough troops," Man says, explaining the failure of the ambush.

The personality of the campaign changed drastically as the North Vietnamese broke off their attack on Plei Me and abandoned the ambush attempt. General Man ordered his 320th and 33rd regiments back to the Chu Pong base-camp area to rest and regroup. The 320th reached a position along the Cambodian border south of Chu Pong practically untouched, but the hard-luck 33rd Regiment, which had suffered heavy casualties and was battle-weary, would endure additional blows on its retreat west, harassed relentlessly by the Air Cavalry troops of the 1st Brigade.

Captured documents and prisoner interrogations revealed that by the time it reached the Chu Pong base area, the 33rd PAVN Regiment was reporting that some forty percent of its officers and men, including two of the three battalion commanders, had been killed. The 33rd had lost virtually all of its eighteen 12.7mm anti-aircraft machine guns and eleven mortars, and the 1st Battalion, 33rd Regiment, which conducted the siege of Plei Me, was down to only one company of effectives. General An says that the 33rd Regiment was given some replacements and built back to a strength of about nine hundred when it reached the base camp. But the general's hopes and plans now revolved around the newly arrived 66th Regiment, which had had no part in the Plei Me attacks.

General Man's three regiments regrouped in the Ia Drang–Chu Pong base area. The region had been a Viet Minh sanctuary during the long war with the French. The Viet Minh's successors, the Viet Cong, had made limited use of the Ia Drang as a hiding place during the years since 1954. General Man could think of no more ideal place for his secret base and staging area for the 1965–1966 campaign. It had ample water for cooking, cleaning, drinking, and caring for casualties. It had deep, wooded defiles and jungle-covered valleys for basing troops, locating hospitals, and storing supplies. Under the jungle canopy were excellent training areas and wide trails on which troops could move, even during the day, without being detected from the air. Best of all, the Ia Drang Valley was convenient to the inviolable sanctuary across the Cambodian border.

The North Vietnamese porters had hauled, on their sturdy bicycles and pack horses, huge quantities of rice, peanuts, and salt, as well as big cans of cooking oil, to stockpile for the troops. Others brought in tons of ammunition, weapons, EE-8 field phones, and WD-30 communication wire. One huge North Vietnamese supply depot was spread over a square mile across the Ia Drang, less than three miles north of a large clearing at the base of the Chu Pong massif.

The 66th Regiment of the B-3 Front was composed of the 7th, 8th, and 9th battalions, each at or near its full strength of forty officers and 515 enlisted men. Still on the trail and scheduled to arrive in mid-November was a battalion of 120mm mortars and a battalion of badly needed anti-aircraft guns. General Man could also call on the local veterans of the H-15 Main Force Viet Cong Battalion, six hundred strong, for duty as porters, guides, and fighters.

October and early November had not been the best of times for General Man. If the old plan to take Pleiku and attack down Route 19 to the coast had indeed been abandoned by Hanoi, and a new one substituted whose focus was to learn how to fight the new American combat troops, the lesson was proving very costly. The game of foxes and hounds, as played by John B. Stockton's 1st Squadron of the 9th Cavalry, had been won hands down by the hounds.

But General Man was about to get what he says he wanted: decisive engagement with a battalion of American cavalry soldiers right in his own backyard. And where were the enemy when the 1st Battalion, 7th Cavalry came calling? Uncomfortably close. According to Man, An, and Phuong, most of the 33rd Regiment was dispersed in a two-mile line along the eastern face of the Chu Pong. The 9th Battalion, 66th Regiment was five hundred yards south and west of a large clearing near the base of the mountain. The 7th Battalion, 66th Regiment was on the ridge line above that clearing, not more than ninety minutes' marching time away. The 8th Battalion, 66th Regiment was half a day's march to the northeast across the Ia Drang. The H-15 Viet Cong Battalion was perhaps eight hours distant. The 320th Regiment was over on the Cambodian border, ten miles northwest.

General An says: "When you landed here, you landed right in the middle of three of our battalions of the 66th Regiment, our reserve force. It was the strongest we had. [At] full strength the battalions each had about four hundred fifty men. Also, there was a headquarters battalion. The regiment's total strength was about sixteen hundred men."

When it came time to give a code name, for map and radio identification, to that clearing we finally chose for our landing at the base of Chu Pong, Captain Dillon, my operations officer, did the honors. He normally picked short words—the names of animals or birds; one-digit numbers; the letters of the alphabet as expressed by the NATO phonetic system. That day, he went with the letter "X"—or "X-Ray," in the NATO alphabet. The North Vietnamese in 1965 also used code letters, to shield the identities of their regiments. General An says the code letter for the 66th Regiment at that time was "X."

Thus was the stage set.

X-RAY

5

INTO THE VALLEY

> The great joy of the Cavalry was to be so far away, out in the
> clean air, the open spaces, away from those damned councils.
> Buford . . . felt the beautiful absence of a commander, a silence
> above him, a windy freedom.
>
> —Michael Shaara, *The Killer Angels*

Sergeant Major Plumley and I rolled out of our ponchos at the old
French fort outside the barbed wire at Plei Me Special Forces
Camp. It was 4:30 on Sunday morning, November 14, and the 1st
Battalion, 7th Cavalry had work to do today. We walked back to
the operations tent, which was manned around the clock. No
change in our orders had come through overnight. But over a cup
of coffee, Matt Dillon passed along one interesting piece of information that the radio relay intercept team attached to our headquarters
had come up with. Says Dillon: "They had made an intercept of a
coded message in Mandarin dialect, like a situation report, from a
position somewhere on a line from Plei Me camp directly through
a clearing at the base of Chu Pong mountain. The intelligence
lieutenant had a map with a line drawn on it. He said that the radio
transmitter was somewhere on this line. I don't remember how long
that message was—that didn't really bother me. It was the direction

it came from. The lieutenant said he thought that possibly there was a North Vietnamese regiment somewhere out there near Chu Pong mountain."

Plumley and I shaved, breakfasted on C-rations, and drank some black coffee. Then I got my pack and ammunition ready and cleaned my M-16 rifle and .45-caliber pistol. As day broke that morning it was cool and fresh at Plei Me, with patches of wispy ground fog. This was the middle of the dry season and the sun just peeking over the horizon promised that the day would be a hot one.

John Herren and his Bravo Company troops were flying in from brigade headquarters in Chinook helicopters; I walked out to the dirt strip to meet him and brief the air-reconnaissance party. The same Chinooks that brought in Bravo Company then picked up the big guns of Alpha Battery, 1st Battalion, 21st Artillery, to move them out to Landing Zone Falcon where they would support our air assault deeper into the valley. Herren's men moved off to relax in the brush south of the airstrip. They had time to eat, refill their canteens, and check and clean their weapons. Unfortunately they were not as fresh as they should have been. Brigade headquarters had kept them on hundred-percent alert all night.

I walked over to Bruce Crandall's Huey and quickly briefed those who would accompany us on the recon flight over the Ia Drang Valley. Colonel Tim Brown had told us generally where he wanted us to operate after the landing, but we now had to select a landing zone, and preferably one that would take as many of our sixteen Hueys as possible at one time.

All of us would have preferred not to make an air-recon flight at all. We didn't want to spook the enemy in the area and possibly alert them to an imminent landing. But we could not choose a landing zone for this assault simply by looking at a 1:50,000 map; we had to overfly the area. We would minimize the chances of discovery by flying high, around 4,500 feet, and pass well to the southeast of the Chu Pong massif on a straight-line flight to the vicinity of Duc Co Special Forces Camp. After orbiting the camp for five minutes we would fly a slightly different return route. Our hope was that any enemy commander in the area would reckon that the two lift ships and the two gunships were on other business in other areas. With binoculars we would be scanning for the right clearing: one with few obstacles and plenty of space.

The flight went precisely as planned. We took no anti-aircraft fire and saw no enemy activity; on our return to Plei Me camp we quickly settled on three possible landing zones: X-Ray, Tango, and Yankee. Major Henri (Pete) Mallet, the 3rd Brigade operations officer, flew in with a half-page "frag"* from Colonel Brown. One of our landing-zone options, Yankee, was about one mile south of the designated area of operations. It was on sloping ground but could take only six or eight Hueys. A possibility. Tango was in the middle of the valley and closer to the Ia Drang by a mile or so, which was good. But it was too small—it could handle only two or three Hueys at once—and, worse yet, it was almost a well, encircled by very tall trees. The pilots hated wells. To land, they had to slow almost to a hover, then drop into the well. Hovering helicopters are juicy targets. We crossed off Tango. That left X-Ray. It was flat; the trees around it weren't all that tall; and it looked as though it could take up to eight helicopters at one time.

I told the command group that I had tentatively decided on the clearing called X-Ray but wanted some more information. Turning to Captain Rickard, the 1st Squadron, 9th Cavalry Scout section leader, I asked him to take his tiny two-man H-13 observation helicopters on a fast nap-of-the-earth flight through the target area to pick up more details on X-Ray, Yankee, and the surrounding area.

By now all the company commanders had assembled at the battalion command post. While we waited for the scout helicopters to return with their reports, I again urged the company commanders to make certain every rifleman had at least the basic load of three hundred rounds of ammo and two hand grenades plus as much additional ammunition as he felt he could carry. Each of the M-79 grenadiers should have at least thirty-six of the fat little 40mm

---

*A frag, or fragmentary order, is an abbreviated version of a commander's directive concerning his plan for a military mission.

rounds. Each squad should be carrying two of the new LAW (light antitank weapon) rockets for bunker-busting and taking out machine-gun crews. And I reminded the commanders of follow-on units waiting for their turn to ride into the landing zone to stay tuned to the command net and listen to what was going on so they wouldn't be in the dark about the situation at X-Ray when they finally got there.

Now the scout pilots returned and reported. Landing Zone Yankee could be used, the scout pilots reported, but it would be risky because it was covered with old tree stumps. X-Ray definitely could take eight to ten Hueys at a time. Finally, they said they had spotted commo wire—a phone line—running east to west on a trail north of X-Ray. That tipped the balance in favor of X-Ray, because it offered certain evidence that there were enemy soldiers in the immediate area. X-Ray would be the assault landing zone, with Tango and Yankee as alternates.

At 8:50 A.M., on the west end of the Plei Me strip, I issued orders to the assembled company commanders, liaison officers, pilots, and staff: Assault into LZ X-Ray to search for and destroy the enemy. Bravo Company lands first, accompanied by my command group, then Alpha, then Charlie, and then Delta companies. Bravo and Alpha will move northwest on my order. Charlie Company will move southwest toward the mountain, likewise on my order. Delta Company will control all mortars. The recon and machine-gun platoons will be battalion reserve. Artillery will fire eight minutes each on Yankee and Tango for deception, then a twenty-minute preparatory fire on X-Ray and adjacent areas. Thirty seconds of aerial rocket artillery and thirty seconds of helicopter gunship prep fire would follow. The battalion rear command post, run by my executive officer, Major Herman Wirth, and our supply point and medical-aid station would both shift forward to Landing Zone Falcon, where the two artillery batteries were located.

Colonel Brown arrived and I walked him through the plan. He agreed with everything, including the selection of X-Ray as the assault landing zone. He chatted with some of the officers and troopers for a few minutes. Then, just before he left, he did something out of the ordinary. Says Matt Dillon: "Colonel Brown called Moore and me aside. He told us: 'I want you two to be especially careful on this operation.' He looked concerned." As we walked Brown to his helicopter he repeated his instructions: "Stay tight" and "Don't let your companies get separated." At 9:15 A.M. the two artillery batteries reported they were going into position and would soon be ready to fire. I set 10:30 A.M. as touchdown time. Commanders returned to their companies, the staff to the command post. The Huey air crews were being briefed by their pilots.

Then we got word that because of air movement delays the artillery was not yet in position in LZ Falcon and could not begin the prep fires on the Ia Drang targets before 10:17 A.M. H hour slid back accordingly, and the word was passed down the line. Dillon lifted off in the battalion command helicopter with the fire-support and helicopter-coordination group. Bruce Crandall and I stood beside his chopper, discussing final details. The precise flying time from liftoff at Plei Me to touchdown at X-Ray came up. Crandall's copilot, Captain Jon Mills, a twenty-five-year-old native of the Panama Canal Zone, worked for a couple of minutes over his maps, flight table, and calculator, looked up and said: "Thirteen minutes fifteen seconds." I bet him a beer he couldn't hit it dead on the nose. He took me up on that bet—he kept an honest log—and collected his beer three nights later at Camp Holloway, near Pleiku.

We loaded aboard and Crandall and Mills preflighted the Huey. Then Crandall fired up both his engine and a big fat cigar. We were enveloped in a choking cloud of red dust as all sixteen Hueys strained toward liftoff. Crandall, in the left seat, looked back. I gave him a thumbs-up and pointed westward. He pulled pitch and lifted off, and we were bound for Landing Zone X-Ray.

We flew over a broad, slightly rolling plain dotted with trees thirty to fifty feet tall, interspersed with a few old Montagnard farm clearings, small winding streams, and dry streambeds. We saw no villages and no people. It was Sunday morning but I didn't realize that: over here we paid attention to the date, not the day. In the field in Vietnam all days were the same: hot and wet, or hot and dry, but always dangerous. Back in Columbus, Georgia, it was Saturday night. My wife had put our five kids to bed and was watching the nightly news on television. Secretary of Defense Robert McNamara announced plans to abolish 751 Army Reserve units, including six reserve divisions. The *Yarmouth Castle* cruise ship burned and sank at sea, and ninety-one passengers were missing. *The New York Times* headlined a James Reston think piece WASHINGTON: WAR ON THE INSTALLMENT PLAN. Joe Namath, who had been paid an unthinkable $400,000 bonus for signing with the New York Jets, was having a great first season in pro football.

The troop doors on the Huey helicopters were open. We flew at two thousand feet to reduce the chances of being hit by enemy small-arms fire as we traversed 14.3 miles of hostile country. We flew in four groups of four helicopters each, with each group in a heavy-left formation, and Crandall's four helicopter gunships guarding our flanks, two on each side slightly forward of us. Captain John Herren, whose Bravo Company troops filled the helicopters, recalls: "It was a misty, cool morning with some low-hanging fog when we lifted off, but shortly after takeoff we broke into the clear and you could see the 105mm artillery pounding the areas around the LZ as we headed in. Vietnam, even in war, was scenic, with the green jungle, heavy forested mountains, and wild-looking rivers crisscrossing the terrain."

About four miles from X-Ray, Bruce Crandall gave the signal and his pilots dropped down to treetop level to fly nap-of-the-earth on the final approach. Birds scattered as we roared along at 110 miles per hour just above their perches. High overhead in the command chopper, Matt Dillon was running the fire support preparations: "The hairiest part of any operation was always the air assault. We had to time the flight and the artillery so close. When the choppers were one minute out the last artillery rounds had to be on the way or you get Hueys landing with the shells. We always sweated because if you shut down the artillery too soon the enemy could be up and waiting when the choppers came in. This one was precisely on time."

We were two minutes out now and could see smoke and dust flying around the landing zone. Minimum fire had been directed on the clearing; if there were enemy they wouldn't be there, but in concealed positions around the clearing's edge. Now the helicopters of the aerial rocket artillery slammed that perimeter with rockets, grenades, and machine-gun fire, using twenty-four of the forty-eight 2.75-inch rockets each carried. They saved the other half in case we needed help after we got on the ground. As the ARA ships banked steeply away to take up an orbit nearby, the four escorting gunships left us and dashed ahead to take over the firing that would keep any enemy heads down on our final approach.

Major Bruce Crandall recalls: "We went low-level and arrived right on schedule at the release point into the landing zone. The landing zone was not as clear of obstacles as we would have liked but we got our flight in without any real problems. The only movement we spotted in the landing zone was something that looked like a dog scampering into some underbrush on the far side. It was probably an enemy soldier." Now the door gunners on the lift ships were firing into the tree line as we dropped into the clearing. I unhooked my seat belt, switched the selector switch on my M-16 to full automatic—rock 'n' roll—and fired bursts into the brush to the left, toward the mountain, as Crandall came in hot and flared* over the dry five-foot-tall elephant grass. As the chopper skids touched the ground I yelled, "Let's go!" and jumped out, running for the trees on the western edge of the clearing, firing my rifle.

It was 10:48 A.M. Sergeant Major Plumley, Captain Metsker, Bob Ouellette, and Mr. Nik, the translator, were right behind me. Herren and his men came out of their Hueys in like fashion. In less than ten seconds Crandall's first lift of eight ships had roared back into the air, banked north, and hightailed it back east. The second wave of eight helicopters was now touching down to disgorge its troops.

I ran across twenty-five yards of open ground, then across a waist-deep, ten-foot-wide dry creekbed, and continued running some seventy-five yards into the scrub brush, leading the command group. We stopped to slap fresh magazines in our rifles. So far we

*Hot; fast; flared: The pilot lifts the helicopter's nose and drops its tail to lose speed suddenly before landing.

had been unopposed. We were in a lightly wooded area, with scraggly trees twenty to fifty feet tall and dry, brown elephant grass between. The area was dotted with large mounds of red dirt, most with brush and grass growing out of the tops. The size of these old termite hills ranged from that of a small automobile to that of a large pickup, and they offered excellent cover and concealment. The valley was a desolate place, with no villages and no civilians, ten miles east of where the Ho Chi Minh Trail turned left out of Cambodia into South Vietnam.

The heavily forested eastern slopes of the Chu Pong rose steep and dark more than a thousand feet above the clearing. The massif's lower slopes were covered with thick green foliage, elephant grass, and tangles of brush. Gullies and long fingers of ground led from the bottom of the mountain and blended into the woods and the dry creekbed where we stood. Plenty of places for people to hide. The creekbed just inside the western edge of our clearing was an excellent route of approach for enemy troops coming from the direction of the mountain or the valley, and for us going the other way. That creekbed was a critical feature.

Heading back toward the clearing, we ran into some of Bravo Company's 1st Platoon troopers, led by Sergeant Larry Gilreath, moving out into the brush. Gilreath yelled: "Moore's fire team has already cleared this area." Plumley grinned. He knew that the troops liked to see the Old Man out with them on the ground, sharing the risks. Gilreath and his men headed deeper into the brush to the west. Plumley and I recrossed the dry creekbed and moved around the clearing, checking on the terrain and on the patrols Herren's troopers were conducting. No enemy contact so far, and I was glad of that. We didn't want a fight before we got the rest of the battalion on the ground.

The clearing was about a hundred yards long, east to west, and kind of funnel-shaped, with the ninety-yard-wide mouth of the funnel on the western edge near that dry creek. The bottom of the funnel was on the forty-five-yard span of the clearing's eastern edge. In the center of the clearing was a copse of scraggly trees, about half the size of a tennis court. All told, the space at X-Ray amounted to no more clear ground than a football field.

Now I stopped and looked up at the steep slopes of the mountain. I had a strong sense that we were under direct enemy observation. That, and the fact that everything had gone so well so far, made me nervous. Nothing was wrong, except that nothing was wrong. I continued reconnoitering. There were no streambeds on the north, east, or south. The southern edge of the clearing was closest to the mountain and to those draws and fingers reaching out from the high ground. The terrain to the north and east was relatively flat. My attention continued to be drawn back to the south and west.

I did two things now. I ordered Herren's 1st Platoon to intensify its search to the west of the creek, and checked to make sure that the rest of Bravo Company was gathered in the clump of trees near the creekbed and ready for action. Herren had most of his troops on the ground; the rest were on the way in the second lift.

This clearing was the only decent helicopter landing zone between the slopes of Chu Pong and the Ia Drang and for two miles east or west. Our assault landing had, so far as we could tell, achieved total surprise. The enemy weren't around the clearing waiting for us. But we had been seen arriving and the North Vietnamese were already moving in our direction.

The People's Army commander on the battlefield, then–Senior Lieutenant Colonel Nguyen Huu An, says, "When you dropped troops into X-Ray, I was on Chu Pong mountain. We had a very strong position and a strong, mobile command group. We were ready, had prepared for you and expected you to come. The only question was when. The trees and brush limited our view of the helicopters landing but we had an observation post on top of the mountain and they reported to us when you dropped troops and when you moved them."

Sergeant Larry Gilreath's memory of this morning is clear and sharp: "The 1st Platoon was told to move straight forward about a hundred and fifty yards from where we landed. And from there each squad would send two or three men out further in all directions. Sergeant John W. Mingo in the 1st Squad went forward with a couple of men and hadn't been out very long when he found 'a boy' wandering around in the area. When Mingo brought him in, my exact words were: 'Boy, hell! That ain't no boy.' " Mingo and his recon squad had spotted the soldier sitting on the ground; surprised, he got up and ran. After a short zigzag chase through the brush, the sergeant tackled him and took him prisoner. Herren passed the word to me. I was pleased that the 1st Platoon had taken him alive, and not surprised when I learned that it was Mingo who caught him. Mingo was a Ranger Company veteran of the Korean War and knew the value of a live prisoner who was able to talk.

It was 11:20 A.M.; just then, Crandall's sixteen helicopters returned, bringing in the rest of Bravo Company and the 3rd Platoon of Alpha Company plus Captain Tony Nadal's Alpha Company command group. They ran into the scrub brush on the northern edge of the clearing near the creekbed. Things were quiet, nothing happening yet, so most of the troopers broke out their C-rations and ate a quick lunch. I was on my way out to question the enemy prisoner and had not yet seen Captain Nadal to give him any instructions. We had been in X-Ray only thirty-two minutes and the countdown was on.

John Herren left the rest of Bravo Company in the copse with his executive officer, Lieutenant Ken Duncan, and joined me and my party as we rushed across the creek into the brush where Gilreath's men were holding the prisoner. He wasn't much, but he was this battalion's first prisoner in Vietnam: about five feet seven inches tall, maybe twenty years old, scrawny, wild-eyed and trembling with fear. He was unarmed and barefooted; he wore a dirty khaki shirt, partly pulled out of his khaki trousers. There was a serial number on one of the shirt epaulettes. He carried a canteen but it was empty. He had no papers, no food, and no ammunition.

When we took a prisoner on the battlefield in Korea, we never got bogged down in long interrogations. No time for that. All I wanted to know was "How many of you are there?" and "Where are they?" A look of apprehension spread over Mr. Nik's face as he shakily translated the prisoner's words: "He says there are three battalions on the mountain who want very much to kill Americans but have not been able to find any." What the prisoner said fit in neatly with what our intelligence people had told us and with that big red star I had seen on the division headquarters map. I still don't know what that soldier was doing out there in the brush without food, water, or a weapon, but he was a godsend.

Three battalions of enemy added up to more than 1,600 men against the 160-plus Americans currently on the ground here. I turned to John Herren and ordered him to immediately intensify the patrols in the area where we had found the prisoner. I told Herren that as soon as enough of Tony Nadal's Alpha Company troops were on the ground to secure the landing zone, Bravo Company would be cut loose to search the lower slopes of the mountain, with special emphasis on the finger and draw to the northwest. If those enemy battalions were on the way, we needed to engage them as far off the landing zone as possible.

We radioed Matt Dillon and told him to come in to pick up the prisoner and take him back to brigade for further interrogation. Dillon landed at 11:40 A.M. The forward air controller, Air Force Lieutenant Charlie Hastings, says that when Dillon put the prisoner aboard the command helicopter and relayed his words that there were many enemy in the area who wanted to kill Americans "the war suddenly had my undivided attention."

Captain Nadal had been hunting for me while I was in the woods with the prisoner. We caught up with each other after the prisoner was put aboard the command helicopter. I quickly briefed Nadal on the situation and told him that Alpha Company would take over security in the LZ as soon as the next lift brought in the rest of his men. Crandall's helicopters returned at 12:10 P.M. on their third trip to X-Ray, bringing in the rest of Tony Nadal's troopers, minus only a few men. Now Nadal had enough men on the ground to be effective.

Suddenly a few rifle shots rang out in the area where the prisoner had been captured. Sergeant Gilreath's men were in contact! It was now 12:15 P.M. We had to move fast if we were going to survive, had to get off that landing zone and hit him before he could hit us. Only if we brought the enemy to battle deep in the trees and brush would we stand even a slim chance of holding on to the clearing and getting the rest of the battalion landed. That football-field-size clearing was our lifeline and our supply line. If the enemy closed the way to the helicopters all of us would die in this place.

Even as the first shots rang out I was radioing Herren to saddle up the rest of his Bravo Company men and move out fast toward the mountain to develop the situation. Turning to Nadal, I told him that the original plan was out the window, that his Alpha Company should immediately take over LZ security and get ready to move up on Bravo Company's left when enough of Charlie Company had arrived on the next lift to assume the job of securing the clearing.

In the small copse, the other two platoons of Bravo Company men had opened C-ration cans and were grabbing a bite when they heard those first shots out in the brush. The older sergeants glanced at one another and nodded. Eat fast, they told the men, and get ready to move.

The battle of LZ X-Ray had just begun.

6

THE BATTLE BEGINS

When first under fire and you're wishful to duck,
Don't look or take heed at the man that is struck.
Be thankful you're living and trust to your luck,
And march to your front like a soldier.

—Rudyard Kipling, "The Young British Soldier"

It was now 12:20 P.M. Bravo Company commander John Herren radioed his four platoon leaders to meet him near that waist-deep streambed that traversed the western edge of the clearing; there, they would organize the assault toward the mountain. Herren talked only briefly with them: "Lieutenant Al Devney of the 1st Platoon, an eager, impulsive officer who was anxious to tie into the enemy; Lieutenant Henry T. Herrick of the 2nd Platoon, an aggressive redhead who pushed his men hard and had told me he hoped to earn the Medal of Honor one day; Lieutenant Dennis Deal of the 3rd Platoon, a low-key but very effective officer; and Sergeant First Class Ed Montgomery, an excellent mortarman who was acting weapons-platoon leader."

The Bravo Company commander says, "I told Devney and Herrick to move out abreast, Herrick on the right, with Deal to follow behind Devney's platoon as reserve. The weapons platoon would support with their one 81mm mortar and forty shells."

It was now near 12:30 P.M., and the Bravo Company contact was continuing to build. Specialist 4 Galen Bungum, twenty-two, the short, muscular son of a Hayfield, Minnesota, dairy farmer, was in Lieutenant Herrick's platoon. He carried a 40mm grenade launcher, which looked like a short, fat, single-barrel sawed-off shotgun, and a .45-caliber pistol. Our grenadiers carried a usual load of thirty-six rounds for the M-79. Galen Bungum this day had only eighteen in his green cloth pouches. His day had started out great, had turned bad, and was about to get a lot worse.

Bungum remembers, "Early that morning First Sergeant Robert F. Mohr told me to pass out all my ammunition to the other troops because I was going back to An Khe to leave for Bangkok on R and R. I had just got that done when he came back and said: 'Bungum, there are no more choppers going that way today, so get your ammo back. You go with us today.' I didn't get all my ammo back, just eighteen rounds." Now Bungum's lunch was cut short. Lieutenant Herrick loped back from his meeting with Captain Herren and shouted: "Saddle up and follow me. We're moving up." Platoon Sergeant Carl Palmer, thirty-nine years old, a native of Pelham, Georgia, married and a veteran of the Korean War, got the four squads formed up and moving out through the elephant grass.

Captain Herren recalls, "The lead platoons moved out smartly and I followed with my radio operators and my artillery observer, Lieutenant Bill Riddle. I planned to tie in with the rear of Al Devney's platoon but had to stop to establish good radio contact with Moore's headquarters." While Herren was doing that his other two rifle platoons passed by his location on the western edge of the creekbed. Because of that pause, Herren would be cut off from his men for the next hour or so.

Al Devney's 1st Platoon was in the lead and was soon some hundred yards west of the creek. Henry Herrick's 2nd Platoon crossed the dry creek and moved through the scrub brush on the right and slightly to the rear of Devney. Galen Bungum could hear scattered rifle shots up ahead as he moved out.

Bungum says, "While we were headed that way Sergeant Palmer

came up behind me, put his arm around me, and said: 'Bungum, I'll be forty years old day after tomorrow, but I don't believe I will live to see it.' I didn't know how to answer Palmer, so I just said: 'Come on, Sarge, you can't be out here with that kind of attitude. You'll make it.' " It was the third time in recent days that Carl Palmer had predicted his own death. Sergeant Larry Gilreath and Captain Herren say they, too, had similar conversations with Palmer and tried to reassure him.

By 12:45 P.M. the contact had grown to a moderate firefight and we were taking casualties. As fast as the fight was growing, I figured that we were in for a long afternoon and that the number of wounded might well exceed the capability of the platoon medics on the ground. Now I radioed Matt Dillon, who was back overhead in the command chopper, and told him to order the battalion surgeon, Captain Robert Carrara, and his medical aid station people to come into LZ X-Ray. Tell them not to bother with the tent, but bring a lot of supplies, I said.

Things were definitely heating up for Al Devney's men at the point of the spear. Sergeant Gilreath recalls: "My 3rd Squad leader, Staff Sergeant Carl R. Burton, spotted a column of troops coming down the mountain. They didn't look like they were in any big hurry, walking along in single file. Some had their weapons on their shoulders. I don't think they knew exactly where we were. We checked with Captain Herren to make sure there were no South Vietnamese units in the area, then we opened up on them. We had no knowledge of what size unit we were tangling with, but we found out very shortly when we were taken under heavy small arms fire and automatic weapons fire. At that time I lost contact with Lieutenant Devney and was mainly concerned with placing the men closest to me in positions where they could return effective fire."

Within minutes Devney's 1st Platoon, which was leading the assault, was attacked heavily by thirty to forty North Vietnamese in khaki uniforms, wearing pith helmets and firing automatic weapons. It was now near one P.M.; Devney's men were under attack on both flanks, and they were in trouble. The North Vietnamese were using a well-worn trail as a general axis of advance. Says Sergeant

Gilreath: "We were virtually pinned to the ground and taking casualties." Lieutenant Dennis Deal remembers that moment: "Devney's platoon was taking moderate fire. We could all hear it through the foliage, and I heard it crackling on my radio. Al was in some sort of trouble. The firing increased in volume and intensity; then I saw my first wounded trooper, probably the first American wounded in LZ X-Ray. He was shot in the neck or mouth or both, was still carrying his rifle, was ambulatory and appeared stunned at what had happened to him. When he asked where to go I put my arm around him and pointed to where I had last seen the battalion commander."

Here's what Sergeant Jimmie Jakes of Phenix City, Alabama, who was leading four men in one of Devney's rifle squads, remembers: "As we were advancing toward the enemy, two of my men and one from another squad were hit by machine-gun fire. I was ordering men to my left and right; some didn't even belong to our platoon. I yelled to them to lay down a base of fire; then I crawled to aid the wounded. I was able to drag two of the wounded back to our defensive line. We had stopped advancing at this point. As I attempted to drag a third back I was wounded." An AK-47 round penetrated Jakes's side and exited through the top of his left shoulder.

Over on the right and slightly behind Al Devney's men, Lieutenant Henry T. Herrick was maneuvering his 2nd Platoon up the slope toward a meeting with destiny. His company commander, Captain Herren, said: "Herrick's platoon was probably my most seasoned unit, with outstanding NCOs. They were led by an old pro, SFC [Sergeant First Class] Carl Palmer, who I relied on to counsel and help develop Lieutenant Herrick, much as I did with my other two platoon sergeants—Larry Gilreath of the 1st Platoon and Larry Williams of the 3rd. But the 2nd Platoon had other NCOs who were exceptional: Ernie Savage, a young buck sergeant from Alabama, was a rifle-squad leader; then there was SFC Emanuel (Ranger Mac) McHenry, who was forty years old but could walk the legs off men half his age; Staff Sergeant Paul Hurdle, the weapons-squad leader, who was a Korean War veteran, and Sergeant Ruben

Thompson, a fire-team leader with a reputation of never quitting."

Henry Toro Herrick was red-haired, five foot ten, twenty-four years old, and the son of an astronomy professor at UCLA. He had joined the battalion in July and been given a rifle platoon; he was a hard-charger. When the battalion recon-platoon leader job, a coveted assignment, came open in October, I briefly entertained the notion of giving it to young Herrick. I mentioned Herrick to Sergeant Major Plumley and his response was forceful and swift: "Colonel, if you put Lieutenant Herrick in there he will get them all killed." We had a gaggle of new second lieutenants in the battalion, and it surprised me that one of them had made such a poor impression on the sergeant major. Herrick, needless to say, did not get the recon-platoon job.

Herrick's platoon sergeant, Carl Palmer, had voiced his own reservations about the lieutenant to Captain Herren after one of his men was drowned in a river crossing while on patrol. "Sergeant Palmer took me aside after the drowning incident and told me that Herrick would get them all killed with his aggressiveness," Herren says. "But I couldn't fault Herrick for that. We were all eager to find the enemy and I figured I could control his impetuous actions."

Devney reported by radio to Captain Herren that his platoon was pinned down on both flanks. Says Herren: "I directed Lieutenant Herrick to alleviate some of the pressure, ordering him to move up on Devney's right and gain contact with Devney's 1st Platoon." The time was now about 1:15 P.M., and the scrub brush was baking in the ninety-plus-degree heat of midday. A few rounds of enemy 60mm and 82mm mortars and some RPG-2 rocket-propelled grenades were bursting in Devney's area. Captain Herren and Lieutenant Bill Riddle, his artillery forward observer, now began working the radios, calling in air and artillery fire support.

Devney's platoon sergeant, Larry Gilreath, was expecting to see Herrick and his men moving up on his right. He did, but not for long. As he moved, Herrick radioed Captain Herren to report that his 2nd Platoon was taking fire from the right, that he had seen a squad of enemy soldiers and was pursuing them. Herren radioed back: "Fine, but be careful; I don't want you to get pinned down or sucked into anything."

Gilreath says: "I saw Lieutenant Herrick at a distance of about fifty yards. His weapons-squad leader, Sergeant Hurdle, was closest to me. I asked him, 'Where the hell are you going?' They were deployed on line and moving fast. I wanted him to stop and set up his two machine guns on my right flank. They kept on moving. I thought they were going to tie in with my men."

Captain Herren was concerned about Devney's situation but enthusiastic about Herrick's contact, which he reported to me by radio. "Shortly after," Herren says, "I moved out again to catch up with Devney. He reported he was under heavy fire and pinned down. I immediately called Lieutenant Deal to move around to the left and help Devney."

Dennis Deal had been running the 3rd Platoon, Bravo Company, for only two weeks. "My platoon sergeant was Staff Sergeant Leroy Williams, a true man. He had spent a year and a half in Korea. My weapons-squad leader was Staff Sergeant Wilbur Curry, a full-blooded Seneca Indian from upstate New York, who was in Korea for two years and was reputed to be the best machine gunner in the battalion, if not the division. Just before we left base camp, Curry got too much firewater in him, got a horse from a Vietnamese, and rode it up Route 19 toward Pleiku. Because Colonel Moore knew what a good trooper he really was, he passed on punishing Curry."

Until now Deal's platoon had not seen any enemy, but as they moved up fifty yards and approached Devney's left flank, they came under heavy fire. Sergeant Gilreath remembers seeing the 3rd Platoon "having the same problems we were having with enemy automatic weapons fire. It was coming from a covered machine gun position and it was giving us fits."

Staff Sergeant William N. Roland, a twenty-two-year-old career soldier who came from Andrews, South Carolina, was one of Deal's squad leaders. "We began to encounter wounded soldiers from the 1st Platoon. Then we started taking enemy fire, including incoming mortar rounds." Lieutenant Deal says, "My personal baptism of fire was occurring and I turned around to Sergeant Curry. 'Chief,

I've never been shot at before. Is this what it sounds like?' And he smiled. 'Yes sir, this is what it sounds like. We are being shot at.' We had to scream at each other to be heard."

The military historian S. L. A. Marshall wrote that, at the beginning of a battle, units fractionalize, groping between the antagonists takes place, and the battle takes form from all this. Marshall had it right. That is precisely what was happening up in the scrub brush above Landing Zone X-Ray this day. And no other single event would have a greater impact on the shape of this battle than what Lieutenant Henry Herrick was in the process of doing. Herrick charged right past Lieutenant Devney's men, swung his platoon to the right in hot pursuit of a few fleeing enemy soldiers, and disappeared from sight into the brush.

Says Sergeant Ernie Savage of Herrick's orders: "He made a bad decision, and we knew at the time it was a bad decision. We were breaking contact with the rest of the company. We were supposed to come up on the flank of the 1st Platoon; in fact we were moving away from them. We lost contact with everybody."

Henry Herrick was in the lead with Sergeant McHenry's rifle squad as the platoon rushed through the brush, chasing the fleeing enemy down a gentle slope to the northwest on a well-beaten jungle path. His platoon was strung out over fifty yards. McHenry's squad was followed by Sergeant Jerry Zallen's rifle squad, and then came Ernie Savage's men. Paul Hurdle's weapons squad with its two M-60 machine guns brought up the rear.

The enemy quickly disappeared but Herrick continued down the trail. He had put more than a hundred yards between himself and the rest of Bravo Company when the path crossed a small streambed four feet deep. Herrick crossed it with McHenry's squad and called for the rest of the platoon to follow. The foliage was thick near the stream but opened up again only five yards out. The platoon closed up and the two lead rifle squads came up on line, with McHenry on the right, Zallen on the left, and Savage and Hurdle in the rear. A small ridge line, hardly more than a finger, sloped down from a small rise of ground to the west, parallel to the streambed and directly across the line of march of the two lead rifle squads.

Captain Herren says, "In a few minutes Herrick reported that he had reached a clearing and asked if he should go through it or around it. He said if he went around he would lose contact with Al Devney." The fact is, Herrick had already lost contact with the 1st Platoon. He pressed on up the south side of the finger as the two squads in the rear were crossing the stream. At the top of that finger the two lead squads suddenly collided with forty or fifty North Vietnamese who were rushing down the trail toward the sound of the Bravo Company firefight. Both sides opened fire immediately and the enemy broke both left and right.

A huge termite hill was between Herrick's two lead squads when the shooting started. Herrick radioed to Savage, signaling him to flank the enemy from the right. With Hurdle's machine guns right behind, Savage and his troops did just that, charging out of the trees while firing their M-16s on full automatic. The enemy were surprised by the flanking charge. Many of them spun or staggered and dropped, lashed by a hail of rifle fire and M-79 grenades from Specialist 4 Robert M. Hill's launcher. Hill pumped grenade after grenade into the screaming Vietnamese. Firing raged from both sides, but suddenly a larger group of fifty or more enemy scrambled out of the trees, attacked toward the termite hill, and were brought under heavy fire by the two squads on the finger and by Savage's squad on the right. An enemy machine gun and its three-man crew were taken out during this fight. Says Savage: "We had one hell of a firefight for three or four minutes and we hadn't lost anyone. We killed a lot of them. I hit a lot of them. I saw them fall. They tried to put a machine gun up on our right and we shot the gunner and two men with him."

On the radio to Captain Herren, Henry Herrick reported that he had enemy on his right and left flanks and was afraid of being cut off. Herren says, "I told him to try and reestablish contact with the 1st Platoon and move back in my direction. Simultaneously I alerted 1st Platoon and told them to see if they could get to Herrick. It seemed like only a few minutes before Herrick was calling again saying he had a large enemy force between him and Devney, was under intense fire, and [was] taking casualties. I told him to grab some terrain and hold, that we would get to him. I also told him to use mortar and artillery support."

Bringing up the rear of Herrick's column, the old Korean War vet and machine-gun wizard, Paul Hurdle, took in all that was happening at a glance and realized that both McHenry's and Savage's squads had their hands full and needed immediate help. Waving to his crews to follow, Hurdle charged out of the heavy vegetation near the stream, slammed both M-60 machine guns down into firing positions aimed over the crest of the finger behind Savage's squad, and opened fire.

Down below in the clearing, I heard the shocking uproar explode up on the mountainside. There were the steady, deep-throated bursts of machine-gun fire; rifles crackling on full automatic; grenade, mortar, and rocket explosions. All of it was much louder and much more widespread than anything we had experienced thus far. Now John Herren was up on my radio reporting that his men were under heavy attack by at least two enemy companies and that his 2nd Platoon was in danger of being surrounded and cut off from the rest of the company. Even as he spoke, mortar and rocket rounds hit in the clearing where I stood. My worst-case scenario had just come to pass: We were in heavy contact before all my battalion was on the ground. And now I had to deal with a cut-off platoon. My response was an angry "Shit!"

Captain John Herren's estimate that his Bravo Company men were trying to deal with two enemy companies was slightly off. One full enemy battalion, more than five hundred determined soldiers, was boiling down the mountain toward Herrick's trapped 2nd Platoon and maneuvering near Al Devney's pinned-down 1st Platoon. Bravo Company had gone into the fight with five officers and 114 enlisted men. In the swirling kaleidoscope of a fast-developing battle, John Herren was trying desperately to get a handle on what the enemy was doing, to keep me informed, and at the same time to keep his company from being overrun.

What was happening with Bravo Company intensified my concern about that dry creekbed approach into the western edge of the landing zone. My instincts told me that the enemy commander was likely to strike on our left flank, heading for the clearing. We needed help fast, and help was on the way.

Old Snake, Bruce Crandall, came up on the radio. Having been delayed by the need to refuel his sixteen ships, he was inbound on the fourth lift of the day with the last few men of Tony Nadal's Alpha Company and the lead elements of Captain Bob Edwards's Charlie Company troops. As the first eight choppers dropped into the clearing at 1:32 P.M., I told Captain Nadal to collect his men and move up fast on John Herren's left to tie in with him. Then, I said, I want you to lend Herren a platoon to help him get to his cut-off platoon. I ran out into the clearing to locate Bob Edwards. I had decided to commit Charlie Company toward the mountain as fast as they arrived, and take the risk of leaving my rear unguarded from the north and east. There would be no battalion reserve for a while.

Captain Edwards's men of Charlie Company jumped off their choppers and ran for the wooded edge of the landing zone—the southern edge, thank God. I grabbed Edwards, gave him a quick briefing, and then yelled at him to run his men off the landing zone to the south and southwest and take up a blocking position protecting Alpha Company's left flank. I screamed *"Move!"* and Edwards and his two radio operators shot off at a dead run, yelling and waving to the rest of the men to follow.

Bob Edwards says, "While organizing the blocking position we received heavy sniper fire, mainly small arms and a few automatic weapons. Then, fifteen or twenty minutes after landing, we received sporadic mortar or rocket fire. We had not yet made contact with enemy foot troops. After getting into the trees, I disposed my three rifle platoons on line: 3rd Platoon on the right, 1st Platoon in the center, 2nd Platoon on the left.

"My command post was just off the edge of the landing zone, close to the rear of Lieutenant Jack Geoghegan's 2nd Platoon. A combination of luck, rapid reaction to orders, and trained, disciplined soldiers doing what they were told enabled the company to rapidly establish a hasty line of defense fifty to a hundred yards off the landing zone. The elephant grass was a problem: When you went to ground your visibility was extremely limited."

By now, my radio operator, Bob Ouellette, and I had rejoined Sergeant Major Plumley and Captain Tom Metsker near the dry creekbed. The interpreter, Mr. Nik, had gone to ground. Captain Metsker dropped to one knee and began firing his M-16 at enemy soldiers out in the open just seventy-five yards to the south. Within minutes, Metsker suffered a gunshot wound in his shoulder, was bandaged by First Sergeant Arthur J. Newton of Alpha Company, and was sent back to the copse.

I was tempted to join Nadal's or Edwards's men, but resisted the temptation. I had no business getting involved with the actions of only one company; I might get pinned down and become simply another rifleman. My duty was to *lead* riflemen.

Just now the snaps and cracks of the rounds passing nearby took on a distinctly different sound, like a swarm of bees around our heads. I was on the radio, trying to hear a transmission over the noise, when I felt a firm hand on my right shoulder. It was Sergeant Major Plumley's. He shouted over the racket of the firefights: "Sir, if you don't find some cover you're going to go down—and if you go down, we all go down!"

Plumley was right, as always. Anyone waving, yelling, hand-signaling, or talking on a radio was instantly targeted by the enemy. These guys were quick to spot and shoot leaders, radio operators, and medics. I had never fretted about being wounded in combat, in Korea or here. But Plumley brought me up short. The game was just beginning; this was no time for me to go out of it.

The sergeant major pointed to a large termite hill, seven or eight feet high, located in the trees in the waist between the two open areas of the landing zone. It was about thirty yards away; the three of us turned and ran toward it with bullets kicking up the red dirt around our feet and the bees still buzzing around our heads. That termite hill, the size of a large automobile, would become the site of the battalion command post, the aid station, the supply point, the collection area for enemy prisoners, weapons, and equipment, and the place where our dead were brought.

Just now, at 1:38 P.M., the second wave of eight choppers dropped in with more Alpha and Charlie Company troops. They picked up some ground fire this time. Edwards and Nadal sorted out their arriving soldiers and married them up with their respective companies.

Tagging along with this lift was a medical evacuation helicopter bringing in my battalion aid station group. The big red cross painted on each side only drew more fire. On board were Captain Robert Carrara, the surgeon; Medical Platoon Sergeant Thomas Keeton; and Staff Sergeant Earl Keith. President Johnson sent us off to war shorthanded in many areas, but no shortages were so critical as those in medical personnel. The aid station was authorized thirteen personnel. Keeton and Keith were all we had. Period. Captain Carrara and his two sergeants performed miracles for the next fifty hours.

Sergeant Keeton describes their arrival: "Between one-thirty and one-forty-five P.M. we came in over X-Ray trailing a flight of four helicopters and you could see our soldiers and the North Vietnamese. The NVA were in the wood line shooting at the helicopter. The medevac pilot kind of froze up on us and was having trouble setting the ship down. We never did come to a complete hover. All aboard had to dive out on the ground from about six feet up in the air. We ran in a crouch over to where Colonel Moore was, near an anthill. There were twenty to twenty-five wounded there, all huddled on the ground. We put the dead over in a separate area and started to work."

There were now about 250 men of my battalion on the ground and still functioning. Casualties were beginning to pile up. As we dropped behind that termite hill I fleetingly thought about an illustrious predecessor of mine in the 7th Cavalry, Lieutenant Colonel George Armstrong Custer, and his final stand in the valley of the Little Bighorn in Montana, eighty-nine years earlier. I was determined that history would not repeat itself in the valley of the Ia Drang. We were a tight, well-trained, and disciplined fighting force, and we had one thing George Custer did not have: fire support.

Now was the time to pull the chain on everything I could lay hands on. I radioed Matt Dillon and the fire support coordinators overhead and told them to bring in air strikes, artillery, and aerial rocket artillery on the lower part of the mountain, especially on the approaches to the landing zone from the west and south. Priority for all fires was to go to specific requests from the infantry companies. When not firing those missions, the other targets should be hit continuously. I told Dillon and the others to keep their eyes peeled for any enemy mortar positions. I hoped the air and artillery would take some of the pressure off my troops as well as cut up enemy reinforcements headed down the mountain for the fight.

Within minutes the air in the valley was filled with smoke and red dust as a blessed river of high-powered destruction rained from the skies. The company commanders and the mortar and artillery forward observers, however, were all having trouble getting an accurate fix on the locations of their forward elements. Colonel Tim Brown, overhead in his command chopper, came up on my radio and urged me to pull the fires off the mountain and bring them in as close as possible.

John Herren had the biggest problem: trying to pinpoint the location of his missing 2nd Platoon. Herrick and his men were not only separated from the rest of Bravo Company, but also engaged in a moving firefight. The fact that this platoon was out in front of Nadal and Herren delayed effective delivery of close-in artillery fire for some time. But by walking the fires back down the mountain the company commanders managed to place some of the artillery where it would do some good. And the torrent of supporting fire farther up the mountain slopes was chopping up enemy reinforcements.

This cannonade was awesome to see, and its thunder was a symphony to our ears. The artillery rounds hissed over our heads with the characteristic sound of incoming, followed by visible detonations nearby. The ARA helicopters wheeled in over X-Ray and with a whoosh unleashed their 2.75-inch rockets, which detonated with shattering blasts. The Air Force fighter-bombers roared across the sky dropping 250- and 500-pound bombs and fearsome napalm canisters. Throughout, there was the constant close-in noise of rifles, machine guns, and exploding grenades and mortar shells.

It was now becoming clear that the large open area, south of the termite-hill command post, where the helicopters had been landing was especially vulnerable. This was the biggest open area, but it was also closest to where the enemy was attacking. I had been eyeing a smaller clearing just east of my command post that could take two helicopters at a time if some trees were removed. This would be our supply and evacuation link to the rear if the landing zone got much hotter.

I turned to my demolition-team leader, Sergeant George Nye of the 8th Engineer Battalion, and told him to get those trees down. Nye, a twenty-five-year-old native of Bangor, Maine, had led six men into X-Ray: Specialist 5 James Clark, Specialist 5 Scott O. Henry, Specialist 4 Robert Deursch, PFC Jimmy D. Nakayama, PFC Melvin Allen, and PFC David Wilson. "All of a sudden the fire became heavier and heavier and the perimeter just seemed to erupt into a mêlée of constant fire," Nye recalls. "You could see the enemy, and suddenly we were part of the 1st Battalion, 7th Cavalry. It's tough to try to be an infantryman and a demolitions specialist at the same time, but we did it. We blew those trees; no sawing. The intensity of fire made working with a saw tough, working without a weapon. By blowing the trees we could spend more time fighting. I heard that one of our people had got killed, a kid named Henry, Specialist Henry of Columbus, Georgia. As the day drew on, I found out we did lose Henry."

During the few minutes I had been involved with Charlie Company's move to the south, and on the radio bringing in fire support, and talking to George Nye about clearing that little landing zone, Captain Tony Nadal had begun moving his Alpha Company troopers southwest across the open ground toward the dry creekbed.

7

CLOSING WITH THE ENEMY

> If your officer's dead and the sergeants look white,
> Remember it's ruin to run from a fight;
> So take open order, lie down, and sit tight,
> An' wait for supports like a soldier.
>
> —Rudyard Kipling, "The Young British Soldier"

Lieutenant Robert E. Taft was leading the 3rd Platoon of Alpha Company at a lope toward the sound of battle. He had gotten orders to move from the company commander, Captain Tony Nadal, and he was carrying them out. Lean, boyish, just twenty-three years old, Bob Taft of Highland Park, Illinois, was setting a pace toward the tree line at the edge of the clearing that his heavily laden radio operator, Specialist 4 Robert Hazen, also twenty-three and a Chicagoan, had trouble matching. Hazen was carrying his M-16 rifle, a bundle of ammunition, and the big PRC-25 field radio strapped to his back.

Captain Nadal was moving two of his platoons toward the dry creekbed in order to secure that critical piece of terrain, as well as to protect the left flank of Bravo Company, as I had ordered. Nadal says, "I was just east of the creekbed, walking through elephant grass, when suddenly there's my West Point classmate, John Herren, laying on the ground with his radio operators. He looked up and told me: 'Lots of VC up there!' " Herren also remembers that chance meeting. "I told him to get down or get his ass shot off. Nadal got down."

Farther out in the scrub brush, John Herren's 1st and 3rd platoons were linking up and moving out to try to reach Lieutenant Henry Herrick's embattled platoon. Nadal had loaned his 2nd Platoon, led by Lieutenant Walter J. (Joe) Marm, to Herren for this attack. There had been a delay in getting Marm's men on line and oriented, and Deal and Devney had already kicked off their attack. Marm was about a hundred yards behind Herren's two platoons.

Lieutenant Deal recalls what happened next: "I'm on the left and Devney on the right, out of physical contact with company headquarters. Both platoons advanced toward Herrick and were met with automatic-weapons and small-arms fire, causing light to moderate casualties in both platoons. Intense fire caused a withdrawal to a position where we could evaluate the situation."

At that moment, Lieutenant Bob Taft and his 3rd Platoon of Alpha Company collided head-on with an enemy force of about 150 men charging down and along both sides of the dry creek. A savage fight now broke out over ownership of the creekbed. Captain Nadal, who had spent a year in South Vietnam with the Special Forces, looked out across the creekbed at the enemy boiling out of the trees and knew these were not Viet Cong guerrillas but North Vietnamese regulars. He got on the battalion net radio and yelled: "They're PAVN! They're PAVN!"

Specialist 4 Carmen Miceli, a native of North Bergen, New Jersey, remembers, "We were told to drop our packs. We got on line and moved forward in the attack. I saw Specialist 4 Bill Beck on an M-60 machine gun out to my left. Captain Nadal was right there with us. We took fire, and guys started going down. We could see the enemy very plainly. We were assaulting. A lot of our guys were hit right away."

Sergeant Steve Hansen was behind and to the right of Lieutenant

Taft. He says, "We moved at a trot across the open grass toward the tree line and heard fire up on the finger to the west where we were headed. My radio operator friend, Specialist 4 Ray Tanner, and I crossed the streambed. Captain Nadal's party and the two other platoons were off to the right. Lieutenant Taft was well forward as we crossed over into the trees. SFC Lorenzo Nathan, Ray Tanner, and I were close, maybe ten yards behind. We were moving fast. Specialist 4 Pete Winter was near me.

"We ran into a wall of lead. Every man in the lead squad was shot. From the time we got the order to move, to the time where men were dying, was only five minutes. The enemy were very close to us and overran some of our dead. The firing was heavy. Sergeant Nathan pulled us back out of the woods to the streambed."

Bob Hazen, Bob Taft's radio operator, recalls: "Lieutenant Taft got out in front of me. I was off to his left. He had the radio handset in his left hand, connected to the radio on my back with that flexible rubber wire. It got tight and I pulled back on the lieutenant and hollered: 'We're getting off line.' He glanced back at me, turned back to his front, and took four more steps. Then he fired two shots at something. I couldn't see what.

"Then he dropped facedown on the ground. Lieutenant Taft was hit. I didn't realize how bad till I rolled him over. He was shot in the throat and the round had richocheted down and came out his left side. He was dead and it was difficult to roll him over, even though he was a slightly built man."

Captain Nadal says, "The enemy on the mountain started moving down rapidly in somewhat uncoordinated attacks. They streamed down the hill and down the creekbed. The enemy knew the area. They came down the best-covered route. The 3rd Platoon was heavily engaged and the volume of firing reached a crescendo on my left. At this time I lost radio contact with Taft's platoon."

In the center of that fury, Bob Hazen struggled and rolled his dead platoon leader over. "He was gone and there was nothing we could do. The first thing I thought of was what they taught me: Never let the enemy get his hands on a map or the signals codebook. I got those from Lieutenant Taft and was kneeling over to try to pull his body back. That's when my radio was hit and the shrapnel from the radio hit me in the back of the head. It didn't really hurt; all of a sudden I was just laying facedown on the ground next to Lieutenant Taft. I felt something running down my neck, reached back, and came out with a handful of blood." Carmen Miceli was on Hazen's right: "We knew what had happened. The word passed fast: 'They got Lieutenant Taft!' "

Lieutenant Wayne O. Johnson's 1st Platoon of Alpha Company was just to the right of Taft's men. Johnson's platoon sergeant, Sergeant First Class Troy Miller, recalls: "We could see the enemy go after the 3rd Platoon like crazy. It was a more exposed area than we were in and the North Vietnamese had a better-covered and [better-]concealed route into them. The enemy was well camouflaged and you could barely see them because their khaki uniform and hats of the same color blended in well with the brownish-yellow grass. They all seemed very well disciplined and did not seem to have any fear of dying at all."

Specialist 4 William A. Kreischer, twenty-one, of Hauppauge, New York, was a rifleman in Lieutenant Taft's platoon. Says Kreischer: "We assaulted on line; then all hell broke loose. It seemed like we were getting hit from behind, in the area of the creekbed."

Like every other unit in the battalion, the 3rd Platoon's weapons squad was understrength. It had two M-60 machine-gun teams, each authorized a gunner, an assistant gunner, and two ammunition bearers. In reality, one team was down to three men, the other to only two. One team consisted of the gunner, Specialist 4 Russell E. Adams, twenty-three, of Shoemakersville, Pennsylvania; assistant gunner Specialist 4 Bill Beck, twenty-two, of Steelton, Pennsylvania; and ammunition carrier PFC John Wunderly. Russell Adams was exactly fourteen days short of completing his Army obligation when he landed in X-Ray. At five feet eight inches tall and 145 pounds, Adams was small but wiry; he handled the heavy M-60 machine gun with ease. Beck was six foot two, lean and hard. The other M-60 crew was made up of Specialist 4 Theron Ladner, twenty-two, a tall, thin native of Biloxi, Mississippi, and his assistant gunner, PFC Rodriguez E. Rivera.

Bill Beck says Russell Adams was his best buddy, a calm, soft-spoken man with big hands. "He didn't talk much, never bitched—just oiled his M-60," Beck says, adding: "We moved toward the creekbed after chow. Suddenly fire was everywhere and Jerry Kirsch, three yards directly in front of me, got hit with machine-gun fire and dropped screaming, rolling on his back, yelling for his mother. That scared the shit out of me and I jumped to the left for cover, beside a soldier on the ground. He was in a firing position and looking at me. It was Sergeant Alexander Williams. He had a small hole in his forehead and he was dead." Williams, twenty-four, was from Jacksonville, Florida.

Beck says: "I jumped up as fast as I jumped down and ran forward toward Adams, who had gone past Kirsch. We were in the open about thirty yards left of the creekbed, moving parallel to it toward Chu Pong. Nobody had told us how far to go, so we kept moving. I heard Bob Hazen yelling about Lieutenant Taft getting hit. I saw him leaning over Taft when an NVA blasted him and his radio exploded into pieces. His back was to the creekbed. That all happened at once, you know, thirty seconds. We kept moving. Adams, firing from the hip, blew away an NVA aiming his AK at us through the fork of a tree."

Over on the east side of the creek Bob Hazen lay, briefly unconscious, beside his dead lieutenant. When he came to, he helped drag Taft's body back to the creekbed. "We were under fire. I looked over to our right and behind us was an NVA leaning up against a tree facing it [the tree]. We had bypassed him. The medic and I saw him up tight against that tree, pith helmet on, tan uniform, pistol belt, and a weapon. I didn't have a weapon. He looked over at us. Then somebody on my left shot him. He slammed into that tree real hard and then just crumpled."

Specialist Bill Kreischer, stunned at the volume of enemy fire, says, "Specialist Jerry Kirsch was hit in the stomach about the same time Lieutenant Taft and his radio operator, Bob Hazen, were hit. Sergeant Travis Poss, Specialist 4 Albert Witcher, and Sergeant [Alexander] Williams were all hit then. We pulled back to the creekbed. Kirsch was screaming with his stomach wound—it was really bad."

Although they had been hit hard and had suffered several casualties, Taft's platoon, now led by Korean War veteran Sergeant Lorenzo Nathan, stood firm and stopped the momentum of the attack. The enemy recoiled and slowly drifted off to their left still trying to find a way to flank Bravo Company. This brought them directly in front of Joe Marm's troopers, who had been moving up to join Bravo. About eighty North Vietnamese soldiers were caught by surprise as Marm's troopers opened up with volley after volley of grazing, point-blank machine-gun and rifle fire and heaved hand grenades into their packed ranks on their exposed right flank. Marm's men mowed them down. Two enemy were taken prisoner.

Several of the men still remember the curious behavior of the North Vietnamese who came under this murderous fire. Captain Tony Nadal says, "It wasn't much of a fight; the 2nd Platoon just mowed them down." Staff Sergeant Les Staley recalls, "Fifty NVA came right across my front and were cut down almost immediately and they did not turn and try to return our fire." The enemy survivors fell back to their right rear, toward the creekbed. That brought them back in front of Tony Nadal's 1st and 3rd platoons, which were now in the four-foot-deep cover of the creekbed. Again the enemy were cut down by close-range flanking fire from their right. They just kept walking into the field of fire.

Sergeant Troy Miller of the 1st Platoon was in the thick of it: "I saw one NVA in the creekbed hit in the upper part of his body, killed by a sergeant from 3rd Platoon and a team leader from my platoon. He was no more than ten feet away. We searched his body later and found he had taken Lieutenant Taft's dog tags."

Captain Nadal, out of radio contact with Taft's platoon, moved toward the furious firing on his left flank to find out what was happening. Nadal says, "My radio operator, Sergeant Jack E. Gell, the company communications chief who had volunteered to carry one of my two radios, ran with me out of the creekbed into the open area toward Taft's position. We ran into Sergeant Nathan and I asked him what was happening. He said the platoon had been attacked on the left flank; the left squad had taken a number of casualties and had pulled back out of the creekbed, refusing their left flank to the enemy. Nathan said Taft had been hit and was left in the creekbed.

"That made me angry. We had been taught never to leave any wounded or dead on the battlefield. Sergeant Gell and I crawled forward of our lines to that creekbed, where the enemy were, to find Taft. We came under grenade attack from the west side of the creekbed but had some cover from a few trees. We located Taft, dead. While bringing him back we saw another soldier who had been left behind. After leaving Taft's body with his platoon, Gell and I went back again and we picked up the other man."

Bill Beck and Russell Adams had by now moved about a hundred yards toward the mountain and were heavily engaged with masses of enemy thirty yards to their south and west around the creekbed. Beck says their charge into battle had been eventful: "As I was chasing after Adams, above the noise of automatic fire someone yelled 'Grenade!' and right in front of me, less than two yards away, one of those wooden-handled potato-masher hand grenades rolled to a stop. I started to go to ground, my knees bent; then came an explosion and flash of bright-white light. I never did hit the ground and continued to move, carrying my boxes of M-60 ammo.

"On the right, twenty yards away, was an anthill with a clump of trees on it, just outside the creekbed. American GIs were on one side and two NVA soldiers were on the other side, not five yards away from each other. I don't think our men could see the enemy. I yelled at the top of my lungs but nobody could hear me because of the overall noise of battle. It was deafening. The only weapon I had was my .45-caliber pistol."

Beck says, "All this time I had been jumping, dodging, hitting the dirt, and moving forward with Adams. Now I pulled my .45 and fired the entire clip of seven rounds at the left side of that anthill and both of the enemy dropped. Adams called for ammo, and I moved up with him beside a little tree. We were now the forwardmost position. I was feeding belt after belt of 7.62mm ammunition into the gun. We were prone and he was firing at the enemy in front and to the right. On the right about ten yards out were our buddies Theron Ladner and Rodriguez Rivera on their gun. We could hardly see them in the grass."

Beck adds, "I would spot movement to the front, point where, and Adams did the firing. This went on for several attacks. The enemy were zeroed in on Russ and me, their bullets hitting the tree trunk, the dirt around us, and crackling over our heads. Russ stopped those assaults and we started looking for our ammo bearer, John Wunderly. He was gone. I can remember the extreme heat and exhaustion taking hold now, like I hadn't taken a breath the entire time. We were soaked with sweat and the sun was very hot as we lay in the brown grass, in the open with really no cover but the grass."

On one of his trips up to collect Taft and the wounded soldier, Captain Nadal spotted Beck and Adams on his left about twenty yards out and running toward the mountain. Beck and his gunner, Russell Adams, and the other M-60 crew ended up at least seventy-five yards out front of Alpha Company's 3rd Platoon. Adams puts it simply: "Nobody told me to stop so I kept going."

In piecing together the mosaic of a confused and fast-paced fight, it is clear to me that those courageous machine gunners inflicted heavy casualties on a large North Vietnamese force that was hurrying down to reinforce the attack on Alpha Company's left flank. Bill Beck and his buddies paid a terrible price, but virtually single-handedly they kept the enemy from turning Nadal's left flank and driving a wedge between Alpha and Charlie companies.

Overhead, some of the best air-support work was being done by the A-1E Skyraider, an antiquated single-engine propeller plane of Korean War vintage that proved of great worth providing tactical air support to ground troops. It was slow, but heavily armored and simply built; it delivered very accurate fire and, best of all, could hang around for up to eight hours.

Captain Bruce M. Wallace, an enlisted man in the Korean War and a 1956 West Point graduate, was on his second Vietnam tour with the Air Force in 1965, this time flying the old "Spads," as the A-1Es were nicknamed. Says Wallace: "The Skyraider was uniquely suited for putting ordnance on the ground at the exact time and in the precise place that the ground commander needed it. It was slow, cumbersome, ungainly, greasy and hot to fly. But you could hang everything under its wings but the kitchen sink. As fighting intensified around the Ia Drang, all available aircraft and crews of the 1st and 602nd Air Commando squadrons were committed to the mission."

At around two P.M. one of those A-1Es was coming in from the south just above the slope of the mountain, very low, just over the trees, on a bombing run directly over the location where the enemy was attacking from. Suddenly there was an explosion, and the Spad burst into flames. It continued on down the creekbed, trailing fire and smoke, passed directly over us and the fighting, turned back east, and staggered on for perhaps two miles before crashing in a black ball of smoke. We saw no parachute. Overhead, Captain Matt Dillon in the command ship had a clear view: "The plane caught fire, veered off and crashed to the east of X-Ray. There was an explosion and fire. We flew over to see if we could see any sign of life. Very soon after the crash a lot of enemy, twenty or thirty of them, came running to the plane. I called the Aerial Rocket ships in on them."

Air Force records indicate that the pilot who died in that crash was Captain Paul T. McClellan, Jr., thirty-four, of West Stayton, Oregon, who flew for the 1st Air Commando Squadron. Captain Bruce Wallace says, "Paul was probably downed by fragments of his own ordnance. We were carrying both bombs and napalm on a single aircraft, and safe separation altitude[s] for the two types of ordnance were different. It was easy to select the wrong switch in the cockpit during the heat of a low-altitude mission under fire. The precise cause of that crash, however, was never officially determined."

Meanwhile, back at 3rd Brigade headquarters, Brigadier General Dick Knowles had been filled in on details of our rapidly developing fight. The prisoner we captured had been debriefed; he identified his unit as a battalion of the 33rd Regiment of the People's Army. Intelligence said the 66th Regiment and the 320th Regiment were also in the vicinity. At Knowles's urging, the division commander,

Major General Harry Kinnard, flew in from headquarters at An Khe for a briefing. Says Knowles: "When General Kinnard arrived I showed him a situation map. He took one look and said, 'What the hell are you doing in that area?' I replied: 'Well, General, the object of the exercise is to find the enemy and we sure as hell have.' After an awkward pause and a few questions he said, 'OK, it looks great. Let me know what you need.' "

While all of this was taking place, John Herren was still desperately trying to reach Lieutenant Herrick's cut-off platoon. His other platoons were battling a large number of enemy who had moved between them and Herrick. During the confusion, Lieutenant Bill Riddle, Herren's artillery forward observer, made his way forward and linked up with Lieutenant Al Devney. Herren was still in the creekbed area, to the right of Nadal's Alpha Company location, trying to get Lieutenant Joe Marm's platoon of reinforcements linked up with Deal and Devney.

The devastating flanking fire Nadal's Alpha Company soldiers poured on the enemy, and the shock of the continuing artillery and air bombardment, caused the North Vietnamese ahead of Devney and Deal to reel back and slack off. This gave Lieutenant Marm and his troops the opportunity to move forward and link up with the two Bravo Company platoons. Now they were able to launch a full three-platoon attack in the direction of Herrick's cut-off men. It was three platoons abreast, left to right: Deal, Devney, and Marm.

Dennis Deal remembers: "We moved on line for about a hundred or a hundred and fifty yards before the volume of firing forced us to stop. We were taking too many casualties. I radioed Herrick's platoon and said: 'I think we are close to you. Shoot one round off; wait to the count of three and shoot two more.' The radioman, or whoever was on the radio, did that, so we had a pretty firm fix on where he was. We got up and started the assault again. We went about ten yards and the whole thing just blew up in our faces. The enemy had infiltrated between Herrick's platoon and us and now were starting to come in behind us.

"I saw Platoon Sergeant [Leroy] Williams shoot into a tree; a weapon fell but the body didn't. It was roped into the treetop. There were at least fifteen of our men, wounded and dead, out front. At this point our medic, Specialist 5 Calvin Bouknight, rose from cover, ran over, and began administering aid to the wounded. He succeeded in treating four or five of them, always by placing his body between the continuous sheets of heavy fire and the man he was treating. Bouknight was mortally wounded less than five minutes after he began performing his stunningly heroic acts." Bouknight, twenty-four, was from Washington, D.C.

Deal says, "Suddenly a lull occurred on the battlefield. During that lull one of the men in my platoon got up on his knees while the rest of us were all flat on our stomachs. He was promptly shot in the upper body, ten feet from me, and I heard the bullet strike human flesh. It sounded exactly like when you take a canoe paddle and slap it into mud. One bullet, one hit, another man down. During the same lull, my radio operator's hip suddenly exploded, if you will, and before the bleeding started I saw white, jagged bone sticking out. We gave him first aid and tried to keep him out of shock. He said: 'I'll be all right. Just show me where to go.' He made his own way back to the aid station."

Lieutenant Deal adds that he and the other two platoon leaders now began planning yet another attempt to break through and rescue Herrick's men. "Leaders were running back and forth coordinating this when all of a sudden firing began. The lull dissipated quickly. It was at this time that my weapons-squad leader, Sergeant Curry, 'the Chief,' was killed. His last words were 'Those bastards are trying to get me!' He was caught rolling around on the ground. Later on, as my men were carrying him back, I had them put him down and I turned his face toward me and looked at him. I could not conceive of the Chief being dead." Staff Sergeant Wilbur Curry, Jr., of Buffalo, New York, was thirty-five years old.

Deal says his platoon and the others got up to launch the attack and again were driven back by extremely heavy fire. "We slugged it out for all we were worth but finally had so many wounded we had to stop and say 'Let's get out of here.' " Sergeant Larry Gilreath says, "We tried fire and movement and on-line attack but the NVA were waiting for us each time."

Less than a hundred yards away Herrick's men were in a running gunfight for their lives, and had been from the first minute of contact. Shortly after Sergeant Ernie Savage cleaned up that enemy machine-gun crew, he spotted movement out of the corner of his eye, back toward the little creek. Turning in that direction he saw a large group of fast-moving enemy. Savage says: "There were fifty, maybe seventy of them. They weren't firing on us; they were going around to our right trying to get in behind us. We fired on them and kept firing to our front also. Then they outflanked us. There was no way we could control it with what we had. We were short on people."

By now Sergeant Paul Hurdle's two machine guns were firing on enemy to the front and to the right. Savage's squad was also fighting on two sides, thirty yards out front of the machine guns, and began withdrawing by fire and movement, one fire team shooting while the other fell back toward the rest of the 2nd Platoon on the lower end of the finger. Says Savage: "The machine gunners were already set up on the lower part of the finger and firing. There was so much noise, I didn't know that at the time. When we started pulling back I saw both gunners sitting there. They were firing just over the rise and downhill. We pulled back past the guns. PFC Bernard Birenbaum was one of the gunners and he damned sure did some damage before he went down. His firing allowed us to get back. We pulled straight back toward him. It was a wonder he didn't shoot us; the enemy were behind us and he was firing past us. Things were going real fast."

Herrick and the other two squads were holding precariously to the small knoll near the bottom of the finger. Savage teamed up with McHenry's squad, which was pinned to the ground. Herrick was with that squad. Sergeant Zallen's squad was to their left rear. Savage checked on his men when he tied up with McHenry. He knew that Specialist 4 Robert M. Hill, the M-79 grenadier, was no longer with them. "Hill got killed in there somewhere. He had his M-79 and a .45 pistol and he was firing both at the same time." The twenty-three-year-old Hill came from Starkville, Mississippi.

Now the men of Herrick's three rifle squads were all grouped together on the small knoll, under heavy fire from enemy troops close in on their north and east. Unfortunately, the two M-60 machine-gun crews were separated from them by a distance of about thirty yards, downhill. As Savage began to deploy his men into firing positions, the North Vietnamese mounted a reinforced attack from three directions: up the finger from the north; down the finger from the southwest; and, worst of all, fifty to seventy attackers coming from the ditch toward the rear of the two M-60 machine guns. Lieutenant Herrick and Platoon Sergeant Carl Palmer were in the middle of the action. By now Savage had personally killed fifteen to twenty enemy. "The machine guns were still firing and we were all fighting as hard as we could to hold the enemy off. There were a lot of them, all over," Savage recalls.

Lieutenant Herrick shouted to the machine-gun crews to come up the hill. One was out on the north end of the finger, with Sergeant Hurdle. The other, closer in, disengaged and scrambled up the knoll and into the tiny American perimeter. Sergeant Hurdle's gun kept firing to cover the withdrawal. It came under attack by a large number of enemy who swarmed all around the crew. It was during this desperate mêlée that Herrick's platoon suffered its worst casualties and lost one of its precious machine guns.

Sergeant Savage again: "The enemy were past the machine gun before it ever quit firing. I could hear Sergeant Hurdle down there cursing. Even over the firefight I heard him. He was famous for that: 'Motherfucker! Son of a bitch!' I could hear him hollering that down there. Then they threw grenades in on him." Hurdle, thirty-six, was from Washington, D.C. Birenbaum, twenty-four, was a native of New York City. PFC Donald Roddy, twenty-two, hailed from Ann Arbor, Michigan. The three of them died in a hail of rifle fire and enemy grenades.

As Sergeant Wayne M. Anderson and his assistant gunner made it up the finger, carrying the other M-60, the enemy down below turned Sergeant Hurdle's M-60 around and began using it on the Americans on the knoll. The only ammo for the platoon's last machine gun was what was left in the belt hanging out of the gun. Sergeant Anderson was screaming and yelling that his face was on fire. It was. Fragments from a white phosphorus grenade were smoking and smoldering in his flesh. Sergeant Zallen tripped Anderson and, with Savage's help, they used bayonets to scrape and dig the burning "Willy Peter" fragments out of Anderson's face.

The enemy, more than 150 strong, now attacked the knoll from three sides—north, south, and east—and soldiers on both sides were falling. Lieutenant Herrick ran from trooper to trooper trying to get a defense organized. An enemy volley cut across Herrick, his radio operator, Specialist 4 John R. Stewart, and the artillery recon sergeant, Sergeant John T. Browne, wounding all three, Herrick and Browne seriously. Stewart took a single bullet through his leg.

Herrick radioed Bravo Company commander John Herren and told him he had been hit bad and was turning command of the platoon over to Sergeant Carl Palmer. Herrick then gave explicit instructions to his men to destroy the signals codes, redistribute the ammo, call in artillery, and, if possible, make a break for it. Herren says, "I give Herrick all the credit in the world for pulling that platoon together so that they could make their stand."

So should we all. Savage and Zallen paint a clear picture of a green young lieutenant who did a superb job in a hailstorm of enemy fire. His platoon stopped a very large North Vietnamese unit clearly headed down to join the attack on the landing zone. I long ago concluded that the very presence of his platoon so far to the northwest confused the enemy commander as to exactly where we were and how far out we had penetrated in all directions, and thus helped us as the battle built.

Sergeant Savage recounts the final moments of Henry Herrick's life: "He was lying beside me on the hill and he said: 'If I have to die, I'm glad to give my life for my country.' I remember him saying that. He was going into shock, hit in the hip and in a lot of pain. He didn't live long. He died early in the fight, next to a little brush pile." Specialist 5 Charles R. Lose, twenty-two, of Mobile, Alabama, was the platoon medic. "Lieutenant Herrick was kneeling when hit. He had a bullet wound to the hip. He told me to go help the other wounded.

"Carl Palmer got hit about the same time as Lieutenant Herrick, just as we came back in. It was alongside his head. Not a fatal wound, but it knocked him out. He fell right behind me. I thought he was dead but he wasn't. Palmer came to and said: 'Let's get these guys out of here.' I told him there was no way we could get out with all our wounded. Palmer was still talking about getting everybody out, fading in and out of consciousness."

It was now 2:30 P.M. and the cut-off platoon's ordeal had been going on for more than an hour. Palmer was lying wounded on the ground, beside a log. The man closest to him was Galen Bungum. Bungum says: "Palmer was lying there with his bandage held on the wrong side of his head, so I helped him get it on the side he was wounded on. As we were getting it changed, a North Vietnamese threw one of our own hand grenades toward us. It landed just behind Sergeant Palmer and exploded, killing him. A piece of that grenade hit me in the knee and I pulled the splinter out. The North Vietnamese that threw the grenade just stood there and laughed at us. Specialist 4 Michael L. Patterson must have put a full magazine in his stomach. I swear I saw daylight through him before he went down."

Sergeant Carl A. Palmer died in action two days before his fortieth birthday. As he predicted, he did not live to see it.

Specialist Bungum had quickly run through his limited supply of M-79 grenades and had begun hunting for something else to fight with. "I was crawling around looking for an M-16. I got my hands on one, and Specialist 5 Marlin T. Dorman said: 'That doesn't work; I'll get you another one.' Then he hollered: 'That doesn't work either.' I headed for a third rifle and PFC Donald Jeffrey hollered: 'It don't work!' Finally I did find an M-16 and some full magazines from our dead. About then PFC Johnnie Boswell [thirty-two, from Eatonton, Georgia] got hit in the buttocks and was bleeding bad. He said to me: 'I am going to get up and get out of here.' I told him, 'You'll never make it.' He started to get up. I grabbed his foot and held him with us, but he died a little later. Sergeant [Robert] Stokes was hit in the leg. Doc Lose bandaged him up and went on to somebody else."

Sergeant Savage had earlier sent PFC Boswell, Sergeant Joaquin

Vasquez, and Private Russell Hicks scurrying on all fours to the three sides of the perimeter under attack. He was also working with Sergeant Stokes on bringing in mortar and artillery fire. He had moved two wounded men, PFC Calix Ramos and Specialist Stewart, over to the north side of the knoll. Specialist Clarence Jackson took a round clean through his left hand, shifted his rifle to his right, and continued firing until he was hit a second time. Sergeant Vasquez and several of the other wounded men likewise fought on, thanks to their own courage and Doc Lose's medical help. Specialist James Blythe had his thumb shot off. Patterson, Hicks, and Jeffrey were all wounded. Sergeant Ruben Thompson was struck by a bullet above his heart that exited under his left arm; bleeding heavily, he grabbed a rifle and fought on. The encircled infantrymen of the Lost Platoon refused to give up.

Specialist Dorman: "We were all on the ground now and if you moved you got hit. Our training really showed then. We shifted into defense positions. We had five men killed in twenty-five minutes. Then all of a sudden they tried a mass assault from three directions, rushing from bush to bush and laying fire on us. We put our M-16s on full automatic and killed most of them." Galen Bungum: "We gathered up all the full magazines we could find and stacked them up in front of us. There was no way we could dig a foxhole. The handle was blown off my entrenching tool and one of my canteens had a hole blown through it. The fire was so heavy that if you tried to raise up to dig you were dead. There was death and destruction all around."

By now eight men of the platoon's twenty-nine had been killed in action; another thirteen were wounded. The twenty-five-yard-wide perimeter was a circle of pain, death, fear, and raw courage. Medic Charlie Lose crawled from man to man throughout the raging firefight, doing his best to patch the wounded with the limited supplies in his medical pack. Although he was wounded twice himself, Lose never slowed his pace. He would keep all thirteen of the wounded alive for twenty-six long, harrowing hours. Lose says, "On several occasions I had to stand or sit up to treat the wounded. Each time the VC fired heavily at me." Lose used his .45 and an M-16 rifle to help defend his patients.

Captain John Herren got a desperate radio call from the weapons-platoon forward observer with Herrick's platoon: "Sergeant Stokes was saying they were finished and he wanted to infiltrate out. I told him if it was hopeless to try and break out. He was hit shortly afterward." In the combined mortar-fire position on the landing zone, Specialist 4 Vincent Cantu, twenty-three, of Refugio, Texas, a Bravo Company mortarman who had only ten days left on his two-year tour as a draftee, says: "We set up and got our elevations and deflections from Sergeant Robert Stokes, the mortar forward observer who was trapped with the platoon up the mountain. His pleas for help over the radio were desperate. We could all hear him. They were surrounded. He called for everything we had. Within minutes all our mortar rounds were gone."

Cantu said the mortar crews were tortured by their inability to provide any further fire support for the trapped platoon and by their friend's pitiful pleas for help. He says, "Sergeant Montgomery told us we were going after Sergeant Stokes. We got our personal weapons and started up but we couldn't advance. The firepower was overwhelming. We moved back.

"By 2:30 in the afternoon it seemed like half the battalion was either dead or wounded. I remember rolling this soldier in a poncho. He was face down when I turned him over. I saw the lieutenant's bars on him. I snapped; I thought to myself, these rounds don't have any regard. Gary Cooper, Audie Murphy, they all came out of it, but that's in the movies."

Sergeant Ernie Savage, who was lying next to Sergeant Stokes, remembers: "There was a lot of fire coming in on us and they had people coming up at us, but they had a hell of a lot of fire coming down on them. The mortarman was calling artillery around us and we were all firing from the perimeter. The only cover we had was the rise of the hill. If you moved, you crawled, and if you crawled you drew fire. After Sergeant Palmer got killed, Sergeant Stokes says: 'We've got to get out of here.' He got up.

"There were a lot of enemy out there, right on the ground, and if they saw your helmet they shot. Well, Stokes got hit right in the head, two shots in the helmet and one below the rim, and fell backward over a log with the radio on his back, laying on the radio. It was underneath him, on the other side of the log from me, but I reached under the log, got the handset, and called in more artillery and mortars." Sergeant Robert L. Stokes, twenty-four, was from Salt Lake City, Utah.

Command had passed from Lieutenant Henry Herrick to Sergeant Carl Palmer to Sergeant Robert Stokes as each, in turn, died fighting. Now it was the turn of buck sergeant Ernie Savage. "Sergeant Savage came up on the radio," Captain Herren recalls. "He said Herrick, Palmer, and Stokes were dead; to give him more artillery and he would direct it in as close as possible. We could never establish the platoon's exact position but Lieutenant Riddle could adjust fire on Savage's sensing, and he began to do that."

The extraordinary, unyielding resistance that the dozen or so effective fighters were putting up, plus the artillery barrages that Ernie Savage was bringing down, finally beat off the heavy enemy attack. During a brief lull, the Americans collected ammunition, grenades, and weapons from the dead and those too badly wounded to shoot, and redistributed them. A few riflemen were shifted to better firing positions. Sergeant Zallen collected maps, notebooks, and signal operating instructions booklets from the dead commanders and burned them all. Lieutenant Herrick's PRC-25 radio was secured. Captain Herren was now talking to Savage, telling him of the desperate attempts to break through to him.

Ernie Savage and his small band hunkered down, determined to hold their ground to the end.

8

THE STORM OF BATTLE

> The most precious commodity with which the Army deals is the individual soldier who is the heart and soul of our combat forces.
>
> —General J. Lawton Collins

Our intention with this bold helicopter assault into the clearing at the base of the Chu Pong massif had been to find the enemy, and we had obviously succeeded beyond our wildest expectations. People's Army Lieutenant Colonel Nguyen Huu An, deep in a command bunker no more than a mile and a half away this Sunday afternoon, November 14, was issuing orders by land-line telephone—remember the commo wire spotted by the H-13 helicopter scouts?—as well as by old, unreliable walkie-talkie radios and by foot messenger. His orders to every battalion in the vicinity were simple: Attack!

Shortly after two P.M., with the battle well under way, Colonel An's boss, Brigadier General Chu Huy Man, was safely in his headquarters hard by the Cambodian border almost ten miles away from the action. My boss, on the other hand, was right over my head. With the battle raging on two sides of the perimeter, Colonel Tim Brown suddenly came up on my radio from his command helicopter, asking if he could land and get a firsthand look at the situation.

I waved him off without explanation. There was too much going on to deal with the distraction of a visit by the brigade commander; besides, his command helicopter, bristling with a large array of radio antennas, would be too tempting a target. Brown did not press the question. He instantly understood.

The reports of continued heavy fighting in both Herren's and Nadal's sectors to the west reminded me again that the entire north and east sides of the landing zone were still wide open. I was praying that the next helicopter lift, bringing the last of the Charlie Company troops and the lead elements of Delta Company, would arrive soon. It was on the way.

Delta Company commander Captain Ray Lefebvre was in the lead chopper, flown by Bruce Crandall. With Lefebvre were members of his command group. In the helicopters behind were his machine-gun platoon, part of his mortar platoon, and the last of Captain Bob Edwards's Charlie Company elements. "By the time I came in around two-thirty P.M. there was plenty going on. We were about eleven minutes out, approaching X-Ray, and I was listening on my radio handset," says Lefebvre. "In the lead chopper were my radio operator, PFC Gilbert Nicklas; the mortar-platoon leader, Lieutenant Raul E. Taboada, and his radio operator and others. I could hear the battalion commander on the radio.

"You could see the artillery and air strikes going in. You're flying in a helicopter and you watch this battle and listen to all this shit going on on the radio. The pilot, Bruce Crandall, turned around, shook his head, and made this face like: 'Man, what are we getting into?' I recall that pilot's expression. We could see a lot of firing. I was trying to figure out exactly where I was going to go. I was sitting on the left side, facing out toward the mountain, in the middle between the two radio operators." Crandall radioed that he was on short final approach, dropping toward the LZ, and I told him to come on in but be quick getting out.

As this fifth lift of the day roared in at treetop level, the landing zone suddenly turned red-hot. The enemy at the creekbed turned their guns on the helicopters and filled the air with rifle and automatic-weapons fire. Says Crandall: "As I was flaring out to touch down we started receiving heavy ground fire. I touched down at the forward part of the LZ, looked out to my left and saw a North Vietnamese firing at my ship from a point just outside the length of my rotor blades. Another enemy soldier was firing from the other side. Everybody and his brother seemed to be shooting either at us or at them.

"It seemed like this went on forever, but in reality the infantry cleaned up these guys rather quickly. Even though the enemy was that close, my door gunners could not take action to defend themselves. Troops on the ground, or those getting out of our birds had to handle the enemy in the landing zone. We couldn't shoot without killing our own people on the perimeter, so our policy was not to shoot.

"I stayed on the ground a little longer on this lift so that I could pick up wounded. As I pulled pitch my flight of four came out and the next four choppers hit the landing zone almost immediately. I reported the heavy fire to the incoming aircraft and directed them to continue with the approach. I knew several helicopters were hit but I couldn't stick around; my job was to get those wounded aboard my helicopter back to Plei Me to medical help and start getting support and reinforcements going for the people on the ground. I had three dead and three wounded on my bird. The wounded included my crew chief, who had been hit in the throat. When we landed we saw that every bullet had struck the wounded in the head or neck. Excellent marksmanship by the other side, and not a happy thought for a helicopter pilot, to say the least."

Captain Ray Lefebvre, commander of Delta Company, was about to earn his Combat Infantryman's Badge, a Silver Star, and a Purple Heart, all in the next seven minutes. He remembers, "When we came in, the mountain was off to our left and we were taking a lot of fire. We settled down near the wood line. There was lots of fire coming from the woods. Taboada was hit in the hand while we were hovering.

"I was starting to unhook my seat belt when I felt a round crease the back of my neck. I turned to my right and saw that my radio operator had been hit in the head; the same round that cut me killed him. He just slumped forward, still buckled in. Nicklas was a young guy, just twenty, came from Niagara Falls, New York. I jumped out. Firing was coming from the mountain, and three or four of us moved about fifty to seventy-five yards toward the trees, to the sound of the firing, and stopped in a small fold in the ground."

With Crandall, flying Serpent Yellow 3, was Chief Warrant Officer Riccardo J. Lombardo, thirty-four, of Hartford, Connecticut.

Lombardo was in the pilot's seat and recalls that lift: "As I approached I saw the battle smoke getting heavy. As my skids touched down, my troops leaped out. I saw men lying on the ground. I felt and heard bangs on the back of my seat. I looked ahead and saw a man about fifty yards ahead on the edge of the LZ. He was standing in plain view, pointing a weapon at us. I thought it was one of our people, but something didn't look right. His uniform was khaki color and he wasn't wearing a helmet.

"Before I even noticed the muzzle flashes, three holes appeared in my windshield. In my mind I was asking, 'Why is that bastard shooting at me?' As fast as that man appeared, he disappeared. Then I was off the ground and banking to the right in a climb, and all the while red streaks were following me. That was the last lift of troops I made into the LZ."

This was Lombardo's only flight into X-Ray, as his Huey was used by Crandall for the next flight into the LZ and was shot up. Crandall went back to his first bird, which had been pronounced flyable. Lombardo spent the rest of the afternoon listening to the battle on the tactical radio at Plei Me and sucking down beer.

First Lieutenant Roger K. Bean was flying a Huey in the second wave of birds behind Crandall's. "When we landed I was flying on Captain Ed Freeman's right wing. We were all taking fire and the number four ship didn't look like he was going to make it out of X-Ray. I was in the pilot's seat and Captain Gene Mesch was in the left seat. I was looking over my shoulder at the number four ship when we got hit by AK-47 fire. A round came through the door in front of Gene, entered the back of my flight helmet, tore a hole in the side of my head and came out through the front of the helmet. I was bleeding like a stuck pig and my flight helmet was turned sideways on my head with the earphone covering my eyes. At first I thought I was blind. That concerned me because I was still flying. Gene took the controls and the door gunner patched me up. I was X-rayed at the Special Forces camp and went back to the unit after they sewed me up."

For the rest of the afternoon Chief Warrant Officer Alex S. (Pop) Jekel, forty-three, of Seattle, Washington, flew in Bean's seat. Pop Jekel was the father of nine children. During World War II, at the age of twenty, he had flown B-24s out of England, and B-29s during the postwar years, until he left the service in 1950. Pop Jekel reenlisted in 1953 and had been flying helicopters since 1963. Pop flew into X-Ray seven times under fire. Says he: "The anxiety of going back into that hell on earth was devastating."

Several of the Hueys in the first wave of eight took hits, but none crashed, none caught fire, none had to be abandoned in the landing zone. I radioed orders for the other eight Hueys in the fifth lift to get out of the area and wait until I got the landing zone cooled down and under control. They headed back east to Plei Me where they landed, off-loaded the troops, refueled, and shut down to wait.

Captain Ray Lefebvre now swung into action. Purely by chance, he and several of his Delta Company men had run toward a critical section of the perimeter, an uncovered gap on the left flank of Tony Nadal's embattled Alpha Company troops. Lefebvre recalls, "My executive officer and first sergeant didn't come in on that lift, so the only sergeant I had was George Gonzales, a staff sergeant from the machine-gun platoon, and he had gone in another direction.

"There was no one between us and the tree line; we had an unobstructed view forty yards to the front. Lieutenant Taboada was to my left. I hollered to him saying I needed his radio and to stay where he was. He yelled back that he had been hit but was OK. When his radio operator got over to me, I contacted Sergeant Gonzales and told him to bring his machine guns to my location. He was about 150 yards to my rear and said he was on the way. I called him three or four times but we never got together."

Although it seemed that the North Vietnamese were attacking purposefully, the enemy commander, Lieutenant Colonel Nguyen

Huu An, was frustrated and angry. He says, "I ordered the 66th Regiment's commander, Lieutenant Colonel La Ngoc Chau, to use his 7th Battalion to attack you constantly, to encircle you, and not to allow you to withdraw by helicopter. In the first attacks [on the Bravo and Alpha Company sectors] by the 9th Battalion and the 33rd Regiment, our reconnaissance soldiers learned your positions—but the 7th Battalion commander did not know where you were. I ordered him to keep searching for you. I told him to move forward personally to the front so he could control the situation and directly encircle you."

The People's Army 7th Battalion commander, Major Le Tien Hoa, thought he had finally found the open door into Landing Zone X-Ray on the southern side of the perimeter, and he swung his battalion in a broad encircling maneuver around Tony Nadal's left flank toward the south side of the clearing. But, thanks to Charlie Company, that open door was closing fast.

Charlie Company's commander, Captain Bob Edwards, raced down the line of newly arrived infantrymen, picking up those who belonged to him and hurrying them into position with the rest of the company on the south and southeast sides of the landing zone. Edwards sited his machine gunners and riflemen along a thinly stretched blocking position that now ran for 120 yards.

No more than five minutes had passed when a huge wave of North Vietnamese, the lead assault units of Major Hoa's 7th Battalion, charged headlong into the thin line of 112 American riflemen. Added to the din of battle in the Alpha and Bravo Company areas was the sudden heavy firing in the woods where Charlie Company was located. Captain Bob Edwards was on the radio to battalion instantly, shouting: "We are in heavy contact. Estimate a hundred and seventy-five to two hundred enemy. Damn! These guys are good!"

Captain Edwards says, "The enemy were moving fast toward the landing zone, headed northwest. More toward the center of the LZ where the helicopters were landing. They had to be surprised to hit us. Right after we got into position there was a lot of fire, then after the initial rush it tended to slack off. You could see them. It was shooting ducks out there."

Simultaneously, the 9th Battalion of the 66th Regiment launched a strong attack against Tony Nadal's Alpha Company, feeling for the forty-yard gap between Alpha Company's left flank and Charlie Company's right flank and desperately trying to seize control of that dry creekbed. Nadal's brave machine gunners—Beck and Adams, and Ladner and Rivera—were covering most of the gap between my companies with their deadly fire. Now a handful of newly arrived Delta Company troopers led by Captain Lefebvre played their part as well in stemming the enemy tide.

Ray Lefebvre had dropped into a fold in the ground in the western edge of the clearing, just short of the tree line. "Captain John Herren came out of the trees to my right and said: 'There's a hell of a lot of enemy up there coming into our area.' Then I saw sixteen or seventeen enemy real close, twenty yards, coming down the creekbed right at the edge of the LZ. They didn't seem to know what they were doing, coming out into the landing zone. We had a machine gun [and] our M-16s, and we were throwing grenades. I fired two magazines of M-16 ammo at them and then they just disappeared. The machine gunner on my right got hit. I think he was killed. About then I was hit also, as was my replacement radio operator. I called Sergeant Gonzales again and told him: 'You get up here quick as you can.' I was on the ground and John Herren helped give me a tourniquet. I radioed Colonel Moore and told him I had been hit."

John Herren says, "After finishing my latest report to Matt Dillon, who was overhead, I looked up to see a North Vietnamese soldier with an AK-47 just over the bank I was standing behind with my two radio operators. I fired a burst from my M-16 which promptly fell apart. The pin holding the trigger mechanism to the barrel had broken off or dropped off. The North Vietnamese, who was obviously the lead man for his unit, dropped down behind another embankment, so I grabbed my one grenade and threw it toward him. It hit a branch above him and bounced back just in front of us and exploded. Not knowing whether the enemy was dead or not, and fearing that there were more enemy in the creekbed behind him, which meant that they had gotten between my platoons, I moved out with my radio operators across the creekbed and back into the LZ, then to the southwest, where I thought Dennis Deal's platoon would be.

"I thought the people in the ditch were Deal's men. I saw a machine-gun crew off to the right. I ran over and told them there were NVA in the creekbed. We immediately came under withering fire from the south and dropped down next to some other troopers behind what little cover there was. It was part of Delta Company, and I was next to Captain Lefebvre. Shortly after, automatic-weapons fire swept over us. My tireless radio operator, PFC Dominic De Angelis, nineteen, from Queens, suddenly turned toward me after a shot ripped into his arm, with the words 'Captain Herren, I'm hit' frozen on his lips. As he turned a bullet hole appeared in the center of his helmet and he was dead.

"On my right, Lefebvre was also hit and the blood was gushing out of his right arm. He tried to stop the bleeding himself. I grabbed my first-aid kit compress and pressed it on the wound, using it and some other cloth to make a tourniquet. Lefebvre began to weaken, and after about twenty minutes—while I was firing and hugging the ground and talking on the radio to Lieutenant Herrick and checking on Ray Lefebvre's wound—I got the nearest man to help me get Lefebvre back to the rear. I returned to find Tony Nadal in the same general area where we were pinned down, dragging some of his dead men back. It was a wrenching, frustrating experience for me, out of physical contact with my platoons and pinned down while Henry Herrick's platoon was in trouble."

Lefebvre, seriously wounded, was fading fast: "I had lost a lot of blood. I could see people shooting but I couldn't hear any sounds anymore. I told John Herren somebody had to take over. I again called Colonel Moore and told him that I was going to turn the company over to Sergeant Gonzales. Then the medic arrived to bandage my wound. Shortly after, I remember someone putting me in a poncho and hauling me over to the area of the battalion command post. When I saw Lieutenant Taboada again later, we never did talk much about it. It was just too damned close a thing."

Ray Lefebvre and his handful of Delta Company troopers had unknowingly joined the Alpha Company fight at a crucial moment. About thirty North Vietnamese were flanking Nadal's men on their left, and Captain Lefebvre's party ran smack into them and killed most of them. Nadal's men dispatched the rest. Unknown to Lefebvre, Sergeant Gonzales had been hit in the face by an enemy bullet. Gonzales simply said, "Roger," when Lefebvre told him he was now in command, and for the next hour and half ran Delta Company.

Lefebvre and Taboada were carried into the battalion aid station at the termite hill in poncho litters. They were shockingly wounded, a terrible sight to see. Lefebvre's right arm and dangling hand were both mangled and shattered, with bones protruding. Lefebvre was quietly moaning. One of Taboada's legs was a gaping, raw, bloody mess from hip to foot; he was screaming in agony. (First Lieutenant Raul E. Taboada was something of a mystery man. One story that made the rounds had it that he was Cuban-born, and that he fought against Fidel Castro in the Bay of Pigs invasion.)

In the dry creekbed with Alpha Company's 3rd Platoon, Sergeant Steve Hansen had fired all his mortar ammunition and had now become a rifleman. His description of these events: "Delta Company landed after our first firefight. They took fire coming in, and several casualties. One was Lieutenant Taboada, who was shot in the hand and the leg. I found him up near Alpha Company. Sergeant Jose Robles-Claudio, an Alpha squad leader, talked to him in Spanish. I remember Taboada was holding a picture of his wife and children in his bloody hand. He was ranting in Spanish. How he came to be in the Alpha Company outer perimeter is something I attribute to a lack of information about the LZ and where the bad guys were.

"The choppers approached the LZ from the east and the lead ships were setting down only a few feet from the NVA marksmen in the tree line. Our Alpha left flank was exposed until later in the day when Charlie Company lengthened its lines and took up positions there. Initially the gap between Alpha and Charlie companies was covered by fire only. It was a critical point, and an open avenue of approach. When Charlie Company came under attack, Alpha Company was attacked down the creekbed. They came down from the massif."

All this time, Bill Beck and Russell Adams and their buddies on the other M-60 were out front, anchoring the far left flank of Alpha Company, and their sheets of machine-gun fire wreaked havoc on the attacking enemy. Beck now briefly became a medic as well. Beck recalls, "I spotted an arm, off to my left about twenty yards, reaching up above the grass with a GI canteen in hand. Right arm. Like he was trying to drain one last drop out of it. Adams covered me and I ran over. It was a radio man, helmet off, radio on the ground. He was tall and thin with brown hair. He asked me for water and said he'd been hit. I opened his shirt and there was a small black hole in his chest. I tried to comfort him, telling him he'd be all right, that it's not bad. I gently rolled him on his side expecting to find half his back blown out, but the same small black hole was there also.

"I wrapped his first-aid pack and a plastic wrapper over both holes, screamed for a medic, got his M-16, and tried to fire it at the NVA shooting at us. It was all shot to hell. I screamed again for a medic and dragged him back ten or fifteen yards till Doc [Donal J.] Nall got him. Then I spotted an officer—I remember the silver bar on his shirt—he was in shock, moaning, his hand blown apart and his thigh equally bad. He was sitting facing the creekbed. I knew he had got hit from that area and I was scared shitless that I was going to get it in the back while tending to him."

Beck, down on his knees, bandaged the wounded officer and screamed for a medic. He adds, "I wasn't with him for more than a minute. I got his M-16 and tried to fire it and it was inoperable. I took his .45 pistol and fired into the jungle toward the enemy. Somewhere along the line I picked up an M-79 grenade launcher from a dead guy and tried to fire it, and it was no good. I fired more .45 rounds into the jungle. The enemy firing picked up.

"Just then I heard Ladner screaming, 'Beck, Beck, *help!* Adams is hit.' I ran back. Russ was on his back staring at me, the M-60 lying on its side. The side of his head was a mess. He was trying to talk to me but nothing was coming out. The enemy knew they had shot him and were closing in on us from the front and right front thirty yards out. I righted the M-60 fast and started firing at them. Every time I fired Adams winced. He was lying right beside the gun, so I tried not firing so often. Besides, we were low on ammo and this was no small firefight.

"Suddenly the M-60 jammed. We were being assaulted and I could see the enemy twenty-five yards out. It's surprising how fast you think and act in a situation like that. Lying prone I opened the feed cover, flipped the gun over and hit it on the ground. It jarred the shells loose. Debris from the ground had caught in the ammo belt when Adams was hit. I flipped it right side up, slapped the ammo belt back in, slammed the feed cover closed and began firing again. It seemed like a lifetime, but wasn't more than five or ten seconds.

"The enemy firing slacked off. Adams's helmet lay in front of me. I could see a bullet hole in it and I reached out and turned it over. It seemed like his entire brain fell out in front of me on the ground. I was horrified! I screamed over and over for the medic and tried to tell Adams that it wasn't nothing, that he'd be all right. I told him the choppers would get him out soon. I took his .45 pistol; now I had three of them. I remember Adams laying there for at least a half-hour. Ladner and Rivera were firing and I saw more movement to the front and right. I started firing again. At one time I stood up and, using a poncho, kicked out a brush fire moving toward us."

Bill Beck, thirsty, exhausted, and shocked by his friend's terrible wound, now heard screams from the other machine-gun position. He says, "Ladner cried out to me, horror in his voice, 'Rodriguez is hit! *Help!* His guts are on the ground!' Doc Nall came, patched Adams's head, and carried him to the rear while I covered for them. Doc then came back for Rodriguez but Ladner had already taken him back."

Beck was soon rejoined by Specialist Theron Ladner and Ladner's ammo bearer, PFC Edward F. Dougherty, the only men left out of the two M-60 crews. They were fifteen yards apart, each one steadily firing at the close-in enemy. Someone brought up a load of ammo for the machine guns. Beck says, "That made me very happy. There was no one on my left for a long time. It was lonely as hell up there until a captain came over to me from my left rear and ordered me to 'stay put. You are with such-and-such a company now!' I'll never forget that. I can't remember what company he said; hell, one company's as good as another. I don't know what the hell's happening. I'm out there by myself. I'm only a twenty-year-old kid. I don't know what's going on. I followed Russell Adams; I'm his assistant gunner so I go where he goes. That's how I got up there."

The captain was John Herren of Bravo Company. Bob Edwards and his Charlie Company men were off on Beck's left but not in direct contact. Beck, Ladner, and Dougherty—and, before they were hit, Russell Adams and Rodriguez Rivera—all of them draftees, none of them with combat experience, were undergoing a profound and shattering experience. Russell Adams somehow survived the traumatic head wound, which left him partly crippled. He recalls the wood and bark chips flying as a stream of enemy fire chewed up the tree next to his machine gun. "The next burst hit me."

It was during all this horror that Beck remembers the fear coming over him: "While Doc Nall was there with me, working on Russell, fear, real fear, hit me. Fear like I had never known before. Fear comes, and once you recognize it and accept it, it passes just as fast as it comes, and you don't really think about it anymore. You just do what you have to do, but you learn the real meaning of fear and life and death. For the next two hours I was alone on that gun, shooting at the enemy. Enemy were shooting at me and bullets were hitting the ground beside me and cracking above my head. They were attacking me and I fired as fast as I could in long bursts. My M-60 was cooking. I had to take a crap and a leak bad, so I pulled my pants down while laying on my side and did it on my side, taking fire at the time."

Over to Beck's left, Charlie Company was getting its baptism of fire. Sergeant First Class Robert Jemison, Jr., was the top sergeant in Lieutenant John Geoghegan's 2nd Platoon. Jemison, a native of Aliceville, Alabama, married and the father of four, was an old veteran who had already helped make history in Korea. Drafted in 1947 at age seventeen, Jemison stayed in the Army. In February of 1951, he was a rifleman in K Company, 3rd Battalion, 23rd Infantry Regiment. At Chipyong-ni, twelve miles behind enemy lines, the 23rd Infantry was surrounded by two Chinese army corps and miraculously defeated them.

Fate and the United States Army hadn't done all that well by SFC Jemison. He was now surrounded again, and making history again. Says Jemison: "We received fire on the landing zone. We had one man killed, a Specialist 4 from Phenix City, Alabama, and one private who was a replacement. We moved into position and started digging in. We sent an ammo and casualty report to the platoon leader, Lieutenant Geoghegan. We reported one killed. He said: 'May God have mercy on his soul.' We were attacked throughout the day, off and on, where we had set up."

Specialist 4 George J. McDonald, Jr., twenty-four years old and a native of Pass Christian, Mississippi, was a mortarman in Charlie Company. When he bailed out of a helicopter onto Landing Zone X-Ray he had precisely fourteen days left to serve in the Army. "LZ X-Ray has never left my mind. Sunday morning my squad saw the LZ. There were troopers laying and firing their M-16s into the trees and waving and signalling to us that they were under fire. As soon as we hit the ground we started getting automatic rifle fire from the left up on Chu Pong. We had to hug the ground for a while; the rounds were hitting all around and very close. I could see muzzle flashes coming from up in the trees. Since they were out of range of my M-79 grenade launcher, I borrowed an M-16 from the trooper next to me who couldn't see them. I fired directly at the muzzle flashes until they stopped.

"Then we grabbed the mortar and moved ahead into the trees and set up and quickly used up our mortar ammo. There were some dead Cavalry troops laying on the ground, and word was being shouted that there was heavy fighting up ahead and they needed help. I went in the direction of the heavy rifle fire and used up what ammunition I had, then returned to the mortar."

From my command post at the termite hill, the enemy were

clearly visible a hundred yards to the south. They were damned good soldiers, used cover and concealment to perfection, and were deadly shots: Most of my dead and wounded soldiers had been shot in the head or upper body. The North Vietnamese paid particular attention to radio operators and leaders. They did not appear to have radios themselves; they controlled their men by shouts, waves, pointing, whistles, and sometimes bugle calls.

The North Vietnamese regulars were good, but Charlie Company was cutting them down with fire that scythed through the tall elephant grass. Bob Edwards and his thin green line were stopping the most serious threat of the afternoon. Edwards had run his company for nineteen months. His company first sergeant, John James, was in the hospital with malaria and the acting first sergeant for this operation was SFC Glenn F. Kennedy, a soft-spoken Mississippian, thirty years old.

Edwards had gotten three brand-new second lieutenants as platoon leaders just before we shipped out of Fort Benning. The 1st Platoon leader was Neil A. Kroger, twenty-four, a recent Officer Candidate School graduate from Oak Park, Illinois. Kroger's platoon sergeant was SFC Luther V. Gilreath, thirty-three years old, a tall, slender paratrooper who hailed from Surgoinsville, Tennessee. The 2nd Platoon leader was John Geoghegan, a handsome, redhaired young officer, commissioned out of the Pennsylvania Military College, who was four days past his twenty-fourth birthday. Geoghegan was married and the father of a baby daughter born three months before we shipped out to Vietnam. His platoon sergeant was Robert Jemison. The 3rd Platoon leader was William Franklin, another OCS graduate, who was older than Kroger and Geoghegan; he was married and the father of two children. The 3rd Platoon top kick was SFC Charles N. Freeman, another old pro.

The attacking North Vietnamese 7th Battalion ran straight into a company of American infantrymen in a sector that had been completely undefended only minutes before. They were violently thrown back. Now Major Hoa tried to regroup under blistering ground fire and murderous air and artillery barrages. Bob Edwards reported that Charlie Company was in good shape, was locked in a heavy fight but had things well in hand.

It was 2:45 P.M. All three of my rifle companies were heavily engaged. We had lost the use of the larger clearing for helicopter landings. Wounded were streaming into the command-post aid station. We were in a desperate fix and I was worried that it could become even more desperate. By now I believed we were fighting at least two People's Army battalions; turns out it was three. They were very tough and very determined to wipe us out, but a major difference between Lieutenant Colonel Nguyen Huu An of the People's Army of Vietnam and Lieutenant Colonel Hal Moore of the 1st Cavalry Division was that I had major fire support and he didn't.

Air Force Captain Bruce Wallace and his fellow A-1E Skyraider pilots, as well as jet fighter-bombers from all three services, helped provide that edge, flying fifty sorties in close air support that Sunday afternoon. Says Wallace, "The importance of airplanes in a vulgar brawl is to be down among the palm trees with the troops, putting ordnance on the ground at the exact time and in the precise place that the ground command needs it."

While he was in the airspace over Landing Zone X-Ray, Captain Wallace observed the attacks of the 1st Cavalry Division's aerial rocket artillery (ARA) helicopters with more than passing interest. He says, "It is always an experience for an Air Force pilot to watch a gaggle of Hueys attack a target. We pride ourselves on flexibility of thought, quick response time, ability to react to ever-changing situations, but we are committed to a somewhat linear thought process. In the attack the target is always directly in front of us. Not so with a Huey. To watch four or eight of them at a time maneuvering up and down and laterally and even backward boggles a fighter pilot's mind. Those guys swarm a target like bees over honey. I had to hand it to those Huey guys. They really got down there in the trees with the troops."

The ARA helicopters chewing up the slopes of Chu Pong on our behalf were from Charlie Battery, 2nd Battalion, 20th Artillery (ARA), commanded by Major Roger J. Bartholomew, the legendary "Black Bart" Bartholomew, who would later be killed in combat in Vietnam. One of Black Bart's pilots, Captain Richard B. Washburn, then thirty-one, recalls, "The Battery fired all day in support of X-Ray. We refueled every third trip, never shutting down the engine. Each helicopter carried 48 rockets, and with six helicopters plus the battery commander we were going through ammo in a hurry. An artillery battalion commander, a lieutenant colonel, and his driver were among the volunteers opening boxes of rockets to help keep us armed. CH-47 Chinook helicopters flew in load after load of ammo to keep us going. We stayed with it all day."

The field artillery, what we called "tube artillery" to distinguish the howitzer folks from the helicopter-rocket folks, proudly calls itself the King of Battle. During training at Fort Benning my battalion's fire-support coordinator, Captain Robert L. Barker, presented me with a print of an impeccably uniformed artillery officer, circa 1860s, lighting a match to a small cannon aimed at a pile of grubby men engaged in swordfights, fistfights, and gunfights. The legend engraved across the bottom said: "Artillery Lends Dignity to What Would Otherwise be a Vulgar Brawl."

By the time of the battle at LZ X-Ray, which was without question a very vulgar brawl, Bob Barker was the commander of Battery C, 1st Battalion, 21st Artillery, whose six 105mm howitzers were firing in support of us from LZ Falcon, just over five miles away. Lieutenants Bill Riddle, the forward observer with John Herren's Bravo Company, and Tim Blake, who was killed with Tony Nadal's Alpha Company, were on loan to us from Barker's Battery C. Also located in Falcon were the six big guns of Battery A, 1st of the 21st Artillery, commanded by Captain Donald Davis, twenty-eight, a native Ohioan.

The brave cannon-cockers in LZ Falcon went without sleep for three days and nights to help keep us surrounded by a wall of steel. Those two batteries, twelve guns, fired more than four thousand rounds of high-explosive shells on the first day alone. Says Barker, "On the first afternoon both batteries fired for effect [directly on target] for five straight hours." One of Bruce Crandall's Huey slick pilots, Captain Paul Winkel, touched down at Falcon briefly that first afternoon and was astounded by what he saw: "There were stacks of shell casings, one at least 10 feet high, and exhausted gun crews. They had fired for effect for three straight hours by then, without even pausing to level the bubbles. One tube was burned out, two had busted hydraulics. That's some shooting!"

No matter how bad things got for the Americans fighting for their lives on the X-Ray perimeter, we could look out into the scrub brush in every direction, into that seething inferno of exploding artillery shells, 2.75-inch rockets, napalm canisters, 250- and 500-pound bombs, and 20mm cannon fire and thank God and our lucky stars that we didn't have to walk through *that* to get to work.

9

BRAVE AVIATORS

> I knew wherever I was that you thought of me, and if I got in a tight place you would come—if alive.
>
> —William Tecumseh Sherman, in a letter to Ulysses S. Grant

Over the twenty months of airmobile training, a bond had been welded between the infantry and their rides, the Huey helicopter pilots and crewmen. Now the strength of that bond would be tested in the hottest of fires. If the air bridge failed, the embattled men of the 1st Battalion, 7th Cavalry would certainly die in much the same way George Armstrong Custer's cavalrymen died at the Little Big-horn—cut off, surrounded by numerically superior forces, overrun, and butchered to the last man.

I asked Bruce Crandall's brave aircrews of the 229th Aviation Battalion for the last measure of devotion, for service far beyond the limits of duty and mission, and they came through as I knew they would. This was the first, and in the view of many of us, the toughest of many missions we would accomplish together in a long, deadly combat tour. We desperately needed ammunition and water and medical supplies—and Crandall's Hueys brought them to us. Our wounded, screaming in pain or moaning quietly in shock, had to be evacuated, or they would die where they lay, on their ponchos behind the termite hill.

Hauling out the wounded was not the slick crews' job. Crandall's people were assault helicopter crews, trained to carry infantrymen into battle. Hauling the wounded off the battlefield was a medical-evacuation helicopter mission. But this was early in the war, and the medevac commanders had decreed that their birds would not land in hot landing zones—or, in other words, that they would not go where they were needed, when they were needed most. Even before I asked, Bruce Crandall had already decided to begin doing everything that had to be done.

As his shot-up Huey, full of wounded, headed back east, Old Snake was thinking about the perilous situation on the ground at Landing Zone X-Ray. Crandall recalls, "Getting back to Plei Me seemed to take forever, although we were flying as fast as it would go. I made up my mind during this flight that if the 1st Battalion lost this fight it would not be because of the failure of the helicopter support. We knew the officers and men on the ground were the best in their business; now it was our time to prove that we were their equals in the air.

"Before I landed at Plei Me I had decided that Colonel Moore needed ammunition more than he needed additional manpower at this point. My plan was to change helicopters, then two of us loaded with ammo would go back to X-Ray. Get the ammo in and bring out the wounded. I felt we could reach the LZ if we came in hard at treetop level. If we couldn't get back out, at least the ammo would be there and the Infantry would protect us if we could just reach the landing zone."

Crandall radioed Orange 1 Lead, Captain Paul Winkel, who was sitting on the strip at Plei Me, and told him to send two of his Hueys to Camp Holloway to load with all the ammunition they could carry. Winkel dispatched his Orange 3 and Orange 4 Hueys, piloted by CWO (Chief Warrant Officer) Dallas Harper and CWO Ken Faba. Round trip plus loading: about one hour.

Crandall now dropped his Huey, loaded with casualties, onto the red dirt strip at Plei Me. "When we hit the ground at Plei Me we were met by medics and the Infantry troops still waiting to be lifted into X-Ray. They removed the dead and wounded from my bird—and this act is engraved in my mind deeper than any other experience in my two tours in Vietnam. A huge black enlisted man, clad only in G.I. shorts and boots, hands bigger than dinner plates, reached into my helicopter to pick up one of the dead white soldiers. He had tears streaming down his face and he tenderly cradled that dead soldier to his chest as he walked slowly from the aircraft to the medical station. I never knew if the man he picked up was his buddy or not. I suspect not. His grief was for a fallen comrade and for the agony that violent death brings to those who witness it."

Crandall called his pilots together and briefly discussed the terrifying situation on the ground in X-Ray. He outlined his plan to take back into the LZ two ships loaded with ammunition and asked for volunteers. He says, "Captain Ed Freeman, my friend for a dozen years who had been leading my second flight all morning, said he was taking that flight. Big Ed misunderstood. I only wanted a volunteer crew for the second bird. I intended to lead the flight myself. I planned to leave Ed behind in charge of resuming the troop lift as soon as Colonel Moore opened the door to the LZ."

Captain Ed Freeman, thirty-six, fought on Pork Chop Hill in Korea as an enlisted man and won a battlefield commission there. At six feet six inches, Freeman was four inches taller than the maximum height limit for Army pilots at the time he went to flight school, hence his nickname: "Too Tall to Fly." Crandall and Freeman had been a close team for years, sharing flying duties over some of the world's toughest terrain. Together they had flown the Arctic, the deserts of the Middle East and North Africa, and the jungles of Central and South America on mapping missions for the Army. The only thing the two of them were ever known to argue about was which of them was the *second-best* helicopter pilot in the world. Pop Jekel describes the Too Tall Ed of that era as "a good old shit-kicker whose poker winnings could pay off half the national debt."

Crandall understood how determined Freeman could be. "Big Ed and I discussed the mission for a few seconds, and knowing that arguing with him was a waste of time, I decided we both would fly the mission."

Until the LZ went hot, Matt Dillon and Mickey Parrish had controlled all flights into X-Ray from the command chopper overhead. No more. I took control because only I knew where my men were, where the enemy ground fire was coming from, and where the safest spot to land was at any given moment. From this point forward, every helicopter coming into X-Ray would radio me for landing instructions.

The Huey crews performed magnificently, running a gauntlet of enemy fire time and time again. They never refused to come when called. In turn, we did our best to call them in only when fire was lightest, and we tried to have teams standing by to unload supplies and load the wounded in record time, to reduce the aircraft's exposure on the ground.

Back on the dirt strip at Plei Me, Crandall and his copilot, Jon Mills, shifted their gear from their crippled bird to Lombardo's helicopter; the new ship and Freeman's were soon filled with ammunition from the remaining 7th Cavalry stocks at the strip. Crandall then assigned one of his section leaders to take command of the eight-ship flight that had been waved off at X-Ray. He told them to stand by to bring in the rest of Delta Company when I gave the word.

Crandall says, "Big Ed and I took off and headed for the LZ. We picked up the radio traffic and knew things hadn't improved. About five minutes out I contacted Colonel Moore, explained what I had on board, and he acknowledged they needed the ammo. That made it mandatory for us to go in, no matter the consequences. Moore knew the problem and gave us instructions on the approach and where to land. We started receiving heavy fire on our approach. I notified Big Ed and he calmly came back with: 'Roger. What do you want me to do about it, Snake? I kind of thought this might happen.'

"Moore's people laid down covering fire for us, and as we broke over the trees into the clearing I could see Hal Moore standing up at the far end of the LZ, exposing himself to enemy fire in order to get us into the safest position possible in the LZ. I landed where he directed and our crews and his people began pitching the ammo boxes off the aircraft as fast as they could. At the same time, the wounded were moved up and loaded aboard."

Some of the wounded being loaded aboard, including Captain Lefebvre and Lieutenant Taboada, were men of Ray Lefebvre's Delta Company, which Crandall had brought into X-Ray on his last trip. One of the walking wounded, standing by to board, was the battalion intelligence officer, Captain Tom Metsker, who had been shot in the shoulder earlier in the creekbed fight with Alpha Company. Lefebvre recalls, "We were standing by the helicopter. I remember Metsker helping me. Metsker helped shove me in. And about that time he said: 'I'm hit.' He was pulled aboard the chopper by the crew chief."

Crandall remembers, "My bird carried out eight of the seriously wounded. While we were in there a wounded captain helping another officer onto my Huey was shot and killed. We took him out, too. Ed was able to get five wounded out on his ship." Captain Tom Metsker, married and the father of a seventeen-month-old daughter, was dead on arrival at Plei Me.

Busy fighting the battle, I did not see the shooting of Captain Metsker in the clearing beside Crandall's Huey, but it was an ominous development. It meant there were North Vietnamese on the eastern side of the clearing, knocking at our unprotected back door.

Crandall now powered his overloaded Huey out of X-Ray, hitting some treetops with his main rotor blades on the way. He recalls, "We almost didn't make it. In training sometimes we would deliberately hit the treetops with our skids, just to scare the shit out of the infantry, especially if they were new guys. But hitting trees with the rotor blades scared the shit out of me. Once we cleared the trees we again received fire. When we got back to Plei Me I switched back to my first ship, which had been checked out and refueled."

At Plei Me, Captain Paul P. Winkel, thirty-four, of Cicero, Indiana, West Point class of 1956, was waiting for his two Orange Flight choppers to return from Pleiku with more ammunition. "The infantry radio channel sounded like an old war movie. Colonel

Moore, Trojan 6, came across calm and commanding. [His voice] rang with courage and sound judgment. It made men of boys in X-Ray that day. 'OK, understand your situation . . . keep steady . . . we are going to drop artillery all around you. Get your men . . . all of them . . . and walk together slowly back as the shells impact. Just walk back with the artillery and you will be OK. Hang in there.' "

CWO (Chief Warrant Officer) Leland C. Komich radioed Winkel that his ship and that of CWO Dallas H. Harper were inbound from Pleiku and asked for disposition of their cargo of ammunition. Winkel replied, "Wait one," switched channels, contacted Bruce Crandall, who was en route to Plei Me with his shipful of casualties, and relayed the question. Old Snake's reply was brief: "LZ X-Ray."

Says Winkel: "I thought, good God, how am I going to get two ships heavily loaded with ammo into X-Ray, now surrounded by the enemy, with air support, ARA support and artillery direct fire all going in there, without getting hit and blowing up. I switched channels and called Komich: 'Land at Plei Me immediately.' When the two ships dusted down, I ran to the ship, saw Lee Komich in the left seat, told his copilot to unass [get out of] his ship, go to my aircraft, and fly with my copilot, CWO Walter Schramm. I told Komich we were going to X-Ray. Lee's eyes narrowed. I knew he was thinking what I was thinking. [We were] loaded with ammo, one hot round could turn us into a brilliant burst of sunshine followed by a dark puff of smoke over the treetops of LZ X-Ray.

"I switched channels to Moore's frequency. 'Trojan 6, this is Orange 1, flight of two with ammo, en route to X-Ray. Directions for landing, please, sir.' The battalion command ship broke in. Captain Vince Panzitta's voice came over: 'Head generally 275 degrees for the downed A-1E, then make a sharp left turn and when you pick up fire, say 10 seconds later, swing immediately right 90 degrees. You should be heading directly to the center of the LZ.' Moore added: 'That's a roger. We will have a panel waving where you should land. Do not overshoot. I say again: Do Not Overshoot. If you miss, turn directly north and bug out for another try. Stay at treetop.'

"We came to the burning A-1E. I said: 'Now left! Hit 80 knots and clip the treetops.' Lee's turn was precise. Then came the pop, pop, pop and right beside us the bright flash of passing green tracers. 'Now right, Lee, right! Watch for the [marker] panel!' I saw it directly in front and below. There it is. Down now. Lee rolled us back just in time to flutter to the ground on top of the panel man. I looked out and saw our troopers lying prone, hugging the ground. Lee and I sat in our seats about six feet above the ground. My crew was quickly dumping the ammo. Boxes flew. I stared straight forward. Directly ahead, looming high, was the Chu Pong. I fully expected to receive a spray of bullets at any moment. All of the color seemingly drained from my vision and it seemed that it took literally hours to unload. Fear does strange things.

"My crew chief called out, 'OK, let's get the hell out of here!' Then Moore called: 'Can you take a couple of prisoners and some wounded?' I said yes. They boarded, Lee pulled pitch and we began translational lift,* so low we began clipping the treetops as we pointed north. Seconds later I glanced over my left shoulder to see if Dallas Harper followed. With disbelief, I saw white smoke burst forth along his engine from vents that normally are not there. I yelled: 'Set her down, you're on fire.' Harper reacted immediately. He was still over the LZ and dropped into a clearing still within Moore's perimeter. Lee began a rapid downward swing, then flared to land next to Harper's crippled bird. Moore called out: 'What are your intentions?' I replied: 'I am returning to drop off these prisoners, pick up my downed crew and pick up your additional wounded. Out.' Moore rogered."

Dallas Harper, his crew, and the wounded from their smoking Huey now loaded aboard Paul Winkel's bird. Says Winkel: "I watched one wounded man hop, limp and stumble toward the trees. I saw his entire back drenched from neck to waist with red, red, blood. I yelled to my gunner: 'That man there! That wounded! Get somebody to get his ass back here. We are not leaving until we get

---

*An overloaded helicopter needs to reach a maximum forward speed before attempting to gain altitude; forward speed translates to lift.

every one we were taking out of here. Go get him!' Two crewmen ran for him. The pop-pop continued. Lee kept the ship running full speed ready for takeoff.

"We loaded 15 or 16 total on board. I hoped we had burned enough fuel to let us lift off. Lee pulled pitch and the Huey lifted, the instrument gauges wobbling a little before steadying. The second ship smoldered over on our left. Our maintenance officer later said that the hydraulics and oil lines of that aircraft had been shot up so badly that had it flown for five more minutes the engine would have frozen and it would have crashed into the jungle at 120 knots. We would have lost a brave crew of four, seven of Moore's wounded plus a passenger, an Infantry captain. Who the hell was that guy? A quarter-century later I learned that he was Captain Gordon P. Rozanski, the battalion supply officer, who rode in and out of X-Ray all day helping unload ammo and load the wounded.

"Our Huey skimmed the trees and headed north out of harm's way. I lit up a cigarette, turned to my left and over my shoulder saw a very bloody trooper laid out with his head in another trooper's lap. I passed the cigarette back, lit another and stuck it in the bloody trooper's mouth. At that moment the trooper with the bloody back looked me squarely in the eyes and gave me one of the most cherished thank you's I have ever received. My windshield was now collecting splats of blood blown by the wind whistling through the open doors. Roughly 30 minutes later we called Pleiku tower: 'Orange 1 inbound with 7 wounded. Need immediate assistance.' I told them to inform the medical unit there would be a lot more ships inbound this afternoon, perhaps 100 wounded. Call for additional medical support now. We have got a bad fight out there. Do you read?

"We landed, off-loaded the wounded, then refueled with our engine still turning. Harper and his copilot ran off to find another aircraft. We hovered for takeoff and Lee said: 'As long as we're going back we can carry some more ammo. I said, 'Roger, hover over there where the battalion has its stores.' We sat down in the middle of the ammo dump and our crew piled the boxes onto our ship. A captain ran up yelling: 'You can't do that. This belongs to the 3rd Brigade and it must be accounted for on paper.' I didn't have time to give this yo-yo an explanation, just said: 'Lee, get us the hell out of here.' We left the captain ranting in a cloud of red dirt.''

Major Bruce Crandall and Big Ed Freeman made two more trips into X-Ray with more ammunition. Crandall recalls, "I lost track of time. Somewhere in the early afternoon I decided to try to get a pair of the division medevac aircraft to go into the LZ. To show them the safest way in and out, my two birds went in at low level, aided by Colonel Moore. Although we were fired on in both directions, we got in and out OK. The medevacs didn't like the setup and particularly didn't like the treetop-level approach. They decided to come in one at a time from fifteen hundred feet in a normal approach. This, of course, gave them a much greater exposure to enemy ground fire, but I didn't care if they flew in backward as long as they got there. One aircraft actually touched the ground and two wounded were loaded before the second aircraft reported being hit and both of them aborted the rescue.

"From then on, instead of flying all the way back to Pleiku, I flew to LZ Falcon, the artillery base supporting X-Ray. This location was much closer and we could transfer the wounded from our aircraft to the medevac helicopters for the flight on to Camp Holloway. We made several more flights between Falcon and X-Ray, carrying ammo and water in and wounded out. By the time we completed the third run, the rest of my company volunteered to go in, so we set up a shuttle. They pitched right in and carried the ball.''

On the ground, the battle had detonated into a series of deafening explosions of firing, now here, now there, as the enemy commander furiously probed for our weak spot, the opening that would permit him to drive a wedge through the thin line of men defending the landing zone. It was a fast-moving bedlam of activity. They were eager to kill us; they hungered for our deaths. Now they were slamming into us at four different locations.

Never before had the Vietnamese enemy carried the fight to an American Army unit with such tenacity. None of the common wisdom born of the American experience in Vietnam to date applied to this enemy. We were locked into a savage battle of fire and maneuver, a battle for survival, which only one side would be permitted to win. A commander in battle has three means of influencing the action: Fire support, now pouring down in torrents; his personal presence on the battlefield; and the use of his reserve.

My reserve had come down to Sergeant Major Plumley, radio operator Bob Ouellette, and myself. I decided that if it became necessary we would join Tony Nadal's Alpha Company in the fight at the creekbed. In preparation for that contingency, I went to the pile of gear taken from the wounded and filled my ammo pouches and pockets, grabbed up some extra grenades, and jacked a fresh magazine into my M-16.

Although the eastern part of the clearing was still under enemy fire, the shooting there had slacked off some thanks to Charlie Company, the actions of Captain Ray Lefebvre and his few men, and the heavy air and artillery bombardment working that area. Charlie Company's commander, Bob Edwards, was doing a great job. Edwards says, "My platoons were holding their own and, aside from ensuring [that] their resupply needs were met and coordinating fire support, I was able to concentrate on other issues. My exposed left flank worried me."

Edwards, knowing that Ray Lefebvre had turned over command of Delta Company to Sergeant Gonzales, found Gonzales and with my approval directed the Delta Company men to his open left flank, tying them in tightly around the southeastern edge of the landing zone. Then Edwards, whose men had just stopped a North Vietnamese battalion in its tracks, showed up at my command post looking for more work. He asked if he could help get the mortars organized.

Edwards had discovered that the mortars attached to each of the three rifle companies, which should have been consolidated under Delta Company control, were still operating independently because of the wounding of both Delta Company officers. He rounded up the rifle-company mortars in the area east of the command post: "I brought them into the perimeter, told my mortar-section leader, Staff Sergeant [Harold] Matos-Diaz, to assume control until a Delta Company officer arrived. Matos-Diaz got them set up and organized, and by the time I got back to Charlie Company he had them on the company radio frequency and ready to fire. We tried to get them registered, but because of the great amount of dust, smoke, confusion of battle, heavy undergrowth, and no prominent observation points, we could not do this effectively."

Now Tim Brown, the brigade commander, was back on the radio asking for a situation report. I told him we were heavily engaged, outnumbered, and taking casualties; we had a hot landing zone and had one platoon cut off, and I still did not have all my troops in. I told Colonel Brown that this fight was going to go down to the wire and that we could use another rifle company for reinforcements. He said he would send one, but we both knew it would be two or three hours before the reinforcements reached X-Ray. Brown had already alerted Bravo Company of the 2nd Battalion, 7th Cavalry, and it was assembling at pickup points.

It was now near three P.M. Charlie Company's defeat of the North Vietnamese assault stopped the enemy efforts to flank us on our left and opened up an opportunity for me to bring in the rest of the troopers. If we brought the Hueys in one or two at a time, and if the pilots followed our directions, we stood a good chance of getting those men in, and I needed them badly.

Still waiting back at Plei Me were a few more Charlie Company troopers; the rest of Delta Company, including its acting commander, First Lieutenant James L. (Larry) Litton, and its first sergeant, Warren E. Adams; and the battalion reconnaissance platoon. I radioed Dillon in the Charlie-Charlie [command-and-control] ship and told him to get them moving.

The last battalion troop lifts began arriving around 3:20 P.M. It was during this period that the second of the helicopters we lost in X-Ray was shot down. The incident stands out in my mind: A pilot came up on my frequency asking for landing instructions. I told him to come in at treetop level from the east and land on the eastern side of the clearing. He came in through the smoke and I saw that he was flying too fast and too high and would overshoot the eastern side into the hotter western side toward the mountain. I told him to drop lower and land on the eastern side. He flew right at me and obviously was not going where he was directed. I yelled at him on the radio: 'You're gonna get hit! You're gonna get hit!'

He thundered right over my head, fifty feet up, shuddered, and banked in a hard right turn to the west and north. Then the pilot, CWO Donald C. Estes, guided his dropping ship, rotor blade whapping, into the trees just across the clearing from the termite-hill command post. The chopper and crew were immediately secured by the nearest troops. Two of our sixteen helicopters were now disabled in the landing zone. Estes, thirty, from Auburn, Alabama, was later killed in action on June 24, 1966.

One of the ships brought in Larry Litton, who immediately took over command of Delta Company from the wounded Sergeant Gonzales. I told him to add the four Delta mortars to the consolidated mortar position set up by Captain Edwards and to control all seven mortars from a single fire-direction center. Principal direction of fire was toward Alpha and Bravo companies, and the mortarmen would also have the mission of defending our two-chopper landing zone from the east.

I also told Litton to spread out the recon platoon, led by Lieutenant James Rackstraw, along the north and east fringes of the clearing to the right of the mortar pits as further security for the little landing zone. The recon platoon was also designated as battalion reserve. For the first time this day, I now had a semblance of a complete perimeter, and our rear was covered.

Bob Edwards's Charlie Company had fought off the enemy for more than an hour. They had the advantage of more open ground. They could adjust artillery and air strikes more accurately, and the pilots overhead could see the enemy swarming in the elephant grass and thus could kill more efficiently. Finally the stunned enemy fell back south and southwest, dragging some of their casualties. As they withdrew from the Charlie Company killing ground, their activity around Alpha Company also slacked off.

Curiously, the North Vietnamese forward of Deal, Devney, and Marm's platoons did not press their advantage. During this lull, many of the Bravo and Alpha Company wounded and dead were carried back to the battalion aid station. Alpha Company's Sergeant Hansen says: "We were carrying out one rather heavy Alpha trooper, Specialist Jerry Kirsch, in a poncho when the man on the left corner of the litter was shot in the back. He went down immediately. He was Specialist Scott Henry. The round that hit him was fired from very close. I comforted Henry; then we got Kirsch on out. Kirsch was gut-shot but survived. When I got back to Henry, he was dead. I think about him often, dying alone on that open field. He was an engineer attached to our battalion."

Up the slope, Lieutenant Joe Marm was trying to evacuate his casualties. "My weapons-squad leader, Staff Sergeant Robert L. Parker, organized a party to get out the wounded. He came back about twenty minutes later saying he could not get out because we were surrounded. Whether we were or not is still a question to me; it may have been friendly fire. But the enemy were maneuvering to our flanks. I asked permission to withdraw with the wounded. We policed up the dead. We had quite a problem with all the wounded, but met little resistance going back. When we reached the ditch which was our forward line of departure, the wounded were evacuated back to the clearing and we were resupplied with ammo. Water was in very short supply."

Among the wounded flowing into the command-post aid station during this brief lull was Specialist 5 Calvin Bouknight, who was the medic with Lieutenant Dennis Deal's 3rd Platoon. Bouknight had been assigned to the battalion aid station for over eighteen months as one of two medical assistants to the surgeon. By late October, our line companies were short a total of eight platoon medics. We checked battalion personnel records and found some soldiers who had previously served as medics. Some of them were pressed into service; others were given refresher training and were designated reserve medics. Joe Marm describes the situation in his platoon: "My platoon medic was a short-timer and did not accompany us to Chu Pong. SFC [George] McCulley, the platoon sergeant, carried the aid kit, and we planned to use Staff Sergeant Thomas Tolliver as our medic when the need arose. He had been a combat medic during the Korean War and was well qualified."

Still, we did not have enough medics to go around, so we sent down Specialist Bouknight and Specialist 5 Charles Lose, a senior medical-aid man, as platoon medics to Bravo Company. Now Calvin Bouknight, still alive but mortally wounded, was gently laid on the ground in his blood-filled rubber poncho before the medical-platoon sergeant, SFC Keeton, his friend and comrade of the last two years: "Bouknight wasn't dead. He was shot between the shoulders, right directly between the shoulders. He reached up and took my hand and said: 'Sarge, I didn't make it.' We got an IV started on him and put a pressure bandage over his back wound. There was just no hope. We were able to get him on an evac ship, but he died." The Scriptures say that there is no greater love than to lay down your life for your friends. This is what Calvin Bouknight did in that fire-filled jungle. He sheltered the wounded he was treating with his own body, his back to the enemy guns, completely vulnerable.

Up on the line canteens had run dry. Rudyard Kipling, in his poem "Gunga Din," writes:

> But if it comes to slaughter
> You will do your work on water,
> An' you'll lick the bloomin' boots of 'im that's got it.

Kipling had it right. The heat, dust, smoke, and fear dried the mouth of every man in Landing Zone X-Ray. The little bit of water left in our canteens went for our wounded. Says Lieutenant Deal: "By three or four P.M. we had used all our water, mostly on our wounded because they kept begging for water. We were horribly thirsty. It must have been terrible on the wounded who had lost blood. Then we went to our C-rations to drink the liquid out of them. I opened a can, and it was ham and lima beans—the saltiest of all the C-rat meals. I drank the liquid and got twice as thirsty. Incredibly dumb."

Deal was helping in the evacuation of casualties when he was brought up short by a strange sight. "It was at this time that one of the things I regret most about that battle occurred. I saw a line, not a column, just a line of men, probably two hundred strong, moving on my right flank in the same direction as we were about to turn, the east, and move in with our casualties. I immediately lifted my weapon, had them in my sights with a clear shot. I started to call for those near me to get their weapons up because I thought they were North Vietnamese. But it was just a little bit too far to distinguish if they were Americans or North Vietnamese, so I elected not to fire.

"There was also fear of drawing attention to our depleted platoon. My men were now all killed or wounded except for the equivalent of two squads, about eighteen or so left. These two hundred troops were parallel to us, making their way to the landing zone. Marm, who had been on my right, had already withdrawn. It turned out that they were some of the North Vietnamese we had to fight later that day, who inflicted fearsome casualties on us. I only regret that we didn't stand there and start shooting them."

No more than a hundred yards away from Deal, the Lost Platoon clung doggedly to its tiny, tortured piece of earth. By now, Sergeant Ernie Savage and his band of survivors from Henry Herrick's 2nd Platoon had withstood four separate enemy assaults. The enemy believed they had the Americans in a vise. Three North Vietnamese clothed in camouflage uniforms walked directly into the perimeter from the direction of X-Ray. All three were killed instantly. Galen Bungum saw several enemy, no more than ten feet away, rise to their feet, rifles slung over their shoulders, laughing "like they were out for a Sunday walk."

From their prone positions, bodies pressed tightly to the earth, the Lost Platoon survivors banged away at a target-rich environment. Ernie Savage rose to fire on three enemy soldiers only a few feet away only to find that his rifle was empty. Savage says: "I didn't know what to do, so I just said "Hi" and smiled. All three looked at me in confusion, but by then I had slipped in a fresh magazine and sprayed them."

Dorman recalls: "They tried to crawl up on us. We put our guns flat on the ground and laid the fire into them two and three inches high. We fired real low and we stopped them. All this time there were snipers ten to fifteen yards away. If you stuck your head up they shot at it. But we were killing them right and left. Every time they stuck a head up we shot it."

It was now 3:45 P.M., and, except for the predicament of Sergeant Savage and the cut-off platoon, I was feeling a good deal better about the situation. We had all our men in; massive firepower had been deployed; a company of reinforcements was on the way; our two-chopper lifeline landing zone was secure; most of our wounded were either evacuated or awaiting evacuation; and we were holding tough. I was determined to make one more attempt to rescue Sergeant Savage and all his wounded and dead up on the slope. I ordered Alpha and Bravo companies to evacuate their casualties, withdraw out of close contact with the enemy under covering fires, and prepare to launch a coordinated attack, supported by heavy preparatory artillery fire, to reach the cut-off platoon. I was tortured by the fate of those men and the need to rescue them.

10

FIX BAYONETS!

There are only three principles of warfare: Audacity, Audacity, and AUDACITY!

—General George Patton

Alpha and Bravo companies, the first units to land, had now been locked in violent battle for more than two hours, had suffered no small number of casualties, especially among the sergeants and radio operators, and had shot up most of their ammunition. The two commanders, Tony Nadal and John Herren, needed time to evacuate their dead and wounded, to reorganize and regroup their diminished platoons and designate new leaders, and to replenish stocks of ammunition and grenades. They would have forty minutes to accomplish this; then heavy artillery fire would rain down ahead of them as they kicked off one more attempt to break through the ring of enemy troops and rescue the survivors of Lieutenant Henry Herrick's 2nd Platoon.

Meanwhile, help was on the way. Back at 3rd Brigade headquarters in the tea plantation the orders were going out: Our sister battalion, the 2nd Battalion, 7th Cavalry, was informed that one of its companies, Bravo, was being detached and sent to Landing Zone X-Ray to reinforce. On arrival in X-Ray, Bravo Company, 2nd

Battalion would come under my operational control for the duration of the fight.

Three platoons of Bravo Company, 2nd Battalion were pulling guard duty around Colonel Tim Brown's 3rd Brigade headquarters this afternoon, and were closest at hand and the easiest to move when Brown cast about for reinforcements. All the other 2nd Battalion companies were dispersed on patrols in the thick brush and would take much longer to assemble. So Captain Myron Diduryk's B Company troops won the toss, hands down.

Bravo Company, 2nd Battalion had good, solid, professional noncoms, and its troops had served together for a long time. It was a good rifle company and I was happy to get it. Captain Diduryk was twenty-seven years old, a native-born Ukrainian who had come to the United States with his family in 1950. He was an ROTC graduate of St. Peter's College in Jersey City, New Jersey, and was commissioned in July of 1960. He had completed paratrooper and Ranger training and had served tours in Germany and at Fort Benning. Diduryk was married and the father of two children. He was with his mortar platoon at Plei Me camp when he got the word by radio of his company's new mission.

Specialist 5 Jon Wallenius, twenty-two and a native of Gloucester, Massachusetts, was in Diduryk's 81mm mortar platoon, which had not moved back to brigade headquarters with the rest of the company. He says, "We waited in the red dust outside Plei Me camp. The constant coming and going of helicopters made conversation almost impossible. Word filtered down that 1st Battalion had got themselves into a fight and that we should be ready to go to their relief at any time. I was assigned to the first bird with Captain Diduryk; his radio operator, PFC Joe Keith; Platoon Sergeant SFC John A. Uselton; and his radio operator, Specialist 4 Virgil Hibbler, Jr."

While our reinforcements were saddling up at Catecka and Plei Me, my Alpha and Bravo companies were about to launch their second attempt to break through to Lieutenant Herrick's trapped platoon. John Herren and Tony Nadal had pulled their men back to the dry creekbed during the lull, so they would begin the attack from there.

Tony Nadal was on the left with his three Alpha Company platoons. John Herren was on the right with his two remaining Bravo Company platoons. Herren would be given priority of supporting fire since he was closest to the cut-off platoon and had only two remaining platoons under his control.

Nadal and his men removed their packs and replenished their ammo. What little water was available was shared out. Nadal was well aware of the threat from the mountain and down the ridge line: "I planned to use an echelon left* initially, since all the enemy movement had been from our left, and then switch to a wedge if we met no resistance." John Herren planned for Bravo to use "fire and maneuver," with one platoon moving forward under covering fire from the other.

Nadal called his three platoon leaders to a conference in the creekbed: "I told them what we were going to do and gave them our formation. I also instructed Joe Marm to guide on Bravo Company because we did not know where their cut-off platoon was located. Then I got most of the company together in the creekbed and gave them a pep talk about going out to rescue that platoon from Bravo, and told them how we were going to do it." Platoon Sergeant Troy Miller remembers the scene: "Our morale was very high after the first contact. Before we went after the cut-off platoon, Captain Nadal got us together, then he said: 'Men, we've got an American platoon cut off out there and we're going after them!' The replies were: 'Yeah!' and 'Let's go get them!' and 'Garry Owen!' "

Nadal was worrying over a major problem that he had discovered during the earlier fight: "There was only one artillery-fire-request radio frequency for all the battalion artillery forward observers. It was difficult to get fires in front of more than one company at a time, and the more experienced and aggressive observer, who happened

---

*In an echelon-left formation, the company commander positions one platoon in the lead; the second follows, staggered left at forty-five degrees, and the third follows that, also staggered left at forty-five degrees. Such a formation is used to counter a perceived threat from the left flank.

to be with Bravo Company, managed to control the fires. As we prepared to move out, I tried to get artillery fire support but my forward observer was unable to communicate with the batteries.''

The troopers came to their feet at 4:20 P.M. and moved out of the creekbed on the attack. They didn't get very far. There was an immediate and furious reaction from the North Vietnamese, who had obviously taken advantage of the temporary American withdrawal to move well down the slope and draw the circle that much tighter around us. Some were in the trees. Others were dug into the tops and sides of the termite hills. Still others were in hastily dug fighting holes. They had gotten well inside the wall of artillery fire, and we would pay dearly as a consequence.

Captain Tony Nadal, Alpha Company, was the first man out of the creekbed, leading the 1st Platoon in the assault. He recalls, "We moved out about fifty yards when we ran into the enemy force which had come down the mountain. I presume they were preparing to launch their attack about the time we launched ours. The fighting quickly became very vicious, at close range. We took many casualties. Lieutenant Wayne Johnson, the 1st Platoon leader, was hit. At least three squad leaders were also hit, two of them killed—one while going forward in an attempt to rescue one of his soldiers against direct orders.''

Sergeant Troy Miller was in the thick of the 1st Platoon fight. "I became the acting platoon leader when Lieutenant Johnson was wounded. We got ahead of Marm's platoon. Right after Lieutenant Johnson was hit, Sergeant Billy Elliott, one of my squad leaders, yelled out: 'We got a man killed.' It was Sergeant Ramon Bernard. [Bernard, who was from Mayagüez, Puerto Rico, would have been twenty-six in five days]. We were pushing fast when we started getting heavy small-arms and automatic-weapons fire, mostly AKs." Sergeant Elliott himself was killed shortly after he reported the death of Sergeant Bernard.

Over on Nadal's right, John Herren's Bravo Company troopers had run into the same deadly buzz saw. The "fire and maneuver" plan was forgotten. By necessity, Bravo Company got on line and attacked toward the sizable enemy force in the brush ahead of them.

Lieutenant Dennis Deal, whose platoon anchored Bravo's right flank, was again in a storm of enemy fire. "We stood up and started the assault—got out of the trench and the whole world exploded. I don't know how many there were. I couldn't see ninety percent of them but I sure heard their weapons. We had men dropping all over the place. Finally, the assault line which had started out erect went down to our knees. And then down to the low crawl. One of my men right in front of me absorbed the full impact of a rocket-propelled grenade. His sergeant, to my rear behind a tree, kept yelling: 'Come on, Joe, come on, you can get back here.' I crawled up to him, took his weapon, and threw it to the rear. That M-16 landed on top of an anthill in full view of the enemy.

"The soldier was a mess. He asked me if I had any morphine. I said no, nothing. I said: 'Joe, crawl toward that tree.' He did. He got there and the sergeant took care of him. I now took his place and was basically a rifleman. As I turned I saw North Vietnamese coming around our right flank, and we were the right flank unit on line. I screamed and yelled and one of my machine gunners got up and walked through all this fire and started shooting them from the hip. I went along with him and we killed them all. We got rid of them. We returned to the assault line, unhurt, and got back down."

Over in the Alpha Company sector, machine gunner Bill Beck, who had now rejoined his company, was in the first group charging out of the dry creek. Beck says, "Captain Nadal was the first man over the top. I was right beside him, to the left five yards or so. I saw the North Vietnamese out front." Tony Nadal had ordered his men to fix bayonets for the attack. Bill Beck, firing a burst from his M-60 machine gun to his right front, was transfixed by what he saw just forward: "Sergeant (John) Rangel bayoneting a North Vietnamese in the chest. It was just like practice against the straw dummies: Forward, thrust, pull out, move on. One, two, three."

Beck kept moving and firing when suddenly a swarm of wasps or hornets—real ones this time—got inside his helmet. This courageous soldier, who had withstood everything the North Vietnamese could throw at him, was momentarily defeated by a swarm of angry, stinging insects. Says Beck, "For a moment I dropped my machine gun and knocked my helmet off. My head was full of welts. I could not believe anything could make me forget the enemy, but I was in such instant pain."

Specialist 4 Bill Kreischer recalls, "We started to come out of the creekbed when we began receiving heavy fire from out front. About this time I was hit on my left side, just below my shoulder. At first it knocked me back, but I got up and started to fire again when I fell back into the creekbed. The pain was intense. My fatigue jacket was turning a dark brownish color from the blood. I tried to get up; I didn't want to be left behind. I fell again and someone helped bandage my shoulder. Before long someone half-carried, half-dragged me to the aid station. I remember being asked if I wanted a cigarette and I took one, even though I had never smoked before. I guess it was what you were supposed to do; in the war movies when someone was shot they always smoked a cigarette. I smoked that cigarette and three others while I lay there on the ground."

Captain Tony Nadal had four men in his command group as he charged into the brush: his two radio operators—Sergeant Jack Gell, a twenty-five-year-old native New Yorker, and Specialist 4 John Clark of Michigan—plus the company's artillery forward observer, Lieutenant Timothy M. Blake, twenty-four, from Charleston, West Virginia; and Blake's recon sergeant, Sergeant Floyd L. Reed, Jr., twenty-seven years old, of Heth, Arkansas. As they moved up Nadal had the radio handset to his ear. A burst of enemy machine-gun fire swept across the group. Sergeant Gell was hit and dropped without a sound. Nadal kept moving until the long black cord pulled back on him. He looked around to see what was wrong. The same burst that killed Sergeant Gell had also killed Lieutenant Blake and struck Sergeant Reed, who died shortly afterward. Sergeant Sam Hollman, Jr., a native Pennsylvanian, knelt beside his mortally wounded buddy Jack Gell and heard him gasp, "Tell my wife I love her."

Tony Nadal had no time to mourn Jack Gell, a man he greatly respected. Too many other lives were in his hands. He swung back into action: "I removed the radio from his back, had some soldiers near me take Gell back to the aid station, and told another soldier to put on the radio." That soldier was Specialist 4 Ray Tanner, a twenty-two-year-old trooper from Codes, South Carolina. Tanner was normally Sergeant Steve Hansen's radio operator, but they had gotten separated and Tanner was tagging along with the 1st Platoon.

On the right flank of the Bravo line, Lieutenant Deal was now rolling around on the ground desperately trying to dodge a volley of machine-gun slugs cutting through the grass all around him. Suddenly, twenty-five yards away, Deal saw an American get up and charge forward while everyone around him was flat on his belly. Says Deal, "I saw him throw a grenade behind an anthill and empty his weapon into it. Then he fell to his knees. I said to myself: 'Please, get up, don't be hurt.' I didn't know who it was; I couldn't make out the form. There was so much battlefield haze, dust, smoke."

It was Lieutenant Joe Marm. He had spotted an enemy machine gun dug into a big termite hill; it was chewing up both the Bravo Company platoons. After failing to knock it out with a LAW rocket and a thrown grenade, he decided to deal with it directly. He charged through the fire, tossed a hand grenade behind the hill, and then cleaned up the survivors with his M-16 rifle. The following day, Lieutenant Al Devney found a dead North Vietnamese officer and eleven enemy soldiers sprawled behind that termite mound. Says Deal, "Joe Marm saved my life and the lives of many others."

Lieutenant Marm suffered a bullet wound to his neck and jaw. Staff Sergeant Les Staley, thirty-eight, of Pike County, Kentucky, ran out and, with a private, got the wounded lieutenant to his feet. Supporting him, they joined a growing stream of walking wounded flowing back toward the battalion aid station. Sergeant Keeton treated Marm's wound, and one of Bruce Crandall's Hueys evacuated him to the rear. Within days, Lieutenant Joe Marm was recuperating at Valley Forge Army Hospital near his home in Pennsylvania. In December of 1966, Joe Marm reported to the Pentagon where the Secretary of the Army, acting on behalf of President Lyndon Johnson, presented him with the Medal of Honor, the nation's highest award for valor.

Here's how Lieutenant Joe Marm himself modestly describes

what happened: "I was located at the right flank of my platoon, with SFC George McCulley on the left flank. On the right of me was Lieutenant Al Devney's platoon. So I was in the center of the action. That bunker was holding up the line and I first shot a LAW into it. There were no apertures in the anthill and the fire was coming from the sides of the bunker. There was heavy tree covering around it which prevented hand grenades from landing effectively. I thought it would be a simple matter to run up to the bunker and toss a grenade over the top. I tried to motion what I wanted done to one of the troops. The noise of battle was very high and the sergeant nearby thought I meant to throw it from our position. It landed short. In order to save time and get the job done as quickly as possible, I told both companies to watch their firing because I was going to rush the anthill. I was wounded immediately after silencing the bunker."

Joe Marm's heroic action unfortunately failed to open the door to the cut-off platoon. Bravo Company had progressed only about seventy-five yards, Alpha Company a bit further. All three of Nadal's platoon leaders were now either dead or wounded, as were many of his noncoms. Worse yet, Alpha Company's 1st Platoon had gotten out ahead of the other two and was heavily engaged with perhaps a hundred enemy. Some of the Alpha troopers bypassed the enemy in dense brush, and those North Vietnamese had opened up on them. Not only were we unable to punch through to rescue Herrick's platoon, we were now in danger of having another platoon cut off.

It was the 1st Platoon's turn. Platoon Sergeant Larry Gilreath recalls that moment: "They must have captured one of our M-60s from the cut-off platoon and turned it on us. We were behind a fallen tree and we were flat pinned down by machine-gun fire and couldn't move. I remember saying that Sergeant Hurdle must be mad at us 'cause he's shooting at us. That was because of the difference in the sound of that particular machine-gun fire and the other automatic-weapons fire we had been receiving."

Sergeant Gilreath and his men weren't really on the receiving end of friendly fire. Sergeant Paul Hurdle had been killed covering the withdrawal of his buddies in Herrick's platoon. But Sergeant Gilreath's sharp ears did not deceive him: The weapon he heard was, in fact, Paul Hurdle's M-60. After Hurdle and his gunners were killed, the enemy first used that gun on the cut-off platoon and then turned it against the troopers trying to fight their way through to rescue Lieutenant Herrick's men.

It was now near five P.M. and Crandall was bringing thirteen Hueys in on final approach to X-Ray, with the reinforcements from Captain Myron Diduryk's Bravo Company 2nd Battalion. Specialist Jon Wallenius was aboard the first helicopter. "There was so much dust and smoke it was difficult to see very far off the LZ, but we could see tracers ahead of us on Chu Pong and hear the sounds of small arms. Then we were on the ground and running away from the chopper. I headed for the anthill area because it was the only cover I could see and it was close. Captain Diduryk ran up and saluted the officer in charge."

Sergeant John Setelin, a slender twenty-two-year-old South Carolinian, led the 2nd Squad of the 2nd Platoon on the third Huey coming into the landing zone. "The crew chief hollered: 'We are going into a hot LZ and hover; get your men out fast and head to the right!' Then from the air I saw what appeared to be soldiers in khaki. I thought we must really be desperate if we're bringing in guys just back from R and R without giving them time to change into their fatigue uniforms. Then I realized their rifles were pointed at us; that was the enemy! When we jumped out, people were firing down on us. The gooks were up in the trees!"

Captain Diduryk ran up to me and shouted: "Garry Owen, sir! Captain Diduryk and Bravo Company, 2nd Battalion, 7th Cavalry, a hundred and twenty men strong, reporting for duty!" His eyes sparkled with excitement and the challenge of the situation. I told Diduryk to assemble his men in a clump of trees thirty yards northwest of the command post to act as battalion reserve for the time being. Another unit came into X-Ray about that same time, unasked, unheralded, and, in fact, unnoticed by me. It was a Department of the Army Special Photographic Office (DASPO) team of two sergeants, Jack Yamaguchi and Thomas Schiro, armed with their 16mm silent movie cameras. It would be a quarter-century before we unearthed their film from military archives and saw the eerie color images of ourselves in battle.

Up in the scrub brush, in the thick of the fight to reach Herrick's cut-off platoon, the Alpha Company commander, Captain Tony Nadal, had come to a decision. He had one platoon pinned down in a hail of enemy fire and he knew that the longer this went on the harder it would be to get them out. It was 5:10 P.M. Nadal ordered his reserve, the 3rd Platoon, to move up on his left in an attempt to circle the enemy forces. It didn't work. They ran into the same buzz saw that was chewing up all the other platoons.

Over on the right, Sergeant Larry Gilreath of Bravo Company wasn't finding the going any easier. Captain John Herren asked Sergeant Gilreath if he knew of any other way that they had not tried. Says Gilreath, "My answer was 'No sir.' Even without all our dead and wounded that had to be taken care of, the time of day was against us."

Captain Nadal says, "The fight continued for another twenty or thirty minutes with neither side making headway. It was getting dark and as the casualties mounted I decided we were not going to be able to break through. I called Colonel Moore and asked for permission to pull back." John Herren, who was monitoring the battalion net, heard Nadal's request and quickly concurred. It was now 5:40 P.M.; I ordered both companies to withdraw to the creekbed under cover of heavy supporting artillery fires.

With night approaching there was no real choice. I did not want to go into the hours of darkness with my battalion fragmented, with the companies incapable of mutual support, and subject to defeat in detail. The cut-off platoon would have to hang onto their little knoll tonight. We had to pull back, get our wounded and dead out, and resupply ammo and water. Then we had to get all units on line, tied in tight, with artillery and mortar fires registered for the long night ahead.

For Nadal and Herren, the hardest part would be breaking contact with the enemy and pulling back. Disengagement is always one of the most difficult military maneuvers to accomplish successfully.

Doctrine calls for a deception plan, covering elements, fire support, security, mapped routes, a precise schedule, and the use of smoke. We had fire support and we could call down smoke, but we had neither the troops nor the time to work out a school solution.

Captain Nadal, with his artillery observer and artillery radio operator both dead, was now calling and adjusting fire support over the battalion command net. He recalls: "I told all platoon leaders that no one was pulling back until everyone, dead or alive, came back. In order to cover my withdrawal, I called Colonel Moore and asked him to give me a smoke mission and to drop the range about a hundred meters closer to us than the high-explosive fire missions. This would put the smoke almost directly on top of us."

Nadal's request went to the battalion command post and was relayed to the command helicopter overhead, where Captain Jerry Whiteside called it back to the fire direction center at LZ Falcon. In seconds the reply came back: 'No smoke available.' Drawing on my Korean War experience, I asked if they had white phosphorus (WP) shells. They said yes. I told them to fire the mission using Willy Peter.

The bursting WP shells release thick clouds of brilliant white smoke and spew out fragments of phosphorus, which ignites on contact with air. I reckoned that if the North Vietnamese had never made the acquaintance of Willy Peter it would be a real eye-opener for them. Within a minute the shells whistled in, low over my head. The explosions were instantly effective in breaking up the NVA and silencing their guns.

Specialist Ray Tanner, pressed into service as Nadal's replacement radio operator, says: "We started to pull back carrying out dead and wounded. We were under heavy fire that made it hard to move. Captain Nadal called for some smoke rounds for cover. Colonel Moore informed artillery to use WP. We got down as low as possible when the shells came in. The noise and bright light was shocking. No one was injured and we managed to make our withdrawal. The WP rounds were landing within yards of our positions. I still remember how bright they lit up when they exploded."

Captain Nadal reacted to the Willy Peter with anger, surprise, and gratitude, in roughly that order. He recalls, "When this WP burst in the middle of us I got rather upset. Miraculously, not a single Alpha Company soldier was hit by any WP. It was very effective. All the firing died down and we started to recover our dead and wounded. The success of this volley now led me to ask for it to be fired again. Once again it fell among us and no one was hurt. I believe it was that WP that enabled us to pull our forces back to the creekbed without taking any more casualties in the process. I remained behind with my radio operators to provide covering fire for the withdrawal and was the last person back to the creekbed." Seeing how well the white phosphorus worked in front of Alpha, we also dropped it in front of Bravo Company. It gave us the edge at precisely the moment we needed it.

Over on the left, Lieutenant Dennis Deal got the word to stop and withdraw to the dry creek—"which we did at a run. The executive officer, Lieutenant Ken Duncan, who was handling casualties, looked up and said: 'Are you guys being chased?' I said no. We had recovered all our radios, but that M-16 was still out there on that anthill, and I knew exactly where it was. One of my sergeants and I took off. No web gear and we both ran fast. He was covering me. We ran out there about a hundred yards. I went right to the anthill, got the missing weapon, and we ran back to the perimeter—straight at two hundred Americans who had their weapons aimed at us. Only then did I realize that I had forgotten to coordinate what I was doing with anybody, and it was almost dark. Thank God they held their fire. Otherwise there would have been a dumb lieutenant and a brave sergeant, both dead."

While the costly effort to reach the remnants of Lieutenant Herrick's platoon was playing out in the brush a hundred yards away, Sergeant Ernie Savage and his surrounded buddies were clinging desperately to their little patch of ground. Savage had walked the artillery in tight around them and each time he heard voices or saw any movement he called in the heavy stuff. "It seemed like they didn't care how many of them were killed. Some of them were stumbling, walking right into us. Some had their guns slung and were charging bare-handed. I didn't run out of ammo—had about thirty magazines in my pack. And no problems with the M-16. An hour before dark three men walked up on the perimeter. I killed all three of them fifteen feet away. They had AKs. At first I thought they were South Vietnamese. They had camouflage uniforms. Sergeant McHenry killed three more of them on the west side."

Captain Herren was on the radio keeping Savage informed of the attempts to break through. Finally Herren told Savage they couldn't make it before dark and were withdrawing. Herren told Savage, "Don't worry. You've won this fight already." Savage and Sergeant McHenry seemed confident they would survive if they could hold out through the night. Specialist Galen Bungum and others had their doubts: "Word came over the radio that we would have to hang on till morning. I could not believe what I heard. I thought there was no way we would be able to do that. Others thought the same thing. PFC Clark kept asking me: 'Do you think we'll make it?' I didn't know, but I said we have to pray and pray hard. It was a big question mark in all our minds. We all had to keep our cool and bear down."

As Bravo Company pulled back toward the creekbed, Sergeant Gilreath was getting the word on who had been killed. "Sergeant Roland told me that Chief Curry had been killed. I went with Roland and helped carry him back. He wasn't going to get left behind. I owed him that much. I had a special feeling for Curry. He was a squad leader in my platoon before he was transferred to the 3rd Platoon. I had known Curry well at Kelly Hill [Fort Benning]. He had never talked much about his family or relatives. He wasn't married. He was known as a barracks soldier."

The Bravo Company commander, Captain Herren, was making dispositions for the night. "I ordered my company to dig in, in front of the creekbed where we could tie in better with Bravo Company, 2nd Battalion on the right and Nadal's Alpha Company on the left. We kept that artillery going around Sergeant Savage."

I had thought the situation over in the interim and decided to strengthen our thin lines by deploying Diduryk's Bravo Company, 2nd Battalion and continuing to hold my recon platoon in battalion reserve. I ordered Diduryk to position two of his platoons between

John Herren's Bravo Company and Litton's Delta Company on the northeastern side of the perimeter. I also told Diduryk to turn his two 81mm mortars and crews over to the Delta Company centralized fire-direction center.

I also ordered Diduryk to send his 2nd Platoon, commanded by Lieutenant James L. Lane, to reinforce Bob Edwards's Charlie Company, which was thinly spread over 120 yards of the perimeter on the south and southeast sides. Says Edwards: "The attachment of the 2nd Platoon was greatly appreciated. I placed it on my right flank, where it filled that critical gap between Alpha Company and my 3rd Platoon. Our ability to trade off platoons with other companies and work with them was important."

As Lieutenant Lane's platoon began settling in, a shocking event occurred. Sergeant John Setelin had moved his men into some of the foxholes vacated by Charlie Company men when they shifted left. "I got everybody down and started scouting to my left to hook in with Charlie Company. As I started out I heard one round sizzle over my head. I heard the crack of the rifle and the sizzle. I had never seen anybody or been that close to anybody who was hit before. The round struck Glenn Willard, our machine gunner, in the left side of his chest. I rushed to him; I thought a lot of Willard. He was a small man but he never let anybody help him carry his M-60 or the ammo. He was gurgling and his eyes rolled back in his head. It was almost like he was having a stroke."

Setelin rolled Willard over and started pulling his web gear and his clothing off. "He had a sucking chest wound and I remembered training to treat that. I must have done it right, protected his wound, but when I tried to pick him up my hands sort of disappeared in the lower portion of his back where the bullet came out. Lamothe ran over to help. Tears were running down my face. I was yelling: 'He's about to die on me!' Willard was my first casualty and I felt like I wasn't doing my job. A tall guy came over and picked Willard up in his arms and carried him to the medics at the battalion CP." The gravely wounded Willard survived.

With the pall of smoke and dust choking the valley, twilight would be brief. We had only a little time to set up the nighttime perimeter around X-Ray. In positioning the five infantry companies I took several things into account: the fighting strength of each company; the need to defend the small, two-chopper landing zone; enemy routes of attack; and placing the Delta Company machine-gun platoon with its six M-60s where they could do the most good and the most damage. I wanted those machine guns in the more open, flat terrain on the eastern edge of the clearing.

I now considered the toll this day's fighting had taken. Tony Nadal's Alpha Company had lost three officers and thirty-one enlisted men killed and wounded, and now reported effective strength of two officers and eighty-four enlisted. John Herren's Bravo Company had lost one officer and forty-six enlisted men killed or wounded, and was down to four officers and sixty-eight enlisted men with one platoon, Herrick's, trapped outside the perimeter. Those two companies were given smaller sectors than Bob Edwards's Charlie Company, which had lost only four casualties and was reporting a strength of five officers and 102 enlisted. Even so, I beefed up Charlie Company with Lieutenant Lane's platoon from Bravo Company, 2nd Battalion. Myron Diduryk and his other two platoons were assigned to the sector northeast of the small landing zone to help protect the clearing, the eight mortars, and the aid station–command post–supply dump near the termite hill. The battalion recon platoon was held back in a reserve assembly area close to my command post. I made certain the machine-gun platoon was tightly tied in to Bob Edwards's left flank in the southeast sector.

At about 6:50 P.M. I radioed Matt Dillon to come into X-Ray as soon as possible, bringing Hastings and Whiteside, two more radio operators, and as much ammo and water as they could carry on two Hueys. We now had good, direct communications with brigade headquarters and no longer needed the command ship overhead relaying our radio traffic. This was thanks to First Sergeant Warren Adams of Delta Company, who brought in a RC-292 field antenna. Installed in a tall tree, the long antenna gave us the range to talk to brigade at the tea plantation, more than twenty-five miles away. Besides, this battle was far from over, and I now needed Dillon at my right hand to help me control the fight. With the fire support coordinators on the ground we would also cut our response time in the fluid, fast-paced situation.

For almost eight hours I had been involved in the minute-to-minute direction of the battle. Now I wanted to personally walk the perimeter and check the preparations for what promised to be a tough night and another tough day tomorrow. Just before dark, Sergeant Major Plumley and I broke away from the command post and set out to check the perimeter, talking with the troopers and getting a feel for the situation on the ground. What concerned me most was the morale of the men, how well the companies were tied in, their defensive fire plans, and the situation with ammunition and water supplies.

Morale among the men was high, although there was understandable grief over the friends we had lost. The men I talked with realized that we were facing a fierce, determined enemy, but he had failed to break through our lines. They knew the fight wasn't over. I heard weary soldiers say things like: "We'll get 'em, sir" and "They won't get through us, sir." Their fighting spirit had not dimmed, and they made me proud and humble. In every one of my companies that had landed in this place this morning there were fifteen to twenty soldiers who had less than two weeks left to go in the Army. Some of those men now lay dead, wrapped in ponchos, near my command post. The rest of them were on that perimeter, standing shoulder to shoulder with their buddies, ready to continue the fight.

With the coming of full darkness, around 7:15 P.M., Plumley and I moved back to the termite-hill command post. When we got back I checked on Sergeant Ernie Savage and his band of survivors in Herrick's cut-off platoon. The report came back by radio that they had taken no additional casualties and were hanging tough. I mulled over possible options for their rescue: a night attack; night infiltration to reinforce the platoon; or a fresh attempt to fight through to them early the next morning. They would be on all our minds this night, that brave handful of men surrounded and alone in a sea of enemies.

11

NIGHT FALLS

If we are marked to die, we are enow
To do our country loss; and if to live,
The fewer men, the greater share of honor.

—*Henry V,* Act IV, Scene 3

The raging battle of the afternoon had faded to sporadic firing. The landing zone was set up for night operations, and the artillery and mortars had registered all around the perimeter. In the aid station Sergeant Keeton and Sergeant Keith jury-rigged a small, blacked-out tent of ponchos so they could safely use a light while working on the wounded. They were now well stocked with morphine and bandages. "About five P.M. we ran out of morphine and Colonel Moore called back to brigade for additional supplies. By dark we had received a hundred and twenty-five or a hundred and thirty styrettes of morphine," says Keeton. "Seems like every American unit in Vietnam heard our request and sent it to us. I had enough morphine when we got back to base camp to do us for the rest of the Vietnam War."

UPI reporter Joe Galloway had spent the afternoon desperately trying to finagle his way into LZ X-Ray, without success. Galloway had been aboard Colonel Tim Brown's command chopper when I waved Brown off shortly after noon. At brigade headquarters Galloway had lined up with the troopers of Bravo Company, 2nd Battalion and boarded a lift helicopter—but only briefly. Lieutenant Rick Rescorla says: "As we boarded the Hueys, a stocky journalist in a sand-colored beret with an M-16 and camera jumped on one of our choppers. Major Pete Mallet came over and pulled him off. We needed the spot for a company medic." Galloway shifted to LZ Falcon and there spotted Matt Dillon loading up the two resupply helicopters. He pleaded for a ride. Dillon said he couldn't make that decision but agreed to put it to me over the radio. I told Dillon that if Galloway was that crazy and there was room, he could bring him on in.

During those walks in the sun around Plei Me I had gotten acquainted with Galloway. He was different from most of the other reporters who flocked to the 1st Cavalry in those early days. He stuck with a battalion through good and bad, rolling up in a poncho on the ground and staying the night instead of scrambling on a supply Huey and heading back to a warm bunk and a hot meal in the rear. During my time in Vietnam I met only two other reporters who displayed the same grit: Bob Poos of the Associated Press and Charlie Black of the *Columbus* (Georgia) *Ledger-Enquirer*.

There was one other thing: I had concluded that the American people had a right to know what their sons were doing in this war, on the ground, in the field. I welcomed visiting reporters to my battalion and, later, to my brigade. I told them they could go anywhere they wanted with my troopers, with only two restrictions: Don't put out any information that will endanger us, and don't interfere with operations. I never had cause to regret that openness.

Shortly after nine P.M. Bruce Crandall came up on the Pathfinders radio.* His message to me, via Lieutenant Dick Tifft, a vigorous young Californian who had brought in a team to run the helicopter landings, was that he and Big Ed Freeman were five minutes out, two slicks escorted by two gunships, bringing in Dillon and party plus more ammo and water.

*Pathfinders served as combat air-traffic controllers.

As the helicopters dropped in on the final approach, Matt Dillon looked out toward Chu Pong. Plainly visible along the mountain slopes were hundreds of small lights winking in the dark forests. He also spotted a blinking light just below the top of the mountain directly above X-Ray, and a second blinking light on the northern slope of a 1,312-foot peak one mile due south. "I am convinced that the blinking lights I saw were signal lights. From where they were located on the mountains they could not be seen in X-Ray," Dillon says.

But it was that other light show that mesmerized Dillon, Galloway, and the others aboard the choppers: an elliptical northwest–southeast stream of tiny, twinkling lights over half a mile long and three hundred yards wide moving down the face of the massif. The moving lights were no more than half a mile from our foxholes on the perimeter facing the mountain. Galloway, sitting atop a pile of grenade and ammunition crates, was frozen by the twinkling lights. For one heart-stopping moment he thought he was seeing the muzzle flashes of rifles firing at the two helicopters.

Dillon knew better: "These lights were being used by the North Vietnamese, hundreds of them, as they moved down the mountain toward the LZ to get in position for attacks in the morning. Artillery was called in on these lights as well as the signal lights on the two mountain tops. Sometime after midnight there was a large secondary explosion on an area on the mountain right over X-Ray."

The Pathfinders momentarily switched on their small, shielded landing lights in the little clearing while Tifft talked Crandall and Freeman down through the thick curtain of dust and smoke hanging over X-Ray. Old Snake and Big Ed powered down into the darkness, clipping the tops of some trees, and within seconds Dillon, Galloway, and party bailed out and heaved the ammo boxes and five-gallon plastic water jugs into the tall grass; then the two choppers were outbound. Galloway recalls, "We crouched there in the darkness, tried to get our bearings, and waited for someone to come get us. Out of the darkness came a voice: 'Follow me and watch where you step. There's lots of dead people on the ground and they're all ours.' The voice, which belonged to Sergeant Major Plumley, led us to the command post."

I welcomed Galloway with a quick handshake and then briefed Dillon, Whiteside, and Charlie Hastings, the Air Force forward air controller (FAC) while Joe listened. The first order of business was to bring artillery and air down on the locations where the lights had been seen. The second was to make sure that Sergeant Savage and the cut-off platoon were getting all the artillery they needed. Dillon and I discussed how to get to Savage's platoon. Galloway found a tree, leaned back against his pack, and waited.

It was a restless night. All the units were on hundred-percent alert. Herren and his Bravo Company troops were into their second straight night without sleep. The enemy commander had at least a rough idea of our strength if he had counted the helicopters coming in during the day, and he knew for a fact that he had whittled us down. A full moon rose at around eleven P.M., giving the enemy commander on Chu Pong a better look at the perimeter. Dillon and I, although grateful that the enemy had not brought any of their anti-aircraft machine guns into play, still feared that they would do so, and soon. We had to keep artillery and air pounding the slopes to suppress those weapons before they could be brought to bear.

Thirty-seven miles to the northeast, Bruce Crandall and Big Ed Freeman finally shut down their Hueys at a huge helicopter pad, nicknamed the Turkey Farm, outside the wire at Camp Holloway, near Pleiku. They had been flying nonstop since six A.M.; it was after ten P.M. when Crandall shut down and tried to get out of the aircraft. "That is when the day's activities caught up with me. My legs gave out as I stepped on the skid, and I fell to the ground. For the next few minutes I vomited. I was very embarrassed and it took some time to regain my composure. Someone slipped a bottle of cognac into my hand and I took a big slug. It was a waste of good booze. It came up as fast as it went down.

"I finally quit shaking and made it to the operations tent to recap the day and plan the next. The aviation unit had quite a day. We had not suffered a single fatality and we had not left a mission undone. When our infantry brothers called, we hauled. The standard for combat assaults with helicopters had been set on this day. I wondered about tomorrow. Would it be worse? I wasn't sure I could handle another day like today. Then I thought again about the troops in X-Ray. The choice was not mine to make."

Bruce Crandall was still steaming over the refusal of the medevac pilots to return to X-Ray to haul out the wounded. "The officer commanding the medevacs looked me up to chew me out for having led his people into a hot LZ, and warned me never to do it again. I couldn't understand how he had the balls to face me when he was so reluctant to face the enemy. If several of my pilots had not restrained me, that officer would have earned a righteous Purple Heart that night. From that day forward, I planned every mission in such a manner that the infantry would never have to rely on anyone but my unit for evacuation of their wounded."

All of our wounded flown out of X-Ray by Crandall's Hueys ended up at Charlie Company, 15th Medical Battalion, 1st Cavalry Division, which was temporarily set up in tents at Camp Holloway. The executive officer of "Charlie Med" was Captain George H. Kelling, twenty-eight, from St. Louis, Missouri. Charlie Med's five surgeons tried to stabilize the soldiers coming off the helicopters. "The treatment we provided," says Kelling, "was designed to keep blood flowing through the patient's system until he could be gotten to a hospital which had the personnel and equipment to perform definitive surgery." Charlie Med's doctors tied off perforated blood vessels to stop the hemorrhaging, and then pumped in whole blood.

Kelling recalls that many of the casualties were rapidly bleeding to death, so it was a race against time to get blood into the soldier faster than he was losing it, even while the surgeons were trying to tie off the bleeders. "We threw caution to the winds and often gave a patient four cut-downs [intravenous tubes tied into blood vessels] with four corpsmen squeezing the blood bags as hard as they could. It was not unusual for the patient to shiver and quake and lose body temperature from the rapid transfusion of so much cold blood—but the alternative was to let him die."

Army Caribou transport planes from the 17th Aviation Company were standing by ready to evacuate the stabilized patients from

Pleiku to Army hospitals at Qui Nhon and Nha Trang. After additional surgical repairs there, the most serious cases were flown to Clark Field in the Philippines, and then on to the United States. Those who were expected to recover within two or three months were evacuated to Army hospitals in Japan—and found themselves back in South Vietnam and back in the field in due course.

In Landing Zone X-Ray this first night, the enemy harassed and probed forward of all the companies, except for Delta on the east and southeast quadrant of the perimeter. In each case they were answered by artillery fire or M-79 grenades. Our M-60 machine gunners were under strict orders not to fire unless ordered to do so; we didn't want to give their locations away.

Captain Bob Edwards and his Charlie Company troopers, reinforced by one of Myron Diduryk's platoons, occupied the longest section of the perimeter, which now stretched across 140 yards on the south and southeast sides, tied in with Alpha Company on their right and Delta Company on their left.

Says Edwards: "The enemy probes occurred mainly in the vicinity of Lieutenant Lane's position on my right. Small probes of about five to ten enemy. I think they were just trying to feel us out for automatic-weapons locations. The troops fired back with M-16 and M-79 fire. I really did not know what the enemy's capabilities were that night, but I expected anything and told my platoon leaders to keep everyone on hundred-percent alert and to expect an attack."

The fact that Charlie Company began fighting right after its arrival had kept the troops on the southern perimeter from digging good foxholes or clearing good fields of fire through the tall grass. The men had hastily dug shallow holes that protected them only if they were prone. Now they had time to dig better holes, but were prevented from doing so by the strict noise discipline ordered at nightfall by Captain Edwards, who didn't want the sounds of digging to give away the American positions or to muffle the noise of enemy movements.

Bob Edwards's reinforcements, Lieutenant Lane's 2nd Platoon detached from Myron Diduryk's company, held down Charlie Company's right flank and tied in on their right with Captain Tony

Nadal's Alpha Company at the creekbed. They had done what they could to dig in but it was hard going because of the tangle of tree roots and rocks just beneath the surface of the hard, dry ground. Sergeant John Setelin, having seen to it that his gravely wounded buddy Willard was being taken care of at the aid station, returned to his squad's position before nightfall.

Setelin got back, regained his composure, and told Lamothe to watch the trees. "I didn't move my men anymore. I kept everybody down until I could find out where this one sniper was, and sure enough in about five minutes he made the fatal mistake of swinging out from his tree. He was in a harness and roped very high in a tree. He swung around that tree like an aerial artist in a circus and sprayed fire indiscriminately when he came around. We waited him out and he came by one more time. When he did, we were ready. We eventually shot the cord holding him and he fell to the ground, dead. We were pretty well satisfied he was the one who had shot Willard.

"They probed us all night long. We had a few men wounded. I had never been in a situation like that. When they would come at us, they would come screaming and we could hear bugles."

Delta Company, now commanded by Lieutenant Larry Litton, held down a shorter section of the line, immediately to the left of Bob Edwards's Charlie Company. Delta was covering the east–southeast sector. The first sergeant of Delta, SFC Warren E. Adams, was in an L-shaped foxhole with Litton and two radio operators. Adams was a veteran of World War II and Korea and had run his company throughout a long succession of company and platoon commanders.

Sergeant Adams had placed the six M-60 machine guns of the company next to and tied in with Charlie Company's leftmost unit, Lieutenant Geoghegan's 2nd Platoon. Those machine guns had flat fields of fire to the south across Geoghegan's left-flank positions to the southeast and directly east. These six guns constituted a most formidable position, capable of laying down a wall of grazing, interlocking fire. The guns and the gunners behind them would play a key role in defending X-Ray over the next forty-eight hours.

To the left of the six M-60 machine guns was the position where the battalion's eight 81mm mortars, now resupplied with hundreds of rounds of ammo, had consolidated. From this position, the mortars could support any section of the perimeter with their high-explosive rounds. The mortar crews were not only responsible for their big tubes but also had to function as riflemen, helping Delta Company defend that side of the perimeter. To their left, with three more M-60 machine guns, was Lieutenant Jim Rackstraw's recon platoon. They were securing the two crippled Huey helicopters sitting on the edge of the perimeter.

Specialist 4 Vincent Cantu, who had been appointed a mortar-squad leader that afternoon to replace a casualty, was alert and alive, and had every intention of staying that way. He recalls, "That night was just like day, thanks to the guys from the artillery that supported us. By that time we were all dug in. I had dug me a custom foxhole with space where I could sit, and places for all my ammo and grenades and weapons. I had a .45-caliber pistol, an AR-15 rifle, [an] M-79 grenade launcher and a 15-inch bowie knife plus my 81mm mortar and ammo for that. Also fifty feet of nylon rope for river crossings."

Captain Myron Diduryk's Bravo Company, 2nd Battalion, minus Lieutenant Lane's platoon, was on the left of Delta Company and the battalion's mortar pits, protecting the north–northeast sector and helping cover the mortar crews and the small landing zone. "Colonel Moore directed me to occupy the sector extending from the Bravo Company, 1st Battalion, right flank at the stream bed to Delta Company left flank. The 1st Platoon led by Lieutenant Cyril R. (Rick) Rescorla was on the left, and the 3rd Platoon led by Lieutenant Ed Vernon was on the right."

Diduryk's troops dug in, cleared fields of fire, and prepared for the night. Lieutenant William Lund, the artillery forward observer, had the artillery fire marking rounds and pre-plotted the coordinates for instant barrages. During the night Diduryk's men were harassed by sniper fire and a few minor probes of the perimeter.

To the left of Diduryk's Bravo Company, 2nd Battalion were the lines of Captain John Herren's Bravo Company, 1st Battalion, defending north and northwest. Herren recalls his men digging in the best they could: "I told the troops to at least dig prone shelters. A big ditch [the dry creek] provided natural cover. I put my command post in it. The fighting positions were forward of that, however. I put my machine guns in a position to cover my direct front. My perimeter had good grazing fire to the front. Diduryk had more of a problem because his terrain was not as open as mine. There were covered approaches leading into his defense line. The enemy could have come up our side, but I wasn't apprehensive because we had fired in some real good defensive concentrations which were so close when we registered them that they blew me around in the ditch."

On John Herren's left, defending along the dry creekbed on the western perimeter, was Captain Tony Nadal's Alpha Company. The bulk of Alpha's men were employed holding the crucial creekbed, but a small section of the line now bent sharply south to tie in with Bob Edwards's right flank twenty yards east of the creekbed. Captain Nadal says, "We repulsed short attacks, primarily on my left flank, where the 3rd Platoon was, and on the 1st Platoon in the center of my line. That attack came between one and two A.M. Artillery support increased, and I mistakenly believed that the crisis was past."

Nadal's new radio operator, Specialist Ray Tanner, said that with the arrival of reinforcements everyone began feeling a little better about the situation. "While things were quiet we had lots of time to think about what had taken place during the day. I think we all became men that day. After that afternoon, I don't remember feeling real fear again. We were going to live and we knew we would win. I remember seeing lights come down the mountain. I got no sleep. There was artillery and mortar rounds going off all night, and small arms fire would flare up every once in a while. It was a very long night."

On the Alpha Company perimeter that night, Specialist Bill Beck remembers "flares, bugles, fear, talk, thoughts of home, shadows, NVA silhouettes, green enemy tracers. We were still out in the open, flat on the ground, and the flares would whistle and burn bright and light us up as well. This worried the hell out of me; I lay very still and held my fire."

Two other troopers in Nadal's Alpha Company were not so conscientious about maintaining fire discipline. Every few minutes we would hear a "plunk" as an M-79 fired, then the explosion of the 40mm grenade out in front of Alpha Company. Every time this happened I told Dillon to call Nadal and find out what's happening. Finally, Dillon told Nadal: "If you don't stop that M-79 firing, Charlie [the enemy] is going to hit you over the head with a sack of shit." Nadal investigated and reported back: Two of his men were short-timers, men who had only a few days left in the Army. They were determined to survive to catch their plane home, and were shooting up the bushes with the grenade launcher just in case anyone was out there. They wanted no North Vietnamese sneaking up on them and ruining their travel plans.

Out in the bomb-blasted scrub, 125 yards due west of the dry creekbed and our perimeter, the Lost Platoon had drained the last drops of water from their canteens and the juice from C-ration tins, and the riflemen, wounded and unwounded, faced the long night with thirst, courage, and trepidation. The men were spread out in two groups inside an oblong east–west perimeter. Ranger Mac McHenry controlled a group of about six men in the western part. Sergeant Savage had a dozen other survivors with him in the eastern part.

It was purely by chance that Savage, a three-stripe buck sergeant and junior to Sergeant First Class McHenry, ended up controlling the fight to save Herrick's platoon: He had been closest to the radio when Sergeant Stokes was killed. Although he was only thirty yards away, Savage's boss, SFC McHenry, was completely out of reach.

As darkness fell, Savage was on the radio with Lieutenant Bill Riddle, Herren's artillery forward observer, walking the high-explosive barrages all around the cut-off platoon. "All of us were lifted off the ground by the impact and covered with dirt and branches," Galen Bungum recalls. "Savage told them on the radio: 'That's right where we want them.' We hollered that was too close. But I looked back where those first rounds hit and saw three men running toward us. We opened up. They must have been crawling up on our position when that artillery came in. They would sneak in as close as ten yards or less, and many times just stand up and laugh at us. We would mow them down. It begins to work on your mind: What are they laughing at? I couldn't believe it."

Anytime Savage heard the enemy moving in the brush he brought artillery down on them, and often had the satisfaction of hearing their shouts and screams after the explosions. The sniper fire faded away at sunset and the enemy attacks lessened once the artillery ring was drawn around the platoon. John Herren, Matt Dillon, Sergeant Larry Gilreath, and others kept in close radio contact with Savage throughout the night. "I took my turn talking with him," says Gilreath. "We both got pretty choked up, but I told him to hang on and we would see him tomorrow." Dillon had previously commanded Bravo Company for eighteen months and he knew most of the men in Herrick's platoon personally. He talked with Savage often during the night.

More than five miles northeast of X-Ray, at Landing Zone Falcon, my battalion's rear-area headquarters detachment monitored and logged every radio transmission on the battalion net. My executive officer, Major Herman L. Wirth, a Pennsylvanian, commanded there. It was standard operating procedure for a battalion in the field to set up a small rear-area headquarters, commanded by the battalion executive officer. This rear headquarters was responsible for keeping the battalion supplied with everything it needed and for keeping track of communications, casualties evacuated, and the hundred other little, but very important, details that an infantry battalion commander has no time to deal with during a shootout.

In the operations tent, Lieutenant Richard Merchant of Pontiac, Michigan, was in charge, assisted by Master Sergeant Raymond L. Wills of the intelligence section, and Master Sergeant Noel Blackwell of the operations section. Merchant had spent more than a year with Bravo Company under both Dillon and Herren. "My emotions welled high. I had been leader of 2nd Platoon, B Company, during the entire airmobile test phase and knew all but the very new replacements. The sergeants in the cutoff platoon were like family to me. We had soldiered together. Major Wirth, sensing my distress, suggested that I take a break from the radio."

The North Vietnamese launched three separate attacks to keep the pressure on the trapped 2nd Platoon during that long night, each time sending about fifty men against the Americans and each time being beaten back by artillery and rifle fire. Savage had seven men unhurt and thirteen wounded. Nine others were dead. Some of the Lost Platoon's wounded continued to fight, including Sergeant Ruben Thompson, who had been shot through the chest.

"Savage would call us and say: 'I hear them forming up below me and I am sure they are going to attack in a matter of minutes.' The men in the platoon later told me they were sure the enemy had run all the way through their positions during the night attacks," says Captain Herren. "They were such a small group, it was dark, and the enemy had to contend with so much artillery, I don't think they were sure of the platoon's exact location."

The first attack, before midnight, came just as Savage's men heard troops heading for the landing zone on two large trails, one to the Americans' south and one to their north. This attack was beaten off by the riflemen and by Savage's employment of the artillery barrages.

At around 3:15 A.M. a series of bugle calls sounded, first faintly, then loudly, up on the mountain and around Savage's platoon. The forward air controller, Charlie Hastings, immediately called for Air Force flare illumination and called down air strikes on the slopes above Savage. The flares and air strikes all arrived within twenty minutes, just before and during the second attack on the Lost Platoon, and helped break up the attack. Savage, though grateful for the assistance, asked John Herren to call off the flares because the trapped men were afraid the bright light would expose their precariously held positions. But in the light of the last flares dropped that night they saw North Vietnamese scurrying around the rough clearing, dragging their dead and wounded into the trees.

The platoon later heard still another large enemy force noisily moving down the northern trail toward X-Ray, and once again brought artillery fire down on them. This was followed by a flurry of hand grenades back and forth at about 4:30 A.M. Within an

12

A DAWN ATTACK

> A brave Captain is as a root, out of which as branches the
> courage of his soldiers doth spring.
>
> —Sir Phillip Sidney

It was 6:20 A.M., Monday, November 15, and in the half-light before
dawn, the battalion operations officer, Captain Matt Dillon, knelt
rummaging through his field pack for the makings of C-ration hot
chocolate. An uneasy feeling nagged at me as I stood nearby peering
into the calm dimness around the clearing. It had nothing to do with
Sergeant Savage and the Lost Platoon. They had survived the night
without further casualties, and Dillon and I had worked out a new
plan for their rescue. No. It was something else that bothered me.
It was too quiet. Too still. Turning to Dillon, I told him to order all
companies to immediately send out reconnaissance patrols forward
of their positions to check for enemy activity. Dillon put out that
order while his radioman, Specialist 4 Robert McCollums, fired up
a heat tab under a canteen cup of water for their hot chocolate.

While the patrols were preparing to ease out of the perimeter to
check for enemy infiltrators, I told Dillon to radio all the company
commanders to meet us at Bob Edwards's command post just behind the Charlie Company lines to discuss the best attack route out

to Savage. I had decided we would try to break through using three companies—John Herren's Bravo, Tony Nadal's Alpha, and Bob Edwards's Charlie—deployed in a wedge formation. I would be with Bravo, leaving Dillon in charge of the LZ. We would jump off from the dry creekbed after heavy, close-in air and artillery prep fires and keep the artillery walking just ahead of us as we moved west toward Savage's platoon. Diduryk and Litton's companies would remain behind in reserve to protect the small landing area. It was a good plan, but it never happened.

Captain Bob Edwards remembers: "At first light Colonel Moore was planning to attack to reach the cut-off platoon. The company commanders were to meet at my command post to discuss this. He also directed us to patrol out from our positions for possible snipers or infiltrators that had closed in on the perimeter during the night. I passed this on to my platoon leaders and told them to send a squad from each of the four platoons out about two hundred yards. The patrols from 2nd Platoon, Lieutenant Geoghegan, and 1st Platoon, Lieutenant Kroger, had moved about a hundred and fifty yards in the search when they began receiving heavy small-arms fire. They returned fire and started back."

Geoghegan's platoon sergeant, Robert Jemison, recalls that just before daybreak he and Lieutenant Geoghegan shared the last few drops of water in a canteen; their other three canteens were bone-dry. "At first light we sent out a patrol. Staff Sergeant Sidney Cohen, Specialist 4 Arthur L. Bronson, and three other men were picked to go," says Jemison. "They saved us from being surprised. They spotted the enemy on their way in to attack our position. They came running back, with Bronson screaming: 'They're coming, Sarge! A lot of 'em. Get ready!' I told the machine gunners to hold their fire until they were close."

At the battalion command post the attack shattered the early-morning stillness like a huge explosion. The intense heavy firing told us with jolting clarity that the south and southeast sections of the X-Ray perimeter were under extremely heavy attack. I yelled to Dillon to call in all the firepower he could get. Fire swept across the landing zone and into my command post. It was 6:50 A.M.

Then–Lieutenant Colonel Hoang Phuong, who was present in the Ia Drang and wrote the North Vietnamese after-action report on the fight, says, "We had planned to launch our attack at two A.M., but because of air strikes and part of the battalion getting lost, it was delayed until 6:30 A.M. The attack was carried out by the 7th Battalion of the 66th Regiment. The H-15 Main Force Battalion, a local-force Viet Cong unit, was also in that attack."

Bob Edwards was on the radio desperately trying to get information from his four platoons. The heaviest firing was in the vicinity of his 1st and 2nd platoons, who were holding down the left side of the lines. He could not get either Lieutenant Kroger or Lieutenant Geoghegan on the radio. Only Lieutenant Franklin and Lieutenant Lane, whose platoons held the right side, responded; they were in good shape. Captain Edwards and the five men sharing the command-post foxhole began shooting at the onrushing enemy.

Moments later, there was a desperate radio call from Edwards: "I need help!" I told him no; he would have to hold with his own resources and firepower for the time being. It would be tactically unsound, even suicidal, to commit my small reserve force so quickly, before we got a feel for what the enemy was doing elsewhere around the perimeter. Charlie Company was obviously in a heavy fight but they had not been penetrated.

Bob Edwards estimated that his men were being attacked by two or three companies and, to make things worse, a large number of the enemy had closed with Geoghegan and Kroger's two platoons before the artillery and air could be brought to bear. The North Vietnamese were now safely inside the ring of steel.

My command post and Alpha and Bravo companies, directly across the flat, open ground behind Edwards's foxholes, were now catching the enemy grazing fire, which passed through and over the Charlie Company lines.

The Bravo Company commander, John Herren, says: "I alerted my men to be ready to swing around and defend in the opposite direction if the enemy broke through into the perimeter behind us." In Alpha Company, Captain Nadal's radio operator, Specialist Tanner, remembers: "When morning broke it all started over again.

I remember using a big log for cover. Every once in awhile I would see muzzle flashes in the trees. We would fire at any muzzle blast seen."

Bob Edwards could not raise Lieutenant Kroger or Lieutenant Geoghegan on his radio because the two platoon leaders and their men were fighting for their lives, blazing away at the onrushing enemy. Sergeant Jemison says Geoghegan's troops were in two-man, foot-deep holes spaced about ten yards apart, in which they could lie prone. Jemison says, "The enemy was wearing helmets with nets on them and grass stuck in the netting. They looked like little trees. There were over a hundred of them, hitting our right flank hard and over in the 1st Platoon. Geoghegan's foxhole and mine were in about the center of our position. They hit us once, then fell back; then they split into two groups. One began trying to flank us on the left but [Specialist 4 James] Comer's machine gun stopped them. The other kept hitting the right. One of the first men to get hit was Sergeant Cohen to my right; then other people got wounded."

PFC Willie F. Godboldt, twenty-four, of Jacksonville, Florida, was hit while firing from his position twenty yards to Sergeant Jemison's right. Jemison remembers, "Godboldt was hollering: 'Somebody help me!' I yelled, 'I'll go get him.' Lieutenant Geoghegan yelled back: 'No, I will!' Geoghegan moved out of his position in the foxhole to help Godboldt and was shot. This was ten minutes or so from the time the firing first broke out." Struck in the back and the head, Lieutenant John Lance (Jack) Geoghegan was killed instantly. The man he was trying to save, PFC Godboldt, died of his wounds shortly afterward.

The enemy now closed to within seventy-five yards of Edwards's line. They were firing furiously, some crouched low and at times crawling on their hands and knees. Others, no taller than the elephant grass they were passing through, came on standing up and shooting. They advanced, screaming at each other and at Edwards's men. Leaders were blowing whistles and using hand and arm signals. A few were even carrying 82mm mortar tubes and base plates. This was clearly no hit-and-run affair. They had come to stay.

Specialist 4 Arthur Viera, Jr., twenty-two, of Riverside, Rhode Island, was armed with an M-79 grenade launcher and a .45-caliber pistol. "Once the firing started, out with the patrol, it all happened fast. They were into us in about ten minutes. I remember one guy hollering: 'Look at 'em all! Look at 'em all!' There were at least two hundred of them coming at us fast. I yelled at him to start firing and shoved him in a foxhole. I kept firing with my M-79. Our medic was shot in both legs and going crazy, trying to push himself up from the ground with his arms."

Sergeant Jemison says, "We had one man run into our position from the 1st Platoon. He was shot in the head and hollered to me: 'Damn, Sergeant, they are messing us up!' " Jemison says one of his squads—under Sergeant Reginald A. Watkins, twenty-five, of Charlotte, North Carolina—was on the far right, next to Kroger's 1st Platoon, and was virtually wiped out when Kroger's platoon was hit so hard. Sergeant Watkins was among the dead.

Playing a key role in keeping Geoghegan's platoon from being overrun were two M-60 machine guns—one manned by Specialist James C. Comer of Seagrove, North Carolina, and Specialist 4 Clinton S. Poley, and the other operated by Specialist 4 George Foxe of Rocky Mount, North Carolina, and Specialist 4 Nathaniel Byrd of Jacksonville, Florida. Comer and Poley were on the left; Byrd and Foxe were off to the right, next to the 1st Platoon. Comer's gun interlocked its field of fire with that of Delta Company on the left, while Byrd and Foxe interlocked their fire with that of the 1st Platoon. Those two machine guns kept cutting down the enemy.

Now Bob Edwards's 3rd Platoon, led by Lieutenant Franklin, came under attack, but fortunately with nothing like the numbers or ferocity of the assault against Kroger's and Geoghegan's platoons. A heavy firefight developed on Franklin's right, involving Lieutenant Lane's reinforcing platoon from Bravo Company, 2nd Battalion. Sergeant John Setelin was in that scrap: "It seemed like half a battalion hit us all at once. He hit us headlong and he hit us strong. I thought we were going to be overrun. When Charlie hit us, he had this strange grazing fire. He shot right at ground level trying to cut your legs off, or, if you weren't deep enough in your foxhole, he shot your head off. When he started firing at us, it came like torrents of rain. You couldn't get your head up long enough to shoot back. You just stuck your weapon up, pulled the trigger, and emptied the magazine."

Back at the battalion command post, I had my ear glued to the radio handset when Captain Bob Edwards's voice broke in with a quick, curt "I'm hit!" I asked him how bad it was and whether he could still function. He replied that he was down and his left arm was useless, but he would do his best to carry on. Specialist 4 Ernie Paolone, sharing the foxhole with his boss, says Edwards was bleeding badly from the back of his left shoulder and left armpit.

Edwards's commo sergeant, Sergeant Hermon R. Hostuttler, was hit in the neck and went down, bleeding heavily. Edwards then saw two or three enemy "right in front of us. I stood, threw a grenade, and immediately felt a tremendous, hard slap on my back. I found myself on the ground inside the foxhole. I had lost the ability to move my left arm but otherwise was conscious. I called Colonel Moore and told him what happened and asked that he send my executive officer up to take command."

Edwards's executive officer was Lieutenant John W. Arrington, twenty-three, a native of North Carolina and a graduate of West Point, class of 1964. I called him over from the ammo storage area, briefed him, and told him to move out and take over Charlie Company. Arrington headed out at a low, crouching run across fifty yards of open ground toward the company command post.

Now Edwards was on the radio to Matt Dillon, telling him he was very worried about the enemy exploiting their penetration. "When I saw those enemy right in front of my position, I knew I needed at least another platoon to assist me. I needed somebody up there to plug the gap. I tried to convince Dillon that my need was as great as anyone's, because I was stretched thin. I pushed the other two platoons over to try and plug this gap. They tried, but were under too much fire to do it effectively."

The penetration Edwards was talking about was in Lieutenant Neil Kroger's 1st Platoon position directly in front of Bob Edwards's command-post foxhole. The enemy had obviously burst through at that point.

Edwards's artillery forward observer was pinned down in the command-post foxhole, unable to adjust the fires. The battalion fire support coordinator, Captain Jerry Whiteside, calmly stood up, peered over the termite hill in the face of enemy fire, and adjusted the artillery and aerial rocket gunship fire forward of Charlie Company.

Lieutenant Charlie Hastings, our forward air controller, had already swung into action. Sensing disaster, Hastings made an immediate, instinctive decision: "I used the code-word 'Broken Arrow,' which meant American unit in contact and in danger of being overrun—and we received all available aircraft in South Vietnam for close air support. We had aircraft stacked at 1,000-foot intervals from 7,000 feet to 35,000 feet, each waiting to receive a target and deliver their ordnance."

Now it was 7:15 A.M., and suddenly fighting broke out in front of the Delta Company machine guns and mortar positions. It was a separate, heavy assault on a section of the perimeter immediately to the left of Edwards's Charlie Company. Initial reports estimated two companies of enemy, many dressed in black uniforms. It was a Viet Cong battalion, the H-15 Main Force Battalion, making its first appearance on the battlefield.

Delta Company's first sergeant, Warren Adams, a three-war veteran, was dug in on the perimeter. He remembers, "There were enemies who sneaked up and hit us. My radio operator and I kept getting fragments from hand grenades popping all around us. One of them hit our fire-direction center foxhole and Sergeant Walter Niemeyer's leg was blown off. My radio operator and I decided to clean up a termite hill where the grenades were coming from. We each pulled the pins on two grenades, one in each hand, and packed off through the trees and brush, got on the back side of the hill and tossed them over. Sure enough, two or three bodies, clothing, a couple of AK-47s were back there when we looked. One must have been an officer; we picked up his pistol."

Specialist 4 George McDonald, a Charlie Company mortarman, was beside his mortar near Sergeant Adams's position. "When our perimeter was attacked it was so close that we weren't able to use the mortars. I was told to use my M-79 and hand grenades and was pleased with the results. I remember talking to a new trooper who had just joined the Army. He told me that he was only seventeen years old. A short time later a rocket round hit a tree close by and riddled his back with shrapnel. He had on a white T-shirt and I bet that it was the only white shirt in the 1st Cav Division. [All the cavalry troopers had dyed their underwear Army green, on orders, before they sailed for Vietnam.] The last I heard was that he had been evacuated."

Across the clearing, hugging the ground under the hail of fire snapping through the battalion command post, was reporter Joe Galloway. "I was down flat, clutching my rifle, expecting at any moment to see the enemy break through into the clearing. I could see blips of dust where rounds hit and an occasional rocket grenade or small mortar explosion. In the middle of all that a kid wearing a white T-shirt stumbled out of the trees, lurching toward us. We all started yelling and waving to him to go back to cover. He kept coming, but finally saw us. When he turned around we could see his back was shredded, the red blood a startling sight against the white shirt. He later made it to the battalion aid station."

By now I was convinced that the enemy was making a primary effort to overrun us from the south and southeast, and I alerted the reserve platoon for probable commitment into the Charlie or Delta Company sectors. The noise of battle was unbelievable. Never before or since, in two wars, have I heard anything to equal it. I wanted to get help to Bob Edwards, but decided it was still too early in the game to commit the reserve force. Instead, I told Dillon to direct Captain Tony Nadal of Alpha Company to quickly move a platoon across the clearing to reinforce Charlie Company.

Not wanting to weaken his critical left flank, which was closest to Charlie Company and was holding that sharp left turn in the line just east of the creekbed, Nadal chose to pull out his right-flank 2nd Platoon—Joe Marm's unit, now led by Platoon Sergeant George McCulley—and send them over to help Edwards. Nadal then ordered his 3rd Platoon leader, Sergeant Lorenzo Nathan, to stretch his men out to fill the gap left by the departure of McCulley's men. McCulley and his sixteen men, all that were left of Lieutenant Marm's platoon, came through the battalion command post. I briefed the sergeant and pointed out where Edwards's command post was located.

McCulley and his men headed out at a low crouch, moving fast in short bounds across the open ground under heavy enemy automatic-weapons fire. They lost two killed and two wounded—including Sergeant McCulley, who was wounded in the neck—during the dangerous move but finally made it to the right center of the Charlie Company sector, about fifteen yards behind their lines. There, taking up positions that gave them good fields of fire, the remnants of the 2nd Platoon men provided some measure of defense in depth to Charlie Company. But the loss of four men crossing the clearing convinced me that further internal movements were inadvisable until we reduced the enemy grazing fire.

Unnoticed at my command post because of the deafening uproar from the Charlie and Delta Company sectors was a stiff little firefight taking place forty yards north, involving Specialist Wallenius and his fellow Bravo Company, 2nd Battalion mortarmen. "About 6:50 A.M. I observed a soldier in a khaki uniform with helmet and web gear stand up to our front, and pump his arm up and down. He was in waist-high grass and obviously signaling. I alerted Sergeant Uselton in time for us to see four more helmeted troops rise from the grass to our left and cross right, carrying a light machine gun. We were convinced we were behind friendly troops and assumed that these strange, well-disciplined soldiers must be Australians. We radioed back and learned that there were no Aussies with us—and our front was not protected. About then, the North Vietnamese machine gun opened up on us.

"There was a small tree that formed a 'Y' four feet from the ground about thirty yards to the left. It was from there that the machine-gun squad had slipped from cover and ran across our front. I saw a man's head peer out between the Y, and snapped off a quick shot. A second or two later the head reappeared and I took a more careful single shot at it. I was surprised when the head showed again in the same spot. I am a good shot and this was close. I took a shooting-range stance and fired again. Again the head disappeared, then reappeared. I stood there and kept shooting this pop-up target. I fired ten more times, methodical single shots until the pop-up target range closed down."

Wallenius's attention now shifted toward the right, where the mortar pits had come under direct fire from the enemy machine gun. "All three mortar pits knocked over their tubes so that the machine gun wouldn't have a direct fix on their positions in the tall grass. The enemy gun team was placed between Sergeant Alvarez-Buzo and Sergeant James Gother's 2nd Squad mortar pits. Sergeant James Ratledge and his 1st Squad crew, along with Gother and the 2nd Squad, had managed to withdraw their men and guns right under the nose of a firing machine gun. That left Alvarez-Buzo and two men still in position. We were afraid to lay down fire for fear of hitting them. Ratledge made an attempt to put M-79 fire on the machine gun. This distraction allowed PFC Fred S. Bush to make a run for it and he headed toward our regrouped positions followed by PFC Jose Gonzalez. Bush made it but Gonzalez was hit several times. Ratledge and several others were wounded from grenade shrapnel that seemed to be buzzing all over.

"We got to Bush and Gonzalez; Bush said that Alvarez-Buzo was still in the mortar pit, wounded. Without hesitation, Virgie Hibbler dropped his web gear and started to crawl toward the 3rd Squad mortar pit. I followed him. We got about halfway, fifteen yards, and the machine gun started firing at the moving grass over our heads. We reached the mortar pit, a shallow two-yard circle not more than ten feet from the machine gun. He was still firing too high. Alvarez-Buzo looked dead. I didn't see any obvious wound but he wasn't breathing and we couldn't feel a pulse."

Hibbler and Wallenius weren't done yet. Wallenius says, "We crawled back and reported Alvarez was dead. When asked where he had been hit, we had no answer. Some doubt surfaced as to whether he was dead, or maybe that we hadn't actually been there. This was our platoon's first casualty and no one wanted to believe it. Somebody said you could put a mirror under their nostrils and it would fog and prove he was alive. Sure enough, somebody had a mirror. Virgie led again and we crawled back out to Alvarez-Buzo to make sure. The mirror didn't fog up, but still we weren't sure. The machine gun had ignored us this time, so we decided to take Alvarez-Buzo back. He weighed about two hundred pounds; the machine gun immediately got our range again. Just when they figured out exactly where we were, our guys saw us and opened up on them. Everyone now agreed that Sergeant Alvarez-Buzo was, indeed, dead. With no friendlies around the machine gun, we decided to dispatch it with hand grenades. After the second grenade, the fire stopped." Sergeant Elias Alvarez-Buzo, from Ponce, Puerto Rico, was twenty-five years old when he was killed.

The enemy commander was getting better at this. His attacks on Charlie and Delta companies were well planned and came close to achieving complete surprise. And, unlike the first day when he committed his forces piecemeal, today he threw perhaps as many as a thousand men against us in a twenty-five-minute span. Then, too, I had spent too much time worrying about Herrick's platoon and how to rescue them. I should have paid more attention to the enemy's capabilities. If I had, I would have gotten the H-13 scout helicopters up at first light, sweeping the approaches at low level and looking for the enemy.

Clearly the enemy commander had moved his troops and reinforcements all night to get them in position. His objective was to position his assault force right under our noses, so close that our artillery could not be effectively used, and then smash through Charlie Company's lines and on out into the open clearing. With that, he could then roll right into the battalion command post and attack into the rear of Alpha and Bravo companies. Only the recon patrols at first light averted complete disaster.

The enemy troops had Geoghegan's and Kroger's understrength platoons in a deadly bear hug. Americans and North Vietnamese were dying by the dozens in the storm of fire.

The bloody hole in the ground that was Bob Edwards's command post was crowded with men. Sergeant Hermon Hostuttler lay crumpled in the dirt, now dead. Specialist 4 Ernie Paolone crouched low, bleeding from a shrapnel wound in his left arm. Sergeant James P. Castleberry, the artillery forward observer, Castleberry's radio operator, PFC Ervin L. Brown, Jr., the only unwounded men in the hole, hunched down beside Paolone. Bob Edwards, shot through the left shoulder and armpit, slumped, unable to move, in a contorted sitting position with his radio handset held to his right ear. "I continued to command as best I could," Edwards says. "An automatic weapon had the CP foxhole zeroed in and we lay there watching bullets kick dirt off the small parapet around the edge of the hole."

Edwards didn't know how badly he had been hurt, only that he couldn't stand up. The two platoons he had radio contact with continued to report that they were under fire but had not been penetrated. No one answered the captain's calls in the two worst-hit platoons, and the enemy had penetrated to within hand-grenade range of Edwards's foxhole. All this had taken place in only ten to fifteen minutes.

Lieutenant Neil Kroger's platoon had taken the brunt of the enemy attack. Although artillery and air strikes were taking a toll on the follow-up forces, a large group of North Vietnamese soldiers had reached Kroger's lines and the killing was hand-to-hand.

Specialist Arthur Viera was crouched in a small foxhole firing his M-79. "The gunfire was very loud. We were getting overrun on the right side. The lieutenant [Kroger] came up out into the open in all this. I thought that was pretty good. He yelled at me. I got up to hear him. He hollered at me to help cover the left sector. I ran over to him and by the time I got there he was dead. He had lasted a half-hour. I knelt beside him, took off his dog tags, and put them in my shirt pocket. I went back to firing my M-79 and got shot in my right elbow. The M-79 went flying and I was knocked over and fell back over the lieutenant."

Viera now grabbed his .45 pistol and began firing it left-handed. "Then I got hit in the neck and the bullet went right through. I couldn't talk or make a sound. I got up and tried to take charge, and was shot with a third round. That one blew up my right leg and put me down. It went in my leg above the ankle, traveled up, came back out, then went into my groin and ended up in my back close to my spine. Just then two stick grenades blew up right over me and tore up both of my legs. I reached down with my left hand and touched grenade fragments on my left leg and it felt like I had touched a red-hot poker. My hand just sizzled."

Sergeant Jemison was over in Lieutenant Geoghegan's 2nd Platoon lines. "My machine guns just kept cutting them down. The enemy drifted to our right front. At least a battalion was out there."

Some thirty-five yards to Jemison's right rear, Lieutenant John Arrington had safely negotiated the open clearing and made it to the Charlie Company foxhole to take over from the badly wounded Captain Edwards. "Arrington made it to my command post and, after a few moments of talking to me while lying down at the edge of the foxhole, was wounded. He was worried that he had been hurt pretty bad and told me to be sure and tell his wife that he loved her.

"I thought: 'Doesn't he know that I am wounded, too?' Arrington was hit in the arm, and the bullet passed into his chest and grazed a lung. He was in pain, suffering silently. He also caught some shrapnel from an M-79 that the enemy had apparently captured and were firing into the trees above us."

The enemy were now closing in on Lieutenant Geoghegan's platoon. They were already intermingled with Kroger's surviving men and were pushing on toward Edwards's foxhole.

At 7:45 A.M. the enemy struck at the left flank of Tony Nadal's Alpha Company, at that critical elbow where Alpha and Charlie Companies were tied in. We were now under attack from three directions. Grazing fire from rifles and heavy machine guns shredded the elephant grass and swept over the battalion command post and aid station. Leaves, bark, and small branches fluttered down on us. Several troopers were wounded in the command post and at least one was killed. My radio operator, Specialist 4 Robert P. Ouellette, twenty-three years old, a bespectacled six-footer from Madawaska, Maine, was hit and slumped over in a sprawl, unmoving and seemingly dead. I kept the handset to my ear. The situation was now so critical that there was no time to deal with Ouellette.

At about this time fifteen or more mortar and rocket rounds

exploded all around the termite-hill command post. We were locked into a fight to the death, taking heavy casualties in the Charlie Company area, and there was no question that we were going to need help. I radioed Colonel Tim Brown to ask him to prepare another company of reinforcements for movement as soon as it could be accomplished without undue risk. Brown, with typical foresight, had already alerted Alpha Company, 2nd Battalion and had it assembled with the helicopters to fly in on call.

Joe Galloway remembers: "The incoming fire was only a couple of feet off the ground and I was down as flat as I could get when I felt the toe of a combat boot in my ribs. I turned my head sideways and looked up. There, standing tall, was Sergeant Major Basil Plumley. Plumley leaned down and shouted over the noise of the guns: 'You can't take no pictures laying down there on the ground, sonny.' He was calm, fearless, and grinning. I thought: 'He's right. We're all going to die anyway, so I might as well take mine standing up.' I got up and began taking a few photographs." Plumley moved over to the aid station, pulled out his .45 pistol, chambered a round, and informed Dr. Carrara and his medics: "Gentlemen, prepare to defend yourselves!"

The enemy commander's assault into the Delta Company line was not going well. In fact, he would have done a good deal better attacking any other sector of the perimeter. Delta Company now had its own six M-60 machine guns, plus three more M-60s from the recon platoon, stretched across a seventy-five-yard front. Each gun had a full four-man crew and triple the usual load of boxed ammunition—six thousand rounds of 7.62mm. To the left rear of the machine guns were the battalion's 81mm mortars, whose crews were firing in support of Charlie Company and, meanwhile, fending off the enemy at closer range with their rifles and M-79s.

Specialist Willard F. Parish, twenty-four years old and a native of Bristow, Oklahoma, was assistant squad leader of one of Charlie Company's 81mm-mortar squads. Parish was one of the mortarmen who had been outfitted with the spare machine guns and rifles collected from our casualties and put on the Delta Company perimeter.

Parish recalls: "When we were hit I remember all the tracer rounds and I wondered how even an ant could get through that. Back to our right we started hearing the guys hollering: 'They're coming around. They're coming around!' I was in a foxhole with a guy from Chicago, PFC James E. Coleman, and he had an M-16. I had my .45 and his .45 and I had an M-60 machine gun. We were set up facing out into the tall grass.

"I was looking out front and I could see some of the grass going down, like somebody was crawling in it. I hollered: 'Who's out there?' Nobody answered so I hollered again. No answer. I turned to Coleman: 'Burn his ass.' Coleman said: 'My rifle's jammed!' I looked at him and him at me. Then I looked back to the front and they were growing out of the weeds. I just remember getting on that machine gun and from there on I guess the training takes over and you put your mind somewhere else, because I really don't remember what specifically I did. I was totally unaware of the time, the conditions."

On that M-60 machine gun, according to extracts from his Silver Star citation, Specialist Parish delivered lethal fire on wave after wave of the enemy until he ran out of ammunition. Then, standing up under fire with a .45 pistol in each hand, Parish fired clip after clip into the enemy, who were twenty yards out; he stopped their attack. Says Parish: "I feel like I didn't do any more than anybody else did up there. I remember a lot of noise, a lot of yelling, and then all at once it was quiet." The silence out in front of Willard Parish was that of the cemetery: More than a hundred dead North Vietnamese were later found where they had fallen in a semicircle around his foxhole.

Specialist 4 Vincent Cantu had been drafted into the Army the day before President John Kennedy was assassinated in Dallas. He had one week left in service and he had been praying that he would live to make it home to Refugio, Texas, where he had been the lead guitarist and singer for a local band called The Rockin' Dominoes. Says Cantu, "The fighting never let up for long. The artillery fired all around us continually. The jets bombarded the hell out of that mountain. I got word that a friend of mine from Houston, Hilario

De La Paz, had gotten killed. He had only four days left in the Army. He had two young daughters back in Houston." Hilario De La Paz, Jr., was killed that morning in the attack on Delta Company. He was just eighteen days past his twenty-sixth birthday.

During that fierce attack on the Delta and Charlie Company lines, Cantu recalls, "I was hugging the ground better than a snake when I saw what appeared to be a soldier in camouflage with 2 or 3 cameras dangling around his neck. He came from behind a tree and took 2 or 3 snapshots, then ducked back behind a big old anthill. I thought to myself: 'Man, he wants pictures for his scrapbook real bad.' I lay there for a moment and I started to think: 'This guy reminds me of someone.' I crawled to the tree because next time this guy appears I wanted a better look—but I also wanted protection. I didn't have to wait long; there was no mistake. It was hot, his face was red; it was my old friend, Joe Galloway. I felt joy at seeing someone from Refugio, but at the same time sadness because I didn't want anyone from home being killed, and he was going about it the right way."

Galloway and Cantu were classmates; in 1959 they graduated from Refugio High School together with fifty-five others. Cantu braved the hail of fire, sprinted across the corner of the open landing zone, and dived under a bush, where Galloway was kneeling. "Joe. Joe Galloway. Don't you know me, man? It's Vince Cantu from Refugio." The two men embraced, agreed that this was "some kind of bad shit," and for a few brief minutes stolen from the battle raging around them, talked of home, family, and friends. Canto told the reporter: "If I live, I will be home for Christmas." Vince Cantu survived and made it back to Refugio, Texas, population 4,944, just in time for the holidays.

13

FRIENDLY FIRE

Dulce bellum inexpertis. ("War is delightful to those who have
no experience of it.")

—Erasmus

The ordeal of rifleman Arthur Viera, crumpled on the ground,
terribly wounded, beside the body of Lieutenant Neil Kroger, was
just beginning. "The enemy was all over, at least a couple of hundred of them walking around for three or four minutes—it seemed
like three or four hours—shooting and machine-gunning our
wounded and laughing and giggling," Viera recalls. "I knew they'd
kill me if they saw I was alive. When they got near, I played dead.
I kept my eyes open and stared at a small tree. I knew that dead men
had their eyes open. Then one of the North Vietnamese came up,
looked at me, then kicked me, and I flopped over. I guess he thought
I was dead. There was blood running out of my mouth, my arm, my
legs. He took my watch and my .45 pistol and walked on. I saw them
strip off all our weapons; then they left, back where they came from.
I remember the artillery, the bombs, and the napalm everywhere,
real close around me. It shook the ground underneath me. But it
was coming in on the North Vietnamese soldiers, too."
Over in the 2nd Platoon sector, Sergeant Jemison was struck in

the stomach by a single bullet. He ignored the pain, continued firing, and exhorted those still alive to fire faster and hang on. Clinton Poley, the Iowa farm boy, was still alive in the fire storm: "When I got up something hit me real hard on the back of my neck, knocked my head forward and my helmet fell off in the foxhole. I thought a guy had snuck up behind me and hit me with the butt of a weapon, it was such a blow. Wasn't anybody there; it was a bullet from the side or rear. I put my bandage on it and the helmet helped hold it on. I got up to look again and there were four of them with carbines, off to our right front. I told Comer to aim more to the right. A little after that I heard a scream and I thought it was Lieutenant Geoghegan." Poley and Specialist Comer, the man on the trigger of the M-60, blazed away at large numbers of plainly visible enemy troops.

There was no wind, and the smoke and dust hanging over the battlefield were getting worse by the minute, making it ever more difficult for the Air Force, Navy, and Marine fighter-bomber pilots, and Army Huey gunship pilots overhead to pick out our lines. On my order, at 7:55 A.M. all platoons threw colored smoke grenades to define our perimeter for the pilots. Then we brought all fire support in extremely close.

Moments after throwing his colored smoke, Sergeant Robert Jemison was struck a second time, by a round that tore into his left shoulder. It had been about twenty minutes since he was first hit in the stomach. He got back up again and resumed firing his rifle. Thirty minutes later Jemison was shot a third time: "It was an automatic weapon. It hit me in my right arm and tore my weapon all to pieces. All that was left was the plastic stock. Another bullet cut off the metal clamp on my chin strap and knocked off my helmet. It hit so hard I thought my neck was broken. I was thrown to the ground. I got up and there was nothing left. No weapon, no grenades, no nothing."

Comer and Poley, thirty feet to Jemison's left, were likewise coming on hard times. Poley says, "A stick-handled potato-masher grenade landed in front of the hole. Comer hollered, 'Get down!' and kicked it away a little bit with his foot. It went off. By then we were close to out of ammo, and the gun had jammed. In that cloud of smoke and dust we started to our left, trying to find other 2nd Platoon positions. That's when I got hit in the chest and I hit the ground pretty hard. I got up and got shot in my hip, and went down again. Comer and I lost contact with each other in the long grass. We had already lost our ammo bearer [PFC Charles H. Collier from Mount Pleasant, Texas] who had been killed the day before. He was only eighteen and had been in Vietnam just a few days. I managed to run about twenty yards at a time, for three times, and finally came to part of the mortar platoon. A sergeant had two guys help me across a clearing to the battalion command post by the large anthill. The battalion surgeon, a captain, gave me first aid."

Captain Bob Edwards was still holding on in his foxhole: "I think that the fire support prevented the enemy from reinforcing when he really could have hurt us. The penetration reached the first line of holes of the two platoons that had the most contact." Captain John Herren of Bravo Company says, "The enemy broke through to Edwards's command post before he was stopped, mainly by the battalion's use of artillery, air, and helicopter rockets and gunships. It was, in my view, the closest we came to being overrun."

Bob Edwards's personal war was far from over. Some thirty yards from his foxhole was a large termite hill covered with brush and grass. Atop that mound was a North Vietnamese with an automatic weapon who was a damned good shot. He had killed Sergeant Hostuttler; he had wounded Bob Edwards and Lieutenant Arrington; and he was still firing. "We were pretty much pinned down by an automatic weapon sited behind an anthill in front of the 3rd Platoon's left side. Lieutenant Bill Franklin tried to reach us but he, too, was hit. I am not sure if this was before or after Arrington was wounded. We had at least four of us hit by that one person within an hour. Then Sergeant Kennedy came up after Arrington was wounded and single-handedly eliminated the threat with grenades and his rifle. This took the bind off of us."

Comer and Poley's machine gun was not the only one which had fallen silent. George Foxe, twenty-five, and Nathaniel Byrd, twenty-two, were slumped across their silent M-60 machine gun, surrounded by heaps of empty shell casings and empty ammunition cans. They had died together, shoulder to shoulder. Sergeant Jemison pays them the ultimate compliment of a professional soldier: "Byrd and Foxe did a great job. They kept firing that gun and didn't leave it. They stayed on it to the end."

It was time to clean out the enemy overwhelming the left side of Charlie Company. Dillon and I talked it over and agreed we now had to commit our reserve. I told Lieutenant James T. Rackstraw to take his recon platoon and counterattack on the left side of the Charlie Company sector. I pointed at the precise area of the perimeter he was to attack and told him to coordinate his movements with Lieutenant Litton of Delta Company. After his platoon secured the left side of Charlie, I told him he was to join Litton and kill the enemy behind the mortars. Then, to reconstitute a reserve, I ordered Captain Myron Diduryk to bring his Bravo Company, 2nd Battalion command group and one of his platoons off the line and into a dispersed position near the battalion command post. He was to stand by to block, reinforce, or counterattack into Bob Edwards's sector of the line, or anywhere else that came under heavy attack.

Diduryk took off at a dead run and was back with Lieutenant Rescorla's platoon by 8:15 A.M. A heavy volume of grazing fire was covering the entire LZ. Rescorla's platoon had one killed, one wounded.

By now most of the men in Bob Edwards's two hardest-hit platoons were either dead or wounded. The job of holding off the enemy fell to the few still up and shooting. Somehow PFC Larry D. Stevenson of Delta Company found himself in Lieutenant Geoghegan's platoon sector, the only soldier left holding a fifty-yard section of the line. He calmly dropped to one knee and methodically shot fifteen enemy before help finally arrived. That help was the battalion recon platoon. They cleaned out the Charlie Company left, then shifted toward the center of Charlie Company's lines and linked up with them for the rest of the fight. That portion of the perimeter was now under control. The maneuver took some of the pressure off the landing zone, and we noticed an immediate slackening in the volume of fire sweeping the clearing. I radioed word to brigade headquarters to send the lift helicopters in with Alpha Company, 2nd Battalion, 7th Cav.

Somewhere in this time frame I noticed that my radio operator, Bob Ouellette, was sitting back up, looking shaky but functioning again. I took a closer look and discovered he had been knocked cold by a bullet which had penetrated his helmet but not his head. I told him: "Ouellette, never give up that helmet. It saved your life." The crusty old medical-platoon sergeant, Thomas Keeton, says, "I remember Colonel Moore's radio operator. He just suddenly dropped. I thought he had laid down and gone to sleep. I was kind of mad at him; went over and kicked the hell out of him; told him to get off his ass and help us with the wounded. No response. I picked up his helmet and a bullet fell out. A round had gone through the steel pot and helmet liner. Knocked him cold as a cube. He had a big lump on his head."

All of us in the vicinity of the battalion command post were now shocked by an event that unfolded, slow motion, in front of our disbelieving eyes. I was on one knee facing south toward the mountain. Ouellette, still dazed, was kneeling beside me. Movement off to the west, my right, caught my eye. I jerked my head around and looked straight into the noses of two F-100 Super Sabre jet fighters aiming directly at us. At that moment, the lead aircraft released two shiny, six-foot-long napalm canisters, which slowly began loblollying end over end toward us.

The fearsome sight of those cans of napalm is indelibly imprinted in my memory. It was only three or four seconds from release to impact and explosion, but it seemed like a lifetime. They were released by the lead F-100 and were on a direct line for the right side of the command post where Sergeant George Nye and his demolition team were dug in in the tall grass. The jets were on a very low pass. I couldn't do anything about those first two napalm cans, but I had to do something to stop the pilot of the second plane, who was aimed directly at the left side of the command post, from releasing his two canisters. If he hit the pickle switch [bomb release button] he would definitely take out Hal Moore, Captain Carrara, Sergeant Keeton, Captain Dillon, Sergeant Major Plumley, Joe Galloway,

Captain Whiteside, Lieutenant Hastings, our radio operators, radios, medical supplies, and ammunition, and the wounded huddled in the aid station. The nerve center—the life center—of this battalion would be instantly killed in the middle of a cliff-hanger battle for survival.

I yelled at the top of my lungs to Charlie Hastings, the Air Force FAC: "Call that son of a bitch off! *Call him off!*" Joe Galloway heard Hastings screaming into his radio: "Pull up! Pull up!" Matt Dillon says, "I can still see the canisters tumbling toward us. I remember thinking, 'Turn your eyes away so you won't be blinded.' I put my face into a reporter's shoulder to hide my eyes. Was Joe Galloway's. I could hear Good Time Charlie Hastings shouting into his radio: 'Pull up!' The second jet did. The napalm from the first hit some people and some ammo caught on fire. Sergeant Major Plumley jumped up to put out the fire around the ammo. I ran out into the LZ to put an air panel out."

Sergeant Nye says: "Two of my people, PFC Jimmy D. Nakayama and Specialist 5 James Clark, were on the other side of me, several yards away. Somebody was hollering and Colonel Moore was standing there hollering something about a wing man, and I looked up. There were two planes coming and one of them had already dropped his napalm and everything seemed to go into slow motion. Everything was on fire. Nakayama was all black and Clark was all burned and bleeding."

Galloway: "Before, I had walked over and talked to the engineer guys in their little foxholes. Now those same men were dancing in the fire. Their hair burned off in an instant. Their clothes were incinerated. One was a mass of blisters; the other not quite so bad, but he had breathed the fire into his lungs. When the flames died down we all ran out into the burning grass. Somebody yelled at me to grab the feet of one of the charred soldiers. When I got them, the boots crumbled and the flesh came off and I could feel the bare bones of his ankles in the palms of my hands. We carried him into the aid station. I can still hear their screams."

Specialist 4 Thomas E. Burlile, a medical-aid man from Myron Diduryk's Bravo Company, 2nd Battalion, rushed out into the clearing with his kit bag to help the napalm victims. Burlile was shot in the head and died within minutes, in Lieutenant Rescorla's arms. An Oklahoman, Burlile had turned twenty-three years old just four days before he was killed.

Sergeant Keeton, in the battalion aid station, quickly shot Nakayama and Clark up with morphine but it gave little relief. They were horribly burned. Their screams pierced the hearts of every man within hearing. Both soldiers were evacuated, but PFC Nakayama, a native of Rigby, Idaho, died two days later, on November 17, just two days short of his twenty-third birthday.

Says Sergeant Nye: "Nakayama was a real friend of mine. A good kid. Used to call me China Joe. He caught me one time with a Chinese girl and that nickname stuck with me through the whole war. I called him Mizo. In Japanese that meant 'Rain God.' The day he died his wife had their baby. A week after he died his reserve commission as a lieutenant came through. Every damned guy on Landing Zone X-Ray was a hero, but the real heroes were guys like Nakayama. I lost good people in there; they gave their all. Every time I hear a helicopter I get all watery-eyed. It's hard to explain."

Back in the command post, our Air Force FAC, Charlie Hastings, was stunned by the tragic consequences of the misplaced air strike. Hastings recalls, "After the napalm strike Colonel Moore looked at me and said something that I never forgot: 'Don't worry about that one, Charlie. Just keep them coming.'"

Shortly after the napalm strike, an enemy soldier staggered and stumbled into the clearing from behind Bob Edwards's far left flank. He had no weapon, was severely wounded, and, judging by his black uniform, was evidently a member of the H-15 VC Battalion. Staff Sergeant Otis J. Hull, a thirty-year-old native of Terra Alta, West Virginia, and one of his recon-platoon men ran to the enemy soldier and brought him into the command-post aid station for medical treatment. He died before we could evacuate him and was buried in a shallow grave nearby.

The battle in the Charlie Company sector raged on. Most of Kroger's men were down. A handful, like Arthur Viera, had escaped the enemy execution squads and were hunkered down in positions where the heavy close-in fire support shielded them. Over on the far right, Lieutenant Lane's platoon was having a hard time of it—perhaps because they were just to the left of that creekbed highway that led into our positions. Sergeant John Setelin: "The air strikes and the artillery were hitting almost in our holes for forty-five minutes, maybe an hour. That's when I was hit by white phosphorus. The attacks came at various parts of our line. They were determined to overrun us. I guess we were determined enough that we were not going to go down, and we didn't."

At about nine A.M. Lieutenant Dick Tifft, who was controlling the helicopter lifts, gave me the welcome news that Alpha Company, 2nd Battalion, 7th Cavalry was a few minutes out on final approach. At 9:10 A.M. Captain Joel E. Sugdinis, twenty-eight, West Point class of 1960, landed with his 3rd Platoon led by Lieutenant William Sisson. That platoon immediately headed south, toward the sound of the guns in the Charlie Company sector, deploying in the scrub brush behind the few survivors of Lieutenant Geoghegan's platoon. I briefed Sugdinis and pointed him to Myron Diduryk's sector, telling Myron to see that Sugdinis was thoroughly oriented.

S. Lawrence (Larry) Gwin, Jr., twenty-four and a native Bostonian, was Sugdinis's executive officer. Commissioned out of Yale University ROTC, Gwin had spent two years in the 82nd Airborne, was Ranger qualified, and had studied the Vietnamese language at the Defense Language School in Monterey, California, for two months. "That LZ was hot. When I got off my ship there were rounds coming in. Out in the LZ, PFC Donald Allred popped up out of the grass and said: 'Lieutenant, I've been hit.' We patched him up and now we knew we were in Zululand. Alpha Company closed up, with the exception of Sisson's platoon, which was almost immediately detached. That is significant because we would not see them again until four days later."

Sergeant John Maruhnich, a thirty-five-year-old career soldier from Scranton, Pennsylvania, was a squad leader in Sugdinis's mortar platoon. "We had no sooner landed than firing grew intense. At that time we of the mortar platoon fought as riflemen. Five of us were told to move to a section of the line which was lightly held. We spotted about twenty enemy and killed them all. One North Vietnamese I killed was running at me screaming and firing a rifle. After I killed him I saw he was an officer. I took his pistol out of the holster and put it in my pack."

After two and a half hours the battle for Charlie Company finally wound down. Sergeant Setelin recalls: "The firing stopped as quickly as it started. The enemy dead were stacked two or three deep in front of us. In the lulls we would kick and shovel dirt up on them to keep the stink and flies down." Lieutenant Lane now made his way over to Bob Edwards's foxhole without incident. All the officers in Charlie Company were either dead or wounded. Captain Bob Edwards had done all that duty demanded, and much, much more. He had also lost a lot of blood. Turning over command to Lieutenant Lane, Edwards was pushed and pulled out of his foxhole by Lane, Sergeant Glenn Kennedy, and Sergeant James Castleberry.

At the termite-hill command post, I called Myron Diduryk over and ordered him to move with his one assembled platoon to Bob Edwards's sector, assume control of the survivors of Charlie Company and Lane's platoon, and clean out and defend that portion of the perimeter. At 9:41 A.M. he and his troopers moved out, followed in minutes by his other platoon after Joel Sugdinis took over that sector. I attached Sugdinis's 3rd Platoon under Lieutenant Sisson to Myron Diduryk's Bravo Company, 2nd Battalion.

By 10 A.M. the surviving North Vietnamese were withdrawing. Charlie Company had held its ground in a stunning display of personal courage and unit discipline. The brave men of Geoghegan's and Kroger's platoons had stood and died fighting for each other and held their ground. The senior-ranking survivor in those two platoons was Platoon Sergeant Jemison. Asked why the enemy failed to overrun his platoon, Jemison says, "First, it was Byrd and Foxe on the machine gun on the right. At the end, what saved us was Comer's machine gun."

Charlie Company, 1st Battalion, 7th Cavalry had begun this day with five officers and 106 men. By noon, it had no officers left and only forty-nine men unhurt. A total of forty-two officers and men had been killed and twenty more wounded in two and a half hours of vicious hand-to-hand fighting. The bodies of hundreds of slain North Vietnamese littered the bloody battleground.

Captain Edwards was helped across the landing zone to the battalion aid station by Specialist 4 Ernie Paolone. The medics at the aid station got him on plasma and IV fluids immediately. Minutes later, Specialist Arthur Viera was carried in on a poncho, bleeding from his many wounds. The most serious was the bullet hole through his throat. Captain Carrara, the battalion surgeon, knelt over Viera under fire and calmly performed a battlefield tracheotomy without anesthesia or even clean hands. Sergeant Jack Yamaguchi, the combat cameraman, leaned forward and captured the impromptu surgery on film. After his film got back to the Pentagon, Yamaguchi and his partner, Sergeant Schiro, were reprimanded for capturing the stark reality of combat so graphically. Against all odds, Arthur Viera survived.

When Myron Diduryk and Rick Rescorla reached the Charlie Company sector, they were shocked by what they saw. Wrote Diduryk: "When I arrived, only a handful from C/1/7 [Charlie Company, 1st Battalion, 7th Cavalry] and my platoon which was attached to them were left. That company suffered heavy casualties. The enemy got as far as the southern edges of LZ X-Ray but didn't quite make it. Some fighting was in progress but for all practical purposes the enemy was beaten."

Dillon assembled the battered survivors of Charlie Company near the termite-hill command post as the new battalion reserve, such as it was, and saw to it that they got ammo, water, and C-rations. Charlie Company had done yeoman's work these two days. Sergeant Kennedy, the senior-ranking survivor, organized his weary men into two provisional platoons and designated subordinate leaders.

Diduryk's men began the grim task of recovering American dead and wounded and policing up enemy documents and weapons. Lieutenant Rick Rescorla will never forget the scene as he moved his men into the battle area: "There were American and NVA bodies everywhere. My area was where Lieutenant Geoghegan's platoon had been. There were several dead NVA around his platoon command post. One dead trooper was locked in contact with a dead NVA, hands around the enemy's throat. There were two troopers—one black, one Hispanic—linked tight together. It looked like they had died trying to help each other. A lot of dead North Vietnamese. They had whitewall haircuts, thick on top. Their weapons were laying all over."

Rescorla traveled the full length of the front when he was ordered to take some men and go help Lieutenant Lane on the far right. "The NVA were laying all over the place. Colonel Moore and Sergeant Major Plumley were out there with us. We policed up all the weapons, packs and ammo and made two piles: One NVA, one American. It looked like the NVA had dragged off some of their dead and wounded. That night when we got hit and various of our weapons jammed or went out, we used the spare Charlie Company weapons. Also, we put their packs to use as we had left ours back in the rear. Later we went out 300 yards; more NVA bodies. We had plenty of time to clear fields of fire, dig in, register the artillery, and get ready for the night."

Although the enemy had withdrawn, he had left stay-behind snipers, and Diduryk's men came under sporadic fire, as did the landing zone and battalion command post. There were marksmen up in the trees and up on the termite hills. The North Vietnamese had been beaten back but hadn't quit yet. Out in the Charlie Company sector Sergeant Major Plumley and I walked through the horrible debris of battle. We found Lieutenant Jack Geoghegan's body; the two of us personally carried him from the battlefield. Then we returned, located Platoon Sergeant Luther Gilreath's body, and brought him back to the landing zone to begin the long journey home.

Off to our east, more help was on the way. Lieutenant Colonel Bob Tully and his 2nd Battalion, 5th Cavalry were marching in overland. Earlier Tully had radioed asking for the best route and formation for a move into X-Ray. As cryptically as possible over an insecure radio net I told him: Come in paying close attention to the left flank, closest to the mountain. Says Tully: "How did I move? One company along the flank of the mountain, one other out beating the bushes. Two up, one back. Initially my concern was that the enemy would try to block us or slow us down near a north–south hill mass. To preclude this, I sent Bravo Company on the right and shot in several artillery concentrations in that area. Once we got past that line of hills I knew we could get to X-Ray in good order."

Tully's battalion encountered no enemy until about ten A.M. when Captain Larry Bennett's Alpha Company ran into a North Vietnamese strongpoint. Says Bennett, "We were about eight hundred yards from X-Ray when my two lead platoons were suddenly pinned down by heavy automatic-weapons fire. The NVA were in the trees, behind and on top of the anthills. We used fire and movement with my two lead platoons. I swung my 3rd Platoon to the right flank on a line and the resistance was broken rapidly. Due to the firefight and maneuvering we hit the southern half of X-Ray."

With the landing zone relatively safe, we called for Bruce Crandall's helicopters to come in and collect the wounded. Warrant Officer Pop Jekel: "I was told to wait for wounded. We sat in the LZ for at least one full enlistment before someone came out to the chopper on all fours and said: 'Get the hell out of here; you're drawing fire!' We did both."

Captain Bob Edwards rode out in one of Crandall's heavily overloaded flying ambulances. Matt Dillon recalls that Lieutenant Franklin, terribly wounded in the lower abdomen, had been set aside, "triaged," as someone unlikely to survive his wounds; his place was taken by someone the medics felt had a better chance of living. Matt Dillon was having none of that: He dragged Franklin back to the Huey and insisted he be taken. Franklin was pulled in, his head hanging out the door. Bob Edwards says: "They threw Lieutenant Franklin in right on top of me."

The chopper unloaded at LZ Falcon and Edwards remembers talking with Major Herman Wirth, the battalion executive officer, and Lieutenant Bobby Hadaway from the supply section. Says Wirth: "Bob Edwards had been hit seriously in the left shoulder and had lost a lot of blood. He was pale-faced, white, near death. There was a real question whether he would live. A transfusion was administered and Bob came fully alert and talkative. Tremendous transformation." Edwards remembers being placed on a stretcher on the ground; his wounded left arm "flopped off the stretcher in the dirt." He shouted loud enough when someone stepped on that arm and they "flopped it back on my stretcher." Although Edwards says he never lost consciousness in X-Ray or on the evac flight, when he finally reached the Army hospital at Qui Nhon it was another story: "I had to take a leak bad. They gave me a shiny container to pee in while lying down. I didn't want that, so I stood up to pee. When I came to I was flat on my back." Lieutenant Franklin, who rode out of X-Ray on top of Edwards, also survived.

Over the radio we got the word that Tully's 2nd Battalion, 5th Cavalry was thirty minutes away from X-Ray. Dillon passed the orders to our eastern and southern perimeters to hold their fire, and about 11:45 A.M. the lead elements of Tully's battalion began arriving. Lieutenant Rescorla was standing near Lieutenant Geoghegan's command-post foxhole, looking southeast: "Most of them were off to my left front, moving toward us in a column formation. The sergeant came up to me and said: 'You boys must have put up a hell of a fight.' I said: 'No, it wasn't us. The credit belongs to them.' I pointed toward some of the American dead—the men of Charlie Company, 1st Battalion, 7th Cavalry."

Tully's Bravo Company marched in directly through the beaten zone downrange from Delta Company where Sergeant Warren Adams's nine M-60 machine guns had been sawing away for the previous two hours. Lieutenant Litton and Sergeant Adams happily watched the reinforcements march in. Says Adams: "I watched the point man as he came right into my position and the first words out of the young man's mouth was 'My God, there's been a heavy battle here. Hell, there's bodies all over this valley down through here. For the last thirty minutes we've just been walking around and over and through bodies to get here. You guys have been playing combat for real here.' "

Specialist Vincent Cantu watched the reinforcements march in and got his second major shock of the day. Cantu had already run into his old high school classmate, Joe Galloway. Now he had a family reunion as well: "The first guy I saw walk in was my cousin, Joe Fierova, from Woodsboro, Texas. He saw me and said: 'What's going on, Cat?' I replied: 'Joe, get down low and stay there.' I motioned to all our dead."

Specialist 4 Pat Selleck, twenty-four and a native of Mount Kisco, New York, says: "I remember one guy had a small American flag on the back of his pack. When I saw that I felt very proud. It's something that's always stuck with me. This American flag was put on top of a blown-up tree, just like Iwo Jima. Another battle we had won for the United States." That little flag flew over Landing Zone X-Ray for the rest of the fight, raising all our spirits.

We had a lot to do now, and I tried to rank the chores by priority. First and foremost was to maintain the highest state of alert against further enemy attacks. Second was to rescue Ernie Savage and the Lost Platoon. Third, I wanted an early and complete accounting of every man killed or wounded, by name. Finally, we needed more ammo, water, and C-rats. Major Wirth had sent the assistant S-4, Lieutenant Bobby Hadaway, to the Charlie Med casualty clearing station at Camp Holloway, where he would keep personal track of arriving casualties and check their names against the company rosters. Lieutenant Hadaway had spent nearly two years in Charlie Company. He knew all the men. It now fell to Hadaway to go down the line of litters and look into the faces of so many friends and comrades and mark them "killed in action." It was a heartbreaking job.

By 12:05 P.M. Bob Tully's battalion had closed on X-Ray. I shook his hand and told him he was mighty welcome. Dillon and I had discussed how we would go about rescuing Savage's men and now had a pretty clear idea. Now we began briefing Tully on his battalion's major role in that plan. In the meantime, we were advised that General Dick Knowles had authorized the movement of two more 105mm howitzer batteries, twelve more big guns, into Landing Zone Columbus, just over three miles away. One was from the 2nd Battalion, 17th Artillery, commanded by my West Point classmate Lieutenant Colonel Harry O. Amos, Jr., a forty-two-year-old Alabama native. The other was from Lieutenant Colonel Bob Short's 1st Battalion, 21st Artillery. Soon we would have four batteries, twenty-four big guns, firing in direct support of us. Things were beginning to go our way at last.

14

RESCUING THE LOST PLATOON

War is fear cloaked in courage.
—General William C. Westmoreland

It was now approaching noon on Monday, November 15, and the time had come to push out again, this time with three companies, and rescue the Lost Platoon. Although the men of my battalion wanted to be the ones who did the job of bringing their comrades back into the perimeter, common sense dictated that Lieutenant Colonel Bob Tully's newly arrived 2nd Battalion, 5th Cavalry, guided by Captain John Herren's Bravo Company, be given the mission. My Garry Owen troopers desperately needed this lull to reorganize their depleted squads and platoons, evacuate their wounded, resupply with water and ammo, and screen the battlefields in front of them. Two of Tully's companies were on the south side of the clearing and could easily continue moving around the outer ring of defenses toward the trapped men. There was no time to waste pulling my companies off the line, replacing them with Tully's, and then assembling them for the mission.

Tully and I were agreed: I would give him Captain John Herren's Bravo Company, 1st Battalion, which knew the ground and the route, and he would leave me his Bravo Company and his Delta Company. Tully would carry out a battalion-size assault, preceded by heavy fire support, with two companies abreast on line, and one company trailing in reserve. Tully: "Hal Moore's proposal was most logical and practical. My unit was still on the move, still mobile. Time was of the essence. My battalion used a simple two up, one back formation—A/2/5 on the left, B/1/7 on the right, C/2/5 following A/2/5. The reason for a heavy left formation was that the main enemy activity appeared to be from the mountainous area on our left. All that was required was to get Herren's company in the act and move out. Outside of a few coordinating instructions, there was little need to tell Herren much. He knew where the isolated platoon was, and he was anxious to extricate it."

Tully's ninety-six-man Alpha Company, on the left, was commanded by Captain Larry Bennett. "We passed through the southern half of X-Ray under rather heavy sniper fire from the south, which made the passage rather hairy to say the least." Behind Bennett was Captain Ed Boyt's Charlie Company, 2nd Battalion, 5th Cavalry. After the prep fires lifted, Tully and his three companies kicked off the attack at precisely 1:15 P.M.

Herren says, "We had no contact en route. We put in a very good helicopter rocket strike between us and the cut-off platoon. Shortly thereafter I saw two North Vietnamese running to the right through the woods about three hundred yards away, getting out of the area. Once we got to the platoon we got some sniper fire from the Chu Pong hill mass on the southwest." Lieutenant Dennis Deal and his surviving troopers were on Herren's left flank, and this time Deal was loaded for bear: "I had a lot of grenades and threw one behind every anthill we saw. We grenaded our way up to the 2nd Platoon position. All that turned out to be unnecessary. We did not meet any opposition. We used grenades extensively and radioed Savage that we were doing so. We didn't want any live enemy between us and the platoon like the day before. I threw eight or ten grenades."

Even so, it was not a quick trip out. Bob Tully was an experienced battlefield commander and he saw no need to make it a race against time. His operations officer was Captain Ronald W. Crooks.

Crooks says, "Fire support consisted mostly of marking rounds to confirm the location if we needed artillery quickly. We were not trying to surprise the enemy. He knew where we were and I am pretty sure he knew what our mission was. We fired additional rounds as Harassment and Interdiction fires to the south along the mountain to help secure Alpha 2/5's left flank, and also forward of their advance."

There was nothing there. No snipers. No ambushes. Nothing but dead North Vietnamese soldiers and their weapons. I was puzzled but delighted at the radio reports. While Tully was advancing, I passed orders to all companies on the X-Ray perimeter to screen forward three hundred yards and police up the battlefield. Sergeant Major Plumley and I again went forward of Bob Edwards's Charlie Company positions.

In my after-action report I described the scene as follows: "Dead PAVN, PAVN body fragments and PAVN weapons and equipment were littered in profusion around the edge and forward of the perimeter. Numerous body fragments were seen. There was massive evidence, blood trails, bandages, etc., of many other PAVN being dragged away from the area. Some of the enemy dead were found stacked behind anthills. We found some of his dead with ropes tied around the ankles and a short, running end free. I saw two of our dead with similar ropes around their ankles. Possibly they had been captured alive and were being dragged off when killed. We found some of our dead's wallets and dogtags on dead PAVN. Artillery and Tac air was placed on all wooded areas nearby into which trails disappeared. Numerous enemy weapons were collected along with other armament. Two prisoners were taken and evacuated. Friendly dead and wounded were collected. Some friendly were killed and wounded in this screening."

Over on the right flank of the Charlie Company sector, Sergeant John Setelin had so far survived the carnage. "We were ordered to sweep out two hundred yards. We had gone maybe fifty yards on line when we could see the enemy right out in front of us. We fired. They returned it. Then we heard somebody on the right flank: 'They're coming down the mountain!' Sergeant Charlie McManus,

PFC Larry Stacey, Lamothe, and I went west toward a creekbed. Then we saw these people behind us like they were trying to encircle us. The rest of the platoon came through and about that time Sergeant McManus shoved Stacey and myself out of the way. Then we heard an explosion and looked down and there was Charlie McManus laying there, dead. He had jumped on a grenade to save our lives. The grenade had come from the creekbed. The enemy had evidently tunneled into the side of it. It didn't take Stacey long to put some M-79 rounds into the hole and eliminate him." Staff Sergeant Charles V. McManus of Woodland, Alabama, was thirty-one years old when he gave his own life to save those of his friends.

Over on the northern side of the perimeter, Specialist Jon Wallenius was about to solve the mystery of the Y-shaped tree trunk and the pop-up shooting-range target: "A sweep was made forward from our positions by a unit who reported that they found seven dead North Vietnamese behind the tree, all shot in the head. I didn't go look."

During this lull the saddest, most painful, and hardest duty to endure was collecting our dead and loading them aboard the helicopters. There were so many that the brigade ordered in the big choppers, the CH-47 Chinooks. One such helicopter lifted out all forty-two of the dead from Charlie Company. They came in together, died together, and now they left together, wrapped in their green rubber ponchos.

Specialist 4 Vincent Cantu says: "We were picking up our dead and placing them in the choppers. Some of these guys I had known for two years, yet I could recognize them only by their name tags. Their faces were blown off. It was hard not to get sick. We would look at each other and without saying a word just continue putting our dead on the choppers."

Mid-morning, before Tully arrived, Colonel Tim Brown flew in for a visit. Plumley recalls: "Lieutenant Colonel Moore saluted Brown and said, 'I told you not to come in here. It's not safe.' Brown picked up his right collar lapel and waggled his full colonel's eagle at Moore and said, 'Sorry about that!' " Dillon and I gave him a situation report. Brown asked whether he should stay in X-Ray, establish a small brigade command post, and run the show. We recommended against that. I knew the area, and Bob Tully and I got along just fine. Brown agreed. Lieutenant Dick Merchant says: "Colonel Brown had trust and confidence in his commanders. I'm aware that some felt he should have landed in X-Ray and established a command post. I've never accepted that. The 1st Battalion, 7th Cavalry was probably the finest battalion in Vietnam, well trained, superbly led, with outstanding officers and NCOs throughout the unit. Brown would have been out of place in X-Ray. Besides there was no room for a Brigade CP. I recall it being rather crowded behind that anthill."

Just before he departed, Colonel Brown told us that we had done a great job but now that Tully's fresh battalion was coming in, along with two rifle companies of the 2nd Battalion, 7th Cav, he would likely pull us out of X-Ray the following day. As we walked past the growing heaps of North Vietnamese equipment, Brown turned and asked if I would bring him a North Vietnamese pith helmet when I came out. He got his helmet.

As the lull lengthened and Tully continued to report no opposition to his movements, Dillon and I tried to puzzle out what the North Vietnamese were up to. Where were the survivors of those enemy battalions? Where had they taken their wounded? They had to have water for drinking, cooking, and taking care of those wounded. There may have been streams and springs in the ravines on the Chu Pong above us, but to carry wounded up those steep slopes would be a slow, difficult process. The nearest flowing stream on our map was the Ia Drang two miles north. To us that seemed a more likely field-hospital site than the slopes of the mountain. Add to that the fact that shortly after noon on November 15 the Air Force's high-flying B-52 bombers out of Guam placed the first of six days of "ARC LIGHT" strikes on the Chu Pong massif. For the first time ever, the B-52 strategic bombers were being employed in a tactical role in support of American ground troops.

The personality of this battle was changing dramatically, and the enemy commander cannot have been a happy man this noon. Lieutenant Colonel Nguyen Huu An was standing in one of the communications trenches up on the slopes of the Chu Pong massif. He remembers seeing and counting, high above him, eighteen B-52 bombers before he dove back in his deep bunker. Minutes later, the first of the five-hundred-pound bombs struck no more than six hundred yards from his bunker, but the huge explosions walked away from Colonel An, not toward him. He would live to fight on, but always with an appreciation of just how close a call he had on Chu Pong this day.

Up on the Lost Platoon's little knoll, Sergeant Ernie Savage had passed the news that help was on the way. That raised the men's spirits but it did not lessen their vulnerability. Savage says, "We got some firing right after daylight. We stayed down. Anytime they saw us they'd fire on us." It's not clear what the North Vietnamese had in mind for the surrounded Americans. Wait them out? Starve them out? Pick them off one by one with sniper fire?

Whatever they had planned, just before three P.M. Herren's and Bennett's companies reached the shallow ditch and immediately came under enemy rifle fire. It was rapidly suppressed by long bursts of machine-gun fire. Savage was following the rescuers' progress: "There was some fighting just before the relief got to us. They ran into something, not much. I could hear talk on the radio about killing some snipers."

The rescuers crossed the ditch, just as Lieutenant Henry Toro Herrick's men had the day before. From the ditch westward, visibility was good as the ground rose to the small knoll on the far northwest side of the clearing. For the rescue to be carried out, the clearing had to be secured. Says Bob Tully: "We secured the platoon by simply surrounding them after we reached their position." Captain Bennett says: "On arrival at the clearing I was told to secure the eastern half of it. It was egg-shaped, maybe two hundred and fifty yards by seventy-five yards, with high grass and tree stumps throughout."

John Herren recalls: "We picked our way through blown-down trees, anthills, and scrub brush until we reached the platoon." By then some of Bennett's troopers had seen the small band of surviving Americans and hollered to them. Sergeant Zallen, up on the knoll with Savage, knew that the long ordeal was coming to a close, but his heart was heavy: "I couldn't bear to look at Sergeant Palmer."

Now the lead elements of John Herren's company approached the clearing, with Herren well forward and anxious to be reunited with what was left of his missing 2nd Platoon. Herren says, "It was a scene I will never forget. First we found the remains of Sergeant Hurdle and his weapons squad, who had been overrun. There were dead North Vietnamese sprawled nearby. Next, the small groups of Savage's and McHenry's men, some heavily bandaged, all of them covered with dirt and tired, but excited at seeing us." Sergeant William Roland of Bravo Company's 1st Platoon says the distance between where Hurdle and his machine gunners fought and died and the rest of Herrick's platoon, sixty to seventy yards, made it plain that the brave machine-gun crews had given their lives buying time so their buddies could withdraw to higher ground.

In that tiny perimeter every man who could fire a weapon still had ammunition left, even after twenty-six hours of combat. There were twenty-nine men in the 2nd Platoon, Bravo Company, 1st Battalion, 7th Cavalry when the fight started. Twenty-nine men were brought out: Nine dead, thirteen wounded, and seven unscratched. All the casualties had been suffered in the first ninety minutes of combat.

Captain Herren said it was a miracle that more of the wounded did not die, and that miracle was named Doc Lose. Herren says, "I am convinced that one of the major reasons that the platoon came through as well as it did was due to the actions of Specialist 5 Charles Lose, the medic. Every man I talked with in the platoon unanimously credited Doc Lose with saving the men who were badly wounded."

Lieutenant Dennis Deal was one of the first to reach the platoon. "We couldn't see each other. I yelled: 'Are you guys still there?' The answer came back: 'Yes, we're here!' I walked over to where my friend Henry Herrick was laying dead and I stood looking down at him. It was so hot, so horribly hot that his body had already begun to smell. I did not want to remember him that way, so I turned away and occupied myself with other duties. But I have." Sergeant Savage says the first men who walked into his perimeter couldn't see him or his men. "All that artillery had blown dirt and dust on us and we looked like part of the ground," Savage says.

"It was curious," Deal says. "The men who had survived didn't stand up. They just lay there in the shallow body holes they had scratched in the ground. They were still in a state of shock because of what they had been through." Specialist Galen Bungum: "The first man I saw was Lieutenant [Ken] Duncan, the B Company executive officer. I hollered at him to get down. He said, 'It's OK, come on, let's go!' Then he threw me one of his canteens. More troops were standing around and I thought they were nuts. We couldn't believe it. None of us would get up. After some coaxing, we got up slow."

Lieutenant Deal saw a lot of dead North Vietnamese soldiers literally within feet of the Americans and one still alive. "One North Vietnamese was sitting against a tree, shot up terribly. But he continued to try to pull a grenade from his pouch. He still wanted, before he died, to get that grenade off. I was very impressed by that total dedication. He tried, until he finally died, to get that grenade out of his pouch, and we stood there and watched him. He couldn't lift it more than a couple of inches and then it would fall back and he would start trying all over again."

Platoon Sergeant Larry Gilreath says, "The thing I remember most was the peaceful way that Sergeant Palmer looked, laying on his back with his hands folded on his chest. We had gotten pretty close, and I almost lost it when I saw him. Then there was the way that each of them asked for water. And here I was with only about half a canteen to give them. That went fast. I was helping one of them, Sergeant Thompson I think. He was wounded, could hardly walk, and he asked me for a drink of water. I don't think at that time there was a gallon of water in the whole battalion. Such a small thing like that, and I couldn't give him a drink of water."

One of the troopers called Lieutenant Deal's attention to something lying on the ground. "The man said, 'Look, there's something red and I don't know what it is.' It was a book that a North Vietnamese soldier had dropped. It was filled with beautiful writing, beautiful script." It was the jottings of a homesick young soldier—poetry, notes, letters. A sample: "Oh, my dear. My young wife. When the troops come home after the victory, and you do not see me, please look at the proud colors. You will see me there, and you will feel warm under the shadow of the bamboo tree."

As Dennis Deal helped prepare the men and weapons for evacuation, he vividly remembers one other scene: "It was the final act of a North Vietnamese soldier who was killed. Before he died he took a hand grenade and held it against the stock of his weapon. Then he had gotten on his knees and bent over double. If anybody tried to get his weapon they were going to activate that hand grenade. When I saw the dedication of those two Vietnamese with their hand grenades, I said to myself: We are up against an enemy who is going to make this a very long year."

Although the relief force had gotten in without major incident, they now began taking more small-arms fire from unseen marksmen. Captain Bennett, securing the eastern half of the clearing, got new orders to spread his platoons out and cover the entire perimeter. In the process of doing that Bennett and two of his men were shot by snipers.

The sudden outbreak of enemy firing lent new urgency to the mission. Bob Tully and I had agreed that the priority task was to collect Savage and his men and their weapons. No body counting; no searching for enemy equipment. No hanging around. Just get the hell out of there. We didn't want to press our luck. It was now 3:30 P.M. and there was plenty of work to be done before dark: Evacuation of our dead and wounded. Resupply flights of ammo and water. Patrols out of the perimeter. Integrating Tully's battalion into the American lines. Clearing fields of fire. Registering defensive fires. Setting out trip flares—flares set off by trip wires close to the ground.

Says Tully: "Our next concern was the actual movement of the personnel of the isolated platoon back to X-Ray. Many of them needed to be carried. Strange as it may seem, evacuating their casualties, plus a few of our own, took the greater part of two companies. Carrying wounded and dead men in the jungle in makeshift litters is no easy job when you have some distance to travel. And trying to maintain a good tactical posture under those circumstances is difficult. Troops are milling around; litter bearers become tired and need to be replaced. I concentrated on moving the casualties out as quickly as possible and securing the movement back to X-Ray in an organized fashion."

Up on the knoll final preparations for the move were under way. Says Sergeant Larry Gilreath: "After we policed up the area, making sure that everyone was accounted for and that all their weapons were picked up, I asked Sergeant Savage if I could help carry Sergeant Palmer. He told me that would be fine."

Lieutenant Deal says, "I remember somebody saying, 'Now we have them all.' I turned around. Just at that point the litter bearers who were carrying Henry Herrick's body set his litter down and I looked back and saw Henry's face in the red dirt. His head was hanging over the end of that litter. I don't know why those kind of memories remain with you so long after the event. It seemed so unnatural for my friend to be laying stomach-down with his face in that red dirt. I recalled as I was looking at him that Colonel Moore had permitted a small number of troops to leave the ship when it docked in Long Beach, California, on the way to Vietnam. Lieutenant Herrick was one of the few people who had family in that area and was given a pass to go visit his mother and father. As I looked at him I remembered that and I was glad he had that last chance to see them. I have since been to Henry Herrick's grave in Arlington. It's right near the Tomb of the Unknowns on a beautiful hillside. A tree grows above it shading the headstone. On the other side of the Tomb of the Unknowns is Captain Tom Metsker's grave."

Lieutenant Colonel Bob Tully took one last look around, then gave the order to head east for X-Ray. Specialist Galen Bungum, his ordeal nearly at an end, had one last unsettling experience as he staggered down toward X-Ray: "I remember stumbling and falling down, ending up face to face with a dead enemy with his eyes wide open. I will never forget that."

Just before four P.M. Matt Dillon got the radio call from Tully's operations officer advising that the relief force was now an estimated fifteen minutes away from X-Ray. Dillon told Lieutenant Tifft to start calling in the helicopters. Then Tully's force began closing on the perimeter. It was a bittersweet moment. Happy, relieved, and grateful to get that platoon back, I walked over to Tully and thanked him and his men. I shook hands with Ernie Savage and told him that he and his men had done a great job in the worst sort of situation. Then there was the sobering, grim sight of the dead and wounded of Herrick's platoon. The dead lay on their poncho litters. Two or three of the wounded came in on their own feet, half-walking, half-carried on the shoulders of their friends. Some of those who had survived without a scratch were so drained that they also required help.

Captain Carrara, Sergeant Keeton, and Sergeant Keith quickly set to work tending the wounded. The dead were gently laid at the edge of the clearing, their booted feet awry and unmoving and somehow so terribly sad. My eyes passed over Sergeant Carl Palmer and, like Larry Gilreath, I was stopped by the peaceful expression, that half-smile, on his face.

Sergeant Gilreath helped cover the faces of the dead with their ponchos and then walked over to Sergeant Major Plumley: "Somewhere along the way I had picked up a .45 caliber pistol and didn't realize I had it until we got to the CP. Plumley asked me if I knew that it was fully cocked, hammer back, and fully loaded. We decided that I would sit down and safe it."

The helicopters began coming in. Lieutenant Dick Merchant was now in charge of the landing zone: "I still remember loading Sergeant Palmer and Sergeant Hurdle. I broke away to see John Herren and Bravo Company. He described the magnificent performance by the 2nd Platoon. His first words were, 'Dick, we almost lost your platoon.' He was exhausted but still the same solid, thinking John Herren I had known as my company commander."

As Savage, Bungum, and the others came into the command post, Joe Galloway talked briefly to each of them: "They were like men who had come back from the dead. We were all filthy, but they were beyond filthy. Their fatigue uniforms were ripped and torn; their eyes were bloodshot holes in the red dirt that was ground into their faces. I asked each man his name and hometown and wrote them down carefully in my notebook, along with something of what they had gone through. The headline writers dubbed them 'The Lost Platoon' when my story moved on the wire."

Somehow, Galen Bungum, Joe F. Mackey, and Sergeant 4 Wayne M. Anderson, who had not been wounded, were put on an outbound helicopter and ended up back at base camp in An Khe. The four other unhurt members of the 2nd Platoon were sent back to duty on the X-Ray perimeter. Says Savage: "We got back on line in the creekbed not far from the anthill. PFC Russell P. Hicks had brought the machine gun back. There was a lot of firing going on that afternoon—no major attack, but a lot of snipers to deal with."

Within half an hour after the Tully task force had returned to X-Ray, Brigadier General Richard Knowles came up on the radio asking permission to land. He says, "We came in fast. I jumped out and my chopper departed. Morale was high and the 1st Battalion, 7th Cav was doing a great job. I gave Hal a cigar and he quickly briefed me on the situation. Lieutenant Colonel John Stoner, our Air Force liaison officer, had accompanied me. I had been riding Stoner to get the air support in close. As Hal finished his briefing an air strike hit a target adjacent to the command post. The ground trembled and a bomb fragment flew into the CP area, ten or fifteen feet away from where we were standing. John Stoner walked over and gingerly picked up the smoking shrapnel, came back and handed it to me: 'General, is this close enough?' "

Before leaving, General Knowles told us that he would direct Tim Brown to pull my battalion and the attached units out of X-Ray the next day and fly us back to Camp Holloway for two days of rest and rehabilitation. But for now we faced the prospect of another long night defending this perimeter.

Dillon and I worked out a way to integrate Tully's battalion into the lines. We tightened our own lines and placed Tully's men on the eastern and northern parts of the perimeter, generally facing away from the mountain toward the valley. I kept my own battalion plus the two attached rifle companies from 2nd Battalion, 7th Cavalry where they were, covering narrower segments of the line but still controlling the areas where most of the fighting had occurred. The officers and men knew that ground well by now and this was not the time to undertake major shifts in the disposition of our forces.

Tully set up his battalion command post in a grove of trees about forty yards north of mine. Ammunition, water, and rations were distributed, with the primary focus again on getting plenty of ammunition down to every rifleman, every machine gun, and every mortar tube.

The four line companies of the 1st Battalion, 7th Cav were now down to a total of eight officers and 260 men. Charlie Company this morning had lost forty-two men killed—two lieutenants, sixteen sergeants, and twenty-four troopers. They had also suffered twenty wounded—their captain, two other lieutenants, two sergeants, and fifteen troopers. Charlie Company was no longer combat-effective as a rifle company. But we had a fresh battalion plus those two rifle companies from the 2nd Battalion, 7th Cav. With only light probes of the perimeter during the afternoon, the line companies had ample time to reorganize for the night ahead.

15

NIGHT FIGHTERS

> There is many a boy here today who looks on war as all glory, but, boys, it is all hell.
>
> —William Tecumseh Sherman

Captain Myron F. Diduryk, commander of Bravo Company, 2nd Battalion, 7th Cavalry, had a strong hunch that he and his men, now occupying the old Charlie Company positions, would be attacked in strength this night, and he lost no time convincing his men that the enemy were coming and they had best get ready for a fight. In Myron Diduryk and Lieutenant Rick Rescorla, Bravo Company, 2nd Battalion had two foreign-born officers whose accents and gung-ho attitudes lent a touch of Foreign Legion flair. The Ukrainian Diduryk and the Englishman Rescorla were destined, over the next seventy-two hours, to become battlefield legends in the 7th Cavalry—as much for their style as for their fearless leadership under fire.

Having spent the afternoon preparing his platoon positions, Rick Rescorla walked back to Diduryk's command post—Bob Edwards's old foxhole—just about dusk. "Are your men up for this?" asked Diduryk. "Do you feel they can hold?"

Rescorla replied: "We're as ready as we'll ever be. But if they break through us, sir, you'll be the first to know. This CP is less than fifty yards behind us." The Mad Cossack had no patience now for Rescorla's usual banter. "Dammit, Hard Corps, cut the shit," Diduryk snapped. "Stay alert. We're counting on you."

Diduryk, then twenty-seven, had commanded this company since May. He was eager and aggressive yet totally professional; over the next three days and nights he would emerge as the finest battlefield company commander I had ever seen, bar none. He operated on the basic principle of maximum damage with minimum loss.

Diduryk's men had had three or four quiet hours of daylight to prepare for what was coming, and they made the most of it. His company, with the 3rd Platoon, Alpha Company, 2nd Battalion, 7th Cav attached, now held the same 140 yards of perimeter that Bob Edwards's men had secured. Lieutenant William Sisson's platoon of the same company was on the left; PFC John C. Martin, twenty-five, of Wichita, Kansas, among them.

Martin says, "We set up our perimeter and started digging our two-man fighting positions. I remember Platoon Sergeant Charles L. Eschbach came around to each position: 'Dig it deeper and build a bigger and higher parapet. Set up fields of fire. Stay alert!' We were all scared out of our wits, but we put being scared in the back of our minds and concentrated on what we were told. We continued to improve our positions even though the ground was hard. It was like digging through concrete. I remember, I'll always remember, First Sergeant Frank Miller standing there, no helmet on, his bald head shining, smoking a cigar."

Myron Diduryk and his soldiers had not yet been sorely tested, but soon they would be. During that lull Diduryk made certain that fields of fire and observation were cleared out to beyond two hundred yards; that good fighting positions were dug; that machine guns were placed in positions that assured flanking, interlocking fire; that trip flares and anti-intrusion devices were installed as far as three hundred yards out; that every man was loaded down with ammunition and that ammo-resupply points were designated; that all radios were checked and double-checked. Then Diduryk worked very carefully with the artillery forward observer registering preplanned fires all across his front. The officer, Lieutenant William Lund, had four batteries, twenty-four howitzers, registered and adjusted and on call.

Bill Lund, a twenty-three-year-old native of Edina, Minnesota, was an ROTC graduate of the University of Minnesota. He spent his first night in Landing Zone X-Ray learning the real world of close-in fire support. Artillery school solutions in those days considered four hundred yards dangerously close. Lund discovered that in X-Ray the big shells had to be brought down to within forty to fifty yards if you wanted to stay alive. Says Lund, "Myron Diduryk and I were side by side all the time, so I had an infantryman's knowledge of what was happening."

Rick Rescorla, 1st Platoon leader, was six months out of OCS at the Infantry School at Fort Benning. But he had arrived there with a wealth of good training already under his belt. He had served in the British army in Cyprus and with the Colonial Police in Rhodesia, and he knew what soldiering was all about. What he did to prepare his position and his men speaks for his professionalism:

"I met with Lieutenant Bill Sisson, A/2/7, who would be on my left flank. Sisson, a personal friend from OCS class of April 1965, looked around at the dead NVA soldiers and wrinkled his nose. They were starting to get ripe. 'Wish you were back in submarines?' I asked. Sisson wore twin dolphins on his chest from Navy Reserve duty in Rhode Island. Convinced that the NVA would come back that night, we vowed to tie in our sectors tight as a duck's ass. No weak links."

Rescorla walked the terrain and tried to see it from the enemy's point of view. Scrub trees, elephant grass, anthills, and some ground cover stretched to the front. The ground was not as flat as it first appeared, but had seams and thick ruts stretching off to the south, with a slight incline away from his positions. The hasty prone shelters dug by Charlie Company, 1st Battalion had been dug after nightfall under enemy pressure. Rescorla moved his men back fifty yards, which not only shortened the sector but meant the enemy would now have to leave the trees and cross forty yards of mostly open area to reach the Bravo Company foxholes.

Rescorla recalls, "Because of our shortened lines, I decreased the number of foxholes. Three-man holes were constructed. The M-60 machine guns were set on principal directions of fire from which they could switch to final protective grazing fire, interlocking with each other and with the machine guns on our flanks. Foxholes and parapets were built in detail. I tested the holes. Some were so deep the occupants could not even see over the parapet. In these cases firing steps were built back up. Two hours before dusk Sergeant Eschbach, A/2/7, and Sergeant Thompson organized a booby-trap detail. Carefully they rigged grenades and trip flares far out on the main avenues of approach. Claymore mines would have iced the cake, but somewhere they had been lost. A screwup, but I felt we were ready to tangle with the best of the North Vietnamese."

Then, after talking with Captain Diduryk about defensive air, artillery, and mortar fires, Rescorla made a final walk of the line, visiting the neighboring 2nd Platoon. He says, "The gap-toothed James Lamothe was part of the group on our right flank. He was the loudest mouth in the company, but a hard worker and good for morale. I asked: 'When the firing starts are you guys going to stick around? If you are going to bug out, let me know.' By this time they understood my gallows humor. 'Sir, we'll still be here in the morning. Just make sure the Hard Corps [Rescorla's platoon] doesn't cut and run.' The troops let their macho humor run wild.

"Sergeant Eschbach, a slightly built, hard-bitten, forty-three-year-old NCO out of Detroit, walked over from Lieutenant Sisson's platoon and joined in. 'I'm selling tickets on the next chopper to Pleiku,' I told him. 'Shit, sir, I wouldn't miss this one,' Eschbach said, then looked down at the Randall knife on my belt and added: 'But if I decide to bug out, I'll come over and pick up that knife from you.' This kind of spirit showed the confidence I was looking for. Men scribbling forget-me-not letters to their next of kin were worthless. But these were men who believed they could win. I left them with some last words of advice: 'They will come at us fast and low. No neat targets. Keep your fire at the height of a crawling man. Make them pass through a wall of steel. That's the only thing that will keep them out of your foxholes.' "

PFC Richard Karjer, a native of Los Angeles who, at nineteen, was one of the youngest soldiers in the outfit, asked Lieutenant Rescorla: "What if they break through?" Rescorla's response: "If they break through and overrun us, put grenades around your hole. Lay them on the parapet and get your head below ground. Lie on your back in your hole. Spray bullets into their faces. If we do our job, they won't get that far." The troops walked back to their holes and Rescorla moved off to his platoon command post, a small termite hill that had been used by Lieutenant Jack Geoghegan the night before. Geoghegan's body had been found there. It was only twenty yards behind the line of new, deep foxholes.

Back at the battalion command post I made my own final checks. We were in excellent shape and morale was high. The perimeter was beefed up; we had plenty of ammo and medical supplies; all our casualties had been evacuated; air and artillery had us precisely fixed and ranged in. Continuous, close-in H and I (harassment and interdiction) fire would begin at dusk and continue throughout the night. Instructions were passed demanding tight fire-and-light discipline. No mortar fires would be permitted without my personal approval, and especially no mortar illuminating rounds. I wanted the mortars to hold back their illumination rounds for our last light in the sky in case the air and artillery folks used up all their flares.

By 7:30 P.M. it was dead dark. We looked forward to the moon rising, it was so black. But in those first four hours of night, except for light probing fire here and there on the perimeter, the North Vietnamese made no moves against us. Before midnight we got a transmission from brigade headquarters: My battalion would be pulled out of X-Ray the next day and sent back to Camp Holloway. The word came down to Dillon through the operations channel.

A bright, near-full moon was out by 11:20 P.M. Around midnight, Lieutenant Colonel Edward C. (Shy) Meyer, 3rd Brigade executive officer, passed me an astonishing message: General William Westmoreland's headquarters wanted me to "leave X-Ray early the next morning for Saigon to brief him and his staff on the battle." I could not believe I was being ordered out before the battle was over! I was also perplexed that division or brigade HQ had not squelched such an incomprehensible order before it reached me. My place was clearly with my men.

Even as that message arrived, North Vietnamese automatic-weapons fire opened up forward of Rick Rescorla's platoon, and a stream of green tracer fire hooked over his command post at a height of fifteen feet. Rescorla and his radio operator crawled forward and rolled into a hole, joining PFC Curtis Gordon, from Detroit. Rescorla, estimating that the enemy guns were at least five hundreds yards out, suspected that the enemy was just testing the perimeter, and ordered his men to cease firing.

Then, at about one A.M., a five-man enemy probe was launched against the center of John Herren's Bravo Company, 1st Battalion lines forty yards due west of the battalion command post. Some enemy rounds snapped over our heads. Two of the five enemy were killed; the others slipped back into the jungle shadows. That probe, added to the firing forward of Rescorla's lines, was ominously similar to the enemy actions of the previous night and a clear-cut warning that the North Vietnamese hadn't given up on X-Ray yet.

Tied up with these actions, I had not had time to respond to the order for me to leave for Saigon. Finally, around 1:30 A.M., I got Shy Meyer on the radio and registered my objections to the order in no uncertain terms. I made it very clear that this battle was not over and that my place was with my men—that I was the first man of my battalion to set foot in this terrible killing ground and I damned well intended to be the last man to leave. That ended that. I heard no more on the matter.

Out on the line it was quiet but tense. Myron Diduryk says, "During the hours after midnight I received reports from my platoon leaders of strange sounds forward of our lines. In addition, a high-pitched sound of some type could be heard during the stillness between firing of artillery H and I fires. Whistles later found on dead enemy soldiers provided the answer. The enemy apparently used the whistles and a prearranged number of long and short blasts to control the assembly and movement of troops as they massed for attack."

Rick Rescorla says that during the periods of silence he encouraged talk between the foxholes to ease the tension. When all else failed, Rescorla sang "Wild Colonial Boy" and a Cornish favorite, "Going Up Camborne Hill"—slow and steady tunes, which were answered by shouts of "Hard Corps!" and "Garry Owen!" that told him his men were standing firm.

Just before four A.M. Captain Diduryk saw and heard indisputable evidence that the enemy was moving against his lines. "At approximately 0400 warning devices—trip flares and anti-intrusion devices—indicated quite a bit of movement in front of the 3rd platoon A/2/7 and my 1st and 3rd platoons. Some devices were as far forward as 300 yards. It appeared that the enemy was spreading out along a probable line of attack. It also appeared that they were executing a non-supported night attack since supporting weapons other than the 40mm rockets were not used by the enemy."

Although the hand-grenade booby traps and trip flares were exploding, no enemy could yet be seen. That rapidly changed. At 4:22 A.M., Lieutenant Sisson radioed Diduryk: "I see them coming. Can I shoot at them?" (The platoons were under strict fire discipline to conserve ammo.) Lieutenant Lund recalls Captain Diduryk asking Sisson, "How close are they?" When Sisson replied, "I can almost touch them!" Myron's immediate response was "Go! Kill them!"

According to Lieutenant Colonel Hoang Phuong, the 7th Battalion, 66th Regiment had come back with reinforcements and was again knocking on the southern and southeastern door to Landing Zone X-Ray. The H-15 Viet Cong Battalion was assisting in the attack as well as carrying ammunition and collecting the wounded.

In his diary, Diduryk described the scene. "My left and center platoons were under heavy attack by a North Vietnamese battalion. You could see those bastards come in waves, human waves. We greeted them with a wall of steel. I called for illumination. Lieutenant Lund called for direct support from four 105mm howitzer batteries. These batteries gave us continuous fires using point detonating and air burst explosions. The foliage and trees to the front favored use of both fuses. We fired some white phosphorous [sic] also."

For Bill Lund it was a forward observer's wildest dream of a target come true. "Enemy in the open!" he radioed back to the gunners. Masses of the enemy swarmed toward Diduryk's lines, clearly illuminated in the eerie light of swinging parachute flares fired by the howitzers.

Diduryk and Lund were in the foxhole command post together, with Diduryk firmly in control. Diduryk wrote: "The artillery was not fired on the same targets continuously. Lieutenant Lund had each of the four batteries fire a different defensive concentration and shifted their fires laterally and in depth in 100-yard adjustments. Later inspection of the battlefield revealed that this type of fire inflicted quite a punishment on the enemy."

The initial enemy ground attack came against Lieutenant Sisson, then slanted toward Rescorla's platoon as well. Rick Rescorla recalls, "M-16s jammed and every third man was down in the bottom of the holes with a cleaning rod, clearing the rifles. Hot brass showered down the neck of the luckless reloader. The NVA came forward in short rushes, dropping, firing, pushing nearer. Whistles. Shrill fierce voices of NVA noncoms kicking their men forward. A rocket-propelled grenade passed by with a rush of air. The spare rifles from Geoghegan's dead platoon kept us up and firing while our own were being cleared of jams."

The first rush, by at least three hundred North Vietnamese, was beaten off in less than ten minutes by small-arms, machine-gun, and artillery fire from the alert and well-prepared Bravo Company, 2nd Battalion troops. At 4:31 A.M., twenty minutes later, they came back. Diduryk: "The intensity of their attack increased and I was under assault aimed at my three left platoon sectors."

Screams, shouts, and whistles split the night as the NVA swept down the mountain, straight into the smoke-clouded killing ground. Now all the mortars of my battalion and Tully's were turned loose, adding their 81mm high-explosive shells to the general mayhem. Rifleman John Martin, who was in Diduryk's lines, says: "We kept pouring rifle and machine gun fire and artillery on them and then they broke and ran. I don't think we had any casualties but they were catching hell."

By now the Air Force C-123 flare ship *Smoky the Bear* was overhead and its crew was kicking out parachute flares nonstop. We halted artillery illumination to conserve it for later use, if needed. Myron Diduryk wrote: "The illumination proved to be of great value. It gave us the ability to see and place effective small arms fire on the enemy. I could see the enemy formations as they assaulted in my sector. My forward observer was able to see the targets and place effective artillery fire on the enemy. The enemy would wait until the flares burned out before attempting to rush our positions. While the flares were illuminating the battlefield, the enemy would seek cover in the grass, behind trees and anthills, or crawl forward. Low grazing fire prevented the enemy from penetrating, but some managed to get within five or ten yards of the foxholes. They were eliminated with small arms and hand grenades."

In the midst of this bedlam a blazing flare under an unopened parachute streaked across the sky and plunged into the ammunition dump near the battalion command post. It lodged in a box of hand grenades, burning fiercely. Without hesitation, Sergeant Major Plumley ran to the stacks and with his bare hands reached into the grenade boxes and grabbed the flare. Plumley jerked the flare free, reared back, and heaved it out into the open clearing. He then stomped out the grass fires touched off by the flare, in and around the ammo crates.

Over on the perimeter Rescorla's men fought on. "Our M-79s switched to direct fire [fire delivered to a visible target] and lobbed rounds out between seventy-five and a hundred yards. Still the shadowy clumps moved closer. RPGs and machine guns crackled and they blasted at us from the dark line of ground cover. Across the open field they came in a ragged line, the first groups cut down after a few yards. A few surged right on, sliding down behind their dead comrades for cover. An amazing, highly disciplined enemy. A trooper cursed and pleaded in a high-pitched voice: 'Goddammit, stop the bastards!' "

For the next thirty minutes the field artillery, four batteries of twenty-four 105mm howitzers firing from LZ Falcon just over five miles away and from LZ Columbus just three miles distant, dominated this field. Lieutenant Bill Lund, with his imaginative in-depth, lateral, and preemptive close-in adjustments of fire from the big guns, was the maestro of the salvoes. The North Vietnamese could be seen dragging off their dead and wounded. On their last attempt, against Bob Edwards's Charlie Company less than twenty-four hours before, they had quickly gotten inside the artillery ring and grabbed Edwards's men in a deadly bear hug. This night they were stopped cold.

At 4:40 A.M. Diduryk called for more ammunition, and under fire the recon platoon of my battalion made the first of two resupply runs, hauling boxes of rifle and machine-gun ammo and M-79 grenades from the termite-hill command-post dump to the foxholes.

The enemy commander had no doubt assumed that the left side of Diduryk's sector would be lightly held by the battered survivors of Charlie Company. When he found the going anything but easy he shifted the weight of his attack, launching against Diduryk's two platoons on the right. At 5:03 A.M. the third attack came, against Lieutenant Lane's platoon. Sergeant John Setelin recalls, "In the afternoon we had set out trip flares and anti-intrusion devices. That device was the size of a cigarette package with a timing wire in it, and compressed air. The wire would break easily and a small alarm and light would go off telling you something was out there. We strung a lot of them. Sometime after four A.M., I saw the little light blink on an anti-intrusion device and heard the tone. I figured something was coming. Lamothe motioned to me to stay down and quiet, and was pointing at his box going off."

Setelin whispered orders to his squad, telling men on either side of him to hold their fire, not to shoot until the enemy stepped out into that open space right in front. "Suddenly a flare and a booby trap went off and they were there in the grass shooting at us. I took a round just above the elbow, nothing really, just a stitch or two and a piece of tape after the fight. Nobody shot back. Then they stepped into that open area. The flares were burning, they were lit up, and it was easy. We opened up and picked 'em off. It was a light attack. Then they hit us harder thirty minutes later, blowing bugles, blowing whistles. We killed them all. Then some white phosphorus came in about fifteen feet in front of my foxhole and I lost most of my web gear and my shirt. Had about eight burns on one arm." John Setelin sat there under the light of the flares and used the point of his bayonet to quickly dig the still-burning WP fragments out of his flesh.

Within half an hour the attack on Diduryk's right was violently repulsed. Lieutenant Rackstraw's 1st Battalion recon platoon now made a second ammo-resupply run out to Diduryk's lines. At 5:50 A.M., forty minutes before daybreak, *Smoky,* the flare ship, ran dry. No more light from the sky. I ordered immediate resumption of artillery illumination and lifted the restriction on use of mortar illumination rounds.

At 6:27 A.M. the North Vietnamese commander launched another heavy attack, this time directly at Myron Diduryk's command post. Again the men of Sisson's and Rescorla's platoons bore the brunt. PFC Martin: "About 6:30 A.M., they hit us again with an 'All or Nothing' attitude. It was like a shooting gallery; waves of NVA were coming in a straight line down off Chu Pong Mountain." Specialist 4 Pat Selleck of the recon platoon was hauling more ammo to the line: "I heard bugles blowing. I saw in the light of the flares waves of the enemy coming down at us off the mountain in a straight line. One had a white hat or helmet on and it was like he was directing the line of march. His weapon was slung over his shoulder. They just kept coming down like they didn't care. The line company was shooting them like ducks in a pond."

From Lieutenant Bill Lund's point of view, the enemy commander could not have picked a better place for this attack. In the light of the flares, clusters of enemy soldiers were clearly visible only fifty to a hundred yards out across a hundred-yard front. Lund literally shredded those units with 105mm airburst shells and a nonstop bombardment of 81mm mortar shells. With their rifles and machine guns, the troopers in the forward foxholes ripped up those who escaped the heavy stuff. After only fourteen minutes of this, the few North Vietnamese survivors broke off the attack and started back the way they had come, to the southeast, dragging some of their wounded comrades.

Forward of Rescorla's troops, the number of moving enemy dwindled. "Suddenly only one NVA was still moving, thrusting his squat body forward in one last effort. Every rifle and machine gun was firing at him. He finally fell three paces from a foxhole on our right flank. For the next five minutes men kept firing at him, refusing to believe he was mortal. A brave and determined soldier. 'Look, he's carrying a pistol,' Sergeant Musselwhite shouted. I started to crawl out through the dust to grab the souvenir, but Staff Sergeant John Leake beat me to it. Specialist 4 Robert Marks spoke up: 'Man, I think I've been hit.' That strong soldier from Baltimore had been hit in the neck long before, but chose not to report it until the battle was over."

Rescorla adds, "A quietness settled over the field. We put more rounds into the clumps of bodies nearest our holes, making sure. Ammunition was again resupplied by the recon platoon. Two full loads had been expended. We stretched in the gray dawn. Suddenly an NVA body bucked high. His own stick grenade had exploded under him. Suicide or accident? We watched our front. Old bodies from the day before mingled with newly killed. The smell was hard to take. Forty yards away a young North Vietnamese soldier popped up from behind a tree. He started his limping run back the way he had come. I fired two rounds. He crumpled. I chewed the line out for failure to fire quickly."

The night attack had failed; it broke against the firepower and professionalism of Myron Diduryk and his officers and men. Hundreds more North Vietnamese soldiers died bravely doing their best to break through Myron's iron defenses. Captain Diduryk's Bravo Company, 2nd Battalion, had borne the brunt of the attack and suffered precisely six men lightly wounded. Not one was killed.

During the two and a half hours of the attack against Diduryk's sector, the rest of the X-Ray perimeter had been quiet—too quiet. Dillon and I discussed the possibility of conducting a reconnaissance by fire to check for presence of the enemy elsewhere on the line. We had plenty of ammunition and, what the hell, the enemy knew where our lines were as well as I did by now. We passed the word on the battalion net: At precisely 6:55 A.M. every man on the perimeter would fire his individual weapon, and all machine guns, for two full minutes on full automatic. The word was to shoot up trees, anthills, bushes, and high grass forward of and above the American positions. Gunners would shoot anything that worried them. By now we had learned to our sorrow that the enemy used the night to put snipers into the trees, ready to do damage at first light. Now was the time to clean up out in front.

At the stated time our perimeter erupted in an earsplitting uproar. And immediately a force of thirty to fifty North Vietnamese rose from cover 150 yards forward of Joel Sugdinis's Alpha Company, 2nd Battalion lines and began shooting back. The "Mad Minute" of firing triggered their attack prematurely. Artillery fire was instantly brought in on them and the attack was beaten off. When the shooting stopped one dead sniper dangled by his rope from a tree forward of Diduryk's leftmost platoon. Another dropped dead out of a tree immediately forward of John Herren's Bravo Company, 1st Battalion command post. A third North Vietnamese sniper was killed an hour later, when he tried to climb down his tree and run for it.

Sergeant Setelin's arm, speckled with the white phosphorus burns, began hurting him now. "I was sent back to the aid station, where my arm was bandaged, and I was waiting to be medevac'd out. The more I sat there the more I realized that I couldn't in good faith get on a chopper and fly out of there and leave those guys behind. So I took the sling off my arm and went on back out. Somebody asked: 'Where are you going?' I said: 'Back to my foxhole.' Nobody said anything else."

GOING TO WAR

Courtesy Col. Greg Dillon

Tony Nadal, left, and Matt Dillon on the first battalion-size operation 1/7th Cav conducted in Vietnam, in Happy Valley near An Khe during October 1965.

Courtesy Lt. Col. L. R. Lefebvre

U.S. Army Photo

The 11th Air Assault (Test) Division's commanding general, Harry Kinnard, left, and 3rd Brigade commander Col. Tim Brown in May 1965.

Hard good-byes: Ray Lefebvre with his wife, Ann, and children the day he left for Vietnam.

John Herren and Bob Edwards aboard the USNS *Maurice Rose* transiting the Panama Canal late in August of 1965.

Air Force pilot Charlie Hastings had a grunt's eye view of war.

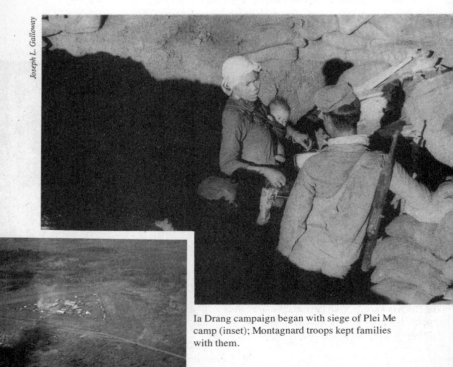

Ia Drang campaign began with siege of Plei Me camp (inset); Montagnard troops kept families with them.

Doc Carrara treats a sick Montagnard child in isolated village five miles east of Plei Me camp on November 10.

Joseph L. Galloway

X-RAY

Clouds of smoke boiling off the X-Ray battlefield made the aviators' jobs all the more difficult and dangerous.

Courtesy CWO Alex Jekel

Battalion command group just before X-Ray: Standing left to right, Basil Plumley, Matt Dillon, Hal Moore, and Tom Metsker. Kneeling left to right, unidentified trooper and radio operator Bob Ouellett

Battalion surgeon Robert Carrara led a sadly understrength crew of medical aid men who worked miracles in the hell that was LZ X-Ray. They saved the lives of many of the 121 men wounded in action there.

Lt. Col. Bob Tully, right, shown here with Gener Dick Knowles, commanded the 2nd Battalion, 5th Cav in the Ia Drang.

Henry Toro Herrick: He led a charge that baffled everyone.

Neil Kroger died holding the line in Charlie Company.

Bob Taft was first casualty in fight for dry creekbed.

Lt. Col. Nguyen Huu An commanded enemy forces in the Ia Drang Valley from a bunker on the slopes of Chu Pong massif. An and his superiors claim a victory in spite of heavy losses, and say they learned how to fight the newly arrived American forces and their helicopters. A North Vietnamese map, captured in 1966, accurately depicts enemy maneuvers and attacks during the Ia Drang campaign.

Galen Bungum, left, and Joe F. Mackey, two of the unhurt survivors of Lt. Henry Herrick's Lost Platoon. They and their buddies fought off hundreds of North Vietnamese with the help of artillery.

Sergeants Carl Palmer, Paul Hurdle, and Ernie Savage (left to right) of Herrick's platoon. Hurdle died fighting a rear-guard action that bought time for his buddies. Palmer commanded only briefly after Herrick's death, then he also was slain. Command then passed to Savage who held the decimated, isolated platoon together for 26 desperate hours under siege. The platoon's losses: 9 KIA, 13 WIA.

Alpha/1/7 machine gunners enjoying warm beer at An Khe: left to right, Edward Dougherty, Russell Adams, Theron Ladner, Rodriguez Rivera, Bill Beck. They held the line with two M-60s.

Top: Rick Rescorla, left, and Myron Diduryk. Clinton Poley, center, in the battalion aid station. Bottom: Doc Carrara works on Arthur Viera.

Medic Charles Lose bandaged wounds with toilet paper and T-shirts and kept 13 men alive by sheer will.

Bill Beck, 22, learned the meaning of fear alone with a machine gun in the tall grass.

Willard Parish says the enemy seemed to be "growing out of the weeds." After Parish ran out of machine-gun ammo, he kept firing with two .45 pistols. More than 100 enemy dead were found around Parish's foxhole.

Rick Lombardo, right, and his good buddy Pop Jekel thought it couldn't get worse than X-Ray. It did.

Ed "Too Tall to Fly" Freeman won a battlefield commission on Pork Chop Hill and flew the world on mapping missions before Vietnam. He and Bruce Crandall claimed the toughest jobs for themselves.

Ancient Serpent 6, Bruce Crandall, led the bravest helicopter pilots in the world into the LZ X-Ray firestorm to deliver ammo and water and bring out the wounded. Greater love hath no man...

Specialist 4 James T. Campbell (left) and a Pathfinder trooper escort two North Vietnamese prisoners taken at LZ X-Ray. During three days of fighting we captured only six PAVN prisoners. Most chose to die fighting.

A badly wounded American is carried to a helicopter. At Charlie Med in Pleiku, corpsmen pumped in four units of whole blood at a time while Army surgeons worked frantically to plug the leaks.

ALBANY

Courtesy Mrs. Frank Henry

Major Frank Henry, left, and Doc William Shucart. Henry called in air and artillery that saved the day at Albany. Shucart tended the wounded at rear of the column.

Joel Sugdinis and his XO, Larry Gwin, watched in horror as the PAVN attack rolled over two Alpha Company platoons.

Courtesy Robert Jeanette

Ghost 4-6, Bob Jeanette, gets a 25-cent haircut at 1st Cav base camp in An Khe.

Charlie Company CO, Skip Fesmire, left, and recon platoon leader Pat Payne in happier days before LZ Albany. Charlie Company lost 46 killed and 50 wounded.

Courtesy Pat Payne

Lt. Col. Bob McDade had just taken over 2nd Battalion, 7th Cav when it was sent into the bloody Ia Drang fighting.

Courtesy Lt. Col. George Forrest

Courtesy James Young

Captain George Forrest ran a gauntlet of enemy fire to reach his Alpha/1/5 soldiers.

Jim Young, wounded and alone, wandered among the enemy but made it home for Christmas.

Sergeant Fred. J. Kluge led a midnight patrol in search of Ghost 4-6 and U.S. wounded.

Sergeant Major James Scott gets a Purple Heart for wounds suffered at LZ Albany. He bandaged himself and, witnesses say, was still "fighting like a demon" hours later.

Bob Towles and a dozen men of Delta Company formed a line, but the enemy flanked them.

Jack P. Smith saw his friends die all around him but lived through a terrifying night.

Purp Lavender was wounded by friendly fire returning from the Kluge night patrol.

James H. Shadden, left, and Snyder Bembry. Shadden heard an NVA officer kill Bembry.

Delta Company mortarmen take a break in the jungle just minutes before the North Vietnamese attacked. Left to right, Duncan Krueger (KIA), A.C. Carter, Osvaldo Amodias (KIA), unknown, James H. Shadden. This eerie photo was taken with a small camera that survived the badly wounded Shadden's journey home.

A 2nd Battalion, 7th Cav trooper on guard beside the body of a fallen comrade. The scene along the column, where more than 150 Americans died, horrified the first relief patrols.

Three lucky survivors from Headquarters Company share a beer at Camp Holloway. They are, left to right, John Howard, Bud Alley, and Dan Boone. Alley and Howard led parties that escaped.

AFTERMATH

Hal Moore and Basil Plumley on the day 1st Battalion, 7th Cav returned to An Khe base camp from the Ia Drang.

Major H. Norman Schwarzkopf leads ARVN paratroopers along a Highlands trail from Duc Co to Pleiku in August of 1965.

Hal Moore, Senior General Vo Nguyen Giap, and Joe Galloway after a meeting in Hanoi in September 1990, to discuss the battles of the Ia Drang.

Tom Metsker with wife, Catherine, and daughter, Karen. Metsker was killed November 14, 1965, in LZ X-Ray.

Jack, Barbara, and Camille Geoghegan at Fort Benning before the 1st Cav left for Vietnam. Geoghegan died trying to rescue a wounded trooper, Willie Godboldt.

Hal Moore and Lt. Gen. Nguyen Huu An during a four-hour discussion of the Ia Drang battles. An arrived with his old battle map and diaries and talked candidly about his actions.

16

POLICING
THE BATTLEFIELD

> Nothing except a battle lost can be half so melancholy as a
> battle won.
>
> —The Duke of Wellington, in a dispatch from
> Waterloo, 1815

In our Mad Minute we had swept the area outside our perimeter.
Now I ordered a sweep inside our lines. At 7:46 A.M. the reserve
elements, the recon platoon, and the survivors of Charlie Company
began a cautious and very deliberate patrol of the territory enclosed
by our troops. I ordered them to conduct the sweep on hands and
knees, searching for friendly casualties and North Vietnamese infiltrators in the tall elephant grass. They also checked the trees inside
the line of foxholes closely. By 8:05 A.M. they were reporting negative results.

At 8:10 all units on line were ordered to coordinate with those on
their flanks and prepare to move five hundred yards forward on a
search-and-clear sweep, policing up any friendly casualties and all
enemy weapons. There was a long delay before this dangerous but
necessary maneuver could begin. Radio checks, ammo resupply,

coordination with flanking units—all these took time for men who were slowing down mentally and physically after forty-eight hours of constant tension and no sleep. My last rest had been those five hours of sleep the night of November 13. I could still think clearly but I had to tell myself what I intended to say before I opened my mouth. It was like speaking a foreign language before you are completely fluent in it. I was translating English into English. I had to keep my head, concentrate on the events in progress, and think about what came next.

The sweep began at 9:55 A.M., and Myron Diduryk's men had moved out only about seventy-five yards when they met enemy resistance, including hand grenades. Lieutenant James Lane, Diduryk's 2nd Platoon leader, was seriously wounded. I stopped all movement immediately and ordered Diduryk's company to return to their foxholes. Sergeant John Setelin, his burned arm still throbbing, was unhappy. "That morning we were ordered to sweep out in front of our positions. I didn't like that. At night I felt fairly safe because Charlie couldn't see me and I was in that hole and didn't have to get out. But when daylight came I wanted to cuss Colonel Moore for making us go outside our holes. We were told to make one last sweep, a final check around. During that sweep, Lamothe and I brought in one of the last of our dead. Big man, red hair, handlebar mustache. We found him next to a tree, sitting up, his rifle propped up on another tree. One round through his chest, another through the base of his throat. We got him back, running and dragging him."

Lieutenant Rick Rescorla, as usual, was in the middle of it all. "I led my platoon forward into the silent battlefield. We followed a twisting path through the clumps of enemy dead. Fifty yards out we crossed a clearing and were approaching a group of dead NVA machine gunners. Less than seven yards away the enemy head snapped up. I threw myself sideways. Everything was happening in slow motion. The grimacing face of an enemy gunner, eyes wide, smoke coming from his gun barrel. I fired twice and went down, looking foolishly at an empty magazine. 'Grenade!' I called back to my radio operator, [PFC Salvatore P.] Fantino. He lobbed a frag to me. I caught it, pulled pin, and dropped it right on those NVA heads. Firing broke out up and down the line and there was a scramble back to the foxholes. Seven more men wounded along the line, including Lieutenant Lane. Sergeant [Larry L.] Melton and I crawled back out with backpacks of grenades while the others covered us. That handful of enemy died hard, one by one, behind the anthills."

When that firing broke out Diduryk reported by radio. I grabbed Charlie Hastings, the forward air controller, and my own radio operator, Specialist Bob Ouellette, and along with Plumley we ran the seventy-five yards to Diduryk's command-post foxhole. Rescorla was thirty to forty yards off to the left front, regrouping his men. I told Hastings to pull out all the stops and bring down all the air firepower he could lay hands on, bring it in now. Orbiting overhead was a flight of A-1E Skyraiders from the 1st Air Commando Squadron. Captain Bruce Wallace, the flight leader, says: "I remember talking to Charlie Hastings on the radio. 'X-Ray, this is Hobo Three-One, four A-1Es, bombs, napalm, and guns. Please key your mike for a steer.' The reply: 'Roger, Hobo Three-One, X-Ray. Your target is a concentration of enemy troops just to our southeast. Want you to come in first with your bombs, then your napalm, then your guns on whatever we see that's still moving around out there.' 'Affirm X-Ray. We are ready for your smoke.' "

The aerial attack began. Hastings had also called in a flight of jet fighter-bombers. Within minutes the brush out beyond Diduryk's lines was heaving and jumping to the explosion of rockets, 250- and 500-pound bombs, napalm, 20mm cannon shells, cluster bombs, and white phosphorus. Peter Arnett, then a reporter for the Associated Press, had hitched a lift into X-Ray this last morning. Arnett was near Myron Diduryk's foxhole busily snapping pictures.

After several minutes of this I told Charlie Hastings: "One more five-hundred-pounder very, very close to kill any PAVN left out there, then call them off." I told Diduryk to order his men to fix bayonets and move out. Within ten seconds we jumped off into the black smoke of that last five-hundred-pound bomb. Overhead, Air Force Captain Bruce Wallace's flight of Spads was reassembling and getting a battle-damage assessment from Charlie Hastings: "On many missions that report would contain estimates that the flight had destroyed suspected enemy truck parks or bamboo hooches or inflicted casualties on suspected enemy pack animals. LZ X-Ray was different. Charlie Hastings would tell it like it was. Tactfully if we didn't do it right: 'Roger, Hobo, no score today, but thanks for your help anyway.' Enthusiastically if we did it right: 'Roger, Hobo, exactly what we needed. The ground commander sends his compliments.'"

Rescorla and his men had been watching the air show appreciatively. "We gathered for the last sweep. Suddenly a fighter-bomber plowed down from above. We buried our noses at the bottom of our holes. An express train screamed down and the explosion shook the earth. The bomb landed thirty yards from our holes. We came up cursing in the dust and debris. The call came to move out. Every available trooper, including Colonel Moore, pushed the perimeter out."

This time it was no contest at all. We killed twenty-seven more enemy and crushed all resistance. I looked over a field littered with enemy dead, sprawled by ones and twos and heaps across a torn and gouged land. Blood, body fragments, torn uniforms, shattered weapons littered the landscape. It was a sobering sight. Those men, our enemies, had mothers, too. But we had done what we had to do.

Aside from wanting to make certain that Diduryk and his men did a clean, safe job, I had one other reason for joining the final assault personally. Rick Rescorla watched. "Colonel Moore, in our sector, was rushing up to clumps of bodies, pulling them apart. 'What the hell is the colonel doing up here?' Sergeant Thompson asked. I shook my head. Later we saw him coming back at the head of men carrying ponchos. By 10:30 A.M. Colonel Moore had found what he was looking for. Three dead American troops were no longer missing in action; now they were on their way home to their loved ones."

Lieutenant Colonel Robert McDade and the rest of his men of the 2nd Battalion, 7th Cavalry had begun marching toward LZ X-Ray from LZ Columbus, three miles east, at around 9:30 A.M. McDade brought with him his headquarters company, plus Charlie and Delta companies of the 2nd Battalion. He had also been given Alpha Company, 1st Battalion, 5th Cavalry. They closed in on our position at about noon. In the forefront of the column was Specialist 4 Jack P. Smith, son of radio and television broadcast journalist Howard K. Smith. Jack Smith wrote of what he saw in a 1967 article for the *Saturday Evening Post:* "The 1st Battalion had been fighting continuously for three or four days, and I had never seen such filthy troops. They all had that look of shock. They said little, just looked around with darting, nervous eyes. Whenever I heard a shell coming close, I'd duck but they kept standing. There must have been about 1,000 rotting bodies out there, starting at about 20 feet, surrounding the giant circle of foxholes."

Others echoed Jack Smith's astonishment. Specialist 4 Pat Selleck, hardened by three days in X-Ray, listened to the newcomers: "I heard one soldier say, 'Jesus Christ, what did you guys do out here? It looks like a bloodbath. All you see is bodies all over the place walking in here.'" Specialist 4 Dick Ackerman, a native of Merced, California, was in McDade's recon platoon as it marched into X-Ray. "Upon entering the LZ the first thing I saw was enemy bodies stacked like cordwood alongside the trail, in piles at least six feet high. I have never forgotten that sight."

At 10:40 A.M., with two fresh battalions—Bob Tully's 2nd Battalion, 5th Cavalry and Bob McDade's 2nd Battalion, 7th Cavalry—now in or on the way to X-Ray, Colonel Tim Brown ordered the weary survivors of my 1st Battalion, 7th Cavalry to prepare to pull out for some needed rest. Brown also told us that Captain Myron Diduryk's Bravo Company, 2nd Battalion and Lieutenant Sisson's platoon from Alpha Company, 2nd Battalion, which fought alongside us would also have the same opportunity to rest and refit. We would fly by Hueys to Landing Zone Falcon, and from there by CH-47 Chinook transport helicopters on to Camp Holloway in Pleiku.

I told Dillon to get the evacuation organized and rolling. Tully and McDade's men would conduct a relief in place, taking our positions along the X-Ray perimeter. Dillon put Lieutenant Dick

Merchant in charge of the extraction, while we coordinated the relief with Bob Tully and his operations officer, Captain Ron Crooks. We would take out of X-Ray not only our troops and weapons but the last of our dead and wounded and an incredible stash of captured enemy weapons and gear.

By now, late morning, Tuesday, November 16, the personality of Landing Zone X-Ray had changed. What previously had been a killing field had become something else. We moved about with impunity in places where movement had meant death only hours before. Except for our own air and artillery, there was nothing to be heard. It was just too quiet, too suddenly, and that made me uneasy. That old principle: Nothing was wrong except that nothing was wrong. Where was the enemy? Headed back into Cambodia? Still on the mountain, preparing to attack again? Headed north to the Ia Drang and its precious water? And again the old question: Where were the enemy 12.7mm heavy anti-aircraft machine guns? If the enemy commander brought those weapons to bear on us from the mountain above, LZ X-Ray with three American battalions crowding the clearing would present a beautiful target. I told Dillon to step up the harassing artillery fire and to keep the air strikes coming in on the slopes above us. I told him I wanted a picture-perfect helicopter extraction, covered by all the firepower we could bring to bear.

Then, still worried about whether we had accounted for everyone, I ordered the battalion rear command post to do a new accounting on all our dead and wounded. And I told Myron Diduryk to take his company out on one final lateral sweep across his front 150 yards out. That area had been the scene of the heaviest hand-to-hand fighting and I wanted it searched one last time. I was determined to keep my promise that this battalion would never leave any man behind on the field of battle, that everyone would come home.

Platoon Sergeant Fred J. Kluge of Alpha Company, 1st Battalion, 5th Cavalry was moving his men into the fighting holes along the old perimeter. "Two of my men called me over and pointed. There was a dead American sergeant in the bottom of the foxhole. I looked at him and couldn't help thinking: *He looks just like me.* I told the two troops: 'Get him by the harness and drag him to the choppers.' Someone came up behind me and said: 'No, you won't do that, Sergeant. He's one of my troopers and you will show respect. Get two more men and *carry* him to the landing zone.' It was Colonel Moore, making a final check of his positions. If we hadn't found that sergeant he would have. I had cause to remember his words, and repeat them, just two days later."

Near noon a Chinook loaded with reporters, photographers, and television crews landed in X-Ray under escort by Captain J. D. Coleman of the division's public-affairs office. Grimed, numbed, and half-deafened by two days and nights of combat, Joe Galloway stood and watched others of his profession fan out nervously and try to make sense of this battle. Frank McCulloch, *Time* magazine's Saigon bureau chief at the time, says, "A helicopterload of us reporters flew into LZ X-Ray on the third day. A few rounds came in and we all flopped down on the ground. We looked up and there was Galloway standing up, saying: 'Bullshit. That stuff ain't aimed at us.' "

Charlie Black, of the *Columbus* (Georgia) *Ledger-Enquirer,* came up and hugged Galloway. The two walked away from the crowd, and Galloway tried to tell Black something of what had happened in this place, something that Black typed up on his battered old portable typewriter for one of the long reports he airmailed home, to be published in the 1st Cavalry Division's hometown newspaper, read by the wives and children of the soldiers: "Charlie, these are the greatest soldiers that have ever gone into a fight! There hasn't been any outfit like this before. It's something I wish every American could understand, what these kids did. Look over there; doesn't that make you feel good?" The young reporter turned the older one toward a section of the perimeter where a GI had planted a small American flag atop the shattered trunk of a tree.

J. D. Coleman describes the moment, and the vision of that little flag, in his book *Pleiku: The Dawn of Helicopter Warfare in Vietnam:* "True, it was a cliché camera shot from every war movie ever made, but there on LZ X-Ray, in the midst of death, destruction and unbelievable heroism, its impact transcended the stereotype."

The other reporters now clustered around me. I told them that this had been a bitterly contested battle, that clearly we were up against a brave, determined, and very tough enemy in the North Vietnamese soldiers—but that American firepower, discipline, guts, and will to win had carried the day at LZ X-Ray. "Brave American soldiers and the M-16 rifle won a victory here," I said. My voice choked and my eyes filled with tears as I told the reporters that many of my men who had been killed in this place were only a matter of days away from completing their Army service—but they fought and died bravely. As I stood there I knew that the telegrams that would shatter the hearts and lives of scores of American families were already being drafted.

Charlie Black came up. I had last seen him at the Catecka plantation airstrip six days earlier as we launched our operation into the Plei Me area. Charlie was on his way out after two hard weeks of covering the 1st Brigade actions. I urged him to come along with us; Charlie Black was welcome in every unit of the 1st Cavalry Division. He wrote for the paper read by our families. Charlie begged off, opting instead for a few days' R and R in Saigon. Now I teased Charlie about missing out on the biggest battle of the war. He flashed his gap-toothed grin and took my ribbing good-naturedly.

Then *New York Times* reporter Neil Sheehan, who had been wandering around the perimeter interviewing the troops all morning, came over to talk to me. I knew he was an old hand in Vietnam, and a sharp, serious observer. Standing near my anthill command post, Sheehan told me: "This could be the most significant battle of the Vietnam War since Ap Bac." He was right.

I turned back to business. The battalion rear command post radioed a report that all the men of my battalion and attached units from the 2nd Battalion, 7th Cavalry had been fully accounted for and evacuated. Not one single man was missing. Diduryk's company reported back from their final sweep across the battlefield: no American casualties found. Those reports convinced me we had no MIAs on our conscience, so I gave Dillon the nod to begin lifting our men out of X-Ray. At 11:55 A.M. the first unit to leave was Bob Edwards's Charlie Company, what was left of it. Dick Merchant says, "My final task was to run the pickup zone for the battalion. It seemed to take forever. Four ships at a time with a load of four troopers each." Why only four men on a helicopter that could carry ten at a pinch? Because each helicopter hauled out not only men but heaps of enemy weapons and our own excess weapons and equipment.

In my after-action report I would urge that the Army establish tighter control on both friendly and enemy weapons evacuated from the battlefield. We lost a lot of our own weapons, which were taken from our wounded men at the hospitals, and many of the enemy weapons captured and sent out for evaluation by our intelligence officers simply disappeared, siphoned off for souvenirs by rear-area commandos, medics, and helicopter crewmen. We shipped out of X-Ray fifty-seven AK-47 assault rifles, fifty-four SKS carbines, seventeen Degtyarev automatic rifles, four Maxim heavy machine guns, five RPG-2 rocket launchers, two 82mm mortar tubes, two 9mm ChiCom pistols, and six enemy medic kits. Engineers collected and destroyed another hundred rifles and machine guns, three hundred to four hundred hand grenades, seven thousand rounds of ammunition, three cases of RPG rockets, and 150 entrenching tools.

Now came the body count. From the beginning of the fight I had known that higher headquarters would eventually want to know what damage we had done to the enemy. So after each major action in this battle, hating it, I asked my company commanders for their best estimates of enemy killed. With the battle raging back and forth over three days and two nights, it was anything but orderly. There was no referee to call time out for a body count. We did the best we could to keep a realistic count of enemy dead. In the end it added up to 834 dead by body count, with an additional 1,215 estimated killed and wounded by artillery, air attacks, and aerial rocket attacks. On my own I cut the 834 figure back to 634, a personal allowance for the confusion and fog of war, and let the 1,215 estimated stand. We captured and evacuated six enemy prisoners.

On our side, we had lost 79 Americans killed in action, 121 wounded, and none missing.

But the body count on both sides, tragic as it was, did not go to the heart of the matter. What had happened here in these three days was a sea change in the Vietnam War. For the first time since Dien Bien Phu in 1954, the North Vietnamese Army had taken the field in division strength. People's Army soldiers were pouring down the Ho Chi Minh Trail in unprecedented numbers, and now they had intervened directly and powerfully on the battlefield in South Vietnam. Seventy-nine Americans had been killed in just three days in X-Ray. The cost of America's involvement in this obscure police action had just risen dramatically. Vietnam was now a whole new ball game militarily, politically, and diplomatically. Decisions would have to be made in Washington and in Hanoi, and they would have to be made soon.

For now, however, my first priority was getting my troopers out of LZ X-Ray safely and quickly and turning responsibility for this battered, blood-soaked piece of earth over to Lieutenant Colonel Bob Tully.

Sergeant Glenn Kennedy and his small group of forty-eight other Charlie Company survivors landed in LZ Falcon at 12:20 P.M. They got off the Hueys and sprawled in the grass in the sun, waiting for the Chinook that would carry them on to Camp Holloway. Delta Company began lifting out of X-Ray at 12:45 P.M.

Specialist Vince Cantu waited to be called. He says, "Chopper after chopper would fill up and take off. It seemed to take forever. The waiting was stressful. But we waited our turn. After we were airborne I remember praying: 'Please, dear Lord, don't let them shoot us down.' I had seen two choppers and a plane shot down. I thought, 'You wouldn't bring us down now after You let us survive three days and two nights of Hell.' God watched over us; He brought us home. When they pulled us out I had six days left in the Army. I came home complete, not even a scratch. Some of my friends weren't so lucky. I think about them often."

Specialist 4 Willard Parish, another Delta Company trooper, recalls his last act in X-Ray: "Some things you remember. We were burying our C-ration cans and things like that, getting ready for choppers to bring us out of the valley. When we dug our foxhole, there had been a small bush on the right corner and it was loaded with leaves. As we were sitting there, getting ready to go, I looked at it and there was only one leaf left on it now. For some reason, I don't know why, I reached over and plucked the last leaf off that bush and left it bare."

Lieutenant Rick Rescorla: "We were flown away, but the stench of the dead would stay with me for years after the battle. Below us the pockmarked earth was dotted with enemy dead. Most of the platoon were smiling. Suddenly a grenadier next to me threw up on my lap. I understood how he felt. He was, like many, a man who had fought bravely even though he had no stomach for the bloodletting. Each soldier would see the battle through his personal lens. Tactically, it had been a 'find 'em, fix 'em, and finish 'em' action—right out of the Benning School for Boys. A tidy show, and the NVA had been defeated piecemeal, feeding their units one by one into a meat grinder."

Joe Galloway shot a few final photos of Tony Nadal's weary soldiers clumped around the termite hill, gathered his own rifle and pack, and approached me to say farewell. We stood and looked at each other and suddenly and without shame the tears were cutting tracks through the red dirt on our faces. I choked out these words: "Go tell America what these brave men did; tell them how their sons died." He flew out to Pleiku and dictated his story over the military telephone system to the UPI bureau in Saigon; next day his story of the fight at the base of Chu Pong mountain stunned our families back at Fort Benning and shocked the world. In Columbus, Georgia, my wife, Julie, got the kids off to school and picked up the *Enquirer* that morning: "The first paragraph of the story—it was written by Joe Galloway—said the battle was the bloodiest in Vietnam history. Then, in the next paragraph, he quoted *my husband*. I had to take a deep breath before I read the rest."

When Galloway finished dictating his story, the UPI assistant bureau chief, Bryce Miller, asked, "By the way, did you hear about Dickey Chapelle? She was killed on an operation with the Marines." Galloway walked out on the steps of the barracks at the MACV (Military Assistance Command Vietnam) II Corps compound, and sat down. Dickey Chapelle, an old pro who had covered a dozen wars and revolutions, had been a good friend and offered good advice to someone new to the game of war. Galloway sat there in the dark, shaking silently and weeping for his old friend and for all the new ones who had died beside him this week. It was going to be a long war. For the job he did in the Ia Drang Valley, UPI raised Galloway's salary from $135 a week to $150. When he later told his mother about the raise, she shook her head and said it was "blood money." Galloway thought that maybe she was right, but it certainly wasn't much money for so great an amount of blood.

Captain Bruce Wallace and his A-1Es covered our withdrawal from X-Ray: "There came a time toward the end of X-Ray when it became clear to me that leaving an area was often as difficult and dangerous as arriving. We put a screen of ordnance between the enemy and the LZ to interrupt his activities long enough to get a flight of choppers in, loaded, and back out again. I remember the sound of the guns through Charlie Hastings' microphone as he was boarding the chopper, and my own feeling of relief when they got airborne. I led that last flight of Skyraiders to cover the 1st Battalion 7th Cavalry's exit from the Ia Drang Valley. That mission ended my personal participation with the 7th Cavalry at X-Ray."

It was almost three P.M. and there were only a few of us left in the command post to load out: Matt Dillon, Charlie Hastings, Jerry Whiteside, their radiomen, Sergeant Major Plumley, Bob Ouellette, and myself. Plumley, Ouellette, and I were the last to leave the termite hill. We trotted over to the fourth Huey in the final lift. It was waiting, blades turning, pointing west. Plumley and Ouellette jumped on; then I hopped in on the left side and we took off in a sharp bank to the north. As I looked down at the battle-scarred earth and shattered trees below, I felt pride in what we had done, grief at our losses, and guilt that I was still alive.

17

IT AIN'T OVER
TILL IT'S OVER

Those who do not do battle for their country do not know with
what ease they accept their citizenship in America.

—Dean Brelis, *The Face of South Vietnam*

It was a short, fast ride to Landing Zone Falcon, just five and a half
miles east of X-Ray. As we landed among the artillery pieces I saw,
seventy-five yards away, a group of my troopers off the northwest-
ern edge of the LZ. They were in the dry, beaten-down elephant
grass, waiting for the Chinooks to fly them back to Camp Holloway.
Sergeant Major Plumley and I headed in that direction and quickly
recognized them as the seventy or so men of Captain John Herren's
Bravo Company. We walked among them and I shook their hands
and thanked them for all that they had done, looking into their
glazed eyes. We were all so worn out, none more so than Bravo
Company. John Herren and his men had been without sleep for
eighty-one hours. We were all terribly saddened by the deaths of our
comrades.

Dean Brelis, an NBC News correspondent, was in LZ Falcon that
afternoon. He captured the scene in his 1967 book, *The Face of
South Vietnam*.

Hal Moore was the last man to come out of the battle. It was the biggest battle he had ever fought. He was a lieutenant colonel, and he carried himself like a proud man. His sergeant major was at his side. It would need a Shakespeare to describe what happened then, but it was something that was love and manliness and pride. It was the moment of the brave. Hal Moore turned and went from group to group of his men, and only a few bothered to get up because there was no exclusivity now, no rank, and Hal Moore did not want them to stand and salute. He was saluting them. He talked with them. He thanked them. He was not solemn, and he did not bring to his greetings the salutations of a politician. There was no poverty of spirit in his handshake, and he shook every man's hand. It was a union of the men who had met and defeated the enemy, not forever, not in a victory that ended the war, but in a victory over their uncertainty. When their hour had come they had done their job, and it was this thought, too, that Hal Moore had in his mind. And he said that if they had won no one else's gratitude, they had his.

After forty minutes or so with Herren's company we walked over to the artillery positions, manned by A and C batteries of the 1st Battalion, 21st Artillery, and commanded, respectively, by Captain Don Davis and Captain Bob Barker. They called themselves the Big Voice of Garry Owen at this point, but in November of 1990, a quarter-century later, Joe Galloway found one of those same artillery batteries supporting the 1st Cavalry Division in the Saudi Arabian desert. A bright young captain from Virginia who knew his history and his man saluted the reporter and told Galloway proudly: "Sir, we call ourselves the Falcons and I expect that you know why better than almost anyone else. We are the artillery that supported you in your time of need in Landing Zone X-Ray." He insisted that Galloway inspect the battery before joining his men for Thanksgiving dinner.

I asked Barker and Davis to gather their gunners. The artillerymen, who had fired more than eighteen thousand rounds over fifty-three straight hours, were exhausted. Huge mountains of empty brass shell casings had grown beside their guns. The gunners who gathered in front of me were stripped to the waist, their skin dyed red from the dirt and sweat. I thanked them from the bottom of my heart. I told them exactly what their barrages of high-explosive shells had done for us in the heat of battle, and what they had done to the enemy. First Sergeant Warren Adams ran into an old friend who was top sergeant of one of the batteries. Says Adams, "He told me: We melted out a few tubes trying to keep you guys warm up there."

SFC Clarence W. Blount of Pensacola, Florida, was chief of a firing section in Captain Davis's battery. Almost twenty years later he wrote me: "I remember you and Sergeant Major Plumley came to our gun position and you gave our entire unit a fine speech for the great artillery support that we provided during the battle at X-Ray. That speech made a lasting impression on me. I felt that my usefulness to my country, the Army and my unit was really at its peak at that time. I have been wanting to say that to someone for a long time."

Barker recalls: "There were numerous times during X-Ray that my battery exceeded sustained rates of fire. Recoil mechanisms failed on two howitzers early the second day. An ordnance team quickly repaired them that morning. When Lieutenant Colonel Moore's battalion was pulled out of X-Ray he talked with all the artillerymen in Falcon. His words made the cannoneers feel they had played a very significant part in the battle."

Later, as the Chinooks began ferrying the troops to Camp Holloway, Plumley and I stayed behind a while longer, talking with the artillerymen, before boarding the Huey for the ride back. We were not present to see what reporter Dean Brelis witnessed at Holloway and recounted in his book:

By late afternoon they were all back at Pleiku. They walked off the big Chinooks and, without anyone giving a command, they straightened up. They were not dirty, tired infantrymen anymore. Hal Moore's battalion voluntarily dressed their lines, as if they were coming back to life. And the GI's who had not been in the Ia Drang glanced at them with something approaching awe because these were the guys who had been in it. No cheers, but they could not conceal their admiration. A few GI's were taking pictures as we went by— there was something dramatic in the scene all right, because Hal

Moore's men had not yet thrown off what they had been through. There was no shouting, no telling off the ones who had been lucky enough to stay back, because that was the luck of the draw. But the signal had passed through these men that they were coming back to base camp and they just couldn't march in as if nothing had happened, because a great deal had. They marched jauntily and smartly, without making it a production. You would have, too, if you had been one of them. The GI's with the clean faces and uniforms watched them to see what they could tell about combat from these men. It was the kind of scene that Hollywood could never produce, because the men had the dirt and gore of combat completely drenched into them. You can only get that dirty and that proud if you have been in combat and survived it. You can't put it on.

In the cockpit of the Huey flying Plumley, Ouellette, and myself toward Pleiku was Serpent 6, Old Snake, Major Bruce Crandall. Beside Crandall was his copilot, Captain Jon Mills. Old Snake had taken us into this thing and now he was taking us out. When we landed and shut down at Camp Holloway, the sergeant major and I left to make sure that our troopers were being well taken care of. But before walking off I told Crandall that after all that had happened I sure could use a drink. Old Snake pointed out a small, gaudily painted Quonset-hut Officers Club nearby, and we agreed to meet there later.

Plumley and I found that the troops were doing all right. They had been given hot showers, clean fatigue uniforms, hot chow, cold beer, and some pup tents for shelter. After the experience of the Ia Drang this was almost wallowing in luxury. Gunner Bill Beck: "We were issued new, clean clothing. How bloody my own clothing was! Shoulders, arms, front, back, legs. Christ, that's what I remember most about the Ia Drang—how goddamned bloody it was." Mortar observer Jon Wallenius: "We were withdrawn back to Pleiku for some R and R. Seems to me we got back in time for a hot supper. We slept near the airstrip on the ground." Specialist 4 Ray Tanner: "When I got back to our staging area at Pleiku we all started trying to find who was missing. I had a home boy in Charlie Company 1/7 so I went looking for him. At the same time he came to Delta Company to find me. Each of us was told that the other had been either killed or wounded. We bumped into each other moments later on the way back. It was a wonderful reunion. Never let it be said that fighting men are afraid to hug and cry. We did both. His name is Hardy Brown."

Sergeant Steve Hansen recalls: "Got damned drunk at Camp Holloway. Also remember the first meal we got: canned B-ration hamburger patties served hot out of Marmite cans. Tasted like steak. One of the cooks apologized to every man because it was all they had. I remember feeling that I had been tested and found to be a man."

Assured that my men were being taken care of, I rejoined Bruce Crandall and Jon Mills and we headed off for that drink. I was still wearing my grimy, frayed old World War II–style herringbone twill fatigues that I had lived in for the last five days. In *Pleiku: The Dawn of Helicopter Warfare in Vietnam,* J. D. Coleman tells what happened next:

> When they walked up to the bar the bartender told them he couldn't serve them because Moore was too dirty. Mills remembers how Moore patiently explained that they had just come out of the field and would really appreciate a drink. The bartender replied: 'You're in the First Cav. This Club doesn't belong to you; you'll have to leave.' Mills says that was when Hal started to lose his patience. He said: 'Go get your club officer and we'll settle this. But right now, I'm here and I'm going to have a drink. And I would like to have it in the next couple of minutes.' The bartender beat a hasty retreat to summon the club officer but still refused the trio service. So Moore unslung his M-16 and laid it on the bar. Mills and Crandall solemnly following suit with their .38's. Moore then said: 'You've got exactly thirty seconds to get some drinks on this bar or I'm going to clean house.' The bartender got smart and served the drinks. By this time, the club officer had arrived. He had heard all about the fight in the valley and knew who Moore was. And, as it turned out, so did most of the customers in the club. From then on, the trio couldn't buy a drink. That was when they knew that the fight on LZ X-Ray was finally over.

Bruce Crandall pulled out a box of Bering cigars, the kind that come sealed in aluminum tubes. He passed them around. I fired one up, sipped a cold gin and tonic, and let my mind go blank. Lieutenant Rick Rescorla, the tough Englishman, remembers that night: "After a shower, but no fresh clothing, I joined the officers of the 1st of the 7th at the Holloway Club. We savored the cold beer but did not go overboard. There was no boisterous celebration of our victory; we had all lost close comrades. We gravitated in a tight circle around Colonel Moore. He could not have moved if he wanted to. The nearest men were jammed up against him like a Rugby scrum. Every few minutes the four or five men closest to him would be gently edged aside and the outer circle would become the inner one. The inner circle locked eyes with the commander. Unspoken mutual respect was exchanged. Now and then someone would grunt 'Garry Owen' or '*shit*' with the same tone as one would say 'Amen.' All twelve or so sweating officers had learned something special about themselves and each other while serving with Hal Moore in the 7th Cavalry in the Ia Drang Valley."

We were all exhausted. That and the drinks and the emotion and the feeling of security did us all in after an hour or two and we drifted off to catch some sleep. I went to the battalion operations tent, which was quiet but operating normally. Staff Sergeant Robert Brown was the NCO on duty. I stretched out, boots and all, on the bare canvas of a folding GI cot and was instantly asleep. When I awoke at daybreak on November 17, I noticed that sometime in the night Sergeant Brown had covered me with a brown wool GI blanket.

Back on Landing Zone X-Ray it had been a relatively quiet night for Bob Tully's 2nd Battalion, 5th Cavalry and Bob McDade's 2nd Battalion, 7th Cavalry. Quiet, but both units were on hundred-percent alert. Sporadic rifle fire, a few mortar rounds, and the continuing American H and I fire kept everyone awake. That, and the growing stench of hundreds of dead bodies ripening in the heat, prevented sleep, even if it had been permitted. Colonel Tim Brown had alerted both battalion commanders to prepare to pull out of X-Ray the next morning; B-52 strikes would be targeted on the near slopes of Chu Pong, and the American troops would have to be at least two miles away from the impact area. Departure time was set for nine A.M.

Both battalions would march northeast, with Tully in the lead, headed straight for Landing Zone Columbus. McDade's battalion would follow Tully's initially, then turn west and northwest toward a small clearing code-named LZ Albany. McDade's battalion had lost Myron Diduryk's Bravo Company and one platoon of Alpha Company, now back at Holloway for much needed rest, but Tim Brown had attached Captain George Forrest's Alpha Company, 1st Battalion, 5th Cavalry to McDade to make up the difference.

Lieutenant Colonel Bob Tully had commanded his battalion for eighteen months. He knew his officers and men personally: He had trained them himself. By the luck of the draw, Lieutenant Colonel Bob McDade, a three-war man, had commanded his battalion less than three weeks. For the previous eighteen months he had been the division G-1, or chief of personnel, and almost ten years had passed since he had been in command of troops. Although McDade had commanded a rifle platoon in the South Pacific in World War II and a rifle company in Korea—and wore two Silver Stars and three Purple Hearts—he was feeling his way into this war and this command very carefully.

McDade had done a good job as personnel chief for the division commander, Major General Harry W. O. Kinnard, and Kinnard had rewarded him with a battalion command. But not without some reservations. He assigned his own personal aide, Major Frank Henry, to go down to the 2nd Battalion, 7th Cavalry as McDade's executive officer "to keep things going until McDade could get his feet wet."

The 2nd Battalion, 7th Cavalry was the same mix of draftees, good NCOs, green lieutenants, and good company commanders that were found in its sister 1st Battalion, 7th Cav. But it had not had the same intense airmobile training that we had gotten in the 11th Air Assault Test. When the 1st Cavalry Division got orders to Vietnam the Army handed two additional infantry battalions to General Kinnard in July of 1965 to fill up the ranks. The 2nd Battalion, 7th Cav was one of those battalions.

Colonel Tim Brown recalls: "When they joined us they were scattered all over the country, some units at Bragg, some at Fort

Jackson, just scattered. I asked the battalion commander, [Lieutenant Colonel] John White, how many men he had. He said he had a hundred men for the whole battalion. So the Army started filling that battalion with people from the 101st, the 82nd Airborne, some from Fort Lewis. They were just a bunch of strangers to each other. Hell, I rounded up some helicopters and had them take the 2/7 troops up for a ride just so they would know what it was like in a helicopter. That was all the airmobile training we had time to give them at Benning."

The battalion sergeant major, James Scott, says: "We got a lot of replacements in, filled up our battalion, prior to joining the cavalry. Airmobile training? We had precisely one helicopter ride at Fort Benning and that was our airmobile training. No more than two percent of the whole battalion had any combat experience. Frightening to think of. We were definitely new and not trained as a unit in airmobile operations."

First Lieutenant J. L. (Bud) Alley, Jr., a native of South Carolina, had joined the 2nd Infantry Division in August 1964, directly out of ROTC at Furman University under an experimental program the Army called U2. It took a new ROTC graduate and put him directly on active duty in command of troops without first sending him through the officers' basic infantry course. "I spent three months directly in the field in Air Assault II. I was in the 1st Battalion, 9th Infantry and we were a mech infantry unit. They were practicing air assault against us. We came back in from the field at Thanksgiving, then on 15 February 1965 I was sent to Fort Sill, Oklahoma, to communications officer school. That took three months. When I came back we were moved to Fort Bragg to take over training duties because the 82nd Airborne Division was in the Dominican Republic and they had a bunch of new people turning up and nobody at Bragg to deal with them. I was there at Bragg in July when President Johnson went on television and said the Air Cavalry Division would be deployed to Vietnam.

"Next day we got called back to Benning. I was immediately assigned to the 2nd Battalion, 9th Infantry, on the day that it was redesignated the 2nd Battalion, 7th Cavalry. It was a remnants outfit, with new people turning up every day. Nobody knew anything, and nobody knew anybody. It was a blur of disposing of POVs [privately owned vehicles] and POE [preparation for overseas embarkation] and packing up. Airmobile training? Hell, I had my first helicopter ride in my life from the beach in Qui Nhon to division headquarters at An Khe in Vietnam."

Lieutenant Alley says he thought the 2nd Battalion, 7th Cav was a pretty decent unit, no better and no worse than most of the rest. "The NCOs and staff people were good. Captain Jim Spires [battalion operations officer] was top-drawer, and I can't say enough good about Major Frank Henry. He was a first-rate guy, a real cool head under fire. The company commanders seemed to know their jobs, especially Skip Fesmire and Myron Diduryk. We had one or two units that had a bit of light contact out in the field. Headquarters Company was a different unit than a regular line company. We were staff people—supplies, communications, and medical people. Noncombatant administrators and support people."

Lieutenant Colonel Edward C. (Shy) Meyer, who later would become Chief of Staff of the U.S. Army, was Tim Brown's executive officer in the 3rd Brigade that fall. He recollects, "A deliberate decision was made in those first operations in Vietnam and later up in Pleiku to put 2/7 in areas where it was clear they would have the opportunity to work on the fundamentals, orchestrating their movement through jungle, so they at least had some time to work together where there were not a lot of enemy. McDade was a very new battalion commander, but I should say that he had very strong company commanders and very strong NCOs with combat experience in Korea and even World War II. I knew some of those people from Korea and they were good. Frank Henry, the executive officer, always knew what was going on; he had a good feel for getting patrols out and taking care of logistics. I thought he was a good adjunct and prop for McDade during his learning period."

One of the strengths of the 2nd Battalion was Sergeant Major James Scott. He had made the landing at Normandy and was wounded in combat three times between June and December of 1944. He served thirteen months in combat in Korea and had been with the 2nd Infantry Division at Fort Benning for six years. "I had twenty-four years' service in 1965; I could have retired, but that was no time to quit, when you know you are going to be needed and you have some experience. Colonel White, the battalion commander that summer, was a World War II veteran. We talked a lot about obtaining experienced personnel."

Scott had his eye on Sergeant First Class Charles Bass, who was in a 2nd Division unit but had not been ordered to Vietnam because he had just returned from a tour there as an adviser to the South Vietnamese army. "He had plenty of experience. I met him on the street in Columbus, Georgia, and he said: 'Promise me a promotion and I'll volunteer to go with you.' I told him he knew there was no way I could guarantee a promotion but I'd see that he was on top of the list. So he came to us as our operations sergeant. He and I shared a tent in Vietnam. The other senior NCOs would come and pick his brain. Charles could talk for hours about how you navigate by artillery fire; never underestimate this enemy—they have patience; be alert to their AK-47s, a good weapon. Watch those anthills. Fire into the trees and anthills when you arrive and when you depart. This Vietnamese enemy is good; he is dedicated to his cause. That was frightening to hear, but it was all truth."

Lieutenant S. Lawrence Gwin was young, blond, six feet two inches tall; he was one of those who heard John F. Kennedy's clarion call and answered it. He was commissioned regular army out of Yale University ROTC in June 1963. Not only was he Ranger and parachute qualified, but he also had three months' schooling in the Vietnamese language. In September 1965 he was advising a South Vietnamese battalion in the Mekong Delta when he was suddenly transferred north and assigned to 2nd Battalion, 7th Cavalry as the executive officer of Alpha Company, under Captain Joel Sugdinis.

Gwin says, "McDade took over and for several weeks he quietly observed, giving only what I would call sotto voce orders. There was a clean sweep in the battalion command structure. Major Frank Henry replaced Pete Mallet. The S-3 was replaced by Captain Jim Spires, whom I liked because he had also been an adviser. The S-2 was Lieutenant Mike Kalla, fairly new at the game. So we went up to Pleiku with a fairly unfamiliar command structure. Basically this battalion was a terrific group of soldiers with solid NCOs. The shortcomings: They were from the 2nd Division, not a cavalry outfit. They were untrained in airmobile operations. Luckily, Captain Sugdinis had transferred in from Delta Company 1/7; he was a West Point graduate, well trained and an outstanding officer."

The one person who lives in a commander's back pocket is his radio operator, connected by that six-foot-long black plastic–covered electrical umbilical cord. Jim Epperson, then twenty-six, a native of Oakland, California, had been John White's radio operator; now he was Bob McDade's. "White was a leader-type person," Epperson recalls. "Perhaps a bit more nitpicky. He ran us more like we were a stateside unit. McDade was more laid-back. He had come to us from a staff position, hadn't been with troops for a long time. I got along with both of them, but McDade was a little more personable. I liked McDade because I used to get double C-rations, mine and his. All he would eat was pound cake and fruit. Regular C-rats tore his stomach up bad, so he just didn't eat. He was tall [and] slender, and wore a gold bracelet."

Lieutenant Colonel McDade has this to say about his battalion: "Until I took command of 2/7 I had no real dealings with the organization. My impression was that everybody seemed competent. I don't think they had had much experience at the time, but then again not many other outfits had either. It was an outfit that hadn't been tested. General Kinnard sent Major Frank Henry down to be with me because he had heavy airmobile and helicopter experience, having worked very closely with Kinnard as his aide. That was to give us the helicopter expertise Frank Henry had; my experience was purely as an infantryman."

Back at Holloway this Wednesday, November 17, we spent the morning finishing the cleanup of men, weapons, and gear, issuing clothing, reorganizing our depleted ranks, and beginning to process the paperwork for men due to return to the United States for discharge from service within the next week or ten days. Now the

ALBANY

18

A WALK IN THE SUN

> I will tell you one thing that sticks in my mind: This was the least airmobile operation that occurred probably in the entire Vietnam War. It was right back to 1950 Korea or 1944 Europe. All we got were verbal orders: Go here. Finger on map. And we just marched off like we were in Korea.
>
> —Colonel Robert A. McDade

Call it fate. Call it Custer's luck. Whatever it was, it sure as hell had nothing to do with airmobility. The two battalions that had inherited Landing Zone X-Ray were about to abandon it, and they were leaving the same way they had arrived: on foot. Whatever the 1st Cavalry Division's 435 helicopters were doing this sunny Wednesday morning, November 17, 1965, they were not available to move Lieutenant Colonel Bob Tully's 2nd Battalion, 5th Cavalry to LZ Columbus or Lieutenant Colonel Robert McDade's 2nd Battalion, 7th Cavalry to the spot on the map that was designated LZ Albany. Grumbling and groaning, the men of both battalions loaded their packs. The word had come down: The big Air Force B-52 bombers were already airborne out of Guam, and their target was the near slopes of Chu Pong mountain. Friendly forces had to be well outside a two-mile safety zone by midmorning when upward of two hundred tons of five-hundred-pound bombs would begin raining down from thirty-six thousand feet. At nine A.M. Bob Tully's men moved out, heading northeast.

Says Tully: "We spent the night there with McDade's battalion. I was told to go to Columbus. We were the lead out of LZ X-Ray and moved out the same way we came in—two companies up, one back. We used artillery to plunk a round out four hundred yards or so every half-hour so we could have a concentration plotted. That way, if we ran into problems we could immediately call for fire."

Ten minutes later Bob McDade's soldiers moved out. The 3rd Brigade's commanding officer, Tim Brown, was on the ground in X-Ray at the time, watching the movement. Brown's instructions to McDade were to follow Tully's battalion. A little more than halfway to LZ Columbus, McDade's battalion would head northwest for LZ Albany. This clearing, at map coordinates YA 945043, was 625 yards south of the Ia Drang.

Chief Warrant Officer Hank Ainsworth, a twenty-eight-year-old native of Weatherford, Oklahoma, had ten years in the Army, the last year and a half as a Huey pilot in the 11th Air Assault Division and the 1st Cavalry Division. Hank was pilot of the 2nd Battalion, 7th Cavalry command helicopter this day: "I was assigned the mission to take the 2/7 command chopper on a recon flight. We flew an area north of X-Ray the morning of 17 November. People on board were looking at two or three different LZs for potential use. They picked Albany, the smallest of those we overflew, really a one-ship LZ. We flew low-level, three or four hundred feet above the trees, checking the route they would take going in there. I saw absolutely nothing to indicate there was enemy on the ground. We drew no fire."

As 2nd Battalion, 7th Cav headed out of X-Ray that morning, what was its mission? The operations journals of the 3rd Brigade and the 1st and 2nd battalions, 7th Cavalry are not available in the National Archives and have not been located despite an ongoing search by the Center for Military History that dates back to September 1967. Why these crucial documents disappeared remains a mystery. The division after-action report of March 1966 states that the 2nd Battalion "was to sweep to the west and northwest toward a map location that appeared it would make a possible landing zone. The map location YA 945043 was named ALBANY."

Colonel Tim Brown, the 3rd Brigade's commander, remembers: "My intentions were that Albany was just an intermediate thing, that McDade was to go on through to LZ Crooks. I wanted to move 2/7 on to Crooks rather than have them all (2/5 and 2/7 and 1/5) congregate on Columbus. We had to support the South Vietnamese who were coming up, so I was going to just swing on out west. The mission hadn't changed; we were still out there to try to find the enemy. So I had them move out by foot. I could move them out by air later if I had to. Albany was just a spot on the route; just pass through and on to Crooks."

The clearing that was called Landing Zone Crooks was 8.1 miles northwest of X-Ray, at map coordinates YA 872126. Across those miles, as the crow flies, lay the Ia Drang Valley. LZ Albany was two miles northeast of X-Ray and 6.8 miles southeast of Crooks.

Shy Meyer says that because of the B-52 strikes the two battalions on X-Ray had to be moved: "The proposal was for 2/7 to move over north and find a suitable LZ. I don't think there was even an Albany plotted on the map. Later, when I had to brief the press, it was clear to me that this thing could not have been a classic ambush, since the enemy did not know where we were going. Hell, nobody knew where this battalion was going."

Lieutenant Colonel Bob McDade, the 2nd Battalion's commander, was in the dark, too. "We really didn't know a goddamned thing, had no intelligence, when Tully and I left X-Ray. We had no idea what to expect out there. They told me to go to a place called Albany and establish an LZ; nobody said we would have to fight our way to that LZ, just go and establish it. There are other things that follow from this. There is the time pressure. They say, Get there and organize the LZ. So you plow through; you don't feel your way or creep along. So I just blundered ahead. 'That is my objective, so let's go.' We were on foot going toward Albany all morning. We had word we were to stop and hold for an hour or so while the B-52 strikes went in. We sat on our asses, then started again."

Captain James W. Spires, McDade's battalion S-3, or operations officer, recalls that their mission was to stop any NVA movement along the Ia Drang. "It was thought they were coming in along that route from Cambodia to attack our fire bases. It was thought that eventually we would be extracted out of that LZ or from another in that vicinity." Asked about intelligence information or any alert of danger, Spires says: "Nothing specific that I was aware of; no reports of anything in there."

Sergeant Major Scott: "On 17 November, early that morning, I heard we would move to another landing zone. I asked Sergeant Charles Bass, 'What's our mission?' He said: 'One of three possibilities: Engage the enemy; evacuate the area for the B-52s; or be picked up and transported back to An Khe.'"

Captain Dudley Tademy, Colonel Tim Brown's 3rd Brigade fire support coordinator (FSC), was to coordinate all the supporting fires: tactical air, artillery, aerial rocket artillery. "My place of duty was wherever Tim Brown was. The FSC stays in the hip pocket of the commander, immediately available to respond to any developing situation. We habitually took off early in the morning and stayed out all day in the command chopper.

"We did have B-52s scheduled to come in on the massif, and we had to get off that LZ. They were moving toward another location, unnamed, just another circle on the map. We needed to get those folks out of that hole they were in, LZ X-Ray. We had had troopers sitting there for four days."

Sergeant Major Scott was with the battalion command group as the battalion left X-Ray: "We started moving out in formation, in company column. We had medical people, the chaplain's assistant, the personnel section, some of the cooks and bakers. The first sergeant and commander of Headquarters Company were with us, too. Captain [William] Shucart was the battalion surgeon. He and the medical-platoon leader [Lieutenant John Howard] and [the assistant medical-platoon sergeant,] Staff Sergeant [Charles W.] Storey, were with the column, too."

Just before Alpha Company, 2nd Battalion moved out, its commander, Captain Joel Sugdinis, put out an unusual order. His executive officer, Lieutenant Larry Gwin, remembers it well: "The company had been on hundred-percent alert for over fifty-two hours. We were in such a state of exhaustion that Captain Sugdinis directed that each man take two APC tablets, aspirin with caffeine, a move designed to increase the mental alertness of the troops. The recon platoon under Lieutenant Pat Payne was attached to us and was designated as the point because they'd led the battalion over-land into LZ X-Ray the previous day over some of the same terrain. Sugdinis said: 'The enemy situation is unclear, but there are NVA in the area. We proceed to Albany, secure an LZ for possible return to Pleiku.' We were tactically deployed and expecting to run into somebody. We had been told by Sugdinis to stay alert."

Before taking over Alpha Company, 2nd Battalion, Sugdinis had served in the 1st Battalion. When Colonel Brown asked for an officer to take over Alpha Company, Sugdinis was immediately nominated. Joel, twenty-eight and a West Point graduate, had a wealth of troop duty behind him, including two years in the 11th Air Assault Test and 1st Cavalry. He also had seen a year of combat—1962–1963—as an adviser to a Vietnamese infantry battalion. Sug-dinis says: "When I requested artillery support to precede our movement to Albany, battalion informed me that we would not recon by fire because it would reveal our presence, or something like that. I was not told that 2nd of the 5th Cav would recon by fire as they moved.

"As point or lead element in the 2/7, I put my company into a 'V' formation. I put the recon platoon, now attached, in the lead or center, and each of my two remaining rifle platoons in echelon to the right and to the left. I placed my own command group in the center on the heels of the recon platoon. We were to initially follow the 2/5 Battalion, which we did."

Captain Henry (Hank) Thorpe, a North Carolinian, was a mus-tang—that is, he had won a direct commission from the ranks in the early 1960s. He was in command of Delta Company, which fol-lowed behind Sugdinis's men in the column. Says Thorpe: "We were just told to follow the outfit in front. It was a walk in the sun; nobody knew what was going on."

Following Delta were Captain John A. (Skip) Fesmire's Charlie

Company troopers, who also began the move in a wedge formation. "During the first halt in the movement, it became immediately apparent that controlling this type [of] formation in the tall grass would be difficult if a firefight were to break out," Fesmire recalls. "Charlie Company platoon and squad leaders had PRC 6's [Korean War–vintage walkie-talkies], but they were unreliable. Furthermore, once a soldier was down in the tall grass, squad leaders had a tough time locating them. Therefore, after the first halt, I put the company in a column formation with platoons in column. We were not the lead element, nor the trail element. We were following D Company, which was the combat support company."

Second Lieutenant Enrique V. Pujals, of Hato Rey, Puerto Rico, had led the 3rd Platoon of Captain Fesmire's Charlie Company for about one month. "My impression was that it was simply a get out as fast as you can thing, because of the B-52 strike. Our company was to move in company column with platoons in column. It sounded like one of those 'admin marches' at Benning right after an exercise ended."

Specialist 4 Jack P. Smith, twenty, Washington, D.C., who had joined the Army to do some growing up after he flunked out of college, was assigned to Fesmire's company: "The order came for us to move out. I guess our commanders felt the battle was over. The three battalions of PAVN were destroyed. There must have been about 1,000 rotting bodies out there. As we left the perimeter, we walked by them. Some of them had been out there for four days."

The next unit of the 2nd Battalion in the line of march was the battalion Headquarters Company of logistics and admin clerks; the battalion aid station medics; supply people; the chaplain's assistant; communications officer and his radio repairmen; and the like.

Second Lieutenant John Howard, a native Pennsylvanian, was a Medical Service Corps officer and administrative assistant to the battalion surgeon. He recalls spending the night of November 16 in X-Ray beside Staff Sergeant Storey. "Charlie Storey came over to me before we moved out of X-Ray that morning and asked me to help him light his cigarette, because he was too nervous to hold the match. I tried to calm him down with casual conversation but he remained very nervous. I think he was having some kind of premonition," Howard says.

Lieutenant Alley, the battalion communications officer, was also with Headquarters Company. "We were told that this would be a tactical move. There was still a lot of stuff on the battlefield: equipment, supplies, captured stuff that had to be policed up and blown up. All in a hurry-up situation. I was personally carrying an RC-292 antenna, in addition to my regular combat load. I weighed about a hundred and forty pounds; my normal combat load was forty or fifty pounds; the 292 antenna weighed sixty pounds. The temperature must have been ninety-six, and the humidity was the same. We were moving as fast as we could through the elephant grass and scrub oaks, some high canopy. We were humping, everyone tired as could be."

At heart almost as much an infantry officer as a medical doctor, Captain William Shucart marched in the column toward Albany. Doc Shucart was one of the most highly regarded officers in the battalion. He went to school at the University of Missouri, then to Washington University Medical School. "I was a resident at Peter Bent Brigham Hospital in Boston when I got drafted. Initially I had a medical deferment, but I lost it when I switched to a surgical residency. I was assigned to the burn unit at Brooke Army Hospital in San Antonio. I got involved in sports with a bunch of great enlisted men in the afternoons. When the Vietnam thing came up, the Tonkin Gulf, a lot of those guys were sent over. I was single and thought it was an important thing to do. So I volunteered to go to Vietnam. I flew to Long Beach and caught up with a troopship that had left the East Coast earlier."

Shucart adds: "The guys who taught me most about the Army were Lieutenant Rick Rescorla, an Englishman, and Sergeant John Driver, who was an Irishman. Driver did tunnel-rat work; he would drop down in there and yell: 'Anybody home?' He didn't throw smoke in first, like everyone else. After his tour, he went back and did OCS, then returned to Vietnam as a lieutenant and got killed. Driver had his own rules of war, and he tried to teach them to me. You know, when you clean a weapon the first rule is always clear the chamber. Not Driver. His first rule was always check to make sure it's your weapon, so you don't end up cleaning somebody else's weapon. He and Rick taught me a lot about being in the infantry. I would march with them to see what life was like. You know, the battalion surgeon thing was a total waste of time. They don't need a medical doctor in that job. I figured the major thing I did was just to provide moral support, not real medical support. There just isn't a hell of a lot you can do in field conditions. I went out on the operations because I liked it."

One of the people Shucart really liked was Myron Diduryk. "He was wonderful. He loved military strategy. He got me reading S. L. A. Marshall, *Men Against Fire,* all that. We would talk about what makes men in combat do what they do. He liked to talk like a tough guy off the New Jersey streets, but he was a very thoughtful, very clever guy. I was proud of the people I knew in the officer corps, very impressed with them."

Captain George Forrest, twenty-seven, of Leonardtown, Maryland, commanded Alpha Company, 1st Battalion, 5th Cavalry. He was bringing up the rear, following McDade's admin and support people. Forrest, who earned an ROTC commission at Morgan State University in Baltimore, had commanded his company for three months. He recalls, "McDade said we'd be the last company out. I knew we were getting the tough job because we were reinforcements. McDade's instructions were very vague. At the time I thought it was because he didn't have a whole lot of information himself. We only had one map, and I had my weapons guy take an overlay and make himself a makeshift map. I told him to plot some fire support for us along this route so if something happens we can support ourselves. I put my company in a wedge formation, sent out some flankers, and moved out."

Although the evacuation of Landing Zone X-Ray had been observed by the North Vietnamese from the ridge line on the Chu Pong massif high above, once the American troopers were deep in the trees and elephant grass they were concealed from overhead observation. People's Army Lieutenant Colonel Hoang Phuong says: "We had many small reconnaissance groups to watch over the area.

We had a position on top of the mountain watching your movements, but it was hard to see from there into the jungle. So we left people behind to watch the landing areas, the clearings. We organized one platoon which attached men to each landing area to cause trouble for the helicopters."

Colonel Phuong's remarks are corroborated in part by Staff Sergeant Donald J. Slovak. Slovak was the leader of the point squad of the recon platoon—at the very front of the men leading this march. "We saw Ho Chi Minh sandal foot markings, which we called 'tire tracks' because the sandals were made from old auto tires. We saw bamboo arrows on the ground pointing north, matted grass and grains of rice. I reported all this to Lieutenant Payne."

After an hour on the march, Sergeant Major Scott checked on things. "I moved up and down the column, visiting A and D companies and the medical platoon. I noticed some of the men getting rid of some of their gear—like ponchos or C-rations. They were exhausted. They'd been up two or three nights. I went back to Sergeant Bass and told him we needed a break."

The battalion after-action report, written by Captain Spires, says that after marching "about 2,000 meters the battalion turned northwest." Lieutenant Larry Gwin says that Alpha Company, in the lead, angled left after crossing a small ridge line. Colonel Tully's battalion continued straight ahead toward the artillery base at Columbus clearing.

Lieutenant Gwin describes the battalion's march toward Albany: "The terrain was fairly open, knee-high grass, with visibility about twenty-five yards through the trees. We hit a small ridge line, crossed it, and angled left. The terrain and vegetation became more difficult. Lots of felled trees and higher grass. Loads were becoming excruciatingly heavy. We drove on, saw some hooches on the left, and Captain Sugdinis held up the company while Lieutenant [Gordon] Grove's men searched them, finding some Montagnard crossbows. Grove was directed to burn the hooches. We continued west. After about four hundred yards we crossed a stream where each man filled his canteens. Now the elephant grass was chest high, the vegetation greener and thicker, and the trees higher. We were getting really tired. We went another three hundred yards when the word came down stopping the battalion column so that elements to our rear could fill their canteens at the stream."

Captain Thorpe and his Delta Company troops were trailing the Alpha Company troops. "As we were moving along there was a small grass hut, and somebody up the column had set it on fire. Anyone in the valley would know we were coming now," Thorpe says. "We crossed a little stream; beyond that they stopped the column. I told my guys to eat, take a break, smoke 'em if you got 'em. Everyone just crashed right there. We hadn't slept in two days and all were pretty tired."

PFC James H. Shadden, twenty-three, of Etowah, Tennessee, was in Thorpe's mortar platoon: "My squad leader, Sergeant Osvaldo Amodias from Miami, asked me to carry the base plate for the 81mm mortar. He said for me to carry it as far as I could; he would then trade me the sights and carry the base plate. We were in three columns spaced twenty to thirty yards apart, which varied as we advanced. The farther we went the greater the weight we were carrying seemed to feel. If anyone fell they had to be helped up. I had the base plate, three 81mm rounds, plus all the items men in the rifle platoon carried. It was awesome. All the men in the mortar platoon were loaded this way. We came to a branch, stopped long enough to fill our canteens, then moved on."

Specialist 4 Robert L. Towles, an Ohioan, was also in Thorpe's Delta Company, assigned to the antitank platoon. These platoons shipped over with jeep-mounted 106mm recoilless rifles and .50-caliber machine guns. Since there were no enemy tanks in Vietnam in 1965, most of these platoons had changed over to machine-gun platoons. But Delta Company's antitank platoon had not. They were carrying their M-16s plus two or three LAWs each. Towles says his platoon had flankers out thirty to fifty yards on either side. Thorpe's headquarters group was in front of him. Shadden and the mortarmen were behind Towles, more with Charlie Company than with Delta Company, as the troopers moved through the jungle.

Towles says: "After we crossed a low hill the jungle closed in, double, then triple canopy. The trees towered above us. It became hard to maneuver across the downed trees and ruts. We took a short break and ate our C-rations in the semidark, not yet noon. We gathered our gear and moved slowly on and the jungle opened up. Visibility greatly improved and we approached a streambed. The water was welcome. As we moved on through trees standing several feet apart, two deer broke out of the heavy wood line about thirty yards off to our right. At that time I thought the flankers had spooked them."

The division forward command post at Pleiku logged Bob Tully's battalion into its objective, Landing Zone Columbus, at 11:38 A.M. "We got into Columbus; somebody there had a good hot meal for us. Hamburgers, mashed potatoes and string beans," Tully says. "Sitting there eating, I heard McDade trying to get hold of somebody on the radio; he couldn't reach them, so I answered and offered to relay anything he had. We relayed his information to Tim Brown. After a while, I think McDade was able to get through directly."

While Bob Tully and his 2nd Battalion, 5th Cavalry troopers were digging into platters of hot chow in the security of LZ Columbus, Bob McDade and his 2nd Battalion, 7th Cavalry troopers were humping and sweating through the tall grass straight into an area saturated with enemy soldiers from the 8th Battalion, 66th Regiment; the 1st Battalion, 33rd Regiment; and the headquarters of the 3rd Battalion, 33rd Regiment. According to General An, while the 33rd Regiment's battalions were severely understrength because of the casualties they had suffered around Plei Me camp and during their retreat west into the valley, the 8th Battalion, 66th Regiment was his reserve battalion, newly arrived off the Ho Chi Minh Trail. The 8th Battalion's only exposure to combat thus far had been the ambush of its heavy-weapons company by Lieutenant Colonel John B. Stockton's 1st Squadron, 9th Cavalry troopers just after the 8th crossed into Vietnam two weeks earlier. They were fresh, rested, and spoiling for a fight with the Americans.

Lieutenant Larry Gwin of Alpha Company says: "The jungle around us got heavier and heavier. That's when things got a little scary. There was a sudden absence of any air cover, the guys were silent, and I wondered where our helos, our aerial rocket artillery ships, were. We had not changed our formation tactically, but physically we had to move in much tighter to maintain visual contact because of the undergrowth. The terrain forced our flankers in."

Having turned the head of the column north northwest, Captain Joel Sugdinis suddenly heard the rolling sound of distant explosions to his left rear: The B-52s were making their run on the Chu Pong. At the same time he also felt a twinge of concern that he still had not seen the Albany clearing, which ought to have been close now. Some 150 yards to Sugdinis's front was Lieutenant D. P. (Pat) Payne, the new leader of the recon platoon. A native of Waco, Texas, and an ROTC graduate of Texas A&M College, Pat had served for fourteen months in the 2nd Battalion. "I was at the very front edge of the platoon," says Payne. "As we were walking around these six-foot-tall termite hills, all of a sudden right by my side was a North Vietnamese soldier, laying down resting. I jumped on top of him, grabbed him, and shouted an alarm. My radio operator grabbed one of his arms. Simultaneously, about ten yards to my left, the platoon sergeant found a second enemy soldier and jumped on him as well. There was quite a bit of shouting and commotion."

Payne reported the capture back down the line, and Captain Sugdinis was quickly on the scene. He says: "I immediately directed Lieutenant Payne to put out observation posts. I remember that one of our men in the immediate vicinity of the North Vietnamese called out that he saw movement on the high ground to our north. I looked and thought I saw something, too, but was not sure."

The men *had* seen something—and what they had seen was another member of the North Vietnamese reconnaissance team escaping to sound a warning of the Americans' approach. Says then–Lieutenant Colonel Hoang Phuong: "Another recon soldier came back to the headquarters of 1st Battalion, 33rd Regiment, reported to the commander, and we organized the battle here."

Gwin says Alpha Company's column order and integrity had been good until the two prisoners were captured and everything came to a sudden halt. "When I arrived Sugdinis was interrogating the two. They were in mint condition: new weapons, grenades, new gear, but both were feverish, terrified, and shaking. None of us in company headquarters had seen a live North Vietnamese up close. These were not the last we would see this day. We gave them water and advised battalion headquarters." Joel Sugdinis looked at one of the POWs, who seemed to be quaking with malaria. He offered the prisoner one of his malaria tablets, but the frightened North Vietnamese refused it. Sugdinis popped one in his mouth and drank it down with a slug from his canteen. Then the prisoner accepted a pill, and the water, gratefully.

Gwin adds that Lieutenant Colonel McDade radioed orders to hold in place and advised that he was coming forward to interrogate the prisoners personally. "The colonel and his S-2 and their radio operators, an interpreter, and the entourage all arrived at the point of our unit. I was getting nervous standing around with all that brass. I backed off to have a cigarette and make sure Alpha Company was OK. It was very still. While the interrogation went on, Alpha Company rested in place. I was surprised to see [that] Lieutenant Don Cornett, the executive officer of Charlie Company and my best friend, had come forward to see what was going on. He was tired but in good spirits, and we commented on how disorganized the march had become. We told each other where our troops were. We parted. It was the last time I spoke to him."

The Charlie Company commander, Skip Fesmire, says, "I sent Cornett up to find out what was happening, why we'd been stopped for so long. Also, I felt that Delta Company was spread out too far and I wanted to know how much."

At 11:57 A.M. the report on the capture of the two enemy prisoners reached division forward at Pleiku and was relayed on to the division headquarters at An Khe, where it was logged into the division journal at 12:40 P.M. The message said that the POWs were policed up at map coordinates YA 943043, a hundred yards from the southwestern edge of the clearing designated Albany.

Captain Jim Spires had come forward with Colonel McDade. The NVA prisoners tried to tell them that they were deserters, Spires says, "but I noticed they had rifles and equipment. We halted there for about half an hour while we questioned these two. They gave the impression they were scared half to death. Our interpreter's English wasn't very good so it was hard to make sense of what they were saying. I spoke a little Vietnamese and I tried to ask some questions myself," Spires says.

Sergeant Major Scott and Sergeant Charlie Bass shared Spires's skepticism: "Bass and the translator were talking to those prisoners. By then their hands were bound behind their backs. Bass told me: 'They say they are deserters and they are hungry.' We looked at each other and I said: 'Charles, they are too well fed. They appear to be an outpost.' "

Jim Epperson, McDade's radio operator: "We had an interpreter: Sergeant Vo Van On. On was an intellectual, college student, spoke good English compared to some of them. His father was a merchant in Saigon. He came to us when we got to Vietnam; he was our first interpreter. We sat down, took a break, while the officers did the questioning. Then McDade called the company commanders up to him."

Specialist 4 Bob Towles of Delta Company tells what happened farther back down the column: "Everyone dropped to the ground. I unslung the LAW rockets I carried, because their weight cut deep. I sat leaning against a tree facing the rear of the column. When the command group closed up, a gap of thirty to forty yards opened in the line of march. We lounged around smoking and bullshitting, just taking it easy. Then the mortar-platoon sergeant came up. He went directly to First Lieutenant James Lawrence, Delta's new executive officer, to learn the situation. The sergeant left his gear behind when he walked over. He wore his web belt and packed a pistol, but carried no rifle and didn't wear his steel pot. Lawrence put out the information that the head of the column took two prisoners. Others could be in the area. We lolled around."

PFC James Shadden, who was in Delta's mortar platoon: "In the column to my left I noticed Sergeant [Loransia D.] Bowen and Captain Thorpe peel off, headed up front. Everyone dropped in a small swag, and lit a cigarette. I believe this to be the time the so-called deserters were captured." Radio operator Specialist 4 John

C. Bratland also went forward with Thorpe for the company commanders' meeting called by McDade.

Captain George Forrest, commander of Alpha Company, 1st Battalion, 5th Cavalry, was more than five hundred yards to the rear. "McDade asked all company commanders to come forward. Lieutenant Adams, my executive officer, had come in on a resupply bird; he was really not supposed to be in there. I told him: 'I'm going forward; you take over and deploy the troops in a herringbone formation, and spread them out good.' I went forward with my two radio operators. As we were going up the column, everyone was just stopped, sitting on their packs. It was just a Sunday walk, and now we're taking a break. I went up that trail, through fairly dense jungle."

Captain Fesmire, the Charlie Company commander, was also moving up the column toward McDade's position. With him were his two radio operators, his artillery forward observer, Lieutenant Sidney Smith, and his radioman, as well as First Sergeant Franklin Hance. Fesmire left First Lieutenant Donald C. Cornett, twenty-four, a native of Lake Charles, Louisiana, and a graduate of McNeese State College, in charge of Charlie Company. Fesmire says that when the column first halted, he sent flank security out on both sides of his company and personally checked it.

At this precise moment, on the brink of disaster, this is what was happening: Sugdinis's Alpha Company was moving forward toward the Albany clearing. Colonel McDade and his battalion-command group were with Alpha Company. The other company commanders had left their companies, under orders, and were moving up to join McDade for a conference. The battalion was strung out along the line of march for a distance of at least 550 yards. The men of Delta Company were lolling around on the ground. Charlie Company had flankers off to each side but most were taking a break, sitting or lying down. George Forrest's men, at the tail of the column, were in a wedge formation and also had flank security posted. The men of the battalion were worn out after nearly sixty hours without sleep and four hours of marching through difficult terrain. Visibility in the chest-high elephant grass was very limited.

Lieutenant Larry Gwin, who was up front: "We picked up again. This time the battalion headquarters group was right with us and McDade was guiding us to a clearing. We broke into an area that looked like it might be Albany. A fairly open area, about the size of a football field, sloping up to a wooded, anthill-studded area. The grass was waist-deep. We'd made it. It was still very quiet. Just about then I was flabbergasted to see McDade and his entourage striding past me heading toward the clearing, moving very quickly.

"I moved forward and Joel Sugdinis was on his knee at the edge of the clearing. He said: 'I sent the 1st Platoon around to the right, 2nd Platoon around to the left, and recon platoon forward to recon the far end of the LZ.' McDade's entourage had walked past us, across the grass, and into a clump of trees. It was swampy to the left, and on the right grassy. I didn't know there was another clearing on the other side of those trees."

The battalion after-action report states that Lieutenant Pat Payne's recon platoon by 1:07 P.M. "had cleared through the western edge of the objective area LZ sites," and that the other two Alpha Company platoons were to the north and south of the Albany clearing. It adds: "The remainder of the battalion was in dispersed column to the east of the objective area."

One hour and ten minutes had passed since the two prisoners had been captured and the other NVA soldiers had fled. The company commanders had reached the clearing.

Sergeant Major James Scott: "Sergeant Bass said: 'Let's question these prisoners some more; I don't believe a word they're saying.' At that point it was Bass and me and the prisoners and the Vietnamese translator. Then Bass said: 'I hear Vietnamese talking.' That interpreter really began to look afraid. 'Yes,' he said. 'They are the North Vietnamese Army.' So what did we have? The company commanders were all up front, and we had NVA all around us. Right about then small-arms fire started up. Bass said: 'They're up in the trees.' Charles Bass was killed in action right there. I joined Alpha Company, no more than thirty yards away. First Sergeant Frank Miller and I went back to back and started firing our rifles."

Lieutenant Gwin: "We had been there a short time, five minutes, when I heard some rounds fired near our 1st Platoon. I thought: 'They must have caught up with those NVA stragglers.' Then everything opened up. The firing just crescendoed. They hadn't found the stragglers. They had run right into the North Vietnamese! I was out in the grass away from the trees when it started. The rounds were so fast and furious overhead they were knocking bark off the trees. I ran to them. One round struck the tree I was crouched next to, about an inch over my head. I said: 'Holy shit!' and ran to join Joel. We all got down. Then I heard the sickening whump of mortar fire landing where I had seen our 2nd Platoon disappear."

Back at the 3rd Brigade command post at Catecka, Captain John Cash, twenty-nine, the assistant operations officer on duty, was writing a letter to his wife. "Suddenly Sergeant Russell leaned close to the radio and said, 'Sir, something is going on.' He could hear radio guys calling for fire support all over, hear them saying, 'We are surrounded!' He had friends in the 2nd Battalion's operations shop. We couldn't hear them on the radio—couldn't hear Sergeant Charlie Bass. Casualty figures kept rising, kept going up," Cash recalls, adding: "I went and woke up Major Pete Mallet, the S-3. This was afternoon. We couldn't get a clear picture. Major Mallet came in and he was concerned. Major Harry Crouch, the S-4 [supply officer], came in, somber look on his face. He said, 'They got Captain McCarn [the 2nd Battalion S-4]. All these things just kept building up."

The most savage one-day battle of the Vietnam War had just begun. The 2nd Battalion, 7th Cavalry had walked into a hornet's nest: The North Vietnamese reserve force, the 550-man 8th Battalion, 66th Regiment, had been bivouacked in the woods off to the northeast of McDade's column. The understrength 1st Battalion, 33rd Regiment, coordinating its movement and actions with the 8th Battalion, was aiming its men toward the head of the American column. And the point men of Lieutenant Payne's recon platoon had marched to within two hundred yards of the headquarters of the 3rd Battalion, 33rd Regiment. A senior lieutenant grabbed up the 3rd Battalion cooks and clerks and joined the attack. Lieutenant Colonel Phuong says other North Vietnamese soldiers in the vicinity

19

HELL IN A
VERY SMALL PLACE

> War is a crime. Ask the infantry and ask the dead.
> —Ernest Hemingway

The North Vietnamese battlefield commander, then–Senior Lieutenant Colonel Nguyen Huu An, had watched the Americans leaving the clearing they called X-Ray. He and his principal subordinate, 66th Regimental commander Lieutenant Colonel La Ngoc Chau, had one thought uppermost in their minds: General Vo Nguyen Giap's dictum "You must win the first battle." As far as Colonel An was concerned, the fight with the Americans that had begun on November 14, in Landing Zone X-Ray, wasn't over. It was simply moving to a new location a short distance away.

An says: "I think this fight of November seventeenth was the most important of the entire campaign. I gave the order to my battalions: When you meet the Americans divide yourself into many groups and attack the column from all directions and divide the column into many pieces. Move inside the column, grab them by the belt, and thus avoid casualties from the artillery and air. We had some advantages: We attacked your column from the sides and, at the moment of the attack, we were waiting for you. This was our reserve battalion and they were just waiting for their turn. The 8th Battalion had not been used in the fighting in this campaign. They were fresh."

Viewed from the American side, the firefight began at the head of the 2nd Battalion column and swiftly spread down the right, or east, side of the American line of march in a full-fledged roar.

Specialist 4 Dick Ackerman was the right-flank point man in the recon platoon, which was itself the point of the battalion. Says Ackerman: "We were going to the left to a clearing. We had gone about 100 feet when we heard some shots, then more shots and finally all hell broke loose. The main brunt of the attack was right where we had been standing just a few minutes before. We hit the dirt. I was laying in the middle of a clearing and bullets were kicking dirt in my eyes and breaking off the grass."

Some of the platoon gathered at a row of trees in front of Ackerman. "I wasn't going to run over there with the bulky pack, so I unhooked it and took off for the trees. We saw NVA sneaking up. We started picking them off and I don't think any of them ever realized we were there. After a while we could hear someone calling us from a circle of trees. We started running back across the field. I fell behind a small tree. I was on my side with my shoulder against the tree when I heard a big thump and felt the tree shake. It had taken a bullet just opposite my shoulder. I decided to lay down flat."

The sergeant major was standing, shouting, and giving directions. "His shirt was off and he was in his tee-shirt. He lifted his left arm to point and I could see where a bullet had ripped open the inside of his arm and part of the side of his chest. He was still giving orders. We were then ordered to another part of the circle that was weak. It was facing the main area of attack. There were people running everywhere. We couldn't just open fire in that direction because our guys were there. We were on semi-automatic and picking off whoever we could be sure of as a target."

Ackerman's recon-platoon leader, Lieutenant Payne, had moved most of his men across the second and larger clearing and into the trees on the western or far side of Albany. Alpha Company had split and sent one platoon around the northeast edge and another around the southwest edge of the clearing. Pat Payne was headed across the clearing to join his platoon when, he says, "all hell broke loose up along the north side of the LZ. I turned to my right and observed some American soldiers moving to the northwest to set up positions and they went down in a hail of bullets. Within minutes we were all under heavy attack and my radio operator and I were pinned down in the middle of the LZ with most of the fire coming from the north and northwest."

Lieutenant Payne's radio came alive as the Alpha Company platoon leaders reported heavy fighting. Payne says, "Mortar rounds began falling, which was a new experience for everyone, since we had never had any kind of mortar fire against us. The noise level was unbelievable. I remember pressing my body flatter against the ground than I had ever been in my life and thinking that certainly the highest things sticking up were my heels. Mortars continued to fall and small-arms and machine-gun fire continued at a hectic pace. Finally my mind seemed to adjust and I once again began to think about the situation we were in and what we were going to do."

Payne raised his head and saw that the North Vietnamese weren't actually ambushing Alpha Company so much as they were attacking it. "I told my radio operator to stay put and I jumped up and ran the twenty-five yards back to the command post in the trees between the two clearings, where I found the battalion S-3, Jim Spires. I explained the situation and recommended that I pull the recon platoon back across the LZ and set up positions so that we could have an adequate field of fire. In LZ X-Ray I had seen the advantages of the fields of fire that the 1st Battalion had set up and how they had successfully repelled heavy attacks. The S-3 agreed and I returned to the middle of the LZ to link up with my radio operator."

Payne was able to get all his squad leaders on the radio, "explained to them what we were going to do, and then we coordinated our movement. I counted down to jump-off; then all of us raced back across the open LZ. Miraculously, we had only one man killed: a new recruit who froze. Just as we reached the tree line, we set up a perimeter and turned to face the first of two or three North Vietnamese attacks across the clearing from the west, where we had just come from. I clearly remember that first attack; we stopped them. They were surprised by the amount of firepower we put across the landing zone."

The recon-platoon leader adds: "As they regrouped I saw what must have been a company commander, North Vietnamese, running back and forth along his line of men encouraging them and rallying them. He then led a second attack. I admired his courage, because there were at least twenty of us all trying to stop him. After a third attempt, the NVA didn't try to come across the landing zone again. Rather, they started coming around to the north side."

Alpha Company's commander, Captain Sugdinis, was in the trees, headed to where he had seen the battalion command group disappear. "Just as I noticed a small clearing up ahead I heard one or two shots to my rear, back where my 1st and 2nd Platoons were. I looked back. There was a pause of several seconds and then slowly all hell began to break loose. Since I was somewhat forward of the remainder of my Company and did not draw fire in the initial exchange, I continued to move forward toward Albany. I knew I had to establish a perimeter that would accommodate helicopters, provide fields of fire and be a distinctive piece of terrain for people to maneuver toward."

Albany was not a typical landing zone—the usual single clearing surrounded by trees. In fact, the small clearing that Captain Sugdinis believed to be Albany was actually only the first of two clearings. A lightly wooded island separated it from a larger clearing up ahead. Within that grove of trees there were at least three giant termite hills: one at the edge of the trees, on the north side; another on the western end; and a third in the middle. The copse was not completely surrounded by open area; the east and west ends were connected to the forest by a few trees about twenty feet or so apart.

Captain Sugdinis says, "Larry Gwin and I hit the edge of Albany on the northeast side of the clearing as the column began to receive intense fire. We began to receive sporadic sniper fire. Part of the recon platoon had already reached the island. I yelled across the opening for someone to cover us. We ran to the island. At this point I called my 1st and 2nd Platoons on the radio. Almost immediately I lost communication with the 1st Platoon. The platoon sergeant for the 2nd Platoon came on the radio. That was SFC William A. Ferrell, thirty-eight, from Stanton, Tennessee. He was a veteran of World War II and Korea, had been a prisoner of war in Korea, and could have chosen to remain in the States. He did not have to deploy to Vietnam with us. Everyone called him Pappy."

Ferrell kept asking Captain Sugdinis where he was, telling him they were mixed up with the North Vietnamese and had several wounded and killed. "I couldn't pinpoint his location. I knew where he should have been—directly east of our island. Pappy then radioed that he was hit; that there were three or four men with him, all hit. I could hear the firing at his location over the radio. I never heard from Pappy again. He did not survive.

"The survivors of my 1st Platoon, with the recon platoon, were the initial defenses at Albany. The battalion command group made it safely into the perimeter. Bob McDade and Frank Henry probably owe their lives to those North Vietnamese prisoners. If they hadn't come forward when they did, and stayed forward, they would have been further back in the column and probably would not have survived. At some point at Albany I asked what had become of the North Vietnamese prisoners and was told that they had attempted to escape when the shooting started and had been shot."

Lieutenant Colonel McDade himself recalls, "When things began happening I got in with Alpha Company. I know I was trying to figure out what was going on. I moved very fast—let's get over here in these trees and let's all get together. The enemy seemed to be all over the woods. We had good tight control in the immediate area and were trying to figure out where everybody else was. One of the things I was very concerned with was people being trigger-happy and just shooting up the grass. I was telling them: 'Make sure you know what you are shooting at because we are scattered!' "

Sergeant Jim Gooden, the battalion's assistant operations sergeant, was with the headquarters detachment, toward the rear of the column. "We were getting fire from three sides. We were getting it from up in the trees, and from both sides. A guy got hit next to me and I grabbed his machine gun. I braced myself against an anthill. Then we got hit by mortars. It was zeroed in right on us. I looked around and everybody was dead. The commo sergeant, SFC Melvin Gunter, fell over hit in the face, dead. The same mortar round that killed Gunter put shrapnel in my back and shoulder. They were closing in for the final assault. I was shooting, trying to break a hole through them, but didn't know which way to go. I went the wrong way, right into the killing zone. I found stacks of GIs." Gunter, thirty-eight, was from Vincent, Alabama.

The battalion operations officer, Captain Spires, believes that the fact that the commanders were absent from their companies when the fight started contributed to the confusion. "It had the most effect, I think, on Charlie Company. Their commander, Captain Skip Fesmire, was up with us and Don Cornett, the Charlie Company executive officer, was killed early on, so they had no commander and they just disintegrated."

Spires also remembers that the shooting began "at the head of the column; then it moved back down the column. I think the enemy battalion ran head on into the recon and Alpha Company troops, withdrew, hooked around, and ran straight into Charlie Company. They also hit part of Delta Company. The battalion command group was just ahead of Delta Company. I had four men back there, including my operations sergeant, and three of them were killed."

Specialist 4 Jim Epperson, McDade's radio operator, says: "We set our radios down behind an anthill. The artillery guys were on their own radio calling in. We honestly did not know much about the situation in the rest of the column. Some of the radio operators were already killed. We were cut off from everyone. Colonel McDade wasn't getting anything from his people down the line. Charlie, Delta, and Headquarters Company weren't reporting because they were either dead or, in the case of Headquarters, didn't have any radios."

By now it was 1:26 P.M. The recon platoon; the Alpha Company commander, Sugdinis, and his executive officer, Gwin; and Colonel

McDade's command group were in the small wooded area between the two clearings. Sugdinis and Gwin were near one of the termite hills, Payne's recon platoon was near another, and McDade and his group were behind the third hill.

Lieutenant Larry Gwin looked back south at the point where he and Captain Sugdinis had emerged from the jungle just minutes before; the entire area was now alive with North Vietnamese soldiers who had obviously cut through the battalion's line of march, severing the head of the battalion from the body. Gwin saw three GIs coming through the high grass, running from the area swarming with the enemy. "I jumped up and screamed to them, waving my arm. They saw me and headed directly to our position. The first man was Captain Kenneth L. Weitzel, our 229th helicopter liaison officer, who was completely spent. I pointed out the battalion command group, which was huddled to our rear at another anthill, and he crawled toward them. He was followed by the battalion sergeant major, Jim Scott, who dropped down next to me. And Scott was followed by a young, very small PFC who was delirious and holding his guts in with his hands. He kept asking, 'Are the helicopters coming?' I said, 'Yes, hang on.' "

"The battalion commander initially thought that the incoming rounds were all friendly fire. He had been hollering for all of us to cease fire and the word went out over the command net but to no avail, as the troops on the perimeter could *see* North Vietnamese. The sergeant major and I were looking to the rear when I heard a loud blast. The sergeant major yelled: 'I'm hit, sir!' He had taken a round in the back under his armpit and there was a large hole underneath his right arm. I told him he would be OK, to bandage it himself. This he did, ripping off his shirt. Then he picked up his M-16 and headed back to one of the ant hills. I saw the sergeant major a few times after that and he was fighting like a demon."

Sergeant Major Scott says, "I took a bullet through my chest, not more than fifteen or twenty minutes into the battle. I could see enemy soldiers to our left, right and front in platoon- and company-size elements. They were up in the trees, up on top of the anthills, and in the high grass. We weren't exactly organized. We didn't have time. Everything happened at once. I did not see a hole being dug prior to eight P.M. that night. We did use the trees and anthills for cover. Within half an hour there was an attempt to organize groups into a defensive position in a company area. Individuals did this, no one in particular. I think that is what saved us."

Lieutenant Gwin rejoined the Alpha Company command group on the western edge of the copse of trees. "Joel Sugdinis told me that our 1st Platoon, on our right, was gone, and that the 2nd Platoon, to our rear, was cut off and all wounded or dead. I stood up to get a better view of the woods on the other side of the clearing to the north and saw about twenty North Vietnamese bent over, charging toward our position and only about sixty yards away. I screamed 'Here they come!' and jumped forward firing. I heard the battalion commander yell 'Withdraw!' and I thought that was odd because there didn't seem like anywhere to go.

"Almost everyone jumped up and ran back to the third anthill. First Sergeant Frank Miller; Joel Sugdinis; the artillery FO, Hank Dunn; and PFC Dennis Wilson, the radio operator; and I stayed and killed all the North Vietnamese. I shot about three with my first burst, and then remember sighting in on the lead enemy, who was carrying an AK-47. I got him with my first round, saw him drop to the ground and start to crawl forward. I was afraid he would throw a grenade. I sighted very carefully and squeezed again, and saw him jolted by my second round, but he continued to move and I stepped out from cover and emptied my remaining rounds into him. He was about twenty yards from our anthill. The rush had been stopped, but we could still see many, many Vietnamese milling around on the other side of the clearing."

The Alpha Company command group now returned to their original position, facing the area where they had first emerged from the forest, to the southwest. Lieutenant Gwin says, "Joel Sugdinis and I had pretty much decided we would make our stand right here. No point in moving. The North Vietnamese were between us and the rest of the battalion column, and that jungle was crawling with bad guys. They were fighting, moving on down the column."

Sugdinis and Gwin agree that it was not long after this that the commander of Alpha Company's missing 2nd Platoon, Lieutenant Gordon Grove, staggered into the American position from the east. Larry Gwin: "I saw Gordy Grove coming across the field along with two wounded men. They were the only ones left of his platoon who could move. Grove was distraught. We got him and his two men in with us, and got our medics working on the wounded. Then Gordy asked for men to go back with him and get his people. Joel Sugdinis said: 'Gordy, I can't send anybody back out there.' It was clear that to leave this perimeter was death. Everywhere you looked you could see North Vietnamese. Gordy asked permission to go talk to the battalion commander. Sugdinis said go ahead. He jogged over, asked McDade for help to go get his men, got a negative response, so he came back to our anthill."

Gwin adds, "There was a tremendous battle going on in the vicinity of where we had come into the clearing and beyond there in the jungle. It was Charlie Company, caught in the killing zone of the ambush, fighting for its life. The mortar fire had ceased—the enemy tubes apparently had been overrun by Charlie Company, because we found them all the next day—but there still were hundreds of North Vietnamese calmly walking around the area we were observing. Now began the sniping phase of our battle. I call it that because for a long period of time all we did was pick off enemy wandering around our perimeter, and this lasted until we started getting air support. Everything that had happened to this point had probably taken less than thirty minutes."

Gwin saw Major Frank Henry, the battalion executive officer, lying on his back using the radio, trying desperately to get some tactical air support and succeeding. "The air was on the way, but there was no artillery or aerial rocket artillery yet. Jim Spires, the S-3, ran over to us and queried Gordy Grove as to the situation outside the perimeter where he had just come from. Grove told him there were still men out there, tightened into a small perimeter, but they were all wounded and dying and the radios had all been knocked out. Captain Spires asked a second time if he thought anyone was still alive and none of us said anything."

Gwin climbed atop the termite hill and began sniping at the

North Vietnamese clearly visible across the clearing in the trees to the south with his M-16 rifle. "There were plenty of targets and I remember picking off ten or fifteen NVA from my position. My memories revolve around the way in which each enemy soldier that I hit fell. Some would slump limply to the ground; some reacted as if they had been hit by a truck. Some that I missed on the first and second shots kept on milling around until I finally hit them. What we did not know at the time was that they were wandering around the elephant grass looking for Americans who were still alive, and killing them off one by one."

After an incoming round snapped past his head, Gwin surrendered his vantage point to Lieutenant Grove, who was eager to settle some scores for his lost platoon. Gwin and his boss, Captain Sugdinis, eased behind the hill, leaned back, and smoked their first cigarettes. Gwin says, "That cigarette brought us back to our senses, and we talked the situation over while those around us poured out fire. We knew we had lost our two Alpha Company rifle platoons, about fifty men, during the first half-hour. Joel was despondent."

The survivors in that thinly held grove of trees at the head of the battalion column could hear the noise of a terrible battle continuing in the forest where the rest of the column was caught. Having hit the head of the 2nd Battalion column hard and stopped it, killing most of Sugdinis's two rifle platoons, the North Vietnamese soldiers immediately raced down the side of the American column, with small groups peeling off and attacking.

As the attack began, all of McDade's company commanders were forward, separated from their men. They had brought their radio operators and, in some cases, their first sergeants and artillery forward observers with them. All of them but one would remain in McDade's perimeter for the rest of the battle.

In answer to the radioed summons from Colonel McDade, Captain George Forrest, a high school and college athlete who was in excellent physical condition, had hiked more than five hundred yards from his Alpha Company, 1st Battalion, 5th Cavalry position, at the tail of the American column, to the head. His two radio operators accompanied him.

Just about the time McDade started to talk to them, a couple of mortar rounds came in. Forrest immediately turned and dashed back toward his company. "I didn't wait for him to dismiss us. I just took off. Both of my radio operators were hit and killed during that run. I didn't get a scratch. When I got back to the company I found my executive officer was down, hit in the back with mortar shrapnel. I wasn't sure about the situation, so I pushed my guys off the trail to the east and put them in a perimeter. It appeared for a time that fire was coming from every direction. So we circled the wagons. I think that firing lasted thirty-five or forty minutes. All my platoon leaders were functioning except Second Lieutenant Larry L. Hess. [Hess, age twenty, from Gettysburg, Pennsylvania, was killed in the first minutes.] My weapons sergeant was wounded."

George Forrest's run down that six-hundred-yard-long gauntlet of fire, miraculously unscathed, and the forming of his men into a defensive perimeter, helped keep Alpha Company, 1st Battalion, 5th Cavalry from sharing the fate of Charlie, Delta, and Headquarters companies of the 2nd Battalion in the middle of the column.

North Vietnamese soldiers climbed into the trees and on top of those brush-covered termite hills, and poured fire down on the cavalry troopers trapped in the tall grass below them in the main body of the column. There was furious firing, including mortar fire, from both sides. The strike at the head of the column was followed so quickly by the enemy encircling assaults that the whole business seemed to erupt almost simultaneously.

Without doubt some platoons of McDade's battalion were alert and in as secure a formation as they could achieve in the elephant grass, brush, and thick scrub trees. But the visibility problem made it difficult to maintain formation, and one result was that the American troops were closer to one another than was tactically sound, providing juicy targets for a grenade, a mortar round, or a burst from an AK-47 rifle. All down the column, platoon leaders, sergeants, radio operators, and riflemen by the dozens were killed or wounded in the first ten minutes, rapidly degrading communication, cohesion, and control.

Captain Skip Fesmire was near the Albany clearing when the

shooting started. He believed his Charlie Company rifle platoons were close enough to the landing zone to maneuver against the enemy and reach the clearing if he moved them quickly and if he was lucky. Fesmire radioed Jim Spires, the battalion operations officer, reported his location, and told Spires he was returning to his men. He never made it.

Fesmire remembers: "The firing became quite intense. My artillery forward observer [Lieutenant Sidney C. M. Smith, twenty-three, of Manhasset, New York] was hit in the head and killed. I was in radio contact with Lieutenant Cornett [Fesmire's executive officer]. He told me that the fire was very intense, particularly incoming mortar fire that was impacting directly on the company. I instructed him to get the company moving forward along the right flank of Delta Company. This was the direction from which the attack was coming. I felt it was necessary to try to consolidate the battalion; to help protect the flank of Delta Company, and to get Charlie Company out of the mortar killing zone."

Captain Fesmire adds, "As I moved back southeast toward my company, I could see the North Vietnamese in the tree line on the other side of a clearing. They were moving generally in the same direction that I was moving, toward Charlie Company. By this time Lieutenant Cornett had Charlie Company moving; they met the elements of the 66th Regiment's battalion head on and were outnumbered. The result was very intense, individual hand-to-hand combat. In the confusion, I had no idea exactly where the company was located. When Lieutenant Cornett died, it was virtually impossible for me to talk to anyone in my company. The battle had clearly become an individual struggle for life. First Sergeant [Franklin] Hance, my two radio operators and I found our return to the company blocked. We were on the edge of an open area and all we could see were enemy."

Specialist 4 Jack P. Smith, who was in Charlie Company, had been a radio operator until a week or so before this operation, when he was shifted to a supply clerk's job. The events of November 17 are etched on his mind. Smith's company commander, Captain Fesmire, had, like the others, been called to the front by Lieutenant

Colonel McDade. "Subsequently, many people pointed to this as a major error, and in light of what happened, it was. The firing began to roll all around us. The executive officer of my company, a man called Don Cornett, a very fine officer, jumped up and in the best style of the Infantry School yelled: 'Follow me!'

"Elements of our 1st and 2nd platoons ran right toward a series of anthills. Within ten feet of them we saw there were machine gunners behind them firing point-blank at us. Men all around me began to fall like mown grass. I had never seen people killed before. They began to drop like flies and die right in front of me. These were the only friends I had, and they were dying all around me."

Charlie Company, 2nd Battalion, 7th Cavalry would suffer the heaviest casualties of any unit that fought at LZ Albany. Before its violent collision with the North Vietnamese, the company had some 112 men in its ranks. By sunrise the next day, November 18, forty-five of those men would be dead and more than fifty wounded; only a dozen would answer "present" at the next roll call.

Captain Henry Thorpe, the Delta Company commander, was a hundred yards forward of his company when the fighting began. He and his first sergeant and radio operator sprinted ahead into the island of trees in the Albany clearing to join the battalion command group and helped organize and control a defensive perimeter. The radio operator, Specialist 4 John C. Bratland, was shot in the leg. They were lucky to be where they were. Delta Company, back down the column, was being torn apart. This day it would lose twenty-six men killed and many others severely wounded.

PFC James H. Shadden was in Thorpe's Delta Company mortar platoon. Shadden says the heavily laden mortarmen, exhausted from the march, had dropped in the trail for a short rest and a smoke. He recalls, "I had carried the base plate a long ways. Sergeant Amodias, true to his word, took the base plate, gave me the sights, and went in front of me. When the enemy sprung the ambush, Amodias was killed instantly. The ones who were not killed in the first volley hit the dirt, with the exception of our radio operator, Duncan Krueger. I saw him still standing a few seconds later, until he was shot down. I have no idea why he didn't get down."

PFC Duncan Krueger, eighteen, of West Allis, Wisconsin, was killed where he stood.

The intensity of the fire rapidly increased to the point where Shadden couldn't hear anything but weapons firing. "Tone Johnson came crawling by me, hit in the cheek and back of the hand. The trees were full of North Vietnamese, but spotting one was almost impossible. They blended in so well. I kept raising up to try to detect a good target. Matthews Shelton, who was lying next to me, kept jerking me down. As I raised up again a bullet pierced my helmet straight through, front to back. I went down again and as I came back up a bullet struck the tree beside my head from behind.

"I don't know if we were surrounded or it was our own men. They were firing wild—anything that moved, somebody shot at it. One trooper crawled up next to me, shooting through the grass a few inches off the ground toward where our own people lay, never thinking what he was doing. I told him to be sure he knew what he was shooting."

The firing eventually began to slack off. Shadden has no idea how much time elapsed. There was no way to keep track of time in a fight like this. "Men were wounded and dead all in the area. Six were alive that I know of: Sergeant [Earthell] Tyler, [PFC A. C.] Carter, [PFC Tone] Johnson, [PFC Matthews] Shelton, [PFC Lawrence] Cohens, and myself. Tyler gave the only order I heard during the entire fight: 'Try to pull back before they finish us off.' Shelton froze to the ground and would not move. [PFC Matthews Shelton, age twenty, of Cincinnati, Ohio, was killed later that afternoon.] The five of us proceeded to try to pull back, but the snipers were still in the trees. Soon I was hit in the right shoulder, which for a time rendered it useless. Tyler was hit in the neck about the same time; he died an arm's length of me, begging for the medic, Specialist 4 William Pleasant, who was already dead. [Pleasant was twenty-three years old and a native of Jersey City, New Jersey.] The last words Tyler ever spoke were 'I'm dying.' " Sergeant Earthell Tyler, thirty-five, was from Columbia, South Carolina.

The soft-spoken Shadden says, "The helplessness I felt is beyond description. Within a few minutes I was hit again, in the left knee.

The pain was unbearable. Cohens was hit in the feet and ankle. We were wounded and trapped. I could see we were getting wiped out. A buddy helped me bandage my leg. He got the bandage off a dead Vietnamese. I got behind a log and there was a Vietnamese there, busted up and dead. This was behind us, so I knew we were surrounded."

Specialist 4 Bob Towles, who was with Delta Company's antitank platoon, heard the firing and mortar blasts forward and could see where the trail disappeared into the brush ahead of him. But he saw no one at all up there. As the front came alive with intense firing, and no information came back to him, Towles's concern redoubled:

"The sound of firing on our right flank got our attention in a hurry. We all faced in that direction. A couple of senior NCOs moved forward and joined the line of enlisted men. We formed a solid battle line about twenty yards long; twelve of us. Bullets whizzed overhead. Still we could see nothing. We waited, expecting to see our men out on flank security break cover and enter the safety of our perimeter. They never did. The sound came closer. Within seconds the wood line changed.

"North Vietnamese troops shattered the foliage and headed straight for us, AK-47 rifles blazing, on the dead run. I selected the closest one and fired twice. I hit him but he refused to go down; he kept coming and shooting. I turned my M-16 on full automatic, fired, and he crumpled. I shifted to another target and squeezed the trigger. Nothing happened. The fear I felt turned to terror. I saw a cartridge jammed in the chamber. I removed it, reloaded, and began firing again. They kept pouring out of the wood line; we kept firing; then finally they stopped coming. On the ground in front of me lay the three magazines I taped together to carry in my rifle plus one other magazine. I had fired eighty rounds."

The lull did not last long. Towles peered beyond the anthill toward the mortar platoon. "It appeared as if the ground was opening up and swallowing the mortarmen, they fell so fast," Shadden recalls. "A brown wave of death rolled over them and on into Charlie Company. Vietnamese intermixed with them. Then reality set in:

The enemy held the ground beyond the anthill. The column was cut in half!

"Incoming gunfire drew our attention back to the tree line. The firing rapidly increased. We returned fire at muzzle flashes. I heard an explosion behind me. Turning, I saw ChiCom grenades landing. All flash and smoke, no casualties. The volume of fire became almost unendurable. Bullets peeled bark from trees. Vegetation disintegrated. I looked to Lieutenant James Lawrence for help. Saw his head violently recoil. He hit the ground.

"A second later I was spun around, then slammed into the dirt. I rose to my hands and knees and started down the line. Blood ran everywhere. The mortar-platoon sergeant's .45 pistol had been shot from his hand. His right hand hung limp from his wrist, and blood poured to the ground. Someone tried to dress his wound. Someone raised Lieutenant Lawrence and attempted to steady him. The firing continued."

Towles's tight twelve-man line was shrinking fast. "I turned back toward the wood line and detected movement. I shifted in that direction and spotted North Vietnamese in the underbrush. Enemy turning our flank! Our position was no longer tenable. I turned back with the warning. Sergeant Jerry Baker took charge now; he realized we needed to pull out. He appointed the unwounded and some slightly wounded to help the severely wounded. An instant later he ordered the move.

"I led this retreat because of my position on the battle line. I rose to my feet and headed in the only direction void of enemy fire—toward our left rear—at a run. Thirty or forty yards and I broke out of the trees into a large clearing of waist-deep grass. The sunlight hurt my eyes. Twenty yards into the field I noticed the man running a half-step to my rear go down. I dove to the ground and turned to see PFC Marlin Klarenbeek struggling with a leg wound."

Captain George Forrest was now back with his Alpha Company, 1st Battalion, 5th Cavalry soldiers at the rear of the column. "I had lost my radio operators, and when I got back and got another radio I found out McDade's lead elements were in heavy firefights to their front and to their west. I got maybe two transmissions from

McDade, then lost contact. We circled up. My parent battalion had come up on my net and I was able to contact Captain Buse Tully, commander of Bravo Company, 1st Battalion, 5th Cav. I have never felt such relief at hearing and recognizing a voice. I knew someone who cared about us was close at hand."

Here's what the Vietnam War looked like in midafternoon of November 17, through the eyes of two of Captain Forrest's Alpha Company riflemen, PFC David A. (Purp) Lavender of Murphysboro, Illinois, and Specialist 4 James Young of Steelville, Missouri.

Says Lavender: "My platoon was bringing up the rear. We started to maneuver and work our way up the column to help those up ahead. Every time we made a move we were hit by mortars. It was something you can't describe. People were dropping like flies. The first blast killed a young soldier named [PFC Vincent] Locatelli. Every time we moved they dropped mortars on us. I know we must have had twelve or fifteen wounded out of our platoon, including our platoon leader.

"These were my buddies I had been in the Army with for two years. [The] majority of our whole battalion had been drafted at age twenty-one [and] had been in service for over eighteen months. All of us were near twenty-three years old. They became my brothers over time. Hearing these fellows scream, hearing them killed, stuck in my heart and mind ever since. The most critical part of this fight was the beginning. It was the surprise. They had us in a U-shaped ambush and they had us cut off with mortars."

Rifleman Jim Young says: "I sat down and took a nap. We had flankers out a hundred yards or so on left and right, so I thought it was safe to grab some sleep. That little bit of shooting up front got a lot worse. That woke me up. Then our 1st Platoon received mortar fire. Five men wounded. I heard them calling for medics. Mortars kept coming in. Heard them order 1st Platoon to pull back out of the area where those rounds were hitting."

Young's platoon was ordered to get on line and move in reaction to the enemy fire. "Everyone had hit the ground when those mortars began coming in. They told us to move ahead toward the enemy. We got on line and we walked right into an enemy ambush. They were behind trees, anthills, and down on the ground. There was waist-high grass and a lot of trees around us. There were enemy soldiers in that grass. They were hard to see and we had to shoot where we thought they were. The medic had his hands full, couldn't take care of all the wounded. One man to my right was hit in the heel. His name was Harold Smith.

"There was a grassy field to my left twenty-five or thirty yards, and a sniper off on my right. I couldn't see him, but I saw a tracer bullet go across my hand. I felt the wind of that bullet. The same bullet passed over the back of Smith's neck. He was lucky he had his head down. Our company commander, Captain Forrest, came running along our line. He was stopping and telling everybody where to go. He acted as though he was immune to the enemy fire. I don't know how he kept from getting hit."

Just ahead of Alpha Company, 1st Battalion, in the hodgepodge of admin and supply staffers, medics, and communications people that constituted Headquarters Company of the 2nd Battalion, 7th Cavalry marched Doc William Shucart, the 2nd Battalion surgeon; Lieutenant John Howard of the medical platoon, and Lieutenant Bud Alley, the communications-platoon leader.

Says Shucart: "Before the fight I remember smelling cigarette smoke. Vietnamese cigarettes. I said: 'I smell the enemy smoking!' The next thing we knew mortars were dropping all around us, then a lot of small-arms fire was coming in, and then everything just dissolved into confusion. We thought that the head of the column had gotten turned and somehow we were getting shot by our own troops. Guys were dropping all around us. It seems like in a very short time I found myself all alone. We had gotten widely dispersed. I was running around with my M-16. I had a .45 pistol, which was useless, and I picked up somebody's M-16.

"I was under direct enemy fire all this time. I got one little zinger up my back; nothing serious, just a grazing wound that left me a nice little scar. This was the most scared I've ever been in my life. I was wearing a St. Christopher's medal around my neck that somebody had sent me. I thought: *This is the time to make a deal.* Then I thought: *I've never been very religious. He isn't likely to want to deal.*

So I got up and started looking for somebody, anybody. I found one of our radio operators, dead, and got on his radio trying to raise somebody. I remember trying to get them to throw some smoke so I could find them."

Lieutenant John Howard remembers: "Soon after the first shots, mortars and grenades started hitting all around us. The small-arms fire then picked up to an intense level and soldiers started going down very quickly with gunshot or shrapnel wounds. There was confusion, and some thought they were being fired at by other American soldiers in the area. This confusion cleared up pretty quickly as the North Vietnamese assault wave moved in so close that we could see them and hear them talking.

"They suddenly appeared behind anthills and up in the trees, sniping at anyone who moved, and we found ourselves shooting at them in all directions. As we crawled around in the tall elephant grass it was very difficult to tell where anyone was, or whether they were friendly or enemy. One thing I caught on to very quickly was how the NVA were signaling to each other in the high grass by tapping on the wooden stocks of their AK-47 rifles."

Lieutenant Bud Alley recalls clearly when "word came back that recon had been shot at. Then that recon had hit an ambush. Then orders to Charlie Company, just in front of us, to move on line and roll up the flank of it. John Howard and I were sitting beside each other. All of a sudden a couple of shots rang out twenty-five yards in front of us. By now we're all standing up, scared. The call comes back: 'Medic! Medic!' The first group of medics in front of us takes off and John Howard takes off with them. Now the leaves begin to shake as bullets are coming in. The infantry in Charlie Company are yelling: 'Get on line!' I pushed my guys up on line, twenty-five yards inside the tree line, and suddenly all hell broke loose. There was lots of shooting and it was difficult to maintain the line.

"A fellow got hit and screamed. My radio operator and I ran up to him and dragged him behind a little tree. He was shot through the wrist and kept screaming. Then he got shot again. I put my M-16 on automatic and fired up high and something fell out of the tree. I crawled down to an anthill where a couple of guys were. I stayed there and found a guy who had a radio. I called in to see what the hell was happening. About then the net went dead; somebody got shot with his finger on the transmit key, or something. The last thing I heard on the net was that Ghost 5 got hit; that was Don Cornett, the Charlie Company executive officer."

Colonel Tim Brown, the 3rd Brigade commander, the man who had the authority to order in reinforcements, was overhead in his command helicopter asking his ground commander, Lieutenant Colonel Bob McDade, for information on the seriousness of the situation. With Brown was the brigade fire-support coordinator, Captain Dudley Tademy, who was eager to unleash all the artillery, air support, and aerial rocket artillery at his command.

Brown and Tademy had just left LZ Columbus where they had been talking to Lieutenant Colonel Tully when the first shots were fired at Albany. Colonel Brown was headed back to brigade headquarters at the tea plantation.

Captain Tademy recalls, "Suddenly I heard Joe Price, the artillery forward observer with McDade's battalion, saying 'We have a problem! I need help!' Price was hollering for everything he could get: air, artillery, ARA. We finally got him to slow down so we could understand what was happening. I notified Colonel Brown that something was going on down there. He tried to get on the command net and talk to McDade. I stayed on the artillery net trying to get some support for them. By then we were overflying their position and we could see puffs of smoke coming out of the woods. When Joe Price would come up on the net I could hear the loud firing over their radio."

Major Roger Bartholomew, commander of the aerial rocket artillery helicopters, was in contact with Captain Tademy and flew a zigzag pattern over the forest trying to get a fix on the location of friendly troops so that his helicopters could support them. He had no luck. Captain Tademy had the artillery fire smoke rounds to try to register defensive fires. No luck there either. "It didn't help because everybody was so mixed up by then on the ground. We had tactical air, ARA, and artillery and still we couldn't do a damned thing. It was the most helpless, hopeless thing I ever witnessed."

Colonel Tim Brown's helicopter was running low on fuel and the chopper had to return to Catecka to refuel. Brown says, "I knew they were in contact. I did not know how severe, or anything else. While I was talking to McDade I could hear the rifle fire, but he didn't know what was happening. I asked: 'What happened to your lead unit?' He didn't know. 'Where's your trailing units?' He didn't know. And he didn't know what had happened to any of the rest of them. Nobody knew what the hell was going on. We were not in [a] position to shoot a bunch of artillery or air strikes in there because we didn't know where to put them."

Captain John Cash, in the center of the now busy Brigade Headquarters at Catecka, recalls the return of Colonel Brown: "Brown was standing there, on our radio, asking McDade what's going on, yelling, 'Goddammit, what is going on out there?' McDade came back with, 'Got a couple of KIAs [killed in action] here and trying to get a handle on the situation. Let me get back to you later. Out.' Captain Tademy, who was at Brown's side in the tactical operations center [TOC] says, "I heard McDade talking. Brown kept asking him what was going on. The radio speakers were all blaring. What I was hearing was that things were not going very well in McDade's area."

After his command helicopter had refueled, Brown flew back into the valley. "All of a sudden I heard all kinds of firing while I was talking to McDade on the radio. He started yelling: 'They're running! They're running!' I thought for one terrible moment he meant that his battalion was running. What it was, the Air Force had dropped napalm on a company-size North Vietnamese unit and *they* were running, not the Americans. About then I began to figure that McDade was in real trouble."

Only now did Colonel Brown begin rounding up reinforcements to send in to help Bob McDade's 2nd Battalion. Brown ordered Lieutenant Colonel Frederic Ackerson to send a company from his 1st Battalion, 5th Cavalry overland from LZ Columbus toward LZ Albany. Ackerson dispatched Captain Walter B. (Buse) Tully's Bravo Company, 1st Battalion, 5th Cavalry on the two-mile march toward the tail of McDade's embattled column. Meanwhile, Brown radioed orders warning McDade's missing component, Captain Myron Diduryk's Bravo Company, 2nd Battalion, 7th Cav, to prepare to be airlifted from Camp Holloway into Landing Zone Albany.

Brown acknowledges that it was too little, too late. "I've thought a good deal about this action over the years, and I believe that most of the casualties occurred in the first hour of fighting. I think the bulk of it was done right at the very first. They did not have decent security for moving through a jungle."

Lieutenant Colonel McDade for his part confirms that he was unable to provide Colonel Brown with detailed reports of what was happening to three of the four companies in his stalled column—most of which were out of sight and out of reach. Says McDade: "In that first hour or so, the situation was so fluid that I was acting more as a platoon leader than a battalion commander. We were trying to secure a perimeter. I was trying to figure out what the hell was going on, myself. I don't think anybody in the battalion could have told you what the situation really was at that time. I can see where I might have left Tim Brown in the dark about what was going on; I didn't really know myself until things quieted down."

The battalion commander adds, "I could have yelled and screamed that we were in a death trap, and all that crap. But I didn't know it was as bad as it was. I had no way of checking visually or physically, by getting out of that perimeter, so all I could do was hope to get back in touch. I wasn't going to scream that the sky was falling, especially in a situation where nobody could do anything about it anyway."

Lieutenant Colonel John A. Hemphill was the operations officer at Brigadier General Knowles's division forward command post at Pleiku. He recalls that he and Knowles flew over the Ia Drang on November 17 and watched the B-52 bombing strike on the Chu Pong massif. They then flew back to Pleiku. Says Hemphill: "When we got back to Pleiku, here came Tim Brown to see Knowles. I brought him to Knowles and he said, 'I have not heard from or made contact with McDade and I am concerned.' So we went piling out and flew out in late afternoon, and that's when I think was the first time we were aware that anything was amiss."

Although Knowles does not recall the Brown visit to his head-quarters described by Hemphill, he does have a vivid memory of how he first learned that McDade's battalion was heavily engaged with the enemy. "I had a warrant officer in the support command at Pleiku. His job was to watch the beans, bullets, fuel, and casualties. He had a direct hotline to me; I wanted to know immediately when things got off track. In the afternoon, around two or three o'clock, he called me and said: 'I got fourteen KIA from McDade's battalion.' All the bells went off. I called my pilot, Wayne Knudsen, and John Stoner, my air liaison officer, and went out to see McDade. I stopped at 3rd Brigade before flying on out to Albany. Tim Brown had nothing to tell me."

Knowles adds, "We got over Albany and McDade was in deep trouble. I wanted to land. McDade said, 'General, I can't handle you. I can't even get medevac in.' I couldn't land. I wanted to get something moving on the ground over there. I told Stoner and Bill Becker, the division artillery commander, 'This guy doesn't know what he's got; put a ring of steel around him.' I could help him with firepower and did. I then went back to see Tim, who still had no information. I was irked. A hell of a mess; no question."

The 2nd Battalion, 7th Cavalry had been reduced from a full battalion in column line of march to a small perimeter defended by a few Alpha Company survivors, the recon platoon, a handful of stragglers from Charlie and Delta Companies, and the battalion command group at the Albany landing-zone clearing—plus one other small perimeter, five hundred to seven hundred yards south, which consisted of Captain George Forrest's Alpha Company, 1st Battalion, 5th Cavalry. In between, dead or wounded or hiding in the tall grass, was the bulk of Bob McDade's command: the fragments of two rifle companies, a weapons company, and Headquarters Company.

Each and every man still alive on that field, American and North Vietnamese, was fighting for his life. In the tall grass it was nearly impossible for the soldiers of either side to identify friend or foe except at extremely close range. Americans in olive-drab and North

Vietnamese in mustard-brown were fighting and dying side by side. It may have begun as a meeting engagement, a hasty ambush, a surprise attack, a battle of maneuver—and, in fact, it was all of those things—but within minutes the result was a wild mêlée, a shoot-out, with the gunfighters killing not only the enemy but sometimes their friends just a few feet away.

There would be no cheap victory here this day for either side. There would be no victory at all—just the terrible certainty of death in the tall grass.

20

DEATH IN THE
TALL GRASS

> I did not mean to be killed today.
>
> —dying words of the Vicomte de Turenne, at the
> Battle of Salzbach, 1675

The North Vietnamese commander on the battlefield, Nguyen Huu An, has a keen memory of that bloody afternoon of November 17, 1965, on the trail to Landing Zone Albany: "My commanders and soldiers reported there was very vicious fighting. I tell you frankly, your soldiers fought valiantly. They had no choice. You are dead or not. It was hand-to-hand fighting. Afterward, when we policed the battlefield, when we picked up our wounded, the bodies of your men and our men were neck to neck, lying alongside each other. It was most fierce." That it was, and nowhere more fierce than along that strung-out American column where the cavalry rifle companies had been cut into small groups.

Lieutenant John Howard was with Headquarters Company near the tail of the column. "At some point early in the battle I was situated next to a large anthill. A sergeant not far from me had received a nasty wound to his foot and he was screaming in pain. I crawled over next to him and started to bandage his foot. No sooner had I told him to try to quit screaming than I was hit by a bullet which spun me completely around on the ground. It had hit me on the right side of my stomach. I pulled up my shirt to see how bad it was and, luckily, it had cut through my flesh but had not gone into my stomach. I had a flesh wound about five inches long."

Bullets continued to hit all around Howard. He grabbed the sergeant and told him they needed to move around to the other side of the anthill. "On the other side we joined up with four other soldiers who were grouped together in the grass. We continued to fire at North Vietnamese soldiers behind trees and anthills and tried to figure out what we should do next."

Although they were now out of sight of each other, Lieutenant Bud Alley, the 2nd Battalion communications officer and Howard's friend, was not far away. "It was consternation," says Alley. "Men on either side of me were being shot. At that point I had not seen any of the enemy. All I could see was the trees and our guys. I tried to move up to my right. I moved into a hail of bullets. Everyone was trying to keep moving up toward the landing zone. I was at a big anthill, pinned down by a machine gun. Fellow on my right, a Puerto Rican, was wounded. I traded the Puerto Rican PFC my .45 pistol for his machine gun.

"I took the machine gun and moved around left of the anthill and tried to move forward, firing to my front. I crawled up on a man behind a little tree; then two enemy automatic weapons opened up, cutting that little tree down. He screamed and hit me in the back. I rolled over on top of him and he had both hands over his face. He told me: 'Don't worry about me; I'm dead.' He opened his hands and he had a bullet hole right in the center of his forehead. He pulled two grenades and threw those grenades. I started crawling back to the big anthill where I had come from. I knew we weren't going forward. By the time I got back to the anthill, the wounded guy, a dead guy or two, another wounded guy, and my radio repairman were there all huddled behind that anthill. Which way do we go?"

William Shucart, the battalion surgeon, was also in that section of the column. "I got up and started looking for somebody, anybody. I ran on, and encountered a couple of enemy soldiers. This meeting scared the shit out of me and them both. I got the M-16 up and fired before they did. That was the end of that. Then I looked over and saw this sergeant leaning against a tree. He said, 'Can I give you a hand, Captain?' Calm as could be. That was Sergeant Fred Kluge of Alpha Company, 1st Battalion, 5th Cav. We went back to a larger group at the rear of the column, maybe fifteen or twenty guys, with several wounded. We were in an area with a lot of wounded and no supplies, only a few styrettes of morphine and some bandages."

Just forward of the headquarters section of the column, Charlie Company was beginning to die. Specialist 4 Jack Smith was with the lead elements in the Charlie Company formation, near Lieutenant Don Cornett, the acting company commander, when the company charged into the teeth of the enemy machine guns. In the first seconds Smith saw one of the radio operators fall dead with a bullet through the chest, his eyes and tongue bulging out. The men of Charlie Company were firing in all directions.

Suddenly, Smith says, he heard a low moan from Lieutenant Don Cornett. He tore off the officer's green fatigue shirt and saw a bullet wound in his back, to the right of his spine. He and another soldier began bandaging the lieutenant's wound. Smith thought how dependent they all were on this one man, now badly hurt, who was the only leader in reach. Then a man beside Smith was shot in the arm and a torn artery began spurting blood. Then a round tore through one of Cornett's boots, tearing away all the toes on his foot.

Now a North Vietnamese with a Maxim heavy machine gun appeared just three feet in front of Smith. The young soldier flicked the selector switch on his M-16 to full automatic and fired a long burst into the face of the enemy machine gunner. An exploding grenade took down another American close by.

Only a few minutes had passed, but Jack Smith's world was being shot to death all around him. Then, he says, something happened that convinced him to keep fighting. Lieutenant Don Cornett, in agony from his wounds, told Smith he was going to do something to try to get his troops organized. Cornett crawled away into the high grass. A brave young lieutenant died doing his duty somewhere out there in hand-to-hand fighting.

Smith recalls: "Within a span of perhaps twenty minutes everyone around me was dead or wounded, except me. You have to understand that in our area the elephant grass was chest-high; once you hit the dirt your world was about as big as a dining-room table. Your world was completely confined to that area and the six or seven men around you. At that point, we were isolated. Alpha Company was in the same shape. Then the North Vietnamese swept through. I believe they came between Alpha and our company and began to shoot people. We didn't know if the noise from five feet away, as they began to shoot people, was friendly or enemy."

Smith saw soldiers take machine guns, lie flat on the ground, and begin firing into the grass. "Often they were firing right into the muzzles of other American machine guns. People were screaming to stop the shooting. It began to have all the elements of a massacre. Nobody was in control because all the officers were to the front and our radio operators had fallen dead on their radio sets."

Just forward of Charlie Company, with the Delta Company mortars, PFC James Shadden was in agony from his two severe wounds. "By this time, some of the NVA were coming through the area killing all who were screaming and calling for medics. Snyder Bembry was killed in this manner by an English-speaking North Vietnamese, probably an officer. He shot Bembry, as Bembry screamed, with a full automatic weapon, and then spoke these words in English: 'Wait a minute. Who are we shooting?' I almost blurted out 'Americans' in answer before I realized what was happening. He had an accent." PFC Snyder P. Bembry of Unadilla, Georgia, was twenty-one years old when he died.

Unable to fight back or do anything to save his buddies from the Vietnamese executioners, James Shadden took the last course left to him: He booby-trapped his own body. "The shot in the arm left me with nothing but a grenade, which I couldn't throw left-handed, so I refrained from trying," Shadden recalls. "And more of the enemy were coming my way from the other side. So I slid the grenade under my armpit, pin pulled. I figured if they got me I might get them."

Specialist 4 Bob Towles of the Delta Company antitank platoon had run into a grassy clearing, leading the way for a dozen of his buddies, several of them badly wounded. He stopped and looked back through the woods toward the column: "I peered through the grass and managed to locate our previous position. There were the North Vietnamese, rummaging what we had left behind. Then they fired bursts from their AKs into the ground. Now I realized what else we had left behind. All of us hadn't made it out of there. I considered shooting at them. Then I thought better about it. It would only attract their attention and we were in no condition to fight."

Most of the people with Towles were wounded, sprawling on the ground and lying on top of each other. "We couldn't function as a combat unit from this pile. At that moment, Sergeant Baker ordered me to move out again. I got up and headed for the wood line on the far side of the clearing. After covering about fifty yards, I noticed movement in the trees off to my right. Americans! I cut to the right and entered the clump of trees. Ten or fifteen yards into the trees two shots rang out. I heard them whiz by behind me. Sergeant Baker lurched and fell. One bullet struck his chest, the other his back. He was a half-step behind and to the left of me. I stopped, knelt, and scanned the trees. Nothing. Sergeant Baker clutched his chest and ordered me to keep going. Just then someone else reached him and helped him to get up."

Towles rose and turned in the direction he had been heading before Baker went down. "I saw Sergeant [Miguel] Baeza kneeling behind a tree and got to him. It took a few moments to catch my breath and compose myself. Then I asked him for information about this sector. He wasn't sure. I informed him the enemy had wiped out the mortar platoon, then overran Charlie Company. Baeza pulled out his bayonet, slit my shirt sleeve, and bandaged my right arm. My hand had frozen to the pistol grip of my M-16, but my trigger finger still worked. No pain; my arm was numb.

"I looked around our position. It seemed pretty good. Trees large enough to give some protection formed an arc facing a clearing opposite the one we had just traversed. The other men formed up, facing the direction we just came from. A few men guarded off west and north. I noticed PFC Lester Becker off by himself facing east. His large tree could easily be occupied by two men. I told Sergeant Baeza I'd go over with Becker and help cover that area. I ran the ten yards to the tree and took position on the right side of it."

From behind that tree Bob Towles and Lester Becker heard moaning nearby in the tall grass of the clearing and decided to investigate. Towles remembers, "I went around the right side of the tree, Becker the left. Instantly two shots. I heard the chilling sound of the bullets' thump as they both hit soft tissue. I stared paralyzed with disbelief as Becker slumped to the ground grasping his stomach. I couldn't move. Others ran across and dragged him to the shelter of the tree. At that moment, Captain Hank Thorpe [the Delta Company commander] appeared behind us. He shouted for us to fall back to his position. We obeyed and carried Becker on a poncho. Once there, we left Becker with the medics. He survived to be medevac'd, but died later." Becker, twenty-five, was from Harvard, Illinois.

Towles's small group of Delta Company survivors had reached the Albany clearing. They joined the thin line of defenders in the cluster of trees where the battalion command post was located.

At the other end of the column, Captain George Forrest was now herding his men of Alpha Company, 1st Battalion, 5th Cavalry off the trail and into a defensive posture.

Alpha Company rifleman James Young remembers Forrest ordering their withdrawal across a grassy clearing that was under enemy fire and then asking for a volunteer for a dangerous mission. Alpha Company was taking incoming fire from a machine gun that, by the sound of it, was an American M-60. Forrest wanted someone to crawl out into the tall grass, locate the machine gun, and tell the gunners that they were shooting fellow Americans.

Young, who had grown up in the Missouri backwoods and knew something about stalking, said he would go. "Another rifleman, a PFC from Chicago, Ronald Fortune, said he would go with me. We started crawling with that machine gun firing over our heads. It was an M-60 and we all assumed it was Americans. When we got close, fifty or sixty yards away, we started yelling at them. Then I realized that they were enemy. It was as though someone told me: 'These are not our men. They are not responding to our calls.' "

Young told Fortune to stop yelling. "I continued to crawl in their direction, trying to locate their exact position. I intended to take them out. Then a bullet struck me in the head. I knew I was hit in the head, and I thought I was going to die. It dazed me good but didn't knock me out. I had my chin strap on so it didn't knock my helmet off. I asked Fortune if he would get in touch with my parents and tell them that my last concern was for them. I thought it was over for me. I asked him to bandage me. He took the bandage off my belt and he patched me up. He was telling me it wasn't too bad, that I was going to be all right.

"Then I tried to crawl in the direction of the machine gun again. Fortune thought I was out of my head and tried to stop me. We were both down low. Every time I would move he would grab me by my legs and hold me. After struggling with me for a while, he said, 'I'm going back,' and he left. I told him I was going to get that machine gun. What it was, I really was afraid to turn my back on that machine gun."

The machine-gun bullet had pierced Young's helmet and crushed his skull on one side of his head. But he was still determined to take out that gun. "As I moved I heard the Vietnamese calling out something. After that I never heard the gun fire again. What I heard were orders for them to pack it up and move. I moved to where I thought it was, still afraid to raise my head on account of snipers. There was lots of shooting. I never found the gun. They were gone."

Lieutenant Enrique Pujals—a Pennsylvania Military College classmate of Lieutenant Jack Geoghegan of Charlie Company, 1st Battalion, 7th Cav, who was killed at LZ X-Ray—was leading the twenty-four-man 3rd Platoon of Captain Skip Fesmire's Charlie Company, 2nd Battalion. His platoon, bringing up the rear of the company, was just ahead of the headquarters detachment. Pujals says he had his men in column formation, but not in single file, when the shooting erupted.

"Then I got the order on the radio: Deploy your platoon and

maneuver right. I used hand and arm signals to get the platoon on line. When I looked back, I was several yards ahead, on my own, and the platoon was still in their positions. I went back, giving verbal commands to get on line and follow me, and to pass the word. Some were getting together when the radio operator called me and said the Company Commander had a message for me: 'Hold where you are. Stop the maneuver and fire only at a target.' I tried to get information on what the hell was going on, but he said, 'Out.'

"The firing was still going on up to my right front. Then bullets started to come our way. I thought they were from the lead American elements. Not many, but they caused me concern. I tried to raise anyone on the radio to get them to watch where they fired and to give me a situation report. Still nothing. I tried to form a perimeter of sorts. Meanwhile, up front, the screams kept on as part of the weird symphony of battle sounds."

Pujals couldn't believe that the entire battalion was firing everything it had just because of a couple of snipers. "I told my radio operator that I was moving up to find the weapons platoon leader. The vegetation changed as I moved. Where my platoon was there were trees and shrubs ten to fifteen feet apart and waist-high grass (for me, five foot six inches tall, sometimes it was nearly neck high). But the weapons platoon had entered a very thick spot with thick grass, and very, very tall clumps of bushes. We were moving in column. The weapons platoon was in file."

Pujals asked a couple of the men he met where their platoon leader was, and was told: Up ahead. Very few men were prone; very few were facing out toward the firing. Most were leaning on something or other, resting. Nobody seemed to know what was going on. "I moved ahead. I was on the outskirts of the thicket when I felt a stabbing shock on my left heel. I thought I had stepped on one of those infamous punji stakes. I grabbed my left leg to pull it off, when I felt like I'd been struck with a sledgehammer on my right thigh. I saw it out of the corner of my eye—a little puff of dust and the trouser leg split and I knew I was hit.

"My thoughts were silly, a little phrase we had used back in the world to signify something was amiss: 'There goes the weekend.' My right leg just twisted all out of shape and began to crumple under me. I tried to shove myself as far back as I could to avoid having it fold under me as I fell. I made it. My leg was stretched in front in a more or less normal position. My thigh was broken. No doubt about it. I was now flat on my back and useless and helpless. What could I do? Yes, call for the medic. But what if they killed my medic as he came to help me? I was bleeding and if I kept this up I'd bleed to death so I chanced it and called.

"He came over with one of my fire-team leaders. They patched me up. I had them splint my M-16 to my right leg, up high. Then the medic took out a morphine ampule. I refused, protested, tried to avoid it, but I still got stuck. They pulled me up to a tree and helped me take off my pack. I had 15 loaded magazines in it and 800 rounds extra I'd picked up at Chu Pong. The guys from the 1st Battalion, 7th Cav had said to take as much ammo as you could carry, and then more. I asked for my two canteens and they got them for me."

Pujals called to his platoon sergeant and told him to take command, and as he did the firing shifted. "My platoon began to get it. The blades of grass were cut at the level of my chest and fell on me. Now the screams were from my men. I did not see them die, but I certainly heard them. One of them screamed, 'Oh my God, forgive me!' I still believed we were under fire by our own troops. I was extremely angry. My men were dying around me and I could do nothing. Those were my thoughts. Later I learned the truth and was ashamed."

At the head of the column, the small group of men and officers with Lieutenant Colonel McDade was locked in a heavy firefight with an enemy determined to overrun them. Captain Joel Sugdinis of Alpha Company, 2nd Battalion, still worried about his missing 2nd Platoon, had shifted to the southeastern side of the grove of trees to watch the area across the clearing where his men had disappeared.

Sugdinis recalls, "I could see movement, but I couldn't tell whether they were our people or the enemy. I saw one soldier stand up and start helping a wounded soldier hobble away from the battle. I picked up binoculars. When I focused in on the two, they were

North Vietnamese and the more healthy one was firing his AK-47 from his hip at what appeared to be objects close to his feet. My thought was that he was executing our wounded. I fired one shot and they both went down. After the battle we removed many of our 2nd Platoon dead from that area and several had been shot in the head.

"Someone from the vicinity of the command group yelled that the North Vietnamese were crawling up on us from the south. There was an open area on the south side with knee-to-waist-high grass. Those of us who were standing turned and began firing into the grass. Several North Vietnamese attempted to flee. One North Vietnamese stood up and continued to advance directly toward us firing his AK-47 from his hip, John Wayne style. I think everyone who saw him fired directly into him. I'm sure it was only a second or two, but it seemed he would never go down."

Lieutenant Pat Payne and his recon platoon had been in the thick of the fight around the Albany clearing since the beginning. "During the first hour, at least, we did not have any artillery coverage at all. We were learning a bitter lesson. The second thing is we had no helicopter coverage. We had no gunships overhead. For that first hour or two, it was belly-to-belly and man-to-man. It didn't make any difference if you were a major, captain, sergeant, or private; we were all standing shoulder to shoulder, shooting it out with the NVA. I can hear the cry 'Here they come!' and we would all rise up and cut loose. There was fear in the air, but I never sensed panic, at least not after the first ten or twenty minutes."

Payne thought the North Vietnamese had done a much better job of anticipating and preparing for the attack, "but the Americans who survived the initial onslaught began to rally. In one respect, you could think of it as the Little Bighorn; we were surrounded, with our packs in front of us, shooting it out. During the course of that long afternoon I never saw a soldier not do his duty. I never saw anyone who cowered in the face of the enemy. Our backs were against the wall and it was a matter of survival. Every person I saw rose to the occasion. Somewhere during the afternoon we started to get some sort of artillery support. However, since we were so spread out I don't recall us being able to use it effectively for close fire support."

The fighting had been under way for well over an hour when Lieutenant Larry Gwin, the Alpha Company executive officer, looked to the northwest, where Alpha Company's 1st Platoon had disappeared in the first assault. He was stunned by what he saw: "Two men were staggering over to our position! They were Staff Sergeant Walter T. Caple, acting platoon sergeant, and Staff Sergeant [Rother A.] Temple, a squad leader. They had fought their way out of the trap. They were exhausted and they indicated they were probably the only ones left alive. They did say that some of the company mortar platoon were in position with the Delta Company people and were OK. But we had still lost our command."

Now came the event that would turn the course of the battle at the head of the column in the Americans' favor. Lieutenant Gwin describes what happened: "Captain Jim Spires, the battalion S-3, comes dodging into our position. He tells us that tactical air is on the way and wants to know where our people are. What's our situation? He asks if any men are still out there. We said nothing. Spires said: 'You mean everybody out there is either dead or captured?' The silence was eloquent. Spires said: 'You sure?' He was satisfied we were. He ran back to the battalion anthill. The air was on the way, but I don't remember any artillery or ARA. Nobody knew where anybody was."

Shortly afterward the command came over the battalion net: Throw smoke. Lieutenant Gwin moved a little way into the grass and the men in the Albany perimeter all began to throw smoke grenades. "I saw Skip Fesmire, Charlie Company commander, throwing smoke. I had no idea what the hell he was doing up here. Our perimeter was marked with all colors of smoke, delineating our positions, and shortly after, the air strikes started.

"They were A-1E Skyraiders with napalm! The first napalm canisters fell right at the point where Sugdinis and I had left the jungle and came into the clearing. We could see masses of North Vietnamese on the other side. I was very sure they were going to come across at us. I think they were cleaning up over there, shooting down at the ground, dispatching our wounded. That first strike was right on target with two napalm cans. I saw them hit the tops of the trees and jellied napalm was coming down through the tree limbs and the NVA were jumping up trying to get away and being engulfed in the flames. I saw that time and time again."

The slow, reliable old Skyraiders worked their way around the tree line surrounding the hard-pressed defenders of the Albany clearing, first using their canisters of napalm—jellied gasoline—then their 250-pound bombs, and then employing their 20mm cannons to strafe the swarming North Vietnamese.

Lieutenant Gwin remembers, "It cleaned out swath after swath. Those fuckers would jump up and try to run. They didn't make it. By now the Americans were cheering and laughing at each strike. The cheering stopped when they dropped two canisters directly onto the position where the remnants of the 2nd Platoon had been making their stand. It might have been me, but all I could hear was the crackling of the unexpended rounds burning in the flames that had engulfed our men. None of us know if there were any still alive at the time, but then none of us want to think about it."

Gwin and others noticed that the enemy firing had slackened, but that as each of the Skyraiders made its bombing run the jungle all around erupted with enemy fire as the North Vietnamese aimed everything they had at the swooping aircraft. Gwin says, "I marveled at how beautiful those birds looked, flying directly at our position and letting fly with all they had."

Then Gwin rolled over, looked up, and saw an A-1E heading his way. "It let go the canister and it was coming right at me. It passed so close overhead I could see the rivets and it struck in the middle of that field. One North Vietnamese jumped up and ran toward us and we shot him dead. I guess they dropped fifteen or twenty cans of napalm. One aircraft dropped his napalm in the field to our front. I thought he'd made a mistake bringing it in so close, but as it crashed to the ground and the flames burst, about five enemy leaped up only thirty yards from our perimeter and were cut in half by our fire. The last incident involved one particular enemy-manned anthill to our front with a heavy machine gun behind it, firing at the A-1Es. The crew never faltered in the face of imminent death and continued firing until one of the last napalm cans dropped smack dab on that gun and cremated the entire anthill."

Lieutenant Pat Payne, the recon-platoon leader, remembers the blessed relief that the Air Force delivered. "They were a sight for sore eyes, and the cheers rang out as they made their first runs. The plane was so close that as the pilot flew by you could see his profile in the cockpit. He made repeated passes to strafe the advancing NVA; he would slow the plane, slow it down, shoot his guns, and literally chew the ground up in front of him. Other planes arrived and began to use napalm. You could see a large number of North Vietnamese, fifty or a hundred, quite a number, within fifty or seventy-five yards of us—massing to attack—when one of the Air Force planes dropped the napalm on a direct hit on them. We began to cheer."

Major Frank Henry and Captain Joe Price, the battalion's fire-support coordinator, not only got the Air Force on target but also, for the first time in the fight, began calling down artillery strikes around the Albany clearing on clearly visible clusters of North Vietnamese soldiers in the tree line. In those areas, at least, they were fairly confident no Americans were alive. The future of what was left of this battalion began to look a little bit better.

Although badly wounded, Sergeant Major Jim Scott remembers the moment: "After the air support arrived, the artillery started coming in. This was about two hours into the fight. They would see groups of the enemy and call down fire on them. All of this was within fifty yards of us. I could actually see from my position, on top of an anthill, the NVA attempting to charge the battalion. They would form up forty or fifty men; then Frank Henry or the artillery officer would adjust the fire on them. All of a sudden there was a lull in the battle, around four or five P.M. It got quiet. I knew the battalion would survive; up till then I didn't believe we could. We had radio reports coming in that the other companies in the column were cut off, in bad shape, taking multiple casualties. They were fighting in isolated platoons and squads. I knew the casualties had to be heavy, but I don't think anyone knew exactly what the situation was at that time. Everyone was scattered."

Lieutenant Colonel McDade was understandably concerned when contact was made with the A-1Es about where they would put down the napalm and how close. "We had to worry about the risk of hitting our other people. I had no idea where George Forrest's A/1/5 company was. I knew they were close and had some general idea which direction, but we had to use the napalm and the question was, Could we use it safely? We decided: Let's bring it in as close as we can to ourselves; that would mean we were backing it away from the other units. It worked."

Back in the column, Lieutenant Bud Alley continued to search for a secure perimeter but couldn't find one. "Lieutenant Butch Aull, Charlie Company platoon leader, and one of his guys came down a little slope; he was looking for his people. He slid right in front of me on his knees. I pulled him down. About then they opened up on us. He said: 'Look where they shot me.' He was wearing a .45 tanker rig holster. He had a slug in the holster and his .45 pistol, which was right over his chest. He said he was OK, 'but they almost got me.' I asked him what we ought to do to get out of this mess. He said we needed to move over to the left side of the column, that they had it under better control there."

There were six or seven in the group. Butch Aull told them they should count out loud and, on the signal, jump up and run. About then the A-1Es made a strafing run right over them. Aull said, "We better go now." Then, says Alley, "Butch took off first, in front of me. We were just going to go five paces and down. He jumped off. I jumped off. I said: 'Butch, where are you?' I never saw or heard him again. [Second Lieutenant Earl D. Aull, twenty-three, of New Orleans, Louisiana, was killed that day.] I tried to move again. Another strafing run by the A-1Es and I jumped up under cover of that and ran again. My mindset at the time was that it was better to get hit by your own than by them."

Forward in the Albany clearing perimeter the situation was improving by the minute. Specialist 4 Dick Ackerman, of the recon platoon, remembers: "Our artillery was supporting us so close we would occasionally get some shrapnel. There were planes flying close support. We started digging in whenever we could. My entrenching tool was still attached to my pack left out in the clearing, so I used my bayonet, my fingers and someone else's tool when it was available. The comfort of a trench just big enough to hold your body is unbelievable."

No more than two hundred yards away, in that tortured column of desperate Americans, one man prayed for a miracle and the U.S. Air Force delivered it. PFC Jim Shadden, Delta Company, who had booby-trapped his own body with a hand grenade, was badly wounded and unable to move. He was directly in the path of a group of North Vietnamese soldiers methodically sweeping the ground, killing his wounded buddies. "Before the North Vietnamese got to me, half a dozen of them, a pilot came over at treetop level, turned straight up, and dropped a canister of napalm dead center on them. I never cease to be amazed at the accuracy of that drop. The heat of the napalm rolled across my face and body like an open door on a furnace. I owe this pilot more than it is possible for a human to pay. May God bless all pilots!"

Specialist Bob Towles, also wounded, was now inside the small perimeter at the head of the column: "We learned of impending artillery fire. This helped us take heart. A minute or so later a violent explosion erupted inside the perimeter. Screams, shouts, and searing white phosphorus flew everywhere. I heard cease-fire being yelled. Finally high-explosive shells exploded in the tree line on the other side of the clearing. The entire jungle disappeared in flame, smoke, and flying dirt. No one could live through that, could they? Wrong."

Towles had one more adventure to endure: "I heard a rushing noise behind me. Staff Sergeant Ronald Benton, the recon-platoon sergeant, charged across the interior of the line and dove for cover. A single shot cut the tree limb directly over my head. The limb fell and hit my helmet. I turned to curse Sergeant Benton for drawing the fire, and saw a scorpion crawling up my leg. I forgot everything else and tried to kick it off. Then I stood up, flailed around and struck it with the barrel of my rifle and ground the thing into the dirt. I realized that what had just happened was absurd. I crawled back to my tree."

Lieutenant Enrique Pujals, badly wounded and with his grasp of reality fuzzed by the morphine injection, did his best to follow radioed instructions to guide the Air Force planes: "At one time I was told to pop smoke; [and] tell the distance and direction of the smoke. My platoon sergeant, off to our rear, also popped smoke to mark the limits of our positions. No air strike at least where I was. The firing increased in our area, off to our rear. My platoon was holding on. The fire changed; it had become a series of intermittent but very intense firefights."

Pujals heard the sing-song voices of the enemy soldiers getting closer. "They sounded excited, pointing out dangers or targets to one another, then short intense bursts of automatic fire. Screams, sometimes. We knew what it was and someone dared utter it: 'They are killing our wounded!' This was terrible. We had lost the fight, the enemy was mopping up and taking no prisoners. We were as good as dead."

Lieutenant Pujals decided to go down with as many of the enemy as he could take. "I had two .45 pistols. One I got from my radio operator. He hadn't cleaned it in a couple of days and I had trouble charging it, I was so weak. Someone else charged it for me. I was ready. I had already died, I figured. How many would I be able to fire off on the dirty .45? I told my radio operator that now he could see why we were always on their asses about cleaning their weapons; now his life might depend on how many rounds I could get off on his dirty .45 pistol."

Pujals thought he was only seconds from oblivion when a huge black cloud formed up right where the voices were coming from. "Napalm, I thought. The Air Force made it! The voices ceased and the noise of battle resumed, only now it was concentrated off to my right. An air strike with all the trimmings. We had won. It was all over. Only a matter of time before our troops could get to us; an hour or so. I drifted off to sleep. But the battle raged. Really intense firefights; my platoon in deep shit."

Specialist Jack Smith's ordeal with Charlie Company, on the other hand, only grew worse: "The NVA were roaming at will shooting people, hurling hand grenades, and if they weren't doing it we were shooting each other. I moved away, napalm falling so close it was making the grass curl over my head. I went to another area and again I was the only man there who wasn't wounded. It terrified me. I was bandaging up a sergeant when all of a sudden some NVA jumped on top of us. I pretended to be dead; it was easy to do since I was covered with those people's blood. The North Vietnamese gunner started using me as a sandbag for his machine gun.

"The only reason he didn't discover I was alive was that he was shaking more than I was. He couldn't have been much older than me, nineteen at the time. He started firing into our mortar platoon; our mortar platoon started firing grenades at him and his gun. I lay there thinking, *If I stand up and say, 'Fellows, don't shoot me,' the NVA will shoot me. And if I lay still like this my own men will kill me.* Grenades started exploding all around; I was wounded, the North Vietnamese on top of me was killed, that sergeant was killed. I moved to yet another position and this went on all afternoon. Everywhere I went I got wounded, but I didn't get killed. All the men around me were dead."

Although the air strikes had broken the back of the assault against the command-post perimeter, there was no shortage of North Vietnamese along the column. The 2nd Battalion commander, Lieutenant Colonel McDade, was isolated in the Albany perimeter and the setting was hardly conducive to clean, clear, and factual radio reports from the embattled companies to the battalion commander, nor from McDade up the line to Colonel Tim Brown, the 3rd Brigade commander. McDade could see what was going on in his little perimeter, but he was dependent on radios for word of what was happening in the ranks of Charlie, Delta, and Headquarters companies, and there was only silence.

Help was on the way, but it would not arrive in time nor in the right place to be of much use to the Americans still trapped and alive in the column. The division journal notes that at 2:30 P.M. the 1st Battalion, 5th Cavalry on Landing Zone Columbus was "alerted to assist" McDade's column. Captain Buse Tully's Bravo Company, 1st Battalion, 5th Cavalry was assigned the mission of attacking "to relieve the pressure and attempt to link up with the beleaguered battalion."

At 2:55 P.M., the 120 men and officers of Bravo Company began marching overland from the artillery base at LZ Columbus toward the rear of the 2nd Battalion, 7th Cav column approximately two miles away. By four P.M. Captain Tully's company was within six hundred yards of Captain George Forrest's Alpha Company, 1st Battalion, 5th Cavalry perimeter. Tully held up there until the Air Force completed its strikes on the North Vietnamese; he then resumed the march. By 4:30 P.M. his company sighted American troops, "remnants of our Company A who had broken out of the death trap."

In an account of the operation written for *Armor* magazine, an Army publication, the following year, Tully said: "Along with them were elements of Headquarters and Charlie Company, 2nd Battalion, 7th Cavalry. Company A had taken many casualties and was missing one whole platoon. You cannot imagine how happy Captain George Forrest was to see friendly faces. I got a great big bear hug from him."

Tully's reinforcements deployed to secure a one-helicopter landing zone at the tail of the column to bring in medical evacuation helicopters. The time was five P.M. "When the majority of the wounded had been evacuated," Tully wrote,

> I gave the order to move out toward where I thought the remainder of 2nd Battalion, 7th Cavalry was located. Our Company A was to follow in column as soon as the remaining wounded were evacuated. We had not moved 400 yards when the very earth seemed to erupt with mortar and small-arms fire. The company was deployed in a wedge and had just passed over a small ridge line. To our front was a densely thicketed wood line. All three platoons came under fire simultaneously.
>
> The NVA were in the wood line. Two men were killed and three wounded in the initial volley. One of the wounded was my 3rd Platoon leader Lieutenant Emil Satkowsky. Another was PFC Martin,* who

---

*PFC Roger Martin of Kenosha, Wisconsin, was the man who disobeyed doctors' orders and returned to join his buddies on the march to Albany. His left hip was shattered by an enemy bullet.

had only 14 days left in the Army and who the night before had burned his hands so badly on a trip flare that he had been evacuated. Before leaving he swore to his buddies he would be back the next day. Sure enough, on the first supply ship into Columbus on the 17th, there he was. He had talked the doctor into just bandaging his hands and letting him come back. He was the point man in the first platoon when we got hit and had his hip torn open. At this point there was no alternative except to press the attack and hope that by taking the wood line the fire could be stopped.

By now Tully's people were beginning to spot the enemy soldiers.

The M-79 grenade launchers proved extremely effective for blowing a man out of a tree. By the time we reached the wood line we had killed enough enemy and driven the remainder far enough into the jungle that the firing subsided to an occasional sniper round. About the same time, Captain Forrest radioed that more wounded had come into the clearing from the west and requested that I hold up so he could med-evac them. This process repeated itself as stragglers continued to filter in. Battalion headquarters had been advised and at 6:25 P.M. orders were received to wrap up in a two-company perimeter and prepare to sweep north to link up with the 2nd Battalion, 7th Cavalry at daybreak. At nightfall, we still had twenty-two wounded in our perimeter. They were made as comfortable as possible for the long wait until morning.

Reinforcements were also on the way for the battalion command perimeter at the head of the column. During the afternoon, Captain Myron Diduryk's battle-weary veterans of the fight at Landing Zone X-Ray, Bravo Company, 2nd Battalion, 7th Cavalry, got a warning to prepare for a night air assault into a hot landing zone. The Bravo Company troopers, delighted to have survived the hellish fighting on X-Ray and enjoying a well-deserved rest and a lot of cold beer back at Camp Holloway, were stunned when told that they were being thrown back into a desperate situation so suddenly. Specialist Jon Wallenius, Bravo Company mortar observer, was doing some serious celebrating. He had not only survived X-Ray without a scratch, but this day, November 17, was his birthday. "I was twenty-two years old. We were fed and showered and new clothes were available. I spent the afternoon at the Enlisted Men's

Club drinking beer with the platoon, exchanging stories and celebrating my birthday. Around four P.M. Diduryk came in and told us to 'saddle up.' We were going to rescue the battalion."

"At about 1600 hours," Lieutenant Rick Rescorla recalls, "Captain Diduryk walked up. 'Get the Company together. Battalion's catching hell. We may have to go in. You're the only platoon leader left in the Company. Help all the platoons get their shit together.' Men spilled out of the Clubs and double-timed to their equipment. They worked quickly, throwing on their harnesses. No protests, but their eyes filled with disbelief. Again? Diduryk then issued the shortest frag order in Bravo Company history: 'We'll be landing from the southeast. Open fire at anything on your left. Run to your right.' A hostile landing with one side of the landing zone held by the North Vietnamese. Sitrep [situation report] from the ground: Grim. Expect to be sandwiched between friendly and enemy fires."

At about 5:45 P.M., Rescorla gathered the platoons. "They pressed in close, listening intently for the word. [SFC John A.] Uselton, the mortar-platoon sergeant, [Staff Sergeant William F.] Martin, [Specialist 4 Andrew] Vincent, [Specialist Jon] Wallenius, the towering [Sergeant Larry L.] Melton. Eighty or more. Young faces, old hollow eyes. 'You know the battalion is in the shit,' I said. 'We have been selected to jump into that shit and pull them out. If you fight like you did at X-Ray you'll come through it. Stay together. Come out of those choppers ready to get it on.'

"Across the field the first lift ships were sweeping in. 'Head 'em up,' Captain Diduryk growled. I turned and walked ahead, Fantino trailing with the PRC-25. The road stretched out past the permanent hooches of the rear echelon at Holloway. Word spread that we were on a suicide flight. Tumbling out of cozy bunks, Holloway's finest lined the road to watch us depart. Hawaiian shirts, aviator shades, jeans, beer cans in hands. Cooks and bottle washers, the shit-burners, projectionists, club runners. Same Army, different species. The Company picked up pace, a tight, dirty brown column."

A few of the men carried AKs, trophies from X-Ray. "No one had shaved," noted Rescorla, "but our weapons sparkled. 'What outfit are you?' one spectator asked. 'The Hard Corps of Bravo

Company, 2nd of the 7th.' 'Where are you headed?' 'To kick ass,' I yelled back. A deep rumble ran through the ranks, men yelling, cursing. Not a man among us would swap places with these lard asses. As we passed I asked Fantino: 'How we looking back there?' His reply: 'No stragglers, Sir. Every swinging dick is with us.' As we made a column-right to the pickup point, I looked back at our crew. No outfit in the Army had ever rendered a route step any better than these men at this moment. We piled onto the Hueys without the usual loading instructions and skidded away into the fading gray light."

At 6:45 P.M. the first lift ships roared into the small Albany clearing and Captain Myron Diduryk's troopers bailed out into the tall grass. The cavalry had ridden to the rescue. But the killing and dying and terror continued unabated outside the American perimeter as the long night began.

21

ESCAPE AND EVADE

One cannot answer for his courage when he has never been in danger.

—François, Duc de La Rochefoucauld, *Maximes,* 1665

In the confusion of a battle as fast-paced, fluid, and disorganized as this one along the trail to the Albany clearing—with leaders killed, wounded, or separated from their men, and unit integrity disintegrating in the tall grass and the storm of enemy fire—soldiers drift away or are forced to move away. This is, perhaps, the ultimate terror: to be lost and alone in a hostile land where the next man you meet wants only to kill you.

The Army solution to the problem calls for the soldier to conceal himself until sure of his ground, and then move as stealthily as possible toward friendly lines. The Army term for this difficult and dangerous pursuit is "escape and evasion" or "E and E." Getting back inside friendly lines in the middle of a firefight is problematic: You are just as likely to be shot and killed by your friends as you are by the enemy.

Late in the afternoon of November 17, E and E was definitely on the minds of many American survivors crawling through the elephant grass in the killing zone along the route of march toward the Albany clearing. Most of them would not make it back alive into the American perimeters at the head and tail of the column. But, against all odds, at least a dozen American officers and soldiers, all of them wounded, stumbled through circuitous routes that took them back to Landing Zone Columbus. Their stories, especially those of James Young and Toby Braveboy, stand as testimony to courage, tenacity, and a tremendous will to live.

Although Lieutenant Colonel Bob McDade and his executive officer, Major Frank Henry, tried to bring in the air strikes close to the head of the column, some strikes hit as far down the line of march as Headquarters Company, where Lieutenant John Howard, a wounded sergeant, and four other Americans were fighting off the enemy from behind an anthill. Howard says, "The A-1Es made a pass and dropped napalm approximately fifty yards to our left. Although they killed some of the NVA, I'm sure they also hit some of our own troops because we were all mixed together, friendly and enemy, at that point. It was utter chaos. The A-1Es made a wide sweep and started to come back around for a second pass."

Lieutenant Howard quickly saw that this next pass might come directly over them, and they had to get out of the way of the napalm. "We decided that we would run down a hill toward a dry streambed to get away from the path of the next strike. The six of us jumped up and ran, crossing the streambed about a hundred yards away, and jumped into a large hole about fifteen feet across that looked like an artillery crater. As we were running down the hill the A-1Es were making their second pass and the North Vietnamese were firing at the planes above, not paying any attention to us.

"After getting into the hole we realized that we were now in no-man's-land on the outside of the enemy and far away from any friendly troops. Intense firefights were still going on a few hundred yards away, but after staying there for maybe an hour, we did not see any more enemy in that area."

Not far away, another desperate little band of Americans was forming and trying to find a way out of the death trap. That group was led by Lieutenant Howard's friend Lieutenant Bud Alley, the communications-platoon leader. Alley had collected five other wounded men, including his platoon sergeant; the assistant operations sergeant, James Gooden; and one soldier from Captain George Forrest's Alpha Company, 1st Battalion, 5th Cavalry.

Alley says, "One of the clerks was pretty bad shot up and he was panicked. We tried to carry him but he was too big; we couldn't handle him. One other guy with me had one of his eyes shot out; had it patched but said he could see. A young enlisted man. We made our way to a ditch. There were other guys in that ditch when I got there.

"I remember one of them said: 'Lieutenant, how about saying a prayer?' We did; then we took off up the ditch to the left, again trying to find a senior person, somebody who could tell us what to do. There was the guy with the eye shot out; Gooden shot in the chest; another guy shot in the arm and leg. We continued to crawl and we realized that we can't go back into that shit; the best thing we can do is go to the artillery if we can make it back."

On the other side was a wide field of elephant grass. "We could see that someone had walked down fields of fire across that field. We skirted around that area real carefully. Somewhere we hit a mud puddle or two and drank the water. It was right at dark when we got outside the American artillery impact area. All of the guys who started out were still with me. It was dark and the flares were out."

Alley and his group crawled, walked, and ran more than two miles through the darkness to the artillery base at Landing Zone Columbus. They knew there was no safe way to approach an American perimeter that was on hundred-percent alert. Alley says, "We were exhausted. We tried to move out of the way of any line of attack. There had been sounds behind us all the way. We got into some real thick elephant grass, made a little burrow right in the middle, and crashed at that point. The sky was lighted with flares and it seemed to us like the Air Force was dropping everything but the atom bomb around Albany. I really thought we were the only survivors from the whole battalion. We had no water, no first aid, no bandages. I took my shirt off and gave it to one of the guys for his wounds."

Lieutenant Howard and the other five men, all wounded, decided after dark that the best way to reach safety was to retrace their steps, first to Landing Zone X-Ray and then to the artillery base at Columbus. Columbus was only about two miles away as the crow flies, but crows don't fly at night. Even though it would add perhaps four extra miles to their route, Howard believed he could locate X-Ray, and once he got there he could then retrace the original route of march back to Columbus.

As they moved, Howard's group could hear Vietnamese voices and the clanking of weapons. They took a sharp turn, and thought they had lost the enemy behind them, but after another hour they heard more enemy voices.

Now, instead of trying to turn away again, Howard and his group just kept moving toward the sounds of distant artillery and helicopters landing and taking off. They reached Columbus before daybreak.

Lieutenant Alley and his group bedded down in their clump of grass waiting for the sun. Alley says, "Once dawn came, the most dangerous thing was trying to get in that perimeter. I moved fifty or a hundred yards away from the rest of them, so if the guys on guard fired on me the others with me wouldn't get hit."

Alley crawled up as close as he could to the perimeter. "I could hear Americans talking in their foxholes. I yelled and asked them to get an officer over right quick. When he came I told him who I was, that I was wearing no shirt and I was going to stand up. I stood with my hands raised. Told him I had a group of people to bring in, please hold your fire. I went back and got them and we came in."

Alley and his group had been inside the Columbus perimeter just a minute or two when Lieutenant Howard and his group came in behind them, no more than twenty-five or thirty yards to the left of where Alley had crossed the line. Howard and his group had also hidden in the grass outside Columbus. At daybreak they spotted two Americans sitting outside a foxhole eating C-rations. Howard stepped into the open and yelled, "Garry Owen!" and "Friendly troops." The reply was "Come on in."

Their ordeal, at least, was over. A helicopter came in and took the seriously wounded out. Alley recalls a medic giving him a shot—"I was shaking like a leaf." John Howard and Bud Alley later rode a helicopter back to Holloway. They discussed how both groups had heard North Vietnamese units moving behind them and in the same direction, toward the American artillery positions at LZ Columbus.

Alley says, "We thought we should tell someone about this. So we hitched a chopper ride to 3rd Brigade headquarters at Catecka and reported our stories to the S-2, intelligence officer. There was so much confusion they seemed not to care. We returned to Holloway, and next day we rejoined what was left of our outfit."

A few hours later, on the afternoon of November 18, a North Vietnamese battalion of the 33rd Regiment attacked the perimeter at LZ Columbus.

An even more remarkable escape-and-evasion saga was that of Specialist 4 James Young of Alpha Company, 1st Battalion, 5th Cav, the attached unit on the end of the column. It may be remembered that Young had volunteered for a dangerous mission to find an American machine gun that was shooting up the Alpha Company position. Out in the tall grass Young was shot in the head and badly wounded before he discovered that the American machine gun was manned by North Vietnamese. The Missouri country boy looked back to find that enemy troops had cut him off from the American lines.

Says Young, "They were shooting at our men, but hadn't spotted me yet. I had two or three frag grenades, a smoke grenade, three hundred to four hundred rounds of ammo, my M-16, two canteens, a notebook, and a little mirror. That was it. Bullets were striking around me. I saw the grass out to my front start moving and suddenly I saw a North Vietnamese. I let him get close, fired on full automatic, hit him in the stomach and chest. I could see more coming. I threw a frag and a smoke grenade and got out of there."

Young was being forced to move away from his company. "Those guys in the grass had cut me off. I began moving in hopes of getting to that artillery base we had passed. I sprayed the treetops as I went, hoping to get those snipers, or at least keep their heads down. I was running and dodging, zigzagging so they couldn't get an easy shot. I ran five hundred to six hundred yards and stopped to rest. I could hear the enemy shooting and coming in my direction. I had killed one of them and put a grenade in their position so I figured they weren't too happy with me."

Jim Young's skills, learned while deer hunting in the Missouri backwoods at an early age, now began to pay off for him. He hit a stream and waded up it for a hundred yards, filling his canteens and drinking all the water he could hold. He left the water at a rocky place where he would leave no trail, moved to an open valley where he would have a clear view of his backtrail, crossed, and took a break, concealed in the brush. It was a game of foxes and hounds, and Jim Young was the fox. He set out again, moving down the valley, hearing the sound of the battle receding to his rear.

It was getting late. Young moved up the mountain, took out his notebook, and started a diary. "I wrote the date and what had happened to me. I figured it was a good chance I wasn't going to make it back and maybe they will find this and at least my mama and daddy would know what happened to me. Artillery started coming in on the mountain. I got between two large trees; had not seen or heard any sign of the enemy. I started looking for a place to hide for the night. I stumbled around those slopes in the dark, falling over rocks, cussing and raising hell but I did some praying too. I found me a good place to hide from the enemy and the artillery if they fired again. A low place by a tree with grass so thick I could crawl in and no one would see me.

"Late in the night I did go to sleep. I was cold and tired and trying to keep ants and bugs out of my head wound. I had a real bad headache. When I would take a drink of water I would throw up. Next morning when I woke up I lay there quite a time just listening. Didn't hear anything except helicopters landing and taking off. I could hear gunfire between me and the ambush site and I wasn't about to try to get through there. If friendly fire didn't get me, the VC would. My next diary entry was: '18 November: I'm on a very large hill with artillery coming in on it along with mortars, but I can't spot them.'"

From the map it is clear that Young had climbed one of the three six-hundred- to seven-hundred-foot-high hills east of LZ Albany. Now he decided to head in the direction he thought was south. He walked a long way, then got off the trail he had been on because it became too narrow. He grew concerned that he was either near or across the Cambodian border, because he had not seen or heard any helicopters or aircraft and he knew they avoided the border. Young then reversed course.

"Later, choppers flew over me. I tried to signal them with my small mirror but had no luck. Late in the day I got close enough to again hear choppers landing and taking off. I estimated I was less than a mile from a landing zone [Columbus]. The enemy made an attack on the troops there in late afternoon or early evening. They had attacked from my side of the perimeter. Friendlies were shooting at the enemy, and their bullets were hitting all around me. There wasn't much cover in the valley so I went to the top of the hill, found a large log, and got behind it. Then the Americans started dropping artillery and mortars. Then the jets and choppers came in bombing and strafing and shooting rockets.

"It was close enough that I was real scared. They were hitting the valley and my hill to cut off the enemy and I was right in the middle. By the time the battle was over it was dark and I knew better than to try to walk in then. Any sound of movement would bring immediate fire. Artillery and mortar fire landed around me all night. There were flares lighting up the area and I didn't dare move. I covered myself with brush and leaves so no one could see me. Another miserable night. I was wet and cold. Ants all over me again and I had a real bad headache. Ants got inside my clothes. If I didn't move around much they were OK, but if I moved they bit me. Had to keep them out of my eyes and ears and my head wound. Shooting off and on all night long. The guys were pretty trigger-happy."

The Americans inside Columbus greeted daybreak of November 19 with a Mad Minute of shooting that sprayed all around Jim Young, hiding up on the slope. When that quieted down he began moving cautiously toward salvation, crossing a wide, shallow creek and finally finding an opening where he could approach the perimeter and be seen for who and what he was. He made it into the

Columbus perimeter only a few hours before the Americans pulled out and abandoned it.

Young talked to some of the men. "They told me where my company was. I had walked in a huge circle, lost, and somehow came back to my own unit on a different landing zone. I walked across the perimeter to my unit. They were as happy to see me as I was to see them. They told me I had been listed [as] missing in action. My family had been sent a telegram saying that and it was a big shock to them. Then they got a telegram saying I was wounded, not missing.

"One of the men from Headquarters Company of the battalion took all my gear. I wanted to keep my helmet with the bullet hole in it. He said I couldn't do that so I asked him to hold it for me, that I wanted it back. Then they took me to the first-aid station. They cleaned my head wound, put me on a stretcher, asked me what I had seen and where I had been. I was bothered by the fact that I had not tried to fight my way back in on the day we were ambushed. One of the officers told me I had done the right thing, that I would never have made it back that day. Finally they flew me out to Holloway and on to Qui Nhon."

Jim Young adds, "The bullet had knocked a place the size of a quarter out of my skull. Both the bullet and shrapnel from my helmet did damage, pressed pieces of skull down into my brain. At Qui Nhon they had to take the bone frags out of my brain, and whatever it was they did medically, it was the first time that had been done in Vietnam, so they wrote me up in the medical journals."

At Qui Nhon a nurse came in and cut off Young's clothes. "When she took my boots off you should have seen her face. It had been five days since I had my clothes off. I had dropped from a hundred and ninety pounds to a hundred and fifty. They sent me to Denver Fitzsimmons Army Hospital because of the type of wound I had. I wanted to go to a hospital in St. Louis near my home. Continued treatment and tests. In mid-December they let me start clearing from the hospital. Release papers were given to me the twenty-second of December but they said I couldn't get a new uniform and my back pay till after Christmas. They were going to have their

Christmas, but I could, by God, sit and wait. Hell with that. I borrowed some money and some clothes from one of the guys, told the pay office where to send my money, and I took off. I arrived home Christmas Eve, sneaked in, and surprised the family."

The last, and most spectacular, escape-and-evasion story would not come to light until a full week after the battle at Albany. A scout helicopter flying in the vicinity of the abandoned Albany battlefield on November 24, the day before Thanksgiving, saw the figure of a man below waving a bloody rag.

The observer-copilot took aim at the man with his M-16 and was about to shoot him when the pilot noticed that the figure was too large for a Vietnamese. He swerved the chopper to get the observer's rifle off the man and radioed a report to a Huey gunship in the area. The extraordinary saga of the survival of PFC Toby Braveboy, an aptly named part–Creek Indian rifleman from Alpha Company, 2nd Battalion, 7th U.S. Cavalry, would now be told.

On November 17, Braveboy—whose hometown, ironically, was Coward, South Carolina—was walking point for Captain Joel Sugdinis's 1st Platoon, the unit that disintegrated in the hail of enemy fire on the eastern side of Albany clearing as the enemy began the battle.

That initial volley of fire shattered Braveboy's left hand and his M-16, and bullet fragments peppered his arm and thigh. Bleeding, weaponless, and in extreme pain, Braveboy crawled into thick brush and hid. When night fell on the seventeenth he crept out and ran into three other American soldiers, all wounded.

He crawled away for help, toward the sound of the firing, and ran into more wounded Americans just as a North Vietnamese patrol moving through the area discovered them. Braveboy played dead for several hours, listening to the other wounded Americans around him being executed.

Finally, when things quieted down, Braveboy, who had lost all sense of direction, again started crawling through the tall elephant grass toward where he thought he would find his company. Bad choice. He was 180 degrees off and moving directly south past the right flank of the Charlie Company survivors.

At daybreak he went to ground on the north bank of a shallow tributary of the Ia Drang, about five hundred yards from the Albany clearing. He had no food but did have two canteens and a small bottle of GI-issue water-purification tablets. He wrapped his T-shirt around his bleeding left hand and stayed put, tortured by mosquitoes, ants, and the chilling cold of the nights. Each day he watched enemy soldiers pass his hiding place in the brush along the creek bank. He could hear American helicopters overhead.

On November 22, his fifth day alone, a North Vietnamese soldier on the tail end of a passing column looked into the hole in the brush and saw the American. Braveboy said: "Four walked by me and the last one looked me right in the eye. He stopped and pointed his rifle at me. I raised my wounded hand and shook my head no. He lowered his rifle and walked away. So young. He was just a boy, not more than sixteen or seventeen."

The U.S. Air Force had begun targeting fighter-bomber missions on the entire Albany area. Braveboy said, "I don't know how I survived. The bombs were landing all around me. All I could do was lay flat on the ground and pray they didn't hit me."

After seven days, terribly weak and sinking fast from loss of blood and lack of food, Braveboy heard and then saw a 1st Cav H-13 scout helicopter wheeling and circling at low level nearby. Desperate, Braveboy crawled to a small open area, took his bloody T-shirt off his gangrenous hand, and waved it, swung it around over his head, until Melvus Hall, the observer in Warrant Officer Marion Moore's scout chopper, saw him and took aim with his M-16.

When pilot Moore realized the figure was an American, he radioed gunship pilot Captain Jerry Leadabrand, who circled the area, wrote "Follow me!" on a box of turkey loaf C-rations, and dropped it to Braveboy on a low pass. Only after the scout helicopter had swept the area and made certain that there were no enemy nearby did Leadabrand land and pick up Toby Braveboy.

Braveboy was flown first to Duc Co Special Forces Camp for immediate treatment of his wounds. Then he was flown to Camp Holloway for surgery.

His Alpha Company commander, Captain Joel Sugdinis, says he

22

NIGHT WITHOUT END

> Any danger spot is tenable if men—brave men—will make
> it so.
>
> —John F. Kennedy

Captain Myron Diduryk's Bravo Company soldiers once again rode
to war, courtesy of Major Bruce Crandall's assault helicopters. In
the front seats of one of those Hueys were Chief Warrant Officer
Rick Lombardo and his good buddy and copilot, CWO Alex (Pop)
Jekel, who thought they had seen and survived everything in Landing Zone X-Ray, but were about to have their horizons expanded
one more time.

Says Lombardo: "Where we were going no one seemed to know
except the flight leader, and he didn't say. We were just following.
Dusk was falling and our fuel situation was critical. About three
miles out I could see battle smoke and that was where we were
headed. I looked at Pop Jekel and said: 'Here we go again!' We were
the second flight of four to go in. As the first flight approached the
landing zone, tracers started arcing up at them. The radio came
alive, people yelling they were hit, or this or that pilot was hit. Our
platoon was forced to go around because the first flight was still on
the ground. On our approach the sight before me was unbelievable.

Grass fires all over the place, tracers crisscrossing the LZ, and the smoke. It looked like Dante's *Inferno*."

About twenty feet from touchdown Lombardo felt and heard a tremendous bang and a rush of air coming between his legs and dirt blowing all around inside his Huey. "Before my skids touched the ground, the troopers were out. I glanced down and saw my left skid on a body. Couldn't tell if it was one of ours or one of theirs. Then I realized I no longer had a chin bubble. My feet were on the pedals but there was no plexiglass beneath them. It wasn't shattered; it just wasn't there! All gauges were in the green so we hauled ass out of there. I told Pop to fly so I could get the dirt out of my eyes. To that point not a word had been spoken over the intercom. Before I could say a word, Pop Jekel keyed the intercom and said: 'I flew thirty-one missions in B-24s in World War II and that's the closest I've ever come to swallowing my balls.' That took the tension out of the crew. I asked if everyone was OK, then I started feeling my legs. I didn't even have a scratch."

Captain Robert Stinnett, thirty-two years old, from Dallas, Texas, had won his ROTC commission out of Prairie View A.&M. College in 1953. On this night he had six years of flying experience under his belt, including two years in the 11th Air Assault Test and 1st Cavalry Division. He led four of the twelve Hueys carrying Diduryk's Bravo Company troops into Albany. He reports that eight aircraft were hit by ground fire and one aviator was wounded on that dusk troop lift.

Captain Diduryk wrote of the flight in and the situation on the ground: "Assaulting Albany we picked up five bullet holes in the helicopter. Things were bad there. I found out when I landed that the battalion [was] shot up pretty bad. So we came in the nick of time to their rescue. The main part of 2nd Battalion, 7th Cavalry was on their last-ditch stand at Albany. Little Bighorn revisited."

Lieutenant Rick Rescorla, 1st Platoon Leader in Bravo Company, recalls: "First pass over Albany I stared down into the smoke and dust. Between the trees [were] the scattered khaki bodies of at least a dozen NVA. They lay face up on the brown gravel of a dry streambed. Firing snapped around us. We circled out to safety.

'NVA bodies. You see them?' I yelled. Fantino shook his head. He had been looking out the other side. 'Lots of American dead down there, Sir. Mucho!' On the second pass I saw the blackened track of the napalm. American bodies and equipment dotted between the anthills and scrub brush. Getting ground fire; the pilot was clearly upset, hunched low. He jabbered into his mike, expressing doubt that we would get down. Darkness was closing in around us. I stood on the skids hovering at least twelve feet over the LZ. Too high."

The sound of two bullets hitting forced Rescorla back. "Looking sideways I saw a trickle of blood down the pilot's sleeve. The chopper dropped a few feet. The pilot yelled at the gunner. The gunner snarled, 'Get out.' I hesitated. *'Get the fuck out!'* Four of us dropped a bone-jarring ten feet. The gunner kicked out the boxes of C-rations and they rained down on us. We were on our own. Lying flat, four of us tried to get our bearings. Sixty yards away three khakis rose like quail and ran for the tree line. Two of us cut loose and they fell headfirst into the brown grass. I popped a round with the M-79 just to make sure. Up ahead we heard sounds of American voices. We sprinted into the perimeter, proudly lugging the precious C-rats."

Now inside the battalion command group perimeter, Rescorla took stock. "The battalion sergeant major sat against a tree with a bandaged chest. 'We got hit bad, Sir. Real bad.' The wounded were gathered thirty yards from the CP. Only half my platoon had arrived. The other ships turned back because of ground fire and darkness. The perimeter was an oval island of trees. Three platoons could man the perimeter but with the exception of our people and Pat Payne's recon platoon there was no unit cohesion. Colonel McDade slumped against a tree. He looked exhausted. He was exceptionally silent. Major Frank Henry, his executive officer, was reassuringly active. A short fireplug of a man, Henry waved a welcome, working the radios. Captain Joe Price, the fire-support coordinator, crouched beside him. Clumps of survivors sprawled inside the perimeter, including several company commanders."

Lieutenant Larry Gwin watched the reinforcements arrive: "I saw Rick Rescorla come swaggering into our lines with a smile on his face, an M-79 on his shoulder, his M-16 in one hand saying: 'Good, good, good! I hope they hit us with everything they got tonight—we'll wipe them up.' His spirit was catching. The troops were cheering as each load came in, and we really raised a racket. The enemy must have thought that an entire battalion was coming to help us because of all our screaming and yelling. Major Henry directed that I round up some men and police up all the ammo resupply which the choppers brought in on the last flight. It was lying in crates on the far side of the LZ. Somehow we got it all into the perimeter. As I came back with the last load I passed right by the body of that North Vietnamese I'd killed early in the fight. There wasn't much left of him and I didn't give a damn."

Lieutenant Pat Payne of the recon platoon was just as happy about the reinforcements as Gwin. "We were all very surprised to see those helicopters come in. We were only securing one side of the LZ so when the guys would jump off the helicopter we hollered at them which way to come. I had the feeling we had actually been rescued, that in fact the cavalry had arrived, just like in the movies. I admired the courage it took to land in Albany. Lieutenant Rescorla was one of the best combat leaders I ever saw during two tours in Vietnam. He walked around and pepped everyone up by telling them they'd done a good job, that there was support now, and that things were under control. He never raised his voice; almost spoke in a whisper. We were awfully glad to see him and the others from Bravo Company."

After walking the perimeter, Lieutenant Rescorla was worried. "We had as many men inside the trees as those on the perimeter. I was uncomfortable with that many rifles to my rear, particularly if they started scare shooting. Worse than the tactical layout was the dark malaise that had fallen over the battalion. Even men who were not wounded were melancholy."

One of the wounded still suffering alone out in the butchered column was PFC James Shadden of the Delta Company mortar platoon. "By this time it was beginning to grow dark," Shadden recalls. "I slipped the pin back into the booby-trap grenade in my armpit, thinking now that I might get out alive. Then artillery began to come in. It felt as if the earth would shake out from under me. This continued on into the night. My thirst was almost unbearable; my leg was so painful I could hardly keep from screaming. I thought help would surely come soon."

Specialist 4 Jack Smith of Charlie Company was also lying wounded in the tall grass. "At dusk the fighting stopped and I had a chance to have a cigarette. I told myself if I lit a cigarette they will find me and kill me, but I didn't care anymore. Then I passed out. I woke up in the middle of the night. The Alpha Company, 1st Battalion, 5th Cavalry sent a group to try to rescue us. A man came up to me and asked if I was wounded. He said they had a few stretchers for the worst wounded. I said, 'Take me out with you.' He said, 'Stand up.' I stood up and passed out. They couldn't take me. They left a medic with us. That night the NVA tried to get to us. They were going around killing people. Our weapons-platoon lieutenant, Bob Jeanette, had been horribly wounded. He called in artillery so close to our tree that it killed some of us. But it also killed the North Vietnamese when they came to try to take us out. This happened two or three times during the night."

Doc William Shucart, the surgeon of the 2nd Battalion, had been guided to safety in the Alpha Company, 1st Battalion, 5th Cavalry perimeter at the tail of the column by one of Captain George Forrest's platoon sergeants, Fred Kluge. Shucart says, "Around dusk, Kluge said he was getting ready to go back up the column. I asked if he was sure he wanted to do that. He said: 'There are other guys like you out there, lost or wounded, who need our help.' I said, 'OK, let's go.' I know we had a radio where we were. We were trying to get the medevac ships to come in but they would not. A couple of Huey slicks came down but we were taking fire and the medevacs wouldn't come. When you are taking fire is precisely when you need medevac. I don't know where those guys got their great reputations. I was totally dismayed with the medevac guys. The Huey slick crews were terrific."

Among the wounded that Captain Shucart and Sergeant Fred Kluge rescued at dusk were Enrique Pujals and some other Charlie Company soldiers. They spent the rest of the night in George Forrest's perimeter at the southern end of the column. Lieutenant Pujals made it through the night and was evacuated the next morning—one of the lucky ones.

Captain Forrest says that late that night he received a radio call from a man identifying himself as "Ghost 4-6" who reported that he was badly wounded, there were dozens of other wounded Americans all around him, and the North Vietnamese were walking around killing them. Forrest sent Sergeant Kluge and a large patrol back up the column at midnight.

PFC 4 David Lavender was part of the patrol sent out to find Ghost 4-6 and the wounded. He recalls, "Our sergeants came around seeking volunteers to go back out and retrieve some men who had been wounded and were bleeding to death. There were twenty-three of us went out on this patrol. One of the wounded had a radio, so we were in radio contact. We wandered around till we found these fellows. There were twenty-three to twenty-six men in a group, trying to take care of each other. All hurt very bad. We had a medic with us and the twenty-three of us tried to carry as many of them back as we could. We left our medic there with the ones we left behind. All we could handle was thirteen. We had men slung on our shoulders, in litters, carrying them any way we could."

Lavender says that on their way back into the American position someone on the perimeter opened fire, wounding three of those carrying the wounded, including Lavender himself, who was shot through the hip. "Last I heard, twelve of those thirteen we brought in lived. The rest of the men our medic watched that night also survived. Jack P. Smith wrote an article in [the] *Saturday Evening Post* about that night, and I read that and suffered flashbacks. He was one of those we left behind with the medic. He went through a long, hard night."

Joseph H. Ibach was the first sergeant of the 2nd Battalion Headquarters Company. He and Captain Daniel Boone, commander of Headquarters Company, were in that mixture of admin and logistics guys inexplicably included in the march across the Ia Drang Valley that day. Says Ibach: "I was with Captain Boone and we had small groups together. More like clusters of men. We did not have radio contact with anyone. Colonel McDade and the command group were 200 to 400 yards up the column. We couldn't locate them so we stayed where we were, all afternoon and the whole night. We were confused and I didn't think we would survive. Finally radio contact was established and we were informed to stay where we were until morning. At first light we started walking and reached the battalion command post."

With the infusion of the Bravo Company reinforcements led by Myron Diduryk, the battalion command post perimeter was expanded to provide better security. That expansion also swept into the American lines several more wounded Americans, some of them near death. Most had suffered their wounds in the initial volley of firing hours earlier. Joel Sugdinis recalls, "We had several badly wounded men in the perimeter and from the sounds of their suffering it was obvious that something had to be done quickly to help them. The perimeter had virtually no medical support and B Company brought only a small amount of medical supplies."

Chief Warrant Officer Hank Ainsworth had been overhead in the 2nd Battalion command chopper all day. "I was overhead when the fight started and orbited overhead till late that night. I was on a freq talking to Major Frank Henry. Later that evening he called me. Henry said we have critically wounded down here; if we don't get them out they are going to die. I called medevac and they came out, made a pass, drew fire and refused to land."

Frank Henry knew exactly what to do about that situation; he told Hank Ainsworth to call the 229th Huey slicks, the old reliables. Ainsworth notified the 229th pilots, told them that LZ Albany was hot, but the 2nd Battalion, 7th Cavalry had critically wounded men who would die if they were not evacuated. Says Ainsworth: "The whole damned unit volunteered. I told them we only needed two ships."

Despite Ainsworth's call for only two ships, four Huey slicks lifted off from the Camp Holloway Turkey Farm at 9:50 P.M. for the forty-minute flight to Albany. Captain Bob Stinnett was again in the lead, followed by Captain Bruce Thomas, CWO Ken Faba, and CWO Robert Mason.

When the flight arrived in the vicinity of Albany, the pilots could not identify the small clearing on the ground. Says Stinnett: "I talked to the guy on the ground [Captain Jim Spires]. He knew we were en route. He had a flashlight and he went out in the clearing to see if we could pick him up. I circled till I picked up his light. We set up the approach. We were drawing tracer fire from the ground. On the way in we started getting pretty heavy small-arms fire. I wasn't sure how big that LZ was, because I couldn't see it. I put the birds in trail formation, one behind the other. I was the first ship in; then another; then a third. I told the fourth ship to circle because there wasn't room."

Normally the Huey pilots throttle back their engines as soon as they touch down to conserve fuel. Not tonight. Stinnett remembers: "Something told me not to do that, to keep the engine turning at full flight rpm's. They had told us the wounded were ambulatory. When we got in there they were all stretcher cases. My crew chief and gunner had to get out and raise the seats so we could get the stretchers in. Then all hell broke loose. Fire was coming in from everywhere. I immediately pulled pitch and, with the rpm's at flight, the ship instantly jumped thirty feet in the air and kept on going up. We went so fast that the crew chief and gunner got left behind on the ground and I didn't even know it. We just flat left them. We had the wounded inside. When we got back we counted thirty holes in my machine. That was enough for me and my Huey. The lift of three that went in after me took in medical stuff and brought back more wounded and my crew. Major Frank Henry was on the flashlight that time."

Joel Sugdinis watched with awe as the brave aviators risked everything for the wounded in Albany. "I remember thinking they were the bravest pilots I had ever seen. They were sitting ducks and I fully expected to see them shot down at any moment. They were guided in by Frank Henry. You could see the tracers. The aircraft didn't hesitate a bit. They landed, loaded and were gone in seconds."

Battalion sergeant major James A. Scott was one of the wounded; he rode out on a helicopter nearly eleven hours after he had been shot in the chest. Says Scott: "About midnight a chopper came in. Eight serious wounded were put on; they pushed me on that chopper. By then I looked like somebody from the Alamo, with blood running down my legs, my clothes torn. Away we went to Holloway."

In early January, six weeks later, Sergeant Major Scott was recuperating at Walter Reed Army Hospital in Washington, D.C. There he read a story in the December 31, 1965, issue of *Time* magazine, which quoted a medic of the 2nd Battalion, 7th Cavalry as saying that Sergeant Major Scott had been killed early in the fight at LZ Albany. The reports of his death, he reckoned, were greatly exaggerated.

The helicopter evacuation of the wounded from Albany clearing was not yet complete. CWO Hank Ainsworth, still overhead, got a call from Major Henry saying he needed one more lift ship for three or four more wounded. Ainsworth volunteered to do the pickup with the command ship. Says Ainsworth, "By the grace of God, I didn't take a hit. I flew in and out through that wall of tracers and did not take a single round. I figured I was one of the luckiest pilots who ever flew in 'Nam. Never a hit the whole time."

Now the Albany clearing perimeter could settle down for what was left of the night. "About five soldiers made it into the perimeter during the night," Rick Rescorla recalls. "Larry Gwin pointed southeast and said what is left of the rest of the battalion is out there in three main groups and then smaller teams. I walked up to the lone figure of Lieutenant Gordon Grove standing in the northwest corner of the perimeter. He was a former sergeant who had come up through OCS. 'My platoon's out there,' he said. 'I came back in to get help but I was ordered not to go back.' He was desolate. He kept looking at the tree line as if expecting his men to show up."

After midnight several shots rang out from inside the perimeter. A trooper twenty yards behind Rescorla, inside the perimeter, had rattled off a panicky three rounds. Rescorla walked back and cussed out the group in the middle of the perimeter. "If I hear one more round out of you we will turn our weapons around and open up. No one fires from inside the perimeter. If you want to fire get out to the perimeter line." Whispered communication took place all night between isolated elements outside the perimeter. If there was heroism, it was out there in the tiny groups of wounded and those who bandaged and protected them through the long night. "They were just like hunting buddies," says Rescorla, "surviving by instinct, looking out after each other."

In the perimeter there were discussions about taking out a night patrol as was being done by Captain Forrest's company at the end of the column. Rescorla recalls: "The idea of crossing through the chaos of the battlefield at night presented problems. We would have to deplete the perimeter. Scare shooting by friendlies was a threat. There was reason to believe the enemy was still effective. Finally, moving the wounded would achieve little unless they could be evacuated immediately. Wait until dawn became the command watchword."

Lieutenant Larry Gwin of Alpha Company recalls that late that night one of Alpha's missing men crawled into the American perimeter. "Sergeant James A. Mullartey from our 1st Platoon made it back to our lines. His story: The NVA had been shooting our wounded. One came up to him, stuck a pistol in his mouth, and fired. The bullet exited the back of his throat, knocked him out and they left him for dead. He survived and when he woke up at night he started crawling to us."

As dawn broke over the Albany battlefield on Friday, November 18, a profound shock awaited the Americans who had survived the night. To this point no one had a clear picture of the extent of the losses suffered by the 2nd Battalion, 7th Cavalry. They were about to find out.

Captain Joel Sugdinis, the commander of Alpha Company, 2nd Battalion, 7th Cav, remembers that at dawn on the eighteenth the area was quiet, though not comfortable. "We did the 'Mad Minute' and it evoked no response. We began to slowly move forward to recon the areas out from the perimeter. No opposition—the battlefield was quiet. We collected as many of our dead as we could. The North Vietnamese had paid dearly but so had we.

"The American dead were retrieved and brought back to the

island perimeter wrapped in ponchos, tagged and literally stacked like cord wood. When the Chinook helicopters arrived to remove them I remember the flight crews were stunned at the cargo. We buried none of the enemy. The battlefield was acquiring that pronounced smell of death."

Lieutenant Gwin, Sugdinis's executive officer, says, "The next day was the real nightmare, as we went out to find our dead and missing. I think each of us cracked up a little bit that day as the true picture of the action began to unfold. Then it came across the radio: Bravo Company had found one other survivor from our 2nd Platoon. He had been badly wounded in the legs and had propped himself up against a tree. He had been burned by napalm, waiting in the night, and some North Vietnamese had put a pistol to his eye and pulled the trigger. Shot him in the eye, blinded him, but he was still alive! I saw him being brought in on a stretcher, smoking a cigarette, all fucked up."

"As they policed up our dead, bringing them in, I lost it," Lieutenant Gwin admits. "I heard that Don Cornett had been killed and that broke my emotional back. I heard that Charlie Company was basically annihilated. That became evident. I saw where our 1st Platoon had been and there was just bodies all over the place, already bloating in the sun. I went to the 2nd Platoon area and we found three of our men all lying together, terribly shot up and clearly hit by napalm. I suppressed those memories for fifteen years."

The terrible task of policing up the battlefield fell to Captain Myron Diduryk's Bravo Company troops and Captain George Forrest's Alpha Company, 1st of the 5th. Diduryk wrote: "Next day, the 18th, I made a tour of the battlefield and I'll tell you it was a hell of a grim sight to see. North Vietnamese and U.S. bodies all over, intermingled. It was a hell of a fight; some North Vietnamese were bayoneted. Again the grim task of recovering friendly dead. This time there were many more. It took the better part of the 18th and 19th to accomplish this."

Specialist 4 Dick Ackerman of the recon platoon remembers, "Just before daylight at the Albany clearing the word was spread:

Do not leave your holes. Do not get up and walk around. At the command there will be a Mad Minute. Somebody was thinking. When the time arrived we opened up. The NVA started jumping up and running, falling out of trees. I don't think this was their main force; possibly just a rear guard group. Then we started spreading out. I was on perimeter defense to enable others to pick up wounded behind us. There was sporadic shooting. What we saw as we expanded our perimeter was unbelievable. The bodies, complete and in pieces, were everywhere.

"Some were still alive. The NVA came into the ambush area at night to recover their dead and wounded. When they found any of our guys alive they would beat them to death, bayonet them or machete them to avoid shooting and drawing fire from us. We policed up all day and pulled back into the circle for the night. Next day, the 19th, we did the same thing except I was on pickup duty, not perimeter guard."

Doc William Shucart hiked up the shattered column from the Alpha Company, 1st Battalion, 5th Cavalry perimeter to the Albany clearing perimeter the morning of the eighteenth. "On the way we found guys scattered all over the place, wounded, who had spent the night out there by themselves. They were so calm. I was thinking: I spent the night with thirty or forty guys and even with all that company I was scared shitless. If I had been out in the woods alone like these guys I would have been scared to death. They were amazing."

Lieutenant Pat Payne, the recon-platoon commander, says, "We moved out very carefully and started finding all our dead and wounded as soon as possible. One of the greatest losses was Lieutenant Don Cornett. I saw his body. He was laid out alongside the edge of the LZ on his stomach. His face was turned to the side. He looked like he was asleep. A helicopter landed and it stirred the wind. Cornett's hair blew in the breeze and it was beyond my comprehension that such a wonderful person had been killed. I covered him up with his poncho and then helped carry his body to the chopper."

Captain Skip Fesmire, commander of Charlie Company: "In sweeping through the area at first light we found dead American and

NVA soldiers locked in mortal combat. Charlie Company, under the control of Lieutenant Don Cornett, had moved forward on the right flank of Delta Company and met head on the hasty attack of the North Vietnamese. Strewn over the battlefield were numerous dead enemy, along with fifty dead and fifty wounded soldiers of Charlie Company and almost all of Sugdinis' lead platoon."

Specialist Jack P. Smith, one of Charlie Company's wounded: "In the morning the place looked like the devil's butcher shop; there were people hanging out of trees. The ground was slippery with blood. Men who were my closest friends were all around me, dead. Then they started to call in artillery and they came and got us. They wrapped me in a poncho and carried me to a helicopter and I was whisked out of there. I was taken to Japan and it all passed. I came back to Vietnam; [I] didn't see any more combat, and left eventually. When I came home on leave my parents were delighted to see me. Couple of days later I was watching the evening news and, lo and behold, I saw my company jumping out of helicopters and I burst into tears and ran out of the room."

Lieutenant Rescorla had a different reaction to the Mad Minute fired at dawn: "This decision was regrettable. Rifle fire shattered the silence and the perimeter was ringed with reckless firing. Little thought had been given that the remainder of our survivors were sprawled among the trees and anthills within 500 yards, the effective range of our M-16s. 'What the fuck is happening? Are you shooting at us?' The frantic radio calls started coming in. How many troops were killed or injured by our wake-up call will never be known. Thank God for the trees, ant hills, uneven terrain."

Rescorla took a path down the western flank of what had been the battalion column. He called it "a long, bloody traffic accident in the jungle. One trooper dead with weapons laid out next to him, pack of cigarettes clenched in his hand. Further on I noticed an officer wearing a Ranger patch. It was Don Cornett. He had been shot several times. Individual troopers looked as if they had not yet received the order to move out. Mortar men were dead, sitting upright against ant hills, rounds still on their backs, as if they were caught during a break. Here and there, between American bodies, lay smaller khaki figures. Coming around an ant hill I saw a concentration of NVA khaki bodies. A movement. I fired twice and we advanced slowly. Three of them. Two riflemen dead. One, wearing a pith helmet, was very young with a soft, round-featured face, lying belly up. He was dying, eyes flickering, shirt soaked with blood. They had all been wounded and had drawn close together, a team of some kind. Charlie or Delta had given them their first crippling wounds."

On the dying enemy soldier Rescorla noticed something shiny. A big, battered old French army bugle carrying a manufacture date of 1900 and the legend "Couesnon & Cie, Fournisseurs de L'Armée. 94 rue D'Ancoïème. Paris." On some long-ago battlefield, perhaps Dien Bien Phu, the victorious Viet Minh had taken it as trophy. And marked their own legend: two crude Chinese characters tattooed onto the brass bell with nailpoint. Rough translation: 'Long and powerful service!' Now, here in the valley of the Ia Drang, in the tall elephant grass, the trophy had changed hands again. The 7th Cavalry had a bugle once more, and Bravo Company, 2nd Battalion would blow it time and again on the battlefields of Vietnam.

Captain Dudley Tademy, 3rd Brigade fire-support coordinator, remembers flying out to Albany at first light the next morning. "Tim Brown, myself, Mickey Parrish. Took a while to get in through the smoke hanging over the whole area. Not much had really taken place in terms of policing the area. The image that is still vivid in my mind is the carnage. Folks were still sitting around in a daze; they hadn't done much, hadn't even taken ponchos and covered up these bodies. I could handle the conversation; I could handle grown men crying; but we are talking twelve hours later. Sitting there feeling sorry for themselves. Colonel Brown was very pissed off. Even if you get caught in a bad situation you have to do something to recover. It was young kids who paid the price. In later years I used to stress that to my young battery commanders: 'It isn't us who die in combat; it's those young kids who die. Those kids we are responsible for training and leading. It's our job to get the job done and get those kids home safe.' "

Colonel Brown recalls that visit to Albany on November 18: "The next morning I finally got into that place. They were busy figuring out who was dead, who was wounded. They never got an accurate count for forty-eight hours or so. I stayed out there wandering around looking while they were bringing the bodies back in. Myron Diduryk was checking them off. I never saw McDade. I asked where he was, where the command post was, but it was all confusion and nobody could tell me where he was. Diduryk seemed to have things under control. When I got back I sent Shy Meyer back out to see if he could make any more sense of it than I had."

Captain Buse Tully of Bravo Company, 1st Battalion, 5th Cav and Captain George Forrest of the same battalion's Alpha Company had laagered their companies together overnight in the tail-end perimeter, venturing out only on the after-midnight patrol to find Ghost 4-6 and all those wounded Charlie Company, 2nd Battalion, 7th Cav soldiers. Captain Tully wrote: "With daylight, re-supply and medevac ships arrived and we moved out toward the 2nd Battalion, 7th Cav position. The battle area was a scene of carnage. One of the few North Vietnamese found alive, when offered assistance, attempted to throw a hand grenade. He was shot. We also found GIs who obviously had been given the coup de grace; hands tied behind their backs and bullet holes in the backs of their heads. The link up had been made at nine A.M. From then until two P.M. we patrolled out of Albany, picking up dead and wounded personnel and enemy and friendly weapons. The job wasn't finished when we had to leave in order to make it back to LZ Columbus and our parent battalion's control by nightfall."

Both the 1st Battalion, 5th Cav companies made the march back to Columbus without incident, closing in at five P.M., well before dark, on November 18. Columbus was a good-sized rectangular clearing, running north–south. George Forrest's A Company moved into position on the northwest while Buse Tully's B Company men secured the southern end of the clearing. Tully immediately put out observation posts forward of his three-platoon defenses. Then he told his men to break out C-rations and take a well-deserved breather. Both the meal and the break were rudely interrupted at 5:35 P.M., when the outposts spotted the lead elements of a North Vietnamese force maneuvering toward Columbus. With that warning, Lieutenant Colonel Fred Ackerson, commander of the 1st Battalion, 5th Cav, had time to get his men in their holes, alert the artillery batteries, and get set for the assault, which came in from the east and southeast.

According to then–Lieutenant Colonel Nguyen Huu An, the NVA battlefield commander, that attack should have been launched against Columbus at two P.M., when half of Ackerson's battalion would still have been marching back from Albany. General An said the commander of the attack battalion of the 33rd Regiment was unable to mass his men, who had dispersed over a wide area of the valley to avoid air strikes, in time to make the deadline. An said his commander also had problems finding a section of the Columbus perimeter where there was sufficient cover to hide his preparations for the attack. The result was a delay of over three and a half hours.

When the attack finally did kick off it was met with a hail of rifle and machine-gun fire from Ackerson's battalion as well as from the artillerymen who had cranked their 105mm howitzers down and were firing canister rounds at point-blank range. The Air Force was quick to provide tactical air strikes close to the perimeter. By nine P.M. the 1st Battalion, 5th Cavalry had beaten off and broken the attack.

An says: "The 33rd Regiment could not destroy this position, but they forced the artillery to withdraw, and the artillerymen left behind about a thousand rounds. We captured a thousand rounds of 105mm ammunition, but we had no guns of that size and never used it." The North Vietnamese commander reckons that even though the attack failed, his men forced the abandonment of Columbus the next day. That's not the way Colonel Tim Brown, 3rd Brigade commander, sees it: "We were in our last days. The 2nd Brigade had already been ordered up. We were just swinging out west so that Colonel Ray Lynch [commander of the 2nd Brigade] could take over. We were also moving artillery out in that direction. Lynch was going to put his brigade headquarters at Duc Co Special Forces Camp. So we were in the process of getting out, but not yet."

In furtherance of that plan, at midday on November 18 Brown

had sent Lieutenant Colonel Bob Tully's 2nd Battalion, 5th Cav on an air assault into a clearing designated Landing Zone Crooks (6.5 miles northwest of Columbus). Once they had secured Crooks, Brown airlifted the artillery from LZ Falcon to Crooks. From there the artillerymen would provide initial support to the 2nd Brigade and to the South Vietnamese Airborne battalions that were planning to move south from Duc Co camp on November 19 and take up blocking positions along the Cambodian border to harass the North Vietnamese on their retreat from the Ia Drang Valley.

On November 19, Brown moved the artillery and the 1st Battalion, 5th Cav from Columbus to a new landing zone designated Golf, 7.5 miles northwest. Now all the pieces were in place for continued operations against the enemy, with Brown's 3rd Brigade handing off the job to Colonel Ray Lynch's 2nd Brigade and to the ARVN Airborne task force.

Back in the Albany area, policing of the battlefield continued. Survivors and witnesses most often use the word "carnage" for the terrible things they saw in the brush and tall elephant grass.

Specialist 4 Jon Wallenius of the Bravo Company, 2nd Battalion, 7th Cavalry mortar platoon, and most of the rest of Myron Diduryk's men were involved in this macabre and depressing duty. "It was incredible carnage. We went to areas where lots of artillery had come in during the night and we saw our guys had been blown up in the trees. The bodies were already decomposed and it had only happened the night before. We were in shock. It was the first, last, and only time I ever saw anything like it and I pray never again. The stench was unbelievable. We started hauling in the whole bodies first; then we brought in the pieces and parts. Two Chinooks came in and we loaded one with about twenty corpses, neatly arranged in litters. The pilot began preparing to take off. One of our officers pointed an M-16 at the pilot and told him to keep the bird on the ground; we weren't through. Bodies were loaded floor to ceiling. When the ramp finally closed blood poured through the hinges. I felt sorry for the poor bastards who would have to unload this chopper back at Holloway."

One of the last wounded Americans recovered from the battlefield that day was PFC James Shadden of the Delta Company mortar platoon. "The next morning and all day long the sun had no mercy. The ants and flies were crawling all over my wounds. My tongue and throat had turned to cotton. I had grown so weak I could hardly move. Captain Henry Thorpe came to me about six P.M. the evening of the eighteenth and said: 'We didn't know where you were.' Well, I didn't know where he was either. After a few days at the 85th Evac Hospital, I was flown back to the hospital at Fort Campbell, Kentucky, where I stayed almost a year recovering."

The nightmares born of this battle have never faded.

23

THE SERGEANT AND THE GHOST

> We have good corporals and good sergeants and some good lieutenants and captains, and those are far more important than good generals.
>
> —William Tecumseh Sherman

Every battle has its unsung heroes, and the desperate fight that raged up and down the column of Americans scattered along the trail to the Albany clearing is no exception. Two of them met after midnight, November 18, when Platoon Sergeant Fred J. Kluge, thirty-two years old, 1st Platoon, Alpha Company, 1st Battalion, 5th Cavalry, led a patrol into the heart of the killing zone in search of the voice on the radio calling himself Ghost 4-6. Kluge eased into a small cluster of wounded and desperate Americans and quietly asked: "Who's in charge here?" There was a long silence and then the faint reply: "Over here." Second Lieutenant Robert J. Jeanette, who had been wounded at least four times that afternoon but had held on to his radio and called deadly barrages of artillery down on groups of North Vietnamese circling the Albany clearing, thought he had been saved. So he had, but not just yet.

Ghost 4-6 and Sergeant Kluge are the stuff of legend, and various versions of their sagas have circulated for years among the survivors of Albany. Literally dozens of men reckon they owe their lives to either the sergeant or the Ghost. Both insist that they only did their jobs, that the real heroes were among all the others who fought in Albany that day and night.

Sergeant Fred J. Kluge was a seventeen-year-old high school dropout when he enlisted in the Army in 1950. He fought in the Korean War with the 187th Regimental Combat Team. Between the wars, Korea and Vietnam, he taught map reading and small-unit infantry tactics in Army schools. In 1965 Kluge was on his way to the Special Forces but ended up in the 1st Cavalry Division, assigned as a platoon sergeant in Alpha Company, 1st Battalion, 5th Cavalry, Captain George Forrest commanding.

When the fighting broke out on the march to Albany clearing, Sergeant Kluge helped establish the perimeter at the rear of the column, and then single-handedly began finding and guiding to safety the Americans staggering out of the chopped-up column. Sergeant Kluge's account:

"We started getting more and more wounded in from the column up ahead. I would go out and collect them. They were staggering out of the kill zone, dazed, badly wounded, shot up. I just moved off in that direction a good ways so I could guide them back. The column up forward of us was gone; it had disintegrated. There was just independent little skirmishes going on, little pockets of men fighting back. I moved on up to where I could see into the kill zone and pick up those people coming out. Some of them were running, some crawling. Almost all of them were wounded.

"I could see the enemy up in the trees—and I could see them on the ground, moving along in groups of three or four, bent over low. They were moving like they had a destination to reach. Some of them shot at me, but mostly they were just moving along. What it looked like to me was their flanking units moving into the ambush zone.

"I picked up the surgeon of the 2nd Battalion, 7th Cav, Doc Shucart, about this time. I told him what we had going and he started dealing with the wounded. By now I started getting some choppers in. The medic, Specialist 5 Daniel Torrez, told me that one of my squad-leader sergeants had put a bandage on his leg but Torrez didn't think he was really wounded. I went over and he was laying down, his pants leg slit up the side and a bandage wrapped around his leg. I asked him: "How bad are you hit?" He said, "Oh, not too bad, just a flesh wound." I said: "Well, how about Torrez and me take a look?" He said no, he didn't want anybody messing with it. I tore that bandage off and there was no wound at all. Right then and there I beat the shit out of him. I ripped his stripes off his arms and demoted him on the spot. I didn't have that authority, of course, but I sure relieved him of his job. I got his assistant squad leader and put him in charge. All this time the doctor had gone on treating the wounded.

"Another captain, I believe an Air Force captain, came in our perimeter around then and asked what he could do. I put him with the doctor. The evac choppers were landing about fifty yards from where I had set up—about two hundred yards from the kill zone. We had three or four choppers come in, one at a time, and I got all my wounded out, but more were coming out of the kill zone all the time, more than I was getting evacuated.

"A pilot called me over and told me there was a clearing two hundred yards further back that was much bigger, where they could bring in two or three choppers at a time. I had my platoon pick up the wounded, and I sent a squad on ahead to recon that clearing, and we moved on back. It was a nice big clearing, with a big anthill in the center. We set up a perimeter around that clearing and I went forward again to guide the people coming out of the ambush.

"Lieutenant Adams and Captain Forrest both came back to us about then. Forrest was really upset; he had lost some friends in this. I was getting reports on who was dead from our company: One lieutenant killed and two lieutenants wounded. One platoon sergeant killed, one wounded. The executive officer wounded.

"A little later Bravo Company 1/5 came in overland from Columbus, led by Captain Tully. He and Captain Forrest conferred, and they wanted my platoon to gather up all the wounded, maybe thirty-five or so, and prepare to move. Bravo Company would lead off. Tully wanted to go forward to the Albany clearing, through the ambush site. I told Tully: "You won't make it even a hundred yards up that trail." He didn't. They took real intense fire, lost one killed and several wounded. He decided that wasn't such a good idea after all, and pulled back.

"Tully and Forrest then decided to set up a joint, two-company perimeter in the big clearing. At that point we were holding the perimeter. Now Tully's people took over three-quarters of it, and we kept the rest. Tully's people took the portion facing the ambush site. By now we had gotten in most of the wounded from the ambush. Only a few straggled in later. I had piles of wounded men, and now the choppers told me they were going to quit flying. It was getting on to dark and they said they wouldn't land after dark.

"I pleaded with them to at least bring us some ammunition. Most of the people coming in from the ambush didn't have weapons or ammo. They had dropped their harness and butt packs when they got hit. Some of my people carrying wounded had dropped their gear, too. I told that pilot I wanted grenades, trip flares and ammo for the 16s and 60s. The pilot said OK, he would do that one last trip. He must have just gone over to Columbus because he was back soon after. He didn't land, just made a low pass over the perimeter and kicked out crates of ammo.

"Captain Forrest had no radio, so we set up my platoon's radio over at the anthill; that's where Forrest set up his CP. I was expecting us to get hit; we were really vulnerable with so many wounded that couldn't move. I kept checking with the doctor and we tried to select an area where the wounded and the medics would be protected.

"Around ten or eleven at night Captain Forrest was fiddling around with the radio when he picked up a plea for help from Ghost 4-6. This was a 2nd Battalion, 7th Cavalry lieutenant. I spoke to him both that night and again, briefly, in the morning. He was telling us over the radio that he was all shot up, that he was going to die, that the enemy were moving around, crawling around in the grass, killing off the American wounded. He said he could hear them shooting and talking out there around him. He said there were a bunch of other American wounded in the area.

"Captain Forrest wanted to take a patrol out to rescue them. I told him it wasn't all that good an idea. We discussed the pros and cons of it. The whole area was lit with flares. I told him there were a lot of arguments against it: Those people are closer to the Albany clearing than to us and we have no contact with Albany. What if Albany has sent out a patrol and we stumble into them and shoot each other up? The wounded Americans out in that grass are scared to death; they may shoot us up as well. Then there's the enemy, and if they don't shoot us, it's damned near guaranteed the Bravo Company guys on this perimeter will shoot us when we come back in.

"He insisted: 'Sergeant, get your people saddled up.' I said: 'OK, but there's no point in both of us going. They are my people, I'll take them out.' It was arranged that Ghost 4-6 would fire his .45-caliber pistol and I would guide in on the sound.

"The medevac guys had kicked out four or five folding-type litters. We got those and an M-60 machine gun and I took the whole bunch of us, twenty-two or twenty-three guys, I think. Captain Forrest stayed back. We traveled as light as we could. I told the guys to leave their steel pots, packs, all that stuff. Just carry rifles, ammo, and grenades. We went out through Tully's lines and I retraced the route back to this ridge I had been on earlier, collecting the stragglers. Then we moved ahead real slow, with Ghost 4-6 firing his pistol. I didn't take a straight line up that column, but kind of looped around.

"We started finding dead everywhere—mostly Americans at that point, on the outskirts of the kill zone, where they had run after they got shot. It was just thick with dead. Then we began to find some enemy dead among them. We picked up three or four American wounded on our way up to Ghost 4-6. If they could walk we helped them along. We were already getting bogged down; we had no real capacity to react quickly if the enemy were to hit us.

"Well, we got to Ghost 4-6, and he was bad shot up, had been hit in the chest and hit in the knees. But of all the wounded we encountered, he was probably the most mentally alert and competent. I really admired him. That guy had a super attitude and spirit. We put up a little perimeter and started policing up the wounded and bringing them in. There were twenty-five or thirty or more that we brought in there.

"I had to make a decision. We could not take them all. There were too many of them. And I knew we would not be able to get back out there that night. There wasn't time enough before daylight. I asked Daniel Torrez the medic to pick out those who were in the worst shape, who didn't look like making it through the night, for us to carry back. Plus those who could walk on their own or with a little help. The rest we gathered close around Ghost 4-6.

"I told Ghost 4-6 I wasn't bringing him back on this trip, that I was putting him in charge of the others and I would be back in the morning. He didn't like it but he accepted it. Then I asked Torrez if he would stay with them. He was the best soldier in my platoon, came from El Paso, Texas, and I thought the world of him. He didn't like the idea of staying out there either, but he said he would.

"I left Torrez the M-60 machine gun. We were gathering up ammo and weapons off the dead and putting those weapons beside the wounded so they could help defend themselves, if it came to that. When we told them we were only taking the worst-wounded plus the walking wounded, some guys said, "I can walk," and got up. Some of them fell right back down, too. When I made the decision to carry out the worst cases, I was hoping that the choppers would come back in and collect those men. Turned out they wouldn't, and that's something that really pissed me off.

"Anyway, we started back in a straggling column; we had to stop every few minutes to let the walking wounded catch up. There were only three of us who were not carrying wounded: myself on point, and my radio operator and another guy riding shotgun at the rear. I was so apprehensive that the enemy would hit us now, when there was no way we could defend ourselves. Those carrying the wounded had their rifles slung on their backs.

"I was even more apprehensive about getting back inside our perimeter; that had worried me from the first minute. When we finally got close I stopped everyone and we clustered in the shadows.

I knew we were real close, less than two hundred yards out from our lines. I was talking to Captain Forrest on the radio, and telling him we were afraid to come in; we were afraid they were gonna shoot us. Forrest came out to the line and shined a flashlight on his face. He was telling me: "We got everyone alerted—everyone has got the word—nobody's going to shoot." I kept saying we are afraid to move. So Forrest came out another fifty yards toward us, still shining that light on his face.

"Finally, I said, 'OK, we're coming in.' We got everyone on their feet and we started in. We had got within a few feet of where Forrest was standing and, sure enough, somebody opened up on us from the Bravo Company 1/5 lines. It was a private in a foxhole and he fired a whole magazine at us. He was firing low, got one guy in the hip and two others in their legs. When he finally emptied his magazine we screamed at him and got it stopped, and we came on in. Turned out that guy had been asleep in his hole when they put the word out and nobody woke him up to tell him. When he woke up and saw that column approaching he figured we were NVA and he opened fire. There's always the one guy who don't get the word and that's the guy who shoots you up coming home. Always.

"And that was that. It was around four A.M., and for the rest of the night we stayed in the perimeter and racked out. I fell asleep. Somebody woke me up before daybreak. The choppers were starting to come in for the wounded. Then Bravo Company 1/5 saddled up. We waited till all the wounded were evacuated and moved off behind Bravo through the ambush site. We never did get inside the Albany clearing. I could see it, maybe a hundred and fifty yards away. We identified our dead and brought them out.

"We went on up, like we promised, and got Ghost 4-6 and Daniel Torrez the medic and that group of wounded. I spoke briefly with Ghost 4-6: 'I told you I would come back for you, didn't I?' He still had a great attitude. I don't know if he lived or died, but if anyone had the will to get through, it was certainly that man.

"They brought in Hueys and Chinooks to pick up the dead. There were bodies everywhere, many of them messed up by the air strikes, bomb strikes, artillery, ARA. I never saw anything in Korea that bad. Captain Forrest sent me out with a roster of the names of the men in our company and a man from each of the other two platoons and we walked the battlefield looking at all the American dead. Then our men and the men from Bravo Company 2/7 got the duty of bringing them all in for evacuation. It was terrible, terrible. Some of them were in pieces from the air and artillery. We had to use entrenching tools to put them on the ponchos to carry them in. We ran out of ponchos so we had to reuse the same ones over and over and they became slippery with blood. When I would see the carrying parties drop one I would go over and use Colonel Hal Moore's words to me at X-Ray: 'Show a little respect. He's one of ours.'

"A week after we got back to base camp I came down with malaria and spent three months in Japan recuperating. When I came back to Alpha Company, Captain Forrest had moved on to some other job. One night I was sitting in the NCO Club at An Khe drinking a beer with some other sergeants. There was a sergeant from Bravo Company, 2nd Battalion, 7th Cav there and he said, 'You know, we won that battle.' Someone else said, 'How do you reckon that?' And the Bravo Company sergeant said: 'I know because I counted the dead and there were a hundred and two American bodies and a hundred and four gooks.' "

Lieutenant Robert J. Jeanette, Ghost 4-6, weapons-platoon leader of Charlie Company, 2nd Battalion, 7th Cavalry, was a big-city boy: grew up in the Bronx, went to the City College of New York. He joined the ROTC program there and was commissioned in the Army in February of 1964. After Officer Basic and Airborne training, Jeanette was posted to Fort Benning in the late spring of 1964. He was assigned to the 2nd Battalion, first as a rifle-platoon executive officer, then as platoon leader. When the battalion got to Vietnam the twenty-three-year-old Jeanette was put in command of the weapons platoon of Charlie Company. Lieutenant Jeanette tells his story:

"My weapons platoon had, I think, three 81mm mortars. We were not really equipped as a rifle platoon. Some of us carried sidearms. I had an M-16 rifle. I think there was one or two M-60 machine guns. Everything was real peaceful up to the point where we were almost at the Albany clearing, the pickup zone. Then we began hearing some small-arms fire up ahead. My platoon set up a little perimeter.

"We stayed put right there for fifteen or twenty minutes. Then the word came down for us to form a skirmish line and move on up to the north. The LZ was to our west, and they were taking small-arms fire up there pretty heavily. We did not get very far with our maneuver. The volume of fire was increasing and now it completely enveloped us.

"There was essentially not much visibility unless you were standing up, and by now nobody was standing up. We could not see the enemy maneuvering at this time. I remember trying to set up a perimeter and fire direction. I was trying to find out where the rifle platoons were. They were reporting a lot of casualties on the radio, saying their medic had gone down, and asking for an aid man. I was crawling forward through the grass trying to move up a bit and see where those other Charlie Company people were. That's when I met my friend, the only enemy I had seen to that point. He fired at me and I fired back. I got off one round and my M-16 jammed. He was still firing at me and I scooted back fast.

"When I got back to my perimeter I picked up a .45 pistol from somebody. By now our group was taking some casualties. Until now the firing had enveloped us but it was not, seemingly, aimed directly at us. Right after I got back, they found us. We were catching automatic weapons, rifle fire, and some light mortar or rifle grenades, airbursts right over our position. I don't remember where our mortar tubes were at this point. Our orders from Captain Fesmire, relayed by Lieutenant Don Cornett, had been to move out in a rifle skirmish line; nothing said about setting up our tubes. We may have left them when we moved out on that very brief maneuver.

"Now we were taking plenty of casualties; we were firing back as best we could, but we really had no visible targets. I tried to get the men to sweep the trees around us. My platoon was all still on our perimeter, all in the same area, spread out but still together. It was becoming very obvious we were surrounded and trapped, because now we began to take fire from all sides, every direction. Two guys volunteered to try to break through and get help. I don't know what happened to them.

"Then I was hit the first time. That round hit me in the right knee. That afternoon I was hit two or three more times, some of it shrapnel from those airbursts. One was a rifle round that hit me square in my steel helmet, right in front. It penetrated but was deflected all the way around. I had a deep crease on my head, could feel the blood running down. Damned if I know how the next wound happened. From the time I was hit in the knee I was flat on my back on the ground. But somewhere in there I was shot in the buttocks. There was no medic, no one to bandage me. I just lay there losing blood. That went for everyone else there as well.

"There was nobody moving, nobody crawling out. There were some other Americans alongside our platoon, under better cover. It is quite possible we were taking some friendly fire, but there was no doubt we were getting enemy fire. The radio we had was on the battalion frequency. I remember hearing conversations that I would not have normally heard on the company net: directions for air support, pilots asking direction where to lay the napalm. I got on once to tell them that their napalm was a little bit hot, a little close to where I thought there were friendlies. It wasn't that close to me but I could see where it landed. I wanted them to know maybe they were hitting friendlies. They told me to get off the net, that they didn't want too many people talking.

"Anyway, I had a radio that was working and a good freq and I wasn't going to give up either one. After I was hit the other channels just went right out of my head and I was afraid to start switching around for fear of losing all contact. Eventually I think they changed channels for the battalion net. I know I stopped hearing all the chatter; later I had communication with some other people.

"By now most everyone near me had been hit, too. I remember the guys who were under deep cover yelling at me: 'Lieutenant, get your ass out of there.' I yelled back that it was hard to move, that I was hit pretty bad. They yelled that they would help me crawl and I told them there was no way I was going to leave the radio behind. That's when an amazing thing happened. We had a young private in the company who was constantly up on charges—a goldbrick, a sad sack. Always in trouble. He got up in all that firing, came over, and said: 'I'll take the radio and help you out of here, Lieutenant.' As he bent over trying to get the radio out from under me he took one right through the heart and fell over dead. Weeks later, in the hospital, I tried to get him a posthumous medal; but I never heard back. And now I can't remember his name.

"As it grew dark I was still in the same position. I was trying to maintain contact with whoever I had talking to me back at brigade. There was a lull in the battle and suddenly I am talking to an artillery outfit. The North Vietnamese were now running around the area and we could see them moving. Bunches of ten, twenty, more of them circling the perimeter of the landing zone. It was maybe a hundred and fifty yards to the LZ perimeter, and the enemy were between us and them.

"I don't know how I got put on to that artillery unit. It took me a good while to convince them to bring artillery into that area. Finally they tried a white phosphorus round or two. I couldn't see any of their rounds land and WP rounds don't make near as much noise as high-explosive rounds. Finally I persuaded them to start using the HE [high-explosive] rounds and then I could hear it and shift that fire into the area where we could see those enemy troops moving.

"I never really knew how effective that artillery fire I directed was until two things happened. Back in the States a few months later, at St. Albans Naval Hospital in New York I met somebody who had been in that fight, a 2nd Battalion, 7th Cav guy, who came over and thanked me for that artillery fire. I was out walking the halls on my crutches for exercise and he came up on crutches, too. He had an empty trouser leg. He told me the artillery fire took his leg but it saved his life and he was grateful. I was stunned. Later on, around 1971, I had to appear as a witness at a court-martial at Fort Leavenworth and I ran into Sergeant Howard of Charlie Company. He and some of his men were together in a position up ahead of me in the fight. Howard told me that every time the enemy got close to them, the artillery would come in close too and really whack them. He said that artillery fire was the only thing that kept the enemy away and kept them alive. It felt good to know that I did some good. And I had to argue with them to give me the HE.

"Somewhere in there I really lose all sense of time. I know before dark and after dark and that's about it. I remember I was on the radio that night talking to someone, telling them that we could hear groups of enemy walk by; we were hearing single rifle or pistol shots; that someone would scream or cry out, and then a single shot. I knew damned well what was going on. The enemy were killing our wounded.

"When the relief patrol came in it was from my south, I think. I guided them to us by firing my .45 pistol. They picked up some American wounded further south who also had a radio on my frequency. When the patrol got to us I could hear the patrol leader saying he never anticipated so many wounded; he was stupefied by the numbers. I know he asked, 'Who's in charge here?' I heard him but my mind didn't react for what seemed like a long time before finally I could say: 'Over here.' They brought a medic and he gave me a shot of morphine. That was the first shot I had, the first treatment I had for, I don't know, twelve hours or more. The medic put a tourniquet on my leg.

"The patrol leader told me that he couldn't take everyone, that he didn't have enough people to carry everyone. He said he had to leave me and the others with the medic and only take the worst-hurt. I know the enemy came back at least once after they left. A party of twenty or thirty of them. We could see the enemy moving; it was a very clear night with a bright moon, maybe full or near full.

"After dawn the relief came for us. Somebody gave me a canteen. I was dry as bone. During the night the medic would only give me a sip or two. When the relief came I know I guzzled a whole canteen. I can remember being triaged somewhere, maybe Holloway. Next thing I know I woke up in a hospital ward at Qui Nhon. A fellow officer, Paul Bonocorsi, from Charlie Company had been shifted out to liaison duty the week before the Ia Drang and he was there checking on C Company people. He told me there had been 108 men on the fit-for-duty report the morning we left for Albany, and only eight on the duty report the day after.

"I arrived at Fort Dix, New Jersey, on Thanksgiving Day, 1965, and was ambulanced over to St. Albans Naval Hospital in the borough of Queens, the hospital closest to my home. I walked out of that hospital on Memorial Day, 1966. I was an outpatient for another three or four months, then was placed on temporary retirement that was made permanent in 1971.

"I was recalled to active duty briefly after that to testify at that court-martial at Leavenworth. That was the case of a Charlie Company enlisted man who got blind, raging drunk the week before Albany. He pointed his rifle at his sergeant and pulled the trigger. It dry-fired; either [it was] unloaded or [it] misfired. Then he went off to try to shoot the company commander. He was sitting in the brig when we were out getting shot to pieces. He was court-martialed and sent to prison but his conviction was overturned on appeal, so they retried him and there weren't many left who could testify."

AFTERMATH

morning of the 18th and staggered into the 1st Cavalry Division press tent, pale and shaken by what he had seen and photographed, and told his colleagues that the 2nd Battalion, 7th Cavalry had been massacred in an enemy ambush. Division public affairs officers swiftly informed Knowles of the report by Merron.

How and why it took more than eighteen hours for the assistant division commander to get the first direct detailed account from the battlefield—and why that information had come, not through command channels, but from a civilian photographer—is a question that lingers. Knowles says, "Lieutenant Colonel Hemphill had been getting pieces of information from the artillery and from all over that fit into a running description of a fight; but nobody, not even McDade, had the full magnitude until the next day. We kept getting body counts and casualty figures all that morning [of the 18th]." The reporters gathering in Pleiku thought they smelled a cover-up. The news conference that followed did little to dispel their suspicions.

Knowles told the news conference that a battalion of the 1st Cavalry Division (Airmobile) had had a "meeting engagement" with an enemy force of equal or larger size, and the American battalion had suffered "light to moderate casualties." Knowles reported that the enemy force had suffered four hundred–plus killed and had broken off the engagement and withdrawn. The cavalry battalion had held its ground and won a victory. The general's summary of what he understood had happened at Albany was greeted by roars of disbelief from the assembled reporters.

In short order the wires were burning up with reports of the heaviest American casualties to date in the Vietnam War; hints of an Army cover-up of a disastrous ambush; reports that the American forces were withdrawing—some accounts said "retreating"—from the valley. Much of the reporting was overstated and oversimplified; some of it was just plain wrong. What had happened at LZ Albany was by no means a classic ambush. The element of surprise worked for the North Vietnamese and against the American column; Colonel An's soldiers had between twenty minutes and an hour to maneuver into position to launch their attack. The battle at Albany encompasses something of *all* these precise definitions:

There were a meeting engagement (with the recon platoon at the head of the column); a hasty attack (on the lead company); and a hasty ambush (of the rest of the column)—all of which occurred within a period of no more than five minutes.

But the reporters were not the only ones who were skeptical about what they had been told, and what they had not been told. That morning, November 18, at 10:15 A.M., the American commander in Vietnam, General William C. Westmoreland, visited 3rd Brigade Headquarters at Catecka. During a thirty-minute briefing, Colonel Brown failed to mention anything at all about the fight at LZ Albany, limiting his report to an overview of the X-Ray fight. Later in the day Westmoreland stopped in Qui Nhon and toured the Army 85th Evacuation Hospital. In his "history notes" (journal) entry covering November 18, General Westmoreland wrote: "I . . . flew down and visited the brigade commanded by Colonel Tim Brown. He gave me a briefing and we flew over the operational area. I then flew down to Qui Nhon where I visited the men in the hospital. They were mostly personnel of the 1st Cavalry who had been wounded in the recent operation in Pleiku. While talking to them I began to sense I had not been given the full information when I had visited the Brigade CP. Several of the men stated they had been involved in what they referred to as an ambush. Most of the men were from the 2nd of the 7th Cavalry."

The Westmoreland history notes entry for the 18th add: "One other thing happened in the afternoon. After returning to my office from a trip to Pleiku, Colonel [Ben] Legare [MACV public affairs chief] came in and informed me that a story had been filed that was highly critical of the 1st Air Cavalry. This came as no great surprise to me since I had suspected it after talking to the men in the hospital. I then called General [Stanley] Larsen and told him to get the facts. I told Colonel Legare to send a planeload of press up the next morning in order to get a briefing on exactly what had happened."

General Westmoreland was now concerned that the Cavalry Division had bitten off more than it could chew, and certainly far more than the American public was able to digest so early in the war. He also worried about sending South Vietnamese forces up against the North Vietnamese in the Ia Drang region.

In his journal entry for Friday, November 19, Westmoreland wrote: "General Bill DePuy returned from Pleiku where I sent him because of my concern that the 1st Air Cavalry and the (ARVN) Airborne task force might get involved in more than they could handle, and a bloody nose for the ARVN general reserve would be adverse to government morale. Further, I feared that intense sustained combat would wear down the Cavalry Division to the point that it might not be capable of performing its mission during the next several weeks. I asked DePuy to look into all these factors and get me a report. After talking to all the commanders and advisers concerned, he recommended that the new phase of the operation be confined north of the river [the Ia Drang] since the river is unfordable and thus would reduce the risk of unsuccessful operations, particularly for the ARVN Airborne."

Whatever his own misgivings, Westmoreland was thunderstruck by the impact those first, negative news accounts of the battle at Albany had back home. The general was catching hell from the Pentagon, and he lost no time giving hell to the Saigon bureau chiefs of the various American media.

In his journal entry for November 20, Westmoreland wrote: "I had my monthly background session with the press. I discussed the battle at Pleiku, starting with the attack on Plei Me camp and going through the subsequent phases. I read a wire I received from Secretary of Defense quoting headlines from the Washington *Post* and *Star* implying the retreat and withdrawal of the 1st Cavalry Division. I then explained to them I had a great respect for the press. I reminded them that I had resisted censorship of the press and was on record to that effect. I stated that stories such as those in the Washington newspapers were having the following effect: 1. Distorting the picture at home and lowering the morale of people who are emotionally concerned (wives). 2. Lowering morale of troops."

During General Westmoreland's November 18 trip to Pleiku, I finally delivered the briefing that I had refused to leave the battlefield and fly to Saigon to deliver. At 8:45 A.M. my surviving company commanders and staff and I were lined up and waiting when two jeeps pulled up and Westmoreland arrived, accompanied by General Cao Van Vien, chief of the South Vietnamese Army Joint General Staff, Major General Harry Kinnard, and Barry Zorthian, chief of the Joint U.S. Public Affairs Office (JUSPAO). I had served with General Westmoreland in the late 1940s on Airborne duty at Fort Bragg, and General Vien had been a classmate of mine in 1956–1957 at the U.S. Army Command and General Staff College at Fort Leavenworth.

We went into a borrowed Quonset hut and each of us who had played a role in the fight at LZ X-Ray briefed General Westmoreland and the others. Things went smoothly, except for one moment. During Captain Matt Dillon's portion of the briefing he mentioned a report by our men that they had seen the body of an enemy soldier they suspected was Chinese—he was large, and was dressed in a uniform different from that of the NVA—which disappeared from the battlefield before we could retrieve it. Westmoreland reacted angrily and forcefully, telling us all: "You will *never* mention anything about Chinese soldiers in South Vietnam! Never!"

The men of the battalion were lined up by their small pup tents. Westmoreland walked down the line of troopers, stopping and chatting with various men, asking them where they were from and making small talk about sports. Then I asked General Westmoreland to address them. Standing atop the hood of his jeep, he thanked the men for their courage and performance in battle. He added that the 1st Battalion, 7th Cavalry would be recommended for a Presidential Unit Citation for the extraordinary heroism displayed in combat.

Westmoreland's sensitivity to the issue of Chinese advisers traveling with the North Vietnamese on the battlefield may well have been provoked by an article by Charles Mohr in the November 17, 1965, issue of *The New York Times*. Filed from Saigon, the article reported that prisoners captured in late October around Plei Me Special Forces Camp had appeared at a news conference in Saigon, telling reporters that they had entered South Vietnam through Cambodia and had received assistance from Cambodian militiamen.

Mohr's article added that the prisoners told the reporters that each of the North Vietnamese People's Army regiments had one Chinese Communist adviser. "An official American spokesman commented, 'We don't have positive knowledge of Chinese advisers but it is a distinct possibility.'"

Clearly that article had touched a raw nerve at the White House, and just as clearly the command posture at MACV had changed radically in the previous twenty-four hours. There would be no more discussion of Chinese involvement in the fighting in South Vietnam. President Johnson remembered Korea, and his fear of Chinese intervention in Vietnam led him to exercise unprecedented personal control over the selection of bombing targets in North Vietnam. The Air Force was forbidden to operate within thirty miles of the Chinese border for fear of provoking an incident.

The question of Chinese advisers was no less sensitive to the North Vietnamese. The battlefield commander in the Ia Drang, then–Lieutenant Colonel Nguyen Huu An, says that it was a point of pride that the People's Army—which had Chinese army advisers down to the regimental level during the French war—did not have any foreign advisers in the field at any time during the war with the Americans. Asked about U.S. Army Signal Intelligence intercepts of radio transmissions in the Mandarin Chinese dialect in the vicinity of his headquarters on the Chu Pong massif on November 14, 1965, An said: "We had that language capability and sometimes used it to confuse whoever might be listening."

Congratulations on a job well done had been pouring in ever since our return to Camp Holloway. I assembled the battalion and read to them this message from the Army Chief of Staff, General Harold K. Johnson, to Major General Harry Kinnard: "On behalf of all members of the United States Army, I salute the intrepid officers and men of the 1st CavDiv for their superb action in the Battle of the Ia Drang Valley. Your Sky Soldiers and their brave Vietnamese allies carry the hopes of free men everywhere as they repel the heavy enemy attacks. The Army and the nation take pride in your display of courage, determination and fighting skill. The brave and resolute performance of the 1st CavDiv in this battle is in keeping with the finest traditions of the American soldier."

Out on the Albany battlefield, as night fell on November 18, all the American dead had still not been recovered. Bob McDade and his men hunkered down for another miserable night on that blood-soaked ground. Captain Joel Sugdinis says: "We remained at Albany all day on the 18th without contact, and again pulled in tight in a defensive perimeter for the night. We did not put out observation posts or patrols, but relied on harassment and interdiction fires around the perimeter to thwart any enemy approach. No one came. The next morning, the 19th, we continued to police the battlefield but the smell of decaying bodies was getting very bad."

Lieutenant Rick Rescorla ran into a sergeant from Alpha Company, 1st Battalion, 5th Cavalry and learned that Lieutenant Larry Hess had been killed. "He was a classmate of mine, OCS Class of April 1965, the son of an Air Force officer and just twenty years old. We pulled out of Albany that day. Several soldiers [were] still unaccounted for, but the press corps had started arriving. Just before we left a member of the press asked: 'What's the official name of this place?' 'The Little Bighorn,' a lieutenant said cynically. 'Don't say that,' Captain Joe Price protested. 'There's been no defeat here.'"

Washington was now thoroughly awakened to the ferocity of the fighting at X-Ray and Albany and to the large numbers of American dead and wounded beginning to arrive from the battlefields. The war was entering a new and much more deadly phase; President Johnson wanted to know what that meant and what it would cost. Defense Secretary Robert S. McNamara, then headed for Europe on NATO business, was told to return by way of Saigon and conduct one of his famous fact-finding missions. He was instructed to focus on the Ia Drang battles and report to the President with his recommendations.

After just two days' rest at Camp Holloway, the men of 1st Battalion, 7th Cavalry were ordered back into the field—trucked back to the Catecka Tea Plantation to mount perimeter guard around 3rd Brigade headquarters. At LZ Albany, on November 19, helicopters began lifting out the survivors of the 2nd Battalion, 7th Cavalry for the short flight to LZ Crooks, just six miles away. At Crooks the exhausted troops were ordered to take over a section of the defense perimeter alongside Colonel Bob Tully's 2nd Battalion, 5th Cavalry. McDade's battalion had still not accounted for all its men. The battalion was reporting 119 killed, 124 wounded, and 8 missing in action. When the final division headquarters report was made on March 4, 1966, the total Albany casualties for the 2nd Battalion, 7th Cavalry, Alpha and Bravo companies, 1st Battalion, 5th Cavalry, and attached artillery observers were: 151 killed, 121 wounded, and 4 missing in action.

McDade's men were exhausted and shaken by the fire storm they had endured at Albany and felt that they should have been withdrawn from the field before nightfall on November 19. As darkness fell, says Sergeant John Setelin of Bravo Company, "we thought if we hung around out there it was all going to happen to us again. That night it got so quiet you could hear a mouse piss on cotton. Every time we did hear a noise in the bush we fired on it. Finally, the 2nd Battalion, 5th Cav people came over and said if we didn't quit shooting they were going to take our ammunition away." The Crooks perimeter passed a generally quiet night with only two rounds of incoming mortar fire and no casualties.

My own battalion, standing guard around the brigade headquarters and airstrip at Catecka, was not so lucky. Sergeant Ernie Savage was in charge of the handful of survivors of Lieutenant Henry Herrick's 2nd Platoon, the Lost Platoon from LZ X-Ray. They had dug deep foxholes in their sector of the Catecka perimeter. At around nine P.M., as I sat in the operations tent, Captain Jerry Whiteside, the artillery coordinator, came in with grief and apprehension written all over his face. He said, "Colonel, our artillery just had a short round land in your Bravo Company lines."

That errant 105mm howitzer shell exploded among the foxholes in Sergeant Savage's sector. PFC Richard C. Clark, nineteen, of Kankakee, Illinois, was asleep on the ground next to the foxhole he shared with Specialist 5 Marlin Dorman. Clark was killed instantly. Specialist 4 Galen Bungum still grieves over what happened. "I just couldn't believe this. He was right next to me in Ia Drang when we were trapped. We made it through that, we got out of there, and then he gets killed by our own artillery. Why did Richard Clark have to die that way?"

The next day a dozen or so of my troopers stood waiting for me outside the operations tent in the chill early-morning fog. They were scheduled to leave that day en route to the United States for discharge upon completion of their terms of service. I had told Sergeant Major Plumley I wanted to speak to each such group before departure. This was the first group to go since the Ia Drang. These young men, each wearing the thousand-yard stare in his old man's eyes, had gone willingly into the inferno at X-Ray knowing that he had only a few days or a week left on Army duty. We had been together for seventeen months now and I knew them well.

I told them how proud I was of each of them, and how they should always hold their heads high for what they had done against such great odds. I told them I would remember them always. Then I walked down the line shaking each man's hand, personally thanking them for what they had done for their country, for their comrades in battle, and for me. It was an emotional moment. They formed in a column of twos and marched off, straight and tall, to the helicopters waiting to take them back to what they called The World.

At LZ Crooks, Bob McDade's 2nd Battalion, 7th Cavalry troopers at last were climbing aboard helicopters that would fly them back to Camp Holloway. Captain Myron Diduryk wrote: "On the 20th, back to Pleiku where we got new fatigues, boots, underwear; had showers, good food, and genuinely rested." Specialist 4 Dick Ackerman remembers it well: "Received new uniforms, boots (they ran out of my size before they got to me), got showers and felt 100 percent better. We spent the night there and next day went back to An Khe base."

Some of the 2nd Battalion officers elected to keep their old fatigues with their name tags and patches. Rick Rescorla says, "We returned to Holloway and for awhile we were buoyed up with the fact that we had survived. All gloomy memories were shoved below the surface. That night, Saturday, Dan Boone, Doc Shucart and a few of us drifted down to the Vietnamese Officers Club. We had showered but still wore our stinking fatigues. The contrast with Albany made the opulent surroundings unreal. The Vietnamese wives and girlfriends were brilliant in red, green, and blue dresses. Some of our group had the nerve to ask the girls to dance, but most of them sniffed our fatigues and retreated to the powder room. You couldn't blame them."

Out at the tea plantation, on November 20, the 1st of the 7th prepared to travel by truck convoy up Provincial Route 5 and Route 14 to Pleiku, and then east on Route 19 over the Mang Yang Pass to An Khe base camp. We would have to drive through the place where the Viet Minh ambushed French Group Mobile 100 in 1954. I was determined there would be no repeat of history this day. We rehearsed counterambush tactics before loading aboard the deuce-and-a-halfs—two-and-a-half-ton Army trucks. The sergeant major and I rode in the back of the first truck in line. The battalion command helicopter would shadow the convoy overhead, with Matt Dillon, Jerry Whiteside, and Charlie Hastings on the radios, just as they were that first day in X-Ray, ready to bring down fire support. The 1st Squadron, 9th Cavalry supplied two Huey gunships and two H-13 scout helicopters to fly the route ahead of us. Just before we pulled out I was informed that the division band would play us into An Khe base on our arrival there.

The trip from Catecka to An Khe was hot, dusty, and completely uneventful. When we arrived the division band was nowhere in sight. The 1st Battalion, 7th Cavalry had come back to a no-key welcome, but who gave a shit? We were home, and the division commander, Major General Kinnard, came by to visit with the men. When we got to Delta Company and Sergeant Warren Adams, I stopped the division commander and described in detail the damage Adams had done to the enemy with his machine-gun platoon at X-Ray. I told him that Adams had been "acting first sergeant" of Delta Company for more than eighteen months and fully merited an immediate battlefield promotion to first sergeant. Both the general and the sergeant were taken by surprise. But General Kinnard gave the order, and Adams was promoted the next day.

At noon, November 20, Colonel Tim Brown turned over control of the Ia Drang Valley operation to the division's 2nd Brigade, commanded by Colonel William R. (Ray) Lynch. Lynch was a battlefield veteran of World War II and Korea. He and his three battalions now assumed responsibility for the continuing operations in Pleiku province.

Late in the afternoon of the twentieth, the 3rd and 6th battalions of the South Vietnamese Airborne Brigade made contact with a battalion of General Chu Huy Man's battle-weary People's Army troops hard by the Cambodian border, north of where the Ia Drang crosses. The hapless North Vietnamese battalion had been a bit slow on the withdrawal toward sanctuary in Cambodia and now they would pay the price.

The radio message received by the American gunners who had twenty-four 105mm howitzers set up on LZ_Golf and LZ Crooks described the target: "Enemy in the open!" The American advisers with the Vietnamese Airborne task force adjusted the artillery fire by radio, ripping the enemy battalion apart. They reported that at least 127 bodies were strewn over the killing field when the barrage lifted, and that the South Vietnamese were amazed and delighted at the pinpoint accuracy of the American artillerymen. A Vietnamese radio message was received by one of the batteries firing during the action. Translated, it said: "Artillery too close! Artillery too close! But very nice! Keep shooting!"

Among the American advisers on the ground with the South Vietnamese Airborne task force in the Ia Drang Valley that day was a big, burly American major, H. Norman Schwarzkopf, West Point class of 1956. Schwarzkopf remembers that the sudden appearance of the South Vietnamese troops on the North Vietnamese route of withdrawal shocked the enemy battalion.

"They were tired and beaten and almost home free," Schwarz-kopf says. "They had had all they wanted. When we opened up with small arms and artillery they threw down their guns and ran for it. No resistance. Later, the Airborne brigade commander and I sat resting under a big tree while the men searched the woods policing up enemy equipment. They brought in rifles and machine guns by the armload, piling them in front of us. The pile of captured gear grew so large that I accused the Vietnamese general of having brought all those weapons out from Pleiku just to impress me. He laughed like hell, but invited me to go out in the brush and see for myself where it was all coming from."

This was the last major action in the Ia Drang campaign. For the next five days, Colonel Ray Lynch's soldiers and the cavalry scouts of the 1st Squadron, 9th Cavalry patrolled widely, screening the western part of the valley up to the Cambodian border with little or no contact. On November 27, the last cavalry unit still in the field returned to home base at An Khe.

The last units of Brigadier General Chu Huy Man's B-3 Front crossed into Cambodia. They were beyond reach now. They would reinforce, reequip, rest, and rehabilitate their surviving soldiers, and then, at a time of their choosing in the spring of 1966, reenter South Vietnam and resume their attacks.

Major Norm Schwarzkopf watched them go and was disgusted with the U.S. policy that permitted the creation of North Vietnamese sanctuaries across the border in supposedly neutral Cambodia. He was not the only military man in the field who was angered by a policy that tied the hands of the American and South Vietnamese forces.

Major General Harry Kinnard and his boss, Lieutenant General Stanley (Swede) Larsen, both appealed to General Westmoreland and U.S. ambassador Henry Cabot Lodge to do everything in their power to persuade Washington to review and revoke the restrictions on American freedom of action along and across the border.

Both Lodge and Westmoreland requested that review in November 1965; they got back a cable from William Bundy, assistant secretary for Far Eastern affairs at the State Department, copied for Defense Secretary McNamara, Joint Chiefs chairman General Wheeler, and Bundy's brother, McGeorge, at the White House. Will Bundy's cable said:

"Separate message through military channels will contain authorization for self-defense measures applicable to existing Silver Bayonet situation. This will include authority to U.S./Government of Vietnam units to return fire, to eliminate fire coming from Cambodia and to maneuver into Cambodian territory as necessary to defend selves while actively engaged in contact with PAVN/VC units. It excludes authority to engage Cambodian forces if encountered, except in self-defense, to conduct tactical air or artillery operations against populated Cambodian areas, *or to attack Cambodian base areas* [emphasis added]. . . . We recognize these distinctions might be most difficult to preserve, but from political standpoint it is essential that this be done."

General Kinnard and the 1st Cavalry commanders said even this slight relaxation of the restrictions on hot pursuit into Cambodia was not communicated or explained to them in time to be utilized during the Ia Drang Valley campaign.

Not long after this, orders came down to all the 1st Cavalry Division brigade and battalion commanders that we were never to speculate or suggest to any reporter that the North Vietnamese were using Cambodia as a sanctuary or that they were passing through Cambodia on their way to South Vietnam. This refusal to admit what we knew was true, and what even the newest reporter knew was true, struck all of us as dishonest and hypocritical.

General Kinnard says this was the point at which, under political direction, the American military surrendered the initiative to North Vietnam. What it said to Harry Kinnard was that this war would never end in an American victory. Initiative had been sacrificed to the polite diplomatic fiction that Cambodia was sovereign and neutral and in control of its territory. By the time another American President lifted the restrictions and the U.S. military crossed into Cambodia, Kinnard says, it was already too late.

Bob McDade's 2nd Battalion, 7th Cavalry survivors had spent the night at Holloway, getting their first decent sleep in a week. Now, on November 21, they were assigned four deuce-and-a-half trucks, more than enough to hold the hundred-plus men left of this battalion, to take them across the Mang Yang Pass and home. While they stood in ranks waiting to climb on trucks, Lieutenant Rick Rescorla wanted to hold a platoon ceremony to honor the men who had fallen. "I called my appointed bugler and asked him to blow Taps. 'Present arms,' I ordered. The bugler blew the sad and bitter notes."

Sergeant John Setelin: "On Sunday they loaded the whole battalion, all that was left of the 2/7, on four trucks. That tells you how many of us were going back on our feet, out of maybe four hundred and fifty who started this thing. It took hours to get there and we were as afraid then as any time in X-Ray or Albany. Figured with our luck we would get hit going home. We all sat facing outward, rifles at the ready, watching every bush, every hole, every rock."

As the 2nd Battalion pulled into An Khe base they rolled past the tents of the 1st Battalion where we were preparing the personal effects of our dead to be sent home. We cheered them as they passed. That little American flag that had flown at X-Ray now decorated one of the trucks. As they approached the clearing by brigade headquarters, the division band struck up the 7th Cavalry regimental march, "Garry Owen," and the division color guard dipped the 1st Cav colors in salute. Darkness fell and someone hollered for "the bugle." Rick Rescorla's battered old French bugle was unlimbered and the designated bugler blew "Garry Owen" on it to the wild cheers of the battalions.

Rescorla adds, "Captain Diduryk came up to me. The band was playing Garry Owen. 'Hard Corps was your platoon nickname, but now I want to use it for our whole company,' Myron said. 'I'd also like to use the bugle as Bravo's bugle for the rest of our tour. OK?' I agreed, saluted, gave him a 'Garry Owen, Sir,' and then trudged off to join the survivors making their way slowly up the hill to the mess. About 150 had been killed, 130 wounded, some maimed for life. I recalled those bright, young faces. They would not grow old with us. If I ever got the chance I would say to them: You were a ragtag bunch but Uncle Sam never sent better men into battle. I wasn't crying. It was the rain. Hell yes, it was only the rain."

Doc William Shucart: "I remember us coming back to An Khe on trucks. They had the division band out playing for us. A victory parade. They played 'Garry Owen.' It was a very emotional, very stirring sight. I thought: *Here we were in the wrong place at the wrong* time, got our asses kicked, and they got a band out playing for us. That was the doctor in me thinking that."

Captain Joel Sugdinis: "I don't believe either side won or lost at Albany. The North Vietnamese did leave first, without destroying us. But is that a U.S. victory? I believe each side was severely battered and each side was grateful to still resemble a military organization when it was over. We both went on to fight other battles, being much wiser for the experiences at the Ia Drang."

Lieutenant Larry Gwin: "We stayed at Albany for another day and night, cleaning up the unspeakable debris of battle, and we slowly realized we must have inflicted a terrible defeat on the enemy. Victory was the only thing that gave us strength to continue. I've tried to forget that day since I've come home, but I realized that those hours of close combat are as fresh in my mind now as if they had just been fought. It will take a long, long time to forget that day at Albany."

Lieutenant Colonel Bob McDade: "I never thought of it as a victory. We got into a scrap. We gave a good account of ourselves and proved to the men that we didn't have to be afraid of [the enemy]. The 2nd of the 7th was a good battalion. The men fought bravely."

Colonel Tim Brown: "The NVA just plain got the jump on them. These two battalions ran into one another; it was like a saloon fight. One of them pulled his gun before the other did. He got the edge."

People's Army Lieutenant General Nguyen Huu An: "This [Albany] was the most savage battle in the Ia Drang campaign. We consider this our victory. This was the first time our B-3 Front fought the Americans and we defeated Americans, caused big American losses. As military men we realize it is very important to win the first battle. It raised our soldiers' morale and gave us many good lessons."

One of the yardsticks for measuring success in those days was captured enemy weapons. The 2nd Battalion, 7th Cav policed up thirty-three light machine guns, 112 rifles, four mortar tubes, two mortar sights, two rocket launchers, and three heavy machine guns on the field at Albany. It reported 403 enemy killed and estimated 150 NVA wounded.

These were emotional days for me as commander of 1st Battalion, 7th Cavalry. I had been on the list for promotion to full colonel for over a year and my number was coming up on November 23. That meant I would have to give up command of my battalion on that date. I had also been pushing my staff hard as we wrote letters of condolence to the families who had lost loved ones killed in action and prepared recommendations for medals and awards.

We had problems on the awards: We had few who could type, so many of the forms were scrawled by hand by lanternlight. Many witnesses had been evacuated with wounds or had already rotated for discharge. Too many men had died bravely and heroically, while the men who had witnessed their deeds had also been killed. Uncommon valor truly was a common virtue on the field at Landing Zone X-Ray those three days and two nights. Acts of valor and sacrifice that on other fields, on other days, would have been rewarded with the Medal of Honor or Distinguished Service Cross or a Silver Star were recognized only with a telegram saying "The Secretary of the Army regrets . . ." The same was true of our sister battalion, the 2nd of the 7th.

Every morning during those final bittersweet days of my command of the 1st Battalion, 7th Cavalry, Sergeant Major Plumley would appear with a group of men bound for the airfield and the plane that would take them home for discharge. Specialist 4 Pat Selleck of the recon platoon, says: "Colonel Moore shook our hands and said, 'Thank you' and 'Go back home.' I was the second or third guy he spoke to and he had tears in his eyes. I remember what he said: 'I see that you are married; you have a wedding ring on. Just go home, pick up the pieces, and start your life all over again.' And basically that's what I did. I came home to a wonderful wife, tried to readjust, did a decent job at it. I did what Colonel Moore said. I tried to put the war behind me. I served. I did my job. I came home. I didn't ask for anything, no fanfare, no parades. I went back to work, back to school, and did my best. He might be a general, but to me he's still Colonel Moore. If it wasn't for him and all his knowledge and training, I don't think any of us would have survived the Ia Drang Valley."

On Tuesday, November 23, the day came for me to turn over command. For the change of command I requested a full battalion formation with officers front and center, the division band trooping the line, honors to the reviewing officer and the colors, and then the pass in review—reminiscent of our weekly Retreat parades back at Fort Benning. I requested that Captain Myron Diduryk's Bravo Company, 2nd Battalion, 7th Cavalry and Lieutenant Sisson's platoon of Alpha Company, 2nd of the 7th be included in the parade of the 1st Battalion, 7th Cavalry in token of the fact that they fought bravely alongside us in the battle at X-Ray. And so it was. The band played "Colonel Bogey" and "The Washington Post March" and "Garry Owen." General Kinnard pinned on my eagles and I spoke briefly and with deep emotion.

Specialist 4 Ray Tanner of Alpha Company, 1st Battalion: "We stood in formation, with some units hardly having enough men to form up. Colonel Hal Moore spoke to us and he cried. At that moment he could have led us back into the Ia Drang. We were soldiers, we were fighting men, and those of us who were left had the utmost love and respect for our colonel and for one another. As I reflect on those three days in November, I remember many heroes but no cowards. I learned what value life really had. We all lost friends but the bravery they showed on the battlefield will live forever."

On Thanksgiving, the 2nd Battalion, 7th Cav troopers were looking forward eagerly to the traditional Thanksgiving feast of hot turkey and all the trimmings. It was a cold and rainy day that Thanksgiving at An Khe, and it lives on in the memory of some of the battalion veterans.

Colonel McDade: "It was a grim Thanksgiving. I met General Westmoreland in the company street near the mess hall. I told him everyone was just about ready to eat their Thanksgiving dinners, but he said, 'Get them all together and let me talk to them.' "

Sergeant John Setelin of Bravo Company, 2nd Battalion remembers the unfortunate consequences of that order: "For Thanksgiving they gave us a hot meal plus a canteen cup of real coffee, not that instant C-ration crap. Turkey and all the trimmings, the best we ever saw. At that time the indoor mess hall wasn't completed, so we collected our dinners in mess kits and were walking back to our squad tents to chow down. It was starting to rain. Somebody hollered attention, stopped us and ordered us to assemble. There stood General William Westmoreland himself. He made a speech there in the rain and while he talked we watched the rain turn that hot dinner into cold Mulligan stew. Who knew what the hell the man said? Who cared? He ruined a decent dinner."

Lieutenant Larry Gwin remembers that General Westmoreland then went off and ate Thanksgiving dinner with the 1st Battalion, 7th Cavalry.

On November 29, 1965, the brass descended on An Khe for detailed briefings on the Ia Drang battles. The party was led by Secretary of Defense Robert S. McNamara and included the Chairman of the Joint Chiefs of Staff, General Earle K. Wheeler; the Army Chief of Staff, General Harold K. Johnson; General Westmoreland; and Admiral U. S. Grant Sharp, commander in chief, Pacific (CINCPAC).

I was told to brief McNamara and party on the fight at LZ X-Ray. I had heard that the secretary of defense had a fearsome reputation as a human computer, insensitive to people. McNamara sat in the front row in the tent briefing room, filled with commanders and staff officers. I talked without notes, using a map and pointer, for perhaps fifteen minutes. When I wrapped up, saying, "Sir, that completes my presentation," there was dead silence. McNamara stood, stepped forward, and without a word extended his hand, looking into my eyes. He asked no questions, made no comments.

After the McNamara briefing, still without a new job, I was given a tent and a typist in 3rd Brigade headquarters and got down to work writing my after-action report on X-Ray. It took nine days and three drafts. I arranged for the Air Force to fly a photo recon mission over the Chu Pong massif, the Ia Drang Valley, and the clearing at X-Ray to illustrate the report. On December 9, 1965, I signed the final version and forwarded it to Colonel Tim Brown. Then it went up to Major General Harry Kinnard, who read it and then made certain that copies were distributed to every branch school in the U.S. Army as a teaching tool.

While I was working on the report I received word that Air Force Lieutenant Charlie Hastings, our fearless and superb forward air controller at X-Ray, had been shot down over the Mang Yang Pass while flying an O-1E Bird Dog spotter plane. The good news was that Charlie was alive; the bad news was that he had been severely burned in the crash. He had been evacuated to the Army hospital at Fort Bliss, El Paso, a town full of retired 7th U.S. Cavalry veterans of World War II and Korea. I passed the word to all of them: Charlie Hastings is one of us, a Garry Owen trooper. Take care of him.

The 2nd Battalion, 7th Cavalry was still carrying four men missing in action after the Albany fight. To the horror of Captain George Forrest, the commander of Alpha Company, 1st Battalion, 5th Cavalry, it became clear in December that one of his soldiers was also missing at Albany. He says, "This was a 2nd Platoon soldier, PFC John R. Ackerman. The one thing that had always been drilled into us was accountability: You must account for every man. I was positive we had gotten all our dead and wounded out. When Ackerman's name came up, before we left, somebody in his squad said they saw him loaded onto a medevac helicopter.

"Then, in December, we got a letter from his mother saying she had not heard from him. I initiated action through the division personnel officer, searching for any record of him in any of the Army hospitals worldwide. There was no record. It was my worst nightmare come true. When we went back to the Ia Drang in April 1966, I spent a day stomping around Albany. At that point I got an appreciation for what we had been in, our position on the ground in relation to the main part of the ambush.

"We found PFC Ackerman's remains, right about where the 2nd Platoon had been. We found his boots and helmet. In those days we tied one of our dog tags into the laces of a boot [and] wore the other around our neck. We found his dog tag with his boots. That put that to rest. On that day they found four more MIAs out there from McDade's battalion. You know, all of this breaks your heart," says Forrest.

By then I was the 3rd Brigade commander; the 2nd Battalion, 7th Cavalry was part of my brigade. I decided if we ever went back into the Ia Drang I would personally lead a thorough search for those four missing men. On the morning of April 6, 1966, Sergeant Major Basil Plumley, Matt Dillon, and I took a platoon of the 1st Battalion, 7th Cav and air-assaulted into Landing Zone Albany. No enemy presence. In a matter of minutes we located the remains of eight soldiers, all in one fifteen-by-twenty-yard piece of ground near the three anthills in the center of the clearing. Some of them were clearly American, as evidenced by fragments of green fatigue uniform material, GI web gear, and GI boots. Their steel helmets lay nearby. Other remains were mixed in; just fragments and bones. We touched nothing, but called in the Graves Registration people, who removed all the remains and associated gear. Four sets of the remains were positively identified as the 2nd Battalion's MIAs; the rest were Vietnamese.

With that operation the 1st Cavalry Division balanced the books and closed a sad chapter on the fight at Albany. Five coffins could begin the long journey home, and five American mothers who had already suffered too much would no longer suffer the agonies of not knowing whether their sons were alive and prisoners, or dead and abandoned in the jungle. And Captain George Forrest and I could sleep a little better at night for the rest of our lives.

25

"THE SECRETARY OF THE ARMY REGRETS . . ."

> Only the dead have seen the end of war.
> —Plato

The guns were at last silent in the valley. The dying was done, but the suffering had only just begun. The men of the 1st Cavalry Division had done what was asked of them. The Army field morgues were choked with the bodies of more than 230 soldiers wrapped in their green rubber ponchos. More than 240 maimed and wounded troopers moved slowly along the chain from battlefield aid station to medical clearing station to field hospital, and onto the ambulance transport planes.

Some whose wounds would heal soon enough for eventual return to duty in Vietnam were flown only as far as Army hospitals in Japan. The most seriously injured were flown to the Philippines; their conditions were stabilized at the hospital at Clark Field, and then they were loaded onto planes that would take them to military hospitals near their homes in the United States.

Sergeant Robert Jemison, Charlie Company, 1st Battalion, 7th Cavalry, would spend thirty-two months in Army hospitals. PFC

James Young of Alpha Company, 1st Battalion, 5th Cavalry, would check out of the Army hospital in Denver with a bullet hole in the side of his skull, borrowed clothes on his back and discharge papers in hand, and make it home to Missouri in time for Christmas, 1965. Specialist 4 Clinton Poley of Charlie Company, 1st Battalion, 7th Cavalry, wearing the terrible scars of three separate bullet wounds and judged seventy percent disabled, got home to Iowa in plenty of time for spring plowing and planting.

But on November 18, 1965, in the sleepy southern town of Columbus, Georgia, half a world away from Vietnam, the first of the telegrams that would shatter the lives of the innocents were already arriving from Washington. The war was so new and the casualties to date so few that the Army had not even considered establishing the casualty-notification teams that later in the war would personally deliver the bad news and stay to comfort a young widow or elderly parents until friends and relatives could arrive. In Columbus, in November and December 1965, Western Union simply handed the telegrams over to Yellow Cab drivers to deliver.

The driver who brought the message of the death in battle of Sergeant Billy R. Elliott, Alpha Company, 1st Battalion, 7th Cav, to his wife, Sara, was blind drunk and staggering. As Mrs. Elliott stood in the doorway of her tiny bungalow, clutching the yellow paper, the bearer of the bad tidings fell backward off her porch and passed out in her flower bed. Then the Army briefly lost her husband's body on its journey home.

When a taxi driver woke up the very young, and very pregnant, Hispanic wife of a 1st Battalion trooper at two A.M. and held out the telegram, the woman fainted dead away. The driver ran next door and woke up the neighbors to come help. The new widow could not speak or read English, but she knew what that telegram said.

The knock on the door at the home of Sergeant Jeremiah (Jerry) Jivens of Charlie Company, 1st Battalion, 7th Cavalry came at four A.M. Betty Jivens Mapson was fourteen at the time: "I have told the story before to friends about how the taxi drivers used to deliver the telegrams to families who'd lost loved ones over there. Today it almost sounds unbelievable. Luckily, my Mom's sister lived with us and was with her when the knock came at our door at 4 A.M. My Mom collapsed completely as this stranger handed the telegram to us. How cold and inhuman, I thought."

In Columbus that terrible autumn, someone had to do the right thing since the Army wasn't organized to do it. For the families of the casualties of the 1st Battalion, 7th Cavalry that someone was my wife, Julia Compton Moore, daughter of an Army colonel, wife of a future Army general, and mother of five small children, including two sons who would follow me to West Point and the Army.

Julie talks of those days as a time of fear; a time when the mere sight of a Yellow Cab cruising through a neighborhood struck panic in the hearts of the wives and children of soldiers serving in Vietnam. As the taxicabs and telegrams spread misery and grief, Julie followed them to the trailer courts and thin-walled apartment complexes and boxy bungalows, doing her best to comfort those whose lives had been destroyed. Two of those widows she can never forget: The widow of Sergeant Jerry Jivens, who received her with great dignity and presence in the midst of such sorrow, and that frightened young Hispanic widow, pregnant with a boy child who would come into this world in March without a father.

When the coffins began arriving home, my wife attended the funeral of all but one of the 1st Battalion, 7th Cavalry troopers who were buried at the Fort Benning cemetery. The first funeral at Benning for a 1st Battalion casualty was that of Sergeant Jack Gell of Alpha Company. Julie turned on the evening news, and there on television was the saddest sight she had ever seen: one of my beloved troopers being buried and Fort Benning had not notified her. She called Survivors Assistance and told them in no uncertain terms that they must inform her of every 1st Battalion death notification and of every funeral for a 1st Battalion soldier at the post cemetery.

Julie recalls, "I was so fearful when I began calling on the widows that I would be very unwelcome, because it was my husband who ordered their husbands into battle. I thought of a million reasons why I should not go, but my father called me and told me to go, so I went. They were so happy to see me and they were so proud of their husbands. That was a little something that they still had to hang onto. There were thirteen widows from the 1st Battalion still living in that little town."

The same duty for the dead of the 2nd Battalion, 7th Cavalry was done by Mrs. Frank Henry, wife of the battalion executive officer, and Mrs. James Scott, wife of the battalion sergeant major, since the battalion commander, Lieutenant Colonel Bob McDade, was a bachelor at that time.

Kornelia Scott's first visit was to the home of Mrs. Martin Knapp, widow of a sergeant in Delta Company, 2nd Battalion, to offer condolences and assistance.

"There was immense grief and bitterness. So immense, that one widow was bitter that her husband had been killed and mine only wounded. Names, addresses and faces became a blur, especially when we started attending the funerals at Ft. Benning in late November and early December," says Mrs. Scott.

Mrs. Harry Kinnard, wife of the commander of the 1st Cavalry Division, and many others went public with their criticism of the heartless taxicab telegrams, and the Army swiftly organized proper casualty-notification teams consisting of a chaplain and an accompanying officer. Nobody intended for this cruelty to happen. Everyone, including the Army, was taken totally by surprise by the magnitude of the casualties that had burst on the American scene at LZ X-Ray and LZ Albany.

But even after the Army teams were formed and the procedure was changed, it was months before a Yellow Cab could travel the streets of Columbus without spreading fear and pain in its wake. My wife remembers: "In December a taxi driver carrying a couple of young lieutenants stopped at my house. I hid behind the curtains, thinking, *If I don't answer the door I won't have to hear the bad news.* Then I decided: 'Come on, Julie, face up to it.' I opened the door and he asked me for directions to some address and I just about fainted. I told him: 'Don't you *ever* do that to me again!' The poor man told me that he understood, that all the taxi drivers had hated that terrible duty."

Far to the north, in Redding, Connecticut, the village messenger, an elderly man, knocked hesitantly on the door of John J. and

Camille Geoghegan. Although the telegram was addressed to Mrs. Barbara Geoghegan, wife of Lieutenant John Lance (Jack) Geoghegan, the messenger knew what it said and he knew that Jack Geoghegan was the only child of that family.

As the Geoghegans read the news, the messenger broke down, quivering and weeping and asking over and over again if there was anything he could do to help them. Before they could deal with their own grief, the Geoghegans first had to deal with his; they hugged and comforted the messenger and helped him pull himself together for the long trip back to town through the deepening gloom.

Barbara Geoghegan was away that day; she had gone to New Rochelle, New York, to stay with her husband's elderly aunt. The aunt's husband had died on this date two years earlier and the family thought someone should be there to comfort her on so tragic an anniversary. When the Geoghegans telephoned Barbara with the news, she was writing her ninety-third letter to Jack, a letter filled, as usual, with news of their baby daughter, Camille. The next morning, in the mailbox at home, she found Jack's last letter to her. He wrote, "I had a chance to go on R and R, but my men are going into action. I cannot and will not leave them now."

When Captain Tom Metsker left for Vietnam in August of 1965, his wife, Catherine, and baby daughter, Karen, fourteen months old, moved home to Indiana to be near her family. Tom's father was in the U.S. Foreign Service, stationed in Monrovia, Liberia. Catherine recalls: "I finally got a teaching job to occupy my time and save some money. The first day was to be Monday, November 15. On that Sunday night, November 14, I was sick with a cold and fever. How could I start my new job? The phone rang. It was my uncle: 'There is a telegram for you.' Probably a message from Tom's parents in Liberia, I thought. 'Open it and read it to me,' I told him. THE SECRETARY OF THE ARMY REGRETS TO INFORM YOU . . . Tom was dead."

The pain and grief of that autumn so long ago still echo across the years, fresh as yesterday for many of the wives and children and parents and siblings of those who died in the Ia Drang Valley. Some of them agreed to write their stories of what one death in battle did to their lives, in hopes that their words might somehow comfort other families who have lost loved ones in war.

Betty Jivens Mapson is forty-two and has grown children of her own today, but she has been haunted for years by the trauma of her father's death on November 15, 1965, in the Ia Drang Valley. She says, "After the initial shock of receiving the telegram announcing Daddy's death, we kids had to go back to school because it would be two weeks or more before his body would arrive home. It seemed everyone was looking at us and whispering, not really knowing what to say except how bad it was our Daddy died over there.

"They mostly left us alone," Mrs. Mapson continues. "There were no support groups or any of that to help us cope. Our family was left alone in our grief. My brothers did not talk about their feelings at all. My mother was devastated. She and Daddy were sweethearts in school but each went on to marry other people. When both were divorced around the same time they met again and were married. Daddy and I used to take trips together on the Greyhound bus, mostly home to Savannah. Whenever he and my mother went out, he would not be ready until he sat in a chair and had me comb and brush his hair. It was cut real close but he made it seem like I had really done something special.

"I remember when he first told us he had to go to Vietnam. We drove him to Fort Benning. I remember the Army trucks filled with soldiers and hearing Daddy say he might not come back. I was young and didn't really see the seriousness of it. He was a good, strict father and my brothers and I thought his being away for so long meant we would be able to stay out later and have more fun. I blamed myself for Daddy being killed because of those selfish feelings when he left. My Daddy was a good man, a preacher's son. His given name is Jeremiah."

She adds: "Two weeks after the initial telegram we got another one stating when to meet the body at the train station. The hearse was already there when we got to the station and soon a wooden cart with a long gray box was being pulled toward us. My Daddy! This is how he came back to us. And the pain started all over again for us, only more so because now he was home. You could have

heard me screaming three states away. At the funeral home I remember looking at him closely and for a long time to make sure it
was really him. Then I saw that little mole on his cheek and I knew.

"I am so very proud of my father and wished that somehow he
could know that and know that he is still very much alive with us.
For a long time it seemed to me that he was just away like he usually
was on Army duty, and one day he would come home. For a lot of
years I waited and watched our driveway because I wanted so much
for him to come home for my Momma and my brothers and me. I
would like to visit the Ia Drang. It is something I have to do for my
own sake. I have to know, have to see that this place really exists.
I need to see and to be where my Daddy died. Then maybe this will
all somehow be complete for me. I just wish with all my heart that
we had not been so alone to deal with such a monumental tragedy
back then. We needed someone to reach out to us, to explain for us,
to help us see why. My mother has passed away now. She never
remarried. She loved Daddy so."

Catherine Metsker McCray, now fifty years old, says the story of
how she met and married Tom Metsker, her dashing young Army
officer, seems to have taken place a lifetime ago. "I didn't know him
in the early days. He absolutely drove his parents crazy—constantly
on the go; accident-prone; strong; never sat still. They were especially proud of his athletic feats—on the state championship football team in high school, Southern Conference pole-vault champion
at The Citadel. Tom was raised in Japan and Korea. His father, also
named Tom, was with the State Department and worked for the
Agency for International Development. High school brought Tom,
his mother Zoe and older sister Ibby back to Indianapolis while his
father was on a hardship tour. The parents were originally from
Indiana; graduates of Indiana University.

"Tom then left for college at The Citadel. While he was there his
family was transferred to the Washington, D.C., area. I was a
sophomore at DePauw University. It was spring break and my
friend Betty Orcutt and I decided to spend the week at my parents'
home. My father was a colonel in the Air Force stationed at The
Pentagon in Washington. I met Tom on a blind date; we were

married on October 5, 1962. We eloped. On October 8, Tom left for
Germany where he was to be stationed for six months. I stayed
home to graduate from DePauw, then joined him when he returned
to Ft. Benning, Georgia.

"I remember these days as the most exciting in my life. He was in
a combat-ready unit. A phone call would come at 4 A.M. and the
troops would assemble and leave Ft. Benning. The wives didn't
know where they were going or whether it was for a day or a month.
It was the time of Cuba and the Dominican Republic. I remember
sitting in our Camellia Garden apartment with the gray and pink
metal furniture and the one plug in the kitchen, behind the fridge.
If you moved the fridge out, you could make toast. I learned to be
patient and brave, but mostly I just missed Tom. When he was
home, I would stay awake at night and stare at him, wondering how
I could be so lucky. Karen Doranne Metsker, 9 pounds 9 ½ ounces,
was born on May 31, 1964, and Tom was ecstatic. Tom had wanted
a boy but he was so happy to have a girl. Ten days after Karen was
born we moved to Washington, D.C., for Tom's language school.
We three camped out in my parents' basement while we looked for
an apartment. Sometime during that school, Tom got orders for
Vietnam. He was excited to be going to Vietnam. It was what he had
trained for. It was his job.

"I didn't share his excitement—not because of the danger but
because of the separation. We were sent back to Ft. Bragg, North
Carolina, to get him ready for Vietnam. I was going to stay there
with the baby. Training went quickly. They received a photo of their
unit. Tom joked it was 'so we can X out the guys who get zapped.'
All our friends were also being transferred, I knew no one at Bragg
and I was pregnant again. I decided to move back to Indiana to my
family during his Vietnam tour.

"Tom left from the Evansville airport in August of 1965. I cried
a lot. We wrote each other every day and Karen and I had a routine
of going to the mailbox every day to mail a letter to Daddy. Tom's
parents were stationed in Monrovia, Liberia, so I didn't see them.
I had a miscarriage in October.

"The telegram came Sunday night, November 14. Tom was dead.

I had to make the arrangements. I had never even been to a funeral before. There was no place for friends to gather, except our motel room. All of our friends from the Army came. All of them had orders for Vietnam. Standing on the sidelines was the wrestling team Tom had coached while we were in Washington. He had meant so much to them.

"I wanted to die but had to stay alive for Karen. I guess she saved my life. I started teaching as soon as I got back from Washington. I was offered tranquilizers. No one knew about counseling back then; it just wasn't an option. When Tom's belongings were returned, I threw them all away. That way, I thought, I wouldn't be reminded of him. It didn't work.

"I stayed numb for so long a time. And smiled. The pain was indescribable. I kept it all inside for years. Twenty years later I went into therapy. With help, I was finally able to put Tom to rest. I am now at peace about that. When I think about Tom I see a smiling young man. I will always miss him."

Karen Metsker Rudel, twenty-seven years old, is married and the mother of two daughters and a son. "One bullet of the billions fired in Vietnam changed the path I would follow for the rest of my days. I wonder how many other lives were just as drastically altered as the result of one bullet? My father, Thomas Metsker, was killed when I was 17 months old. I have no memory of him, although I have seen pictures of the two of us together. We look alike. He was a career Army man, a 1961 graduate of The Citadel. I have spent much of my life asking, 'Why?' Why did he go to Vietnam knowing he might not come back? Why did he have to die? Why would anyone imply that he deserved it for being in Vietnam? Why did it have to be me?

"My mother remarried when I was four. He was a lawyer who was divorced and had two children from his previous marriage. Michael McCray adopted me, so my given name Karen Doranne Metsker was left behind and I became Karen Metsker McCray. Just before my fifth birthday my younger half brother was born, followed a year later by my half sister.

"With the his, hers and theirs meld of our family, I often felt like an outsider. I suppose that how I dealt with it was no better nor worse than any other child. After all, who ever taught me how? I became an over-achiever. I wanted desperately to fit in, but never quite figured out how to do so, at home or at school.

"My father was not discussed. I knew no one else who had lost a relative in the War and sensed at an early age that it was not an acceptable topic of conversation. I would often sneak down to our basement to investigate the trunk where what remained of my father's things were stored. For some reason, my mother threw away most everything that was his after he died. I remember well the musty smell of the triangular flag which had been draped over his coffin at his funeral in Arlington Cemetery; the scrapbook full of condolence letters from a multitude of meaningless officials; the old musical white Teddy bear my parents had bought for me when I was a baby; a bunch of medals including a Purple Heart; and the handful of photographs that, to me, was my Dad. I once found a card which my mother had given my Dad from me on his first Father's Day. I don't recall the outside of the card, but the inside said: 'cause I'll always be Daddy's Little Girl.' I cried a lot when I went through that trunk. On April 25, 1987, Scott Rudel and I were married and that was the first of the four happiest days of my life. The others were: March 1, 1988, when we had our first daughter, Alison Elizabeth; on October 11, 1989, when Abigail Catherine was born; and on March 1, 1992, when Thomas Alexander was born.

"An amazing chain of events happened in the fall of 1990. An article in *U.S. News & World Report* described my Dad's death in Vietnam. It told how my Dad had been shot and was waiting to be evacuated when he got out of the helicopter to help load a much more severely wounded comrade, Captain Ray Lefebvre, and was mortally wounded. My mother wrote a letter to the author of the article, who put her in touch with Hal Moore. There were a few lengthy calls and a letter to Ray Lefebvre asking him to come to the Ia Drang Alumni reunion marking the 25th Anniversary of the battle. I was so excited and nervous to meet these men who had fought alongside my Dad. I anticipated meeting a group of chest-beating macho types, all pro-war, pro-killing and all the other things I had heard about over the years.

"I am a pacifist but felt compelled to meet with them. My notions about these men were absurd. What I met, and I hope they don't mind the analogy, was a bunch of Teddy bears. Even my husband was pleasantly surprised to meet what I eventually came to feel was another family.

"Ray Lefebvre received my letter asking him to attend the reunion in the middle of his daughter's wedding week. He didn't hesitate a second. He told me of the wounds he had received and said that had it not been for my Dad he probably would not be alive today. I spent a lot of my childhood detesting the anonymous man that my Dad loaded onto that helicopter; the man mentioned in the letter in the trunk. I had always felt that my Dad traded his life for that man. It meant so much to me to be able to look that man in the eyes. I know now if the roles had been reversed Ray Lefebvre would have done the same for my Dad.

"I made my first trip to the [Vietnam Veteran's Memorial] Wall that weekend. I walked its length while its power consumed me. I have never before been so moved by any work of art. I suppose I never will be again. I feel that things have come full circle and I can go on. I will always mourn my Dad's death, but I feel now that I can put to rest the hurt, the anger and the feeling that I was cheated out of knowing half of myself. I know myself now and finally I like who I am. I can only hope that we learned something from Vietnam and that all was not for nothing."

Edward Dennis Monsewicz was seven years old when word came that his father, Sergeant Lloyd Joel Monsewicz, had been killed on November 17, 1965, in Landing Zone Albany. "My story begins in France, the country where my father met my mother and the place of my birth. I was a year old when we came to the United States. I can remember living in Missouri at Ft. Leonard Wood. A few years later he got orders for Korea. He moved us to Jacksonville, Florida, to be close to his family. We lived there for a year. From there we went to Ft. Benning, Georgia. By this time I had three brothers. My mother was still learning to speak English. The things I remember most about my Dad are how much he enjoyed working in the yard, spending time with us, and listening to Marty Robbins. Every Sunday we would go to church at Sand Hill. I couldn't wait till the services were over because I knew that I would get cookies and milk.

"In the few months before he left for Vietnam, I remember him training for his mission, coming home and dyeing his tee-shirts green and sorting out his field gear. During the last few days before he left he spent a lot of time with us. The day before he left he put me on top of his car and tried to explain to me, the best way he could, what was happening. He told me that I had to be the Daddy of the family while he was gone and look after my brothers and help Mom. Through the years that has stuck in my mind. My Mom was left alone to raise four boys on her own. I remember receiving several letters from Vietnam in which my Dad mostly talked about the weather and how much he missed home. In one letter he talked about having to go into An Khe Village and feeling very nervous because he never knew who the VC might be. He said he felt safer in the jungle than in the village, because he could blend in with the foliage. We got along the best way that we could, hoping for his return home.

"The first telegram came by taxi stating that he was missing in action. One week later the second telegram arrived stating that he was killed by hostile fire. About a week later we were laying him to rest at Ft. Benning. I was seven years old and I am now thirty-four. Through the years I wondered why this had to happen. Within the last two years I have finally been able to talk to other Vietnam veterans about this battle, and I am hoping one day to be able to find someone who knew my father during that time or was with him when he was killed. Now I have my own family: two boys ages four years and nineteen months and a beautiful wife who has stood beside me for the last thirteen years. My mother is still living and my brothers have all made lives of their own.

"These men fought and died for their country and it affected a lot of people in so many ways. President Bush said on national television that the Vietnam syndrome is over and done with. Not for me, and not for so many others. We can never do enough to help the

Vietnam veterans. May God bless and keep all the loved ones who are still affected by this senseless war."

His career at Pennsylvania Military College from 1959 to 1963 may have made some think that Jack Geoghegan was born to be a great captain in war. He was president of his class in his junior and senior years; cadet brigade sergeant major his junior year; cadet brigade commander his senior year. He won every medal and award of distinction the college granted. But Jack Geoghegan postponed his Army ROTC obligation to complete a master's degree in international relations at the University of Pennsylvania.

While there he married his college sweetheart, Barbara Weathers. Then Jack and Barbara left for East Africa, where they spent almost a year working for Catholic Relief Services in the villages of Tanzania. In May of 1965, he reported for duty as a new second lieutenant at Fort Benning. His daughter, Camille Anne, was born there. In July he was assigned to Company C, 1st Battalion, 7th Cavalry, and in August he sailed with his unit to Vietnam. Here is Barbara Geoghegan Johns's story:

"I never really believed he would die. At twenty-three and untouched by the sorrows of life, even sending my husband off to war didn't shake my feeling that Jack would live. I felt that God had great plans for him. Jack would complete his commitment to the Army and then return to Tanzania—the place that fulfilled his spirit, the place where we had spent most of our first year of marriage in Africa. He was extraordinarily idealistic. His nature was not warlike. The goal of his life was to help people in need. Even in Vietnam he volunteered his platoon to help rebuild a school, and ultimately he died as he lived, going to the aid of one of his men, Willie Godboldt. Their names are next to each other on the Vietnam Memorial.

"When Jack left for Vietnam I chose to move to Redding, Connecticut, so that Cammie and I could be near his parents. We would support and sustain each other for the year that Jack would be gone. They owned a small house on six acres and were having a large house built nearby. We shared the little house until their home was completed. When they moved to the big house, I stayed on in the little house. They named their home 'Wind Ridge.' I named the little house 'Dar es Salaam' or Haven of Peace. Cammie was only two months old when her father left for Vietnam, and she was the focal point for all of us. She kept us all smiling and, because she looked like her father, she was a constant happy part of him in our presence.

"When my world turned upside down on November 17, 1965, the night the telegram came, I felt thrust into another existence, as in a dream. I couldn't comprehend that what I firmly believed wouldn't happen had happened. I was with Jack's Aunt Pat in New Rochelle when Mom called. I remember looking out the window and being surprised that there were people driving by, that everything looked the same as it did before her call. I wanted to scream to everyone to stop. I went upstairs to look at Cammie, sleeping peacefully, not knowing how her life was so altered. In a recent letter, Jack had said: 'How about giving Cammie a little brother when I get back?' Now there would be no more little Geoghegans. I picked up my sleeping baby and hugged her hard, still not believing that an end had come to everything we had hoped and dreamed and planned.

"The news came on November 17, Jack's Dad's sixty-second birthday. Jack was buried in Bethel, Connecticut, on December 2. The funeral Mass was held in Pelham, New York, where he grew up, and the church was filled to overflowing. That week the newspaper of the Pennsylvania Military College devoted most of three pages to tributes to Jack.

"Afterward his mother wrote this letter published in *The Pelham Sun,* January 13, 1966:

Dear People of Pelham:

On November 17, the dreadful telegram arrived notifying us of Lance's death in Vietnam in the Battle of Ia Drang. He was, as you know, Barbara's husband, the father of little Cammie, and our only child.

While we awaited the return of his body, we tried to gather up the pieces of our broken hearts. We said to ourselves: It is God's will.

He knows best. And for a minute or for an hour, we managed some degree of resignation, but then suddenly an old sweater, a bowling ball, a photograph, and that bright red-headed boy was bounding up the stairs, three at a time, or rounding the curve on Manor Circle, tooting the horn to let us know he was home from college—from Africa—or from Fort Benning, and our resignation dissolved in the unalterable knowledge that he was dead. We would never, never see his dear face again.

We began to make funeral arrangements. We reasoned that since Lance's grammar and prep school companions lived in the Pelham–New Rochelle area, we would bring him to his hometown for the services. We phoned the Pelham Funeral Home. We did not wish to inflict our sorrow on others and I think we also felt deep down inside that perhaps no one was too much interested, so we asked Mr. Flood to put a short notice in the paper and to arrange for a brief, simple service.

Lance's body arrived by plane from Vietnam. We gathered what courage we could find and went to the funeral home. As we looked down at his dear face, we felt that the world had fallen in on us. He had fought in an action that was not termed a war; he had died thousands of miles from his beloved country; his blood and the blood of his men, whom he had loved so much, had now become part of the soil of Vietnam, and there were no bands, no parades, no anything—just three desolate people standing beside his coffin. Never had we been so alone.

Behind us a door quietly opened. Someone came into the room. It was a man. He was crying. He knelt. He prayed. He came over to us. He said fond, kind things about our boy. He left. But that was the beginning of what [one friend] said was 'a spontaneous outpouring of love for a boy.' Again the door opened, and again and again. People poured into that room—people who had known Lance— people who wept for him unashamedly—people who cared—people, blessed wonderful people.

Through Bob Cremins [a family friend], a service was held for him at the monument. Braced against the evening's cold, clergymen of all faiths voiced their tribute. The American Legion was there; the

Veterans of Foreign Wars, men who had made possible our boy's growth in a free country, through their own sacrifices. And again the people, hundreds of them crowding the street for this lovely ceremony—and that beautiful flag at half staff with the wind gently raising its folds like a benediction over all.

We cried, the tears streaming down our faces in sheer gratitude to everyone in Pelham for such a remembrance. The day of burial came and the police quietly cleared a path for the funeral cortege through the streets. They stood straight and tall at each intersection with arms raised in a last salute. St. Catherine's Church was filled to overflowing. Lance's flag-draped coffin rested at the feet of his God.

This boy had loved people so much. He didn't care if they were black or white. If they needed him, he always came a'running. He had fed and cared for them in Africa, and he was in Vietnam because he had heard the same summons and was answering it, and suddenly we realized that Lance was really all the boys in Vietnam— the weary, the courageous, the wounded, the dead—and Pelham had said: We love you all, opened its arms and gathered them all to her heart in the person of one young man, Lieutenant Lance Geoghegan.

On behalf of our boy, his men of the 2nd Platoon and all the young Americans in Vietnam, we thank you from the bottom of our hearts. God bless you.

His Family.

Barbara continues her story: "Quite a while after Jack's death, two battered boxes arrived in the mail. They had been returned from Vietnam, marked 'Verified deceased.' They were the chocolate chip cookies I had sent two months before. There was also a camera Jack had asked for and never received. Then there was the shipment of his personal effects, among them his wallet in which he had kept a picture of the 'little house' in Connecticut to which he longed to return. Also in that wallet was a letter from his mother. It says, in part, 'Dad is asleep and I am sitting in the den—thinking of you—

loving you—wishing you well—wishing you home—thanking God for our wonderful son. Dad and I pray so constantly for you and your men that the seconds, the minutes, the hours are full of you.'

"I don't know how I would have managed had it not been for Jack's parents. Years later they said the same thing about me and, of course, Cammie. I guess we kept each other going. When one was weak, another was strong.

"Not long after Jack's death I received a beautiful letter from Jack's battalion commander, Colonel Hal Moore. He also wrote to the Geoghegans, and reached out to us across all those miles, bringing us consolation and courage and wonderful words about Jack. In one of his letters, Colonel Moore suggested that he might stop by to see us. The day came, in 1967. We would be grateful for even five minutes with him. He was with us for five hours. He came first to my house. I picked up Cammie and went outside to greet him. He walked slowly up the stone stairway to us, staring at us with sorrow in his piercing eyes, and surrounded both of us in his arms. This man who had carried my husband's body off a bloody battlefield thousands of miles away was now here at our home. What a painful and difficult task he had, coming to speak of war in a setting so full of tranquility. We hurried up the hill to the Geogheghans' house and there were more hugs and tears. Then we sat and talked and talked. It was cathartic, sitting together, sharing the pain and grief that enveloped us all. Then Colonel Moore asked where Jack was buried. When I told him St. Mary's Cemetery was two miles away, he wanted to go there, so I took him. We walked to Jack's grave. After standing there a minute, Colonel Moore asked if he could spend some time alone at the grave. I sat in the car while he did so. I glanced at him just once, and saw him kneeling by the grave, his head in his hands. I quickly looked away, not wanting to intrude on this private moment. The healing effect of that visit lasted to the end of Mom and Dad Geoghegan's lives, and the memory of it will stay with me always.

"About two years after Jack's death, Mom Geoghegan chose a moment to tell me something that she and Dad felt I should know. They wanted me to know that they wanted me to marry again; that

I should not feel tied to them because of our deep closeness; or that I would somehow betray Jack by loving someone else. I could not imagine loving someone else. I loved them so much. In December, 1968, a neighbor asked Mom and Dad how they felt about him introducing an old friend to me. Since they wanted me to meet people, they agreed and invited him to bring Lieutenant Colonel John Johns over for cocktails when he visited from West Point where he was stationed. John and I met on December 21, 1968, and we were married on April 5, 1969. John adored children and instantly fell in love with Cammie and she with him. She was almost four when we married. For years we'd talk about when WE married Daddy. In May, 1970, a son was born and two years later we added a sister. Mom and Dad Geoghegan remained a vital part of our lives all of their lives. They were a third set of grandparents and all three of our children loved them. Our family was their family.

"America at War! That's how NBC News started out every night during the recent Persian Gulf War. A war. Not a skirmish. Not a police action. A war. Back home the country was in fervent support; flag companies did record business; tons of care packages were shipped to the troops; children wrote letters by the thousands to Any Soldier. What a contrast to Vietnam. Was it guilt feelings? America should feel guilty for its collective treatment of the Vietnam veteran and so should our government—or at least those who governed during the Vietnam conflict. They wouldn't even call the long, long siege in Vietnam a war, because war was never declared.

"Jack's original death certificate read that he died 'as the result of gunshot wounds to head and back, received in hostile ground action.' In 1978, I had to write for another death certificate for insurance purposes. What a shock when the certificate arrived in the mail. Under 'Casualty Status' the box titled 'Non-Battle' was checked. I looked up the one remaining original certificate. That whole section was blanked out. I was horrified and wondered for a moment if I had been lied to; maybe Jack had been killed by friendly fire and no one wanted to tell me. My husband worked in the Pentagon and checked it out. A written answer was forthcoming that very day: 'the policy in 1965 was that hostile deaths were treated as non-battle since the conflict had not been recognized as a war or battle. Because of numerous comments received, the policy was later changed to properly classify combat deaths as battle casualties.'

"Even after 26 years, it is still there, that golden thread in the tapestry. I may see an expression on Cammie's face for an instant that brings a feeling. Or it may be a dream. The doorbell rang in the dream. Cammie, age 8, was beside me; Bobby, age 3, on the other side. The baby, Barbi, age 1, was in my arms. I opened the door and there was Jack, in his tan uniform. He stared at the four of us through the glass storm door and I, my children surrounding me, stared back. Nothing was said. His face broke into a smile, and then his image faded way. When I awoke, at first I felt deep sadness, then a feeling of guilt that my life had taken such an unexpectedly happy turn when once I thought I would never be happy again. But I focused on the smile on Jack's face as his image faded. I knew that if Jack could be present in any sense, he would have been profoundly happy for me."

They are the Gold Star children, war's innocent victims, and their pain shimmers across the years pure and undimmed. They pass through life with an empty room in their hearts where a father was supposed to live and laugh and love.

All their lives they listen for the footstep that will never fall, and long to know what might have been.

26

REFLECTIONS AND PERCEPTIONS

The enemy will pass slowly from the offensive to the defensive. The blitzkrieg will transform itself into a war of long duration. Thus, the enemy will be caught in a dilemma: He has to drag out the war in order to win it and does not possess, on the other hand, the psychological and political means to fight a long-drawn-out war. . . .

> —General Vo Nguyen Giap, in an early and prescient analysis of the future course of the Viet Minh war with the French.

Lessons were drawn and political decisions were made in the closing days of 1965, both in Washington and in Hanoi, that flowed directly out of the head-on collision of two determined armies in the Ia Drang Valley. Projections of the eventual cost in human lives and national resources, and even the eventual outcome, were promptly drawn for the American President, Lyndon Johnson, by his cool, numbers-crunching secretary of defense, Robert S. McNamara, and just as promptly set aside. This was America's war now, and America had never lost a war.

In Hanoi, Senior General Vo Nguyen Giap looked hard at what

he perceived as the important lessons of the Ia Drang campaign and was heartened by what he saw: "After the Ia Drang battle we concluded that we could fight and win against the Cavalry troops. We learned lessons from this battle and disseminated the information to all our soldiers. These were instructions on how to organize to fight the helicopters.

"We thought that the Americans must have a strategy. We did. We had a strategy of people's war. You had tactics, and it takes very decisive tactics to win a strategic victory. You planned to use the Cavalry tactics as your strategy to win the war. If we could defeat your tactics—your helicopters—then we could defeat your strategy. Our goal was to win the war."

In Saigon, the American commander in Vietnam, General William C. Westmoreland, and his principal deputy, General William DePuy, looked at the statistics of the thirty-four-day Ia Drang campaign—3,561 North Vietnamese estimated killed versus 305 American dead—and saw a kill ratio of twelve North Vietnamese to one American. What that said to two officers who had learned their trade in the meat-grinder campaigns in World War II was that they could bleed the enemy to death over the long haul, with a strategy of attrition.

In Hanoi, President Ho Chi Minh and his lieutenants considered the outcome in the Ia Drang and were serenely confident. Their peasant soldiers had withstood the terrible high-tech fire storm delivered against them by a superpower and had at least fought the Americans to a draw. By their yardstick, a draw against such a powerful opponent was the equivalent of a victory. In time, they were certain, the patience and perseverance that had worn down the French colonialists would also wear down the Americans.

There was one man in a position of power in Washington that fall who knew that the name of the game had changed in Vietnam. Secretary of Defense McNamara was on a trip to Europe when President Johnson asked him to return home by way of Saigon for first-hand briefings on the Ia Drang battles. McNamara talked with Ambassador Lodge and General Westmoreland in Saigon, and then flew to the An Khe base camp for briefings by General Harry Kinnard and myself.

During my twenty minutes I did my best to convey to McNamara and his party a vivid picture of the North Vietnamese soldiers who had fought against us at X-Ray: well-disciplined, determined to the point of suicidal fanaticism, and boiling down off the mountain in the kind of human-wave attacks not seen since Korea.

McNamara's silence as I concluded was significant. He now knew that the Vietnam War had just exploded into an open-ended and massive commitment of American men, money, and matériel to a cause that he was beginning to suspect would be difficult to win. By the time he got back to Saigon, McNamara began tempering his usual public optimism. Before boarding the flight back to Washington, he told reporters: "It will be a long war."

On the plane, McNamara dictated a top-secret memo to President Johnson, which stated that it was now clear that North Vietnam was not only matching but exceeding the American buildup, and would continue to do so. McNamara wrote that only two options were open: The United States could go for a compromise solution—withdrawal under whatever diplomatic cover could be arranged—or the President could approve General Westmoreland's requests to more than double the number of U.S. battalions fighting in Vietnam from thirty-four to seventy-four by the end of 1966. He concluded with these words: "Evaluation: We should be aware that deployments of the kind . . . will not guarantee success. U.S. killed-in-action can be expected to reach 1,000 a month, and the odds are even that we will be faced in early 1967, with a no-decision at an even higher level."

A more detailed memo to LBJ, dated December 6, 1965, reflecting the consensus among McNamara, General Westmoreland, Ambassador Lodge, the Pacific commander, Admiral U. S. Grant Sharp, and the Joint Chiefs of Staff, declared:

> We believe that, whether or not major new diplomatic initiatives are made, the United States must send a substantial number of additional forces to Vietnam *if we are to avoid being defeated there* [empha-

sis added]. We recommend: That the U.S. be prepared to increase its deployment of ground troops by the end of 1966, from 34 combat battalions to 74 combat battalions. . . . If the 74 U.S. battalions, together with increases in air squadrons, naval units, air defense, combat support, construction units and miscellaneous logistic support and advisory personnel which we also recommend, were to be deployed it would bring the total U.S. personnel in Vietnam to approximately 400,000. The end 1965 strength of 200,000 would increase during 1966 at the rate of approximately 15,000 a month. It should be understood that further deployments (perhaps exceeding an additional 200,000 men) may be needed in 1967.

McNamara again repeated his estimate that the North Vietnamese would match any American escalation and that by 1967, the number of Americans killed in action would reach a thousand per month. And again he reiterated the bottom lines: "If the U.S. were willing to commit enough forces—perhaps 600,000 men or more— we could ultimately prevent the Democratic Republic of Vietnam/ Viet Cong from sustaining the conflict at a significant level. When this point was reached, however, the question of Chinese intervention would become critical."

The McNamara memo added: "It follows, therefore, that the odds are about even that, even with the recommended deployments, we will be faced in early 1967 with a military standoff at a much higher level. . . ."

In mid-December, President Johnson convened a White House meeting of his top advisers. Will Bundy says that McNamara's option number one—get the hell out of Vietnam now, while the getting is good—was never seriously considered nor was it pressed by McNamara. Option number two—the huge buildup of American combat and support troops—was readily approved by all, including McNamara. Ever the numbers cruncher, McNamara told the gathering, "The military solution to the problem is not certain; [the odds of success are] one out of three, or one in two." McNamara did push for a bombing pause to prepare U.S. public opinion for the coming escalation.

Those of us who commanded American soldiers in the opening

days had already undergone one crisis of confidence in the political leadership's commitment to the struggle when President Johnson refused to extend enlistments and sent us off to war sadly under-strength and minus many of our best-trained men. Now, in the wake of the Ia Drang, American political determination was tested again, and again found wanting.

We knew for a fact that the three North Vietnamese regiments that we had fought in the Ia Drang had withdrawn into Cambodia. We wanted to follow them in hot pursuit, on the ground and in the air, but could not do so under the rules of engagement. Washington had just answered one very important question in the minds of Hanoi's leaders.

General Kinnard says: "I was always taught as an officer that in a pursuit situation you continue to pursue until you either kill the enemy or he surrenders. I saw the Ia Drang as a definite pursuit situation and I wanted to keep after them. Not to follow them into Cambodia violated every principle of warfare. I was supported in this by both the military and civilian leaders in Saigon. But the decision was made back there, at the White House, that we would not be permitted to pursue into Cambodia. It became perfectly clear to the North Vietnamese that they then had sanctuary; they could come when they were ready to fight and leave when they were ready to quit."

General Kinnard adds, "When General Giap says he learned how to fight Americans and our helicopters at the Ia Drang, that's bull-shit! What he learned was that we were not going to be allowed to chase him across a mythical line in the dirt. From that point for-ward, he was grinning. He can bring us to battle when he wants and where he wants, and where's that? Always within a few miles of the border, where his supply lines were the shortest, where the prepon-derance of forces is his, where he has scouted the terrain intensely and knows it better than we do."

Will Bundy was then assistant secretary of state. Of that period and that decision, he says, "I suppose from a strictly military point of view, going into Cambodia would have been a net plus. But there was a good deal more at stake. We were trying to preserve a façade of Cambodian neutrality. Lyndon Johnson had a friendly feeling toward Prince Sihanouk; Richard Nixon did not. But it seems to me that if you started playing that game the other side would simply say, all right, let's fight on a wider field. Unless my initial conclusions are wrong, Nixon's secret bombing of Cambodia did exactly that. We began bombing a ten-mile strip over the Cambodian border, and the North Vietnamese began operating twelve miles inside. By the time we went in on the ground a year later we had to go twenty miles deep. It simply shoved the war deeper into Cambodia, and the other side would just keep moving deeper, unless you moved in and took over all of eastern Cambodia, and that is a very large piece of terrain."

For me, the next hint that something was terribly wrong in the way we were pursuing the war came early in 1966, when I led the 3rd Brigade—including the battalions that had fought at X-Ray and Albany—into another meat-grinder campaign, this time into the heavily populated Bong Son plain on the coast of Central Vietnam.

The Bong Son, a densely populated rice-farming region, had been under Viet Cong control for years. Now North Vietnamese regulars had moved into the area. It was my understanding that our job was to clear the armed enemy from the region and then turn it over to the South Vietnamese army and civilian authorities to secure and administer over the long haul.

Our first problems came with operating in so heavily populated an area. The same awesome firepower—artillery, air strikes, and ARA—that had saved our lives in the unpopulated Ia Drang Valley now, despite our best efforts, began taking a toll of innocent civilians killed and maimed, villages destroyed, and farm animals slain.

On our air assault into the Bong Son on January 28, 1966, I was on the first lift, and charged into the tree line. There was a small thatch-roofed house in the trees; inside, a peasant family huddled, frightened out of their wits by the artillery prep fires that had landed all around them. A lovely six-year-old girl was bloody from a shrapnel wound. She was the same age as my daughter Cecile, back home. I summoned the medics, but I left there heartsick. None of us had joined the Army to hurt children and frighten peaceful farm families.

The fighting was vicious and, by the time the enemy had been routed, 82 of my men were dead and another 318 wounded. A high price to pay, but the Bong Son had been liberated. Right? Prime Minister Nguyen Cao Ky and his wife, Mai, dressed in matching black flight suits with purple scarves, arrived at my headquarters for a briefing on the battles. I emphasized that we were turning control back to the Vietnamese government.

Within one week after we pulled out, the North Vietnamese and Viet Cong Main Force units had returned to the villages of the Bong Son. My brigade would be sent back in a show of force in April and again in May when we lost many more men killed and wounded. After the May operation it was very clear to me, a battlefield commander not involved in the politics of it all, that the American Mission and the Military Assistance Command Vietnam had not succeeded in coordinating American and South Vietnamese military operations with follow-on Vietnamese government programs to reestablish control in the newly cleared areas. If they couldn't make it work in Bong Son—where the most powerful American division available had cleared enemy forces from the countryside—how could they possibly hope to reestablish South Vietnamese control in other contested regions where the American military presence was much weaker. But this was 1966, and early in the war. All I could do was hope and pray that our terrible sacrifices would eventually contribute to achievement of America's objectives in Vietnam. Late in 1966, the entire 1st Cavalry Division was moved to the Bong Son, where it remained for nearly eighteen months as an army of occupation.

One more fatal flaw in American policy soon began to bite hard. Largely in order to pacify the public and to demonstrate that so powerful a nation as the United States was hardly troubled by this distant police action, the Johnson administration decreed that the tour of duty for American troops would be twelve months (thirteen for the hard-luck Marines). No citizen-soldier would have to stay in Vietnam a day longer. Those who had survived and learned how to fight in this difficult environment began going home in the summer of 1966; with them went all their experience and expertise. Replacing them was an army of new draftees, which in due course would be replaced by newer draftees. The level of training drifted ever lower as the demand for bodies grew.

Even more devastating to the morale and effectiveness of every American unit in combat was the six-month limit on battalion and brigade command. This was ticket-punching: A career officer had to have troop-command time for promotion. The six-month rule meant that twice as many officers got that important punch. It also meant that at just about the time when a commander learned the terrain and the troops and the tricks and got good at the job—if he was going to get good—he was gone. The soldiers paid the price.

In late June 1966, my turn was up as commander of the 3rd Brigade. When my replacement, a colonel straight out of the Pentagon, showed up to take over, my brigade was in the field, fighting near Dong Tre. It would have been criminal, in those circumstances, to relinquish command to a man who was still pissing Stateside water, and I flatly refused to do so. The change of command was delayed ten days, until the fight was over. A month later, on August 8, 1966, my replacement sent Alpha Company, 1st Battalion, 7th Cavalry back into the Ia Drang Valley by itself, and twenty-five men were killed in one terrible day.

I had hoped that my next assignment would be to the Infantry School at Fort Benning, where I could pass along what I had learned in Vietnam to the young officers who were headed for combat. It was not to be. In fact, only one of the hundreds of officers who had gone through airmobile training and a year in the field with the 1st Cavalry Division was assigned to the Infantry School. I was sent instead to Washington, D.C., where I was told my next job would be on the Latin American desk at the U.S. State Department. Great job for someone whose only foreign languages were French and Norwegian.

In short order, those orders were changed to a one-year assignment to the office of Secretary of Defense McNamara's International Security Affairs Directorate, under John McNaughton. As half of a two-man Vietnam section, I was primarily charged with putting together "trip books" for the Vietnam visits of McNamara and key Defense and State Department officials, and with fielding "Congressionals," constituent questions and complaints about Vietnam policy passed along by senators and representatives.

For the next year I watched Bob McNamara and John McNaughton, both brilliant men, go through hell as they struggled unsuccessfully to get a handle on the war and the pacification process in Vietnam. At the end of that year neither of them was any closer to finding or creating such a handle. An office wit summed up what was happening in Vietnam sadly and succinctly: "Although we have redoubled our efforts, we have lost sight of our objective."

What, then, had we learned with our sacrifices in the Ia Drang Valley? We had learned something about fighting the North Vietnamese regulars—and something important about ourselves. We could stand against the finest light infantry troops in the world and hold our ground. General Westmoreland thought he had found the answer to the question of how to win this war: He would trade one American life for ten or eleven or twelve North Vietnamese lives, day after day, until Ho Chi Minh cried uncle. Westmoreland would learn, too late, that he was wrong; that the American people didn't see a kill ratio of 10–1 or even 20–1 as any kind of bargain. But we had validated both the principle and the practice of airmobile warfare. A million American soldiers would ride to battle in Huey helicopters in the next eight years, and the familiar "whup, whup, whup" of their rotors would be the enduring soundtrack of this war.

Finally—even though it took ten years, cost the lives of 58,000 young Americans and inflicted humiliating defeat on a nation that had never before lost a war—some of us learned that Clausewitz had it right 150 years earlier when he wrote these words:

"No one starts a war—or rather, no one in his senses ought to do so—without first being clear in his mind what he intends to achieve by that war and how he intends to conduct it."

EPILOGUE

> We few, we happy few, we band of brothers;
> For he to-day that sheds his blood with me
> Shall be my brother.
>
> —Shakespeare, *Henry V,* Act IV, Scene 3

It's easy to forget the numbers, but how can we forget the faces, the voices, the cries of young men dying before their time? Between October 23 and November 26, 1965, a total of 305 young American soldiers were killed in combat in the Pleiku campaign. Their names march down the lines inscribed on Panel 3-East of the Vietnam Veterans Memorial, each one a national treasure, each one a national tragedy. Some tell a story by their very juxtaposition: Lieutenant John Lance Geoghegan's name is frozen in the black granite beside that of PFC Willie F. Godboldt, the man he died trying to save. What would they have become, all of them, if they had been allowed to serve their country by their lives, instead of by their deaths?

Yes, there is an organization, the Ia Drang Alumni, our own Band of Brothers, and we have a dinner before Veteran's Day in Washington every November and a lunch wherever the 1st Cavalry Division Association holds its reunion each summer, for we find pleasure and healing in the company of the friends and comrades of our youth.

We begin by calling the roll, first reading the names of all those who fell and those who have joined them since. Then, one by one, we stand to call out our own names, ranks, military occupations, companies and battalions, and where we fought in the valley. There are no dues—those were paid in blood long ago—and no officers. Two ex-sergeants, Bill Kreischer of Alpha Company, 1st Battalion, 7th Cavalry and John Setelin of Bravo Company, 2nd Battalion, 7th Cavalry, run the organization out of their hip pockets as a labor of love.

Each year one or another stands before us and tells what he remembers of the men on his right and on his left and what they saw and did in the valley. Only now do we begin to understand why old soldiers have always gathered to murmur among themselves of days gone by. Those *were* the days, my friend.

And what of the others, our old and former enemies of the 320th, 33rd, and 66th People's Army regiments? For them there was no expiration of enlistment, no rotation home at the end of one year. They fought on for ten more years. *Death or victory* was their term of enlistment, and for most death came first.

Ho Chi Minh's old soldiers and sergeants of these regiments and others of the People's Army do their best to take care of each other, unofficially, of course. On a given evening once a week, or once a month, the men of a particular unit gather at one of the Hanoi coffeehouses that cater to old soldiers, there to talk among themselves, share news and gossip about their friends and families, and, occasionally, to tell a war story of their days in the Ia Drang. Since 1975, the Vietnamese army has worked to recover the remains of almost one million men and women who fell in battle during the American war. They have been reinterred in war cemeteries that dot the rice paddies, each marked by a low wall and a tall obelisk.

In the small, closed world of the military, great victories, great defeats, and great sacrifices are never forgotten. They are remembered with battle streamers attached to unit flags. Among the scores of streamers that billow and whirl around the flags of all the battalions of the 1st Cavalry Division there is one deep-blue Presidential Unit Citation streamer that says simply: PLEIKU PROVINCE.

Schoolchildren no longer memorize the names and dates of great battles, and perhaps that is good; perhaps that is the first step on the road to a world where wars are no longer necessary. Perhaps. But we remember those days and our comrades, and long after we are gone that long blue streamer will still caress proud flags.

APPENDIX

Where Have All the Young Men Gone?

The men, women, and children of this story are America's neighbors, living quiet lives in every corner of the nation they served. They are representative of the more than three million Americans who served the United States of America in its long and bitter war in Vietnam, representative of those who loved one of the more than 58,000 Americans who died in that war. The following is a partial accounting, prepared in 1992 and updated for the paperback edition, of where some of them are and what they have done with their lives:

ADAMS, Russell, fifty-one, machine gunner, Alpha Company, 1st Battalion, 7th Cav in the Ia Drang, helps run the family dairy farm on five hundred acres outside Shoemakersville, Pennsylvania. He is partly paralyzed as a result of his terrible wound. Adams and his wife have a three-year-old daughter.

ADAMS, Warren, sixty-two, first sergeant, Delta Company, 1st Battalion, 7th Cav in the Ia Drang, retired in 1968 as the best-educated command sergeant major in the Army. Assigned to intelligence duty in Europe in the late 1940s and early 1950s, Adams earned a bachelor's degree from the University of Austria in Vienna, a master's degree in history at the University in Innsbruck, and a doctorate of psychology from Munich University—all under an assumed name. He owns a property-management firm in Tampa, Florida.

AINSWORTH, Hank, fifty-four, who flew the 2nd Battalion, 7th Cav command helicopter in the Ia Drang, retired a chief warrant officer 4 on May 30, 1977, after twenty-two years' service. He lives in Colorado Springs, Colorado, and owns and operates a real estate brokerage firm.

ALLEY, J. L. (Bud) Jr., fifty, communications officer, 2nd Battalion, 7th Cav in the Ia Drang, completed a full tour with his battalion and left Vietnam and the Army in August 1966. He worked as a sales executive in the corrugated-box industry and went to school nights to earn his MBA. Alley is general manager of a box factory in Dayton, Tennessee. He and his wife have two college-age children.

BARKER, Robert L., fifty-five, artillery-battery commander in LZ Falcon, served a second tour in Vietnam with the 1st Cavalry Division in 1969–1970 and later served a third combat tour. He retired a lieutenant colonel in 1980 with twenty years' service, and is now a plastics-plant manager. He lives in Vicksburg, Mississippi.

BARTHOLOMEW, Roger J. (Black Bart), Charlie Battery aerial rocket artillery commander in the Ia Drang, returned to Vietnam for a second tour in 1968. On November 27, 1968, Lieutenant Colonel Bartholomew was killed in action. He had just turned thirty-six years old.

BEAN, Roger, fifty-two, Huey pilot who was wounded in LZ X-Ray, was wounded again in early 1966 in the Bong Son campaign. Still on active duty, he is a major general, and is deputy to the Army inspector-general.

BECK, Bill, forty-nine, assistant machine gunner, Alpha Company, 1st Battalion, 7th Cav in the Ia Drang, left the Army in 1966 and went home to his native Steelton, Pennsylvania. He is a free-lance commercial artist in Harrisburg and occasionally turns his hand to fine-art drawings of his war experiences. He and Russell Adams are still best friends.

BRAVEBOY, Toby, rifleman, Alpha Company, 2nd Battalion, 7th Cav, recovered from his wounds and his week-long ordeal alone on the abandoned battlefield at Albany and returned safely to his family in Coward, South Carolina. After leaving the Army, Braveboy worked as a roofer. He was killed in an automobile accident less than ten years later.

BROWN, Thomas W. (Tim), seventy-three, the 3rd Brigade commander in the Ia Drang, retired a brigadier general in 1973, after thirty-plus years of service and a second tour in Vietnam, with two Silver Stars and two Bronze Stars from his three wars. He and his wife, Louise, live in San Antonio, Texas, and Brown plays a round of golf most days.

BUNGUM, Galen, forty-nine, rifleman in Lieutenant Henry Herrick's Lost Platoon, Bravo Company, 1st Battalion, 7th Cav, left the Army in April 1966 and went home to Hayfield, Minnesota. Bungum operated a 161-acre dairy farm until 1988, when he sold his cows and took a job in town. He still grows soybeans and corn on the farm in his spare time.

CANTU, Vincent, fifty-one, mortarman, Bravo Company, 1st Battalion, 7th Cav, left the Ia Drang battlefield and immediately rotated home for discharge, two weeks late, in December 1965. When he got back to Refugio, Texas, he called on Joe Galloway's parents but mercifully concealed the true circumstances of their meeting on the battlefield in X-Ray. Vince Cantu never went back to his music. Today he is a city bus driver in Houston, Texas. He is married and has a daughter in college and a son in the U.S. Marines. He says he "did a lot of praying" during the Persian Gulf War, when his son, his brother, and his old friend Galloway were all on the battlefield.

CARRARA, Robert J., fifty-four, battalion surgeon of the 1st Battalion, 7th Cav in LZ X-Ray, served eleven months in Vietnam and was discharged in July 1966. A Chicago native, Doc Carrara returned home, changed his specialty to pathology. He retired in 1990. He and his wife live in St. Charles, a suburb of Chicago. They have four children and three grandchildren. Carrara says, "I don't dwell on Vietnam, but now and then I hear something or smell something and flash back to those days. I have one very vivid memory of the second morning in X-Ray. We were crawling around under intense machine-gun fire when Sergeant Major Plumley walked up, pulled his .45-caliber pistol, chambered a round, and said: 'Gentlemen, prepare to defend yourselves.' You never forget a thing like that."

CASH, John, fifty-six, assistant operations officer in 3rd Brigade Headquarters, later commanded a rifle company in the 1st Battalion, 7th Cavalry for more than six months in 1966. Cash served a second tour in Vietnam as an adviser to the Royal Thai Army forces. He added a masters degree in Latin American studies to his M.A. in history. He served in both Brazil and El Salvador, was a history instructor at West Point and served in the Center of Military History for a number of years. His last project on active duty was researching and writing a history of the all-black 24th Infantry Regiment during the Korean War. Cash retired from active duty as a colonel in September of 1992 and lives in the Washington, D.C., area.

CRANDALL, Bruce, fifty-nine, who commanded the helicopters in the Ia Drang Valley, returned to Vietnam for a second tour in 1967. In January 1968, over the Bong Son plain, Crandall's Huey was blown out of the sky by an air strike while flying a nap-of-the-earth search for a downed helicopter. Crandall's back was broken; he spent five months in an Army hospital recovering. Crandall won the first Helicopter Heroism Award of the Aviation/Space Writers Association, for two daring nighttime landings under fire to rescue twelve badly wounded troopers from Captain Tony Nadal's Alpha Company, 1st Battalion, 7th Cav in Operation Masher–White Wing in January 1966. During his two tours in Vietnam, Crandall flew lead ship on 756 separate missions. He earned his master's degree in public administration in 1976 and retired in 1977 as a lieutenant colonel. He served as city manager of Dunsmuir, California, from 1977 to 1980, when he moved to Mesa, Arizona, where he is the city's manager of public works. He and his wife, Arlene, have three sons—a banker in São Paulo, Brazil; a lawyer in Connecticut; and a divinity student in college.

DEAL, Dennis, fifty, platoon leader, Bravo Company, 1st Battalion, 7th Cav in the Ia Drang, left the Army as a captain in 1968 and returned to his native Pittsburgh, Pennsylvania. He is now a financial officer with the U.S. Postal Service in Oklahoma City, Oklahoma.

DIDURYK, Myron F., commander of Bravo Company, 2nd Battalion, 7th Cav in LZ X-Ray and LZ Albany, completed his tour in Vietnam with Bravo Company in 1966, and later returned to Vietnam and the 1st Air Cavalry Division as a major. Assigned as the operations officer of the 2nd Battalion, 12th Cavalry, Diduryk was killed in action on April 24, 1970, in a Huey helicopter at an abandoned fire base near the Cambodian border. The battalion commander had ordered his command helicopter to land and check out a North Vietnamese soldier killed by the door gunner. As the command ship touched down, other NVA soldiers opened up; Myron Diduryk was struck in the stomach in the doorway of the chopper. Thus died one of the finest officers who fought in the Ia Drang. On November 27, 1965, Diduryk wrote a detailed account of Bravo Company's actions at X-Ray for the ROTC students at his alma mater, St. Peter's College in Jersey City, New Jersey. The instructor of that class, Colonel John F. Jeszensky (ret.), provided the authors with a copy of Diduryk's journal and maps for this book. Diduryk is buried at the Fort Benning cemetery; his widow, Delores, lives in Jacksonville, Florida.

DILLON, Gregory (Matt), fifty-nine, operations officer of the 1st Battalion, 7th Cav in the Ia Drang, served a second tour in Vietnam as a battalion commander in the 9th Infantry Division and was a brigade commander at Fort Carson, Colorado. He retired a colonel in December 1981, after twenty-four years' service. He and his wife and their four Saint Bernard dogs live in Colorado Springs, Colorado. Dillon is a scratch golfer who does his best to get in eighteen holes every day, even if it means a drive downslope to find a course that isn't closed on account of snow in the Colorado winter.

DUNCAN, Ken, fifty-three, executive officer of Bravo Company, 1st Battalion, 7th Cav, left the Army in August 1966, and returned to his hometown of Thomaston, Georgia, where he works with a textile-manufacturing company. He is married and the father of two children.

EDWARDS, Robert, fifty-four, commander of Charlie Company, 1st Battalion, 7th Cav, served a second tour in Vietnam as an adviser. He was director of training development at Fort Benning when he retired as a colonel in 1983. Edwards is the acting borough manager of Dublin, Pennsylvania; he and his wife, Nancy, live in nearby New Hope.

FESMIRE, John A. (Skip), fifty-three, commander of Charlie Company, 2nd Battalion, 7th Cav in the Ia Drang, is still on active duty. Fesmire is a colonel assigned as the Army attaché to the U.S. Embassy in Buenos Aires, Argentina. He returned for a second Vietnam tour as an adviser in IV Corps in August 1968; in the 1970s he earned bachelor's and master's degrees.

FORREST, George, fifty-four, who commanded Alpha Company, 1st Battalion, 5th Cav in the Ia Drang, retired a lieutenant colonel in 1980 after twenty-one years' service. For the next ten years he was a football coach at Morgan State University in Baltimore, his alma mater. Since August 1990, he has been the dean of students and basketball coach at St. Mary Rynken Catholic High School in Leonardtown, Maryland, his hometown.

FREEMAN, Ed (Too Tall to Fly), sixty-five, Bruce Crandall's wingman, retired a major in 1967 after twenty-one years' Army service. Freeman won a battlefield commission in the Korean War. He was first sergeant of Bravo Company, 36th Engineer Battalion and one of 14 men in his 257-man company who survived the opening stages of the fight for Pork Chop Hill. His lieutenant's bars were pinned on by General James Van Fleet and, at Freeman's request, his first assignment was as commander of Bravo Company. Freeman reconstituted the unit and led it back up Pork Chop. After retiring from the Army, Freeman became the northwest area director of aircraft services for the U.S. Department of the Interior. Too Tall Ed retired from that job on January 3, 1991. Between the Army and the Interior Department, Freeman logged a total of seventeen thousand hours' flying time in helicopters and eight thousand hours in fixed wing. Freeman and his wife, Barbara, live in Boise, Idaho. They have two sons, one an oil-industry consultant, the other an Air Force sergeant who served in the Persian Gulf War.

GALLOWAY, Joe, fifty, war correspondent attached to the 1st Battalion, 7th Cavalry at X-Ray, served sixteen months in Vietnam on his first tour for United Press International, 1965–1966. When the last of his old friends in the 1st Cavalry and the U.S. Marines rotated home, Galloway also left, vowing never to return. But UPI sent him back to Vietnam in 1971, in 1973, and again in 1975 for the final chapter. Galloway served a total of fifteen years overseas with UPI, assigned to Tokyo, Saigon, Jakarta, New Delhi, Singapore, and Moscow. In 1982, he joined *U.S. News & World Report* magazine. He won a National Magazine Award for his October 29, 1990, cover article on the Ia Drang battles. Now a senior writer for *U.S. News,* Galloway recently had one last combat tour. In January 1991, General H. Norman Schwarzkopf summoned the reporter to his headquarters in Saudi Arabia and said: "I'm sending you to the commander out here who is most like General Hal Moore, and the division which has the most challenging and dangerous mission in my battle plan." Galloway rode with then–Major General Barry McCaffrey and the 24th Infantry Division (Mechanized) on a hairraising tank charge through the western Iraq desert to the Euphrates River valley. He and his wife, Theresa, live on a farm in northern Virginia with their sons Lee, fifteen, and Joshua, twelve.

GEOGHEGAN, Camille, twenty-seven, daughter of Lieutenant John Lance (Jack) Geoghegan, Charlie Company, 1st Battalion, 7th Cav, killed in action November 15, 1965, is a human resources specialist at a company in McLean, Virginia. She is an active member of Sons and Daughters in Touch, an organization sponsored by the Friends of the Vietnam Veterans Memorial. The group is devoted to bringing together the families and friends of men killed in Vietnam.

GILREATH, Larry M., platoon sergeant, Bravo Company, 1st Battalion, 7th Cavalry, did two more tours in Southeast Asia and retired a master sergeant in April 1972. He went home to Anderson County, South Carolina, where he is a deputy sheriff.

GWIN, S. Lawrence (Larry), fifty-one, executive officer, Alpha Company, 2nd Battalion, 7th Cav in the Ia Drang, stayed with his company through July 4, 1966. Alpha Company arrived in Vietnam with 146 officers and men. At the end of a year only fifteen of the original contingent were still there, Gwin included. Gwin left the Army at the end of his ROTC commitment and went home to his native Boston, where he teaches and writes. He is working on a book on Alpha Company's year in Vietnam.

HASTINGS, Charlie W., fifty-three, forward air controller at LZ X-Ray, retired as a colonel from the U.S. Air Force on March 1, 1992, after thirty years' service. After the Ia Drang campaign, Hastings was badly burned when the O-1E Bird Dog spotter plane he was piloting was shot down over the Mang Yang Pass and crash-landed in the old French Group Mobile 100 cemetery beside Route 19 on Christmas Eve 1965. The plane hit several tombstones and flipped over. Charlie's foot was pinned in the wrecked cockpit when the white phosphorus target-marking rockets under the wings cooked off. "I pulled the muscles in that leg so badly yanking it free that I couldn't walk for three months," he said. His hands were burned in the escape from the wreckage, and it was doubted that he would ever fly again. But Charlie was back in the air, flying F-4 Phantoms, less than a year later. He served another Indochina tour in 1975, planning and helping run the final American air evacuation of Vietnam from a base in Thailand. Charlie Hastings moved back home to Tucson after retiring, and he lives there with his wife and children.

HAZEN, Robert D., fifty, Lieutenant Bob Taft's radio operator in Alpha Company, 1st Battalion, 7th Cav, retired from the Army a master sergeant in 1988 after twenty-seven years' service. He now manages the quartermaster laundry at Fort Campbell, Kentucky, and lives in Clarksville, Tennessee. After Vietnam, Hazen maintained a correspondence with the mother of the young lieutenant who died in his arms.

HENRY, Frank, executive officer of the 2nd Battalion, 7th Cavalry in LZ Albany, served a second tour in Vietnam as a battalion commander in the 1st Cavalry Division, later commanded a brigade of the 101st Airborne Division, and was promoted to chief of staff of the 101st Airborne in the summer of 1977. In August 1977, at the age of forty-four, Colonel Frank Henry died when when an aneurysm ruptured. In the spring of 1992, Frank Henry was posthumously inducted into the Army Aviation Hall of Fame. His widow, Emma Lee, lives in Austin, Texas.

HERREN, John, fifty-eight, commander of Bravo Company, 1st Battalion, 7th Cav, served a second tour in Vietnam as a staff officer at MACV/Saigon, was a battalion commander in Germany, and served in the office of the secretary of defense until his retirement in 1985 as a colonel. He is a civilian specialist on NATO affairs for the Defense Department; he and his wife, Sally, live in Bethesda, Maryland. They have a son and two daughters.

HOWARD, John, fifty-four, medical-services officer, 2nd Battalion, 7th Cav in the Ia Drang, retired a lieutenant colonel in 1983, after twenty-five years' service. He remained with the medical platoon in Vietnam until July 1966. When he retired, Howard moved to Carlisle, Pennsylvania, where he works as a consultant in emergency-management planning. His primary job is helping communities located near Army chemical-weapons depots write their emergency-response plans. He and his wife, Martha, have four children. His son is a staff sergeant in the 82nd Airborne Division and a veteran of both the Panama invasion and the Persian Gulf War.

JAKES, Jimmie Sr., forty-nine, a fire-team leader of Bravo Company, 1st Battalion, 7th Cav, was wounded in LZ X-Ray, but recovered and returned to complete his tour. He retired from the Army as a master sergeant and, in 1988, became the pastor of a church in Fort Mitchell, Alabama.

JEANETTE, Robert J., fifty, Ghost 4-6, weapons-platoon leader, Charlie Company, 2nd Battalion, 7th Cav in the Ia Drang, lives in Monsey, New York, a suburb of New York City. He is assistant principal of a public high school in the Bronx. Jeanette spent the better part of a year in a military hospital while his shattered leg was repaired. "I still have my leg, and I can walk on it. There's a lot of pain but at least I lived." Jeanette says: "When I was in the hospital in 1966, I was down in the doldrums, feeling sorry, and they tried to nudge me out of that. They had this 'Learning to be a Teacher' program; I tried it and loved it. I guess I was an oddball; everyone else that year was going into teaching to avoid the draft, and then there was me." Jeanette and his wife, Sandra, were married five days before he shipped out for Vietnam. They have a son, who is in college, and a daughter, still in high school.

JEKEL, Alex (Pop), seventy, Huey pilot in X-Ray and Albany, retired in the late 1960s as a chief warrant officer-4. Since then he has taught industrial arts, electronics, and mathematics, has flown for the U.S. Forest Service, and for a time was a crop duster pilot. He lives on a farm near Rainier, Washington, and has been writing down his memories of Vietnam duty for his children and grandchildren.

JEMISON, Robert Jr., sixty-one, platoon sergeant, Charlie Company, 1st Battalion, 7th Cavalry, retired as a sergeant first class in 1976, after twenty-four years' service. He spent thirty-two months in the hospital recovering from the wounds he suffered in LZ X-Ray. Jemison works part-time as a security guard in Columbus, Georgia, and he says: "Each night I go back to Vietnam to fight that same battle, over and over."

JOHNS, Barbara Geoghegan, fifty, widow of Lieutenant John Lance (Jack) Geoghegan of the 2nd Platoon, Charlie Company, 1st Battalion, 7th Cavalry, killed in action in X-Ray, married Lieutenant Colonel John Johns in 1969. Her daughter, Camille, was soon joined by a brother, Robert, and a sister, Barbara. Johns retired a brigadier general and is now dean of faculty at the Industrial

College of the Armed Forces in Washington, D.C. Mrs. Johns, whose two youngest children are in college, does volunteer work and writes for her own pleasure in her spare time. She and her husband live in Annandale, Virginia.

KEETON, James, fifty-nine, battalion aid station medic, 1st Battalion, 7th Cavalry, served a second tour in Vietnam with an adviser group. He retired a first sergeant in June 1973, with twenty years' service. He was chief of security at a hospital in Columbus, Georgia, until his death on April 18, 1992.

KELLING, George, fifty-four, who ran Charlie Med, the rear-area casualty receiving station during LZ X-Ray and LZ Albany, retired a lieutenant colonel in 1978. He earned a doctorate in history and now lives in San Antonio, where he works in the public-affairs office at Wilford Hall Air Force Medical Center.

KENNEDY, Glenn F., first sergeant, Charlie Company, 1st Battalion, 7th Cavalry, was killed in action on May 6, 1966, during Operation Davy Crockett in the Bong Son plain. A native of Mendenhall, Mississippi, Kennedy was thirty-one years old at the time of his death.

KINNARD, Harry W. O., seventy-seven, former commanding general of the 1st Cavalry Division, retired from the Army as a lieutenant general in 1969. After a second career as a consultant to defense industries on the West Coast, he retired again and lives in Arlington, Virginia, with his wife, Libby.

KLUGE, Fred J., fifty-nine, platoon sergeant, Alpha Company, 1st Battalion, 5th Cavalry in Albany, retired in 1973, as a first sergeant, after a total of twenty-two years' service. He moved back to his hometown of Tucson, Arizona. A high school dropout, he went back to college, earned a B.A., and was working on an M.A. "when I said to hell with it." He and his wife own and manage a trailer park, and Kluge's night job is corrections officer for the Arizona State Department of Corrections. They have two grown children.

KNOWLES, Richard, seventy-five, assistant division commander of the 1st Cavalry Division, served a second consecutive tour in Vietnam, commanded the 196th Light Infantry Brigade, and then was commanding general of Task Force Oregon (precursor to the Americal Division). Knowles retired from the Army in 1974 as a lieutenant general. He and his wife, Elizabeth, live in Roswell, New Mexico, where they run an antiques shop. Knowles has served in the New Mexico legislature since 1982.

KOMICH, Leland C., fifty-two, Huey pilot with Bravo Company 229th in X-Ray and Albany, retired a chief warrant officer 4 with more than twenty years' service. He and his wife live in Alexandria, Virginia.

KREISCHER, Bill, forty-eight, rifleman, Alpha Company, 1st Battalion, 7th Cavalry, recovered from his wounds and returned to duty with the battalion in Vietnam. He served seventeen months and rotated home in January of 1967. In June of that year he left the Army as a staff sergeant. Today, Kreischer runs his own private-investigation agency in New York, specializing in copyright and trademark infringement. He is a member of the board of trustees of the 1st Cavalry Division Association, president of the 7th Cavalry Association, and a founder of the Ia Drang Alumni—and he gives generously of both time and money to all three. Kreischer is working on a night-school law degree in his spare time; he lives in Hauppauge, New York.

LADNER, Theron, fifty, machine gunner with Alpha Company, 1st Battalion, 7th Cavalry in X-Ray, lives in Baton Rouge, Louisiana, where he owns a nightclub and a stable of Thoroughbred racehorses.

LARSEN, Stanley R. (Swede), seventy-seven, commanding general, II Field Force Vietnam, retired a lieutenant general in 1972 and for seven years was president of a large company in San Francisco. He and his wife, Nell, now are retired and living in Shoal Creek, Alabama.

LAVENDER, David A. (Purp), fifty, rifleman, Alpha Company, 1st Battalion, 5th Cavalry, was evacuated to Japan. He underwent four operations on his shattered hip and then was shipped home for discharge on December 21, 1965, ten days overdue on his two-year hitch and judged fifty percent disabled. He went home to Murphysboro, Illinois. Purp is married, the father of three daughters, and cuts hair at Gibb's Barber Shop, where he has worked for the last nineteen years. "Our town is only ten thousand people and we lost eleven young men from here killed in Vietnam," says Purp. "I attended every one of those funerals."

LEFEBVRE, L. R. (Ray), fifty-nine, commander of Delta Company, 1st Battalion, 7th Cavalry, spent eighteen months at Martin Army Hospital, Fort Benning, recovering from the wounds he suffered at X-Ray. He retired a lieutenant colonel in 1977 and returned to Georgia, where he is an executive for a trucking firm. Lefebvre earned graduate degrees in secondary school administration and public administration. He and his wife, Ann, live in Lilburn, Georgia, a suburb of Atlanta. They have four children and five grandchildren. His twelve-year-old granddaughter recently interviewed Ray about his experiences in Vietnam and wrote a school essay she titled: "My Grandfather: An American Hero."

LOMBARDO, Riccardo, sixty-one, Huey pilot in X-Ray and Albany and Pop Jekel's good buddy, was retired on one hundred percent disability after a serious back injury in 1967, when he was thirty-six. He lives in Columbus,

Georgia, and is a serious collector of firearms and active in a local shooting club.

LOSE, Charles R., the medic of the Lost Platoon, Bravo Company, 1st Battalion, 7th Cavalry, lives quietly in Biloxi, Mississippi, on a small veterans' disability pension. Doc Lose once told his old company commander, John Herren, "Nobody out here understands what we went through." After attending the 1992 reunion of the Band of Brothers and reading this book, he changed his mind. In a Christmas 1992 note to the authors, Doc wrote: "Thank you for giving me the tools to heal myself."

LUND, Bill, fifty, who was Myron Diduryk's artillery forward observer in LZ X-Ray and LZ Albany, left Vietnam in March 1966, upon completion of his two-year reserve officer obligation. He and his wife, Kathie, live on a seventy-acre ranch near Aspen, Colorado, where he owns and operates an outfitting company for fishing and boating trips.

MAPSON, Betty Jivens, forty-two, daughter of Sergeant Jerry Jivens, Charlie Company, 1st Battalion, 7th Cavalry, killed in action at X-Ray on November 15, 1965, is married, the mother of two, and works as a secretary at the Medical Center Hospital in Columbus, Georgia. Her mother, who never remarried, died in 1986. Of Mrs. Mapson's five brothers, three served in the Army, one made a career in the Air Force, and one is a lawyer. Mrs. Mapson is a member of the Columbus chapter of the 1st Cavalry Division Association.

MARM, Walter J. (Joe), fifty, platoon leader, Bravo Company, 1st Battalion, 7th Cavalry and the only man to receive the Medal of Honor, America's highest decoration for valor, in the Ia Drang campaign, is a colonel and still on active duty after twenty-eight years. He is senior Army adviser to the 79th Army Reserve Command in Willow Grove, Pennsylvania.

MARTIN, John C., fifty-one, rifleman in Lieutenant Sisson's platoon detached from Alpha Company, 2nd Battalion, 7th Cavalry for duty in X-Ray, served a second combat tour in Vietnam. He retired from the Army as a staff sergeant in 1976, and now serves in the Alabama National Guard. He and his wife live in Anniston, Alabama, where Martin is employed at the Army Depot.

MARTIN, Roger, fifty-two, rifleman, Bravo Company, 1st Battalion, 5th Cavalry, spent eleven months at Great Lakes Naval Hospital recovering from a hip wound suffered at LZ Albany. He was discharged in October 1966, and went home to Kenosha, Wisconsin. He works for a firm that restores classic automobiles. Martin and his wife, Carole, have six children, four of them adopted. One of their daughters is Vietnamese.

MARUHNICH, John, sixty-two, mortar sergeant, Alpha Company, 1st Battalion, 7th Cavalry in LZ X-Ray, retired a sergeant first class in 1974 with twenty-four years' service. He lives in Falls, Pennsylvania.

McDADE, Robert, seventy, who commanded the 2nd Battalion, 7th Cavalry in the Ia Drang, retired a colonel in 1975. He and his wife live in Sag Harbor, New York, where they operate a summer season shop that deals in contemporary original art.

McDONALD, George J., fifty-two, mortarman, 1st Battalion, 7th Cavalry, left the Army in 1966 and went home to Pass Christian, Mississippi, where he is a commercial fisherman.

MERCHANT, Dick, fifty-four, assistant operations officer, 1st Battalion, 7th Cavalry, served a second tour in Vietnam in 1968 as Lieutenant Colonel Matt Dillon's battalion executive officer. Merchant retired a lieutenant colonel in 1982. He lives in Olympia, Washington, and works for the state government.

MEYER, Edward C. (Shy), sixty-three, 3rd Brigade executive officer in the Ia Drang, retired as Army Chief of Staff, a four-star general, in 1983 after thirty-two years' service. Since retiring he serves on the boards of half a dozen major corporations and also works as a consultant to defense industries. He is president of the Army Relief Fund and a trustee of the Association of Graduates of the U.S. Military Academy. Meyer and his wife, Carol, live in Arlington, Virginia.

MICELI, Carmen, forty-eight, rifleman, Alpha Company, 1st Battalion, 7th Cavalry at LZ X-Ray, completed a full tour in Vietnam and left the Army in September 1966. He is married and the father of two daughters. For the last twenty-two years he has worked for the North Bergen, N.J., fire department. He is a captain and the commander of Engine Company Number One.

MILLS, Jon, fifty-four, Bruce Crandall's copilot in the Ia Drang, retired a lieutenant colonel in 1980. He is an executive with a major defense-contracting firm and lives in Centreville, Virginia.

MOORE, H. G. (Hal), now seventy, commanded the 1st Battalion, 7th Cavalry in the Ia Drang and served six more months in Vietnam, commanding the 3rd Brigade. On January 31, 1966, *The New York Times* profiled Moore as "The Man Who Can Find the Viet Cong." He pressed for another assignment to troop command in Vietnam, only to be told that he had already had his turn. Moore commanded the 7th Infantry Division in Korea, was commanding general at Fort Ord, California, and then was the Army's deputy Chief of Staff for personnel. Moore, who says he graduated from West Point "by the skin of my teeth," was the first Army officer of his class (1945) to achieve one-, two-, and three-star rank. He retired in August 1977, with thirty-two years' service. For the next four years he was executive vice president of the company that developed the Crested Butte, Colorado, ski area. He then formed a computer-software company. He and his wife, Julie, divide their time between homes in Auburn, Alabama, and Crested Butte, Colorado. They have five grown children: sons Steve, Dave, and Greg; and daughters Cecile and Julie. Moore lectures at military academies and at several colleges and universities. In his spare time he camps, climbs, skis, and fishes for trout in the Rockies.

MORENO, Francisco (Frank), copilot in Ed "Too Tall" Freeman's Huey in X-Ray, was commissioned a second lieutenant in Vietnam and retired as a major after twenty years of service. He and his wife live in Phoenix, Arizona.

NADAL, Ramon A. (Tony), fifty-six, commander of Alpha Company, 1st Battalion, 7th Cavalry, later earned a master's degree in psychology and taught at West Point and at the Army War College. He retired a colonel in 1981, and is vice president of human resources for a large corporation in Carlisle, Pennsylvania. He and his wife, Billie, have a son in college and a daughter still at home.

NYE, George (China Joe), demolition-team leader, 8th Engineers, attached to the 1st Battalion, 7th Cavalry in Landing Zone X-Ray, died of an apparent heart attack at age fifty-one on December 8, 1991, at his home in Bangor, Maine. After the Ia Drang, Nye finished his tour with the 8th Engineers and the 1st Cav and volunteered for three more tours in combat with the 5th Special Forces Group. He was evacuated, badly wounded, on January 5, 1970, after serving four years, eight months, and ten days in Vietnam. He spent eighteen months in Army hospitals, and was retired, disabled, in June 1975. On his chest he wore the Silver Star, the Bronze Star, and five Purple Hearts. George found solace in hiking the Maine woods, shooting nothing more deadly than a 35mm camera. In March 1991 he found a new purpose in life: meeting the chartered airliners touching down at Bangor International Airport, the first American landfall, bringing American soldiers home from the Persian Gulf. George Nye was a sparkplug of Operation Welcome Home, which brought veterans' groups, brass bands, and Bangor townsfolk to the airport by the hundreds to hug and shake hands with the Desert Storm veterans. Most of the planes touched down between midnight and six A.M., but George Nye was always there, rain or shine. He personally shook the hands of at least fifty thousand returning soldiers. One of those soldiers was Army Captain David Moore, 82nd Airborne Division, son of his old battlefield commander in X-Ray, and that homecoming gave George the greatest pleasure of all. He wanted the Gulf veterans to have the welcome-home that none of the Vietnam veterans got. The day before he died, George picked up a Christmas tree, which he planned to decorate with yellow ribbons and small American flags for the airport terminal; soldiers from the Gulf were still arriving and he didn't want them to think they had been forgotten. His friends completed the tree for him and dedicated it to Sergeant China Joe Nye. God rest you, George.

OUELLETTE, Robert, fifty, battalion commander's radio operator in LZ X-Ray, left the Army in August 1966. He now lives in Dublin, New Hampshire, and works for a firm that sells office supplies.

PAOLONE, Ernest E., Bob Edwards's radio operator, Charlie Company, 1st Battalion, 7th Cavalry, died of a massive heart attack on March 30, 1992, at the age of fifty. Ernie had gone back to his native Chicago and drove a truck for the city. He was the father of four children, aged twelve through twenty. At a surprise fiftieth-birthday party for Ernie, he was presented a plaque engraved with sergeant's stripes and inscribed with a message from Colonel (ret.) Bob Edwards saying that these were the stripes Paolone earned at LZ X-Ray but never got.

PARISH, Willard, fifty-one, mortarman in Charlie Company, 1st Battalion, 7th Cavalry, who won the Silver Star for his work as a machine gunner in LZ X-Ray, was among the draftees who rotated home in December 1965 for discharge. For a number of years he was a country-and-western band leader and disc jockey. Parish now runs the Bristow, Oklahoma, toll gate on the Turner Turnpike. He married in 1981 and is the father of four daughters: an eight-year-old, a five-year-old, and infant twins.

PARKER, Neal G., a Naval Academy graduate who transferred to the U.S. Army and was a Huey pilot in Bravo Company 229th in the Ia Drang, retired a colonel after thirty years' service. He now lives in Mobile, Alabama.

PAYNE, D. P. (Pat), fifty, recon-platoon leader, Delta Company, 2nd Battalion, 7th Cavalry in the Ia Drang, served two tours in Vietnam and left the Army as a captain in June 1969. He joined IBM as a salesman in Austin, Texas, and spent twenty years with them, rising to the post of Midwestern regional manager. Today he is president of a major chemical-waste management corporation in Oak Brook, Illinois. Payne and his wife, Patty, live in Hinsdale, Illinois, and have three children.

PLUMLEY, Basil, seventy-two, the 1st Battalion, 7th Cavalry's sergeant major, retired from the Army as a command sergeant major on December 31, 1974, after thirty-two years, six months, and four days on active duty, and a second tour in Vietnam with the U.S. Advisory Group, Pleiku. His awards include the Combat Infantryman's Badge with two stars; two Silver Stars; two Bronze Stars; four Purple Hearts; a Master Parachutist Badge with five combat-jump stars; a European Theater Service ribbon with eight campaign stars and four invasion arrows; a Korean Service ribbon with three campaign stars and one invasion arrow; a Vietnam Service ribbon with one silver and three bronze campaign stars; and the Presidential Unit Citation badge. He worked an additional fifteen years as a civilian employee at Martin Army Hospital at Fort Benning, Georgia, and retired again in 1990. He and his wife, Deurice, live in Columbus, Georgia, where he is president of the 1st Cavalry Division Association local chapter and an occasional quail hunter. Basil Plumley is a grandfather now, kind and soft-spoken, but do not be deceived: He is the lion in winter.

POLEY, Clinton, forty-eight, assistant machine gunner, 2nd Platoon, Charlie Company, 1st Battalion, 7th Cavalry in the Ia Drang, was discharged from Fitzsimmons Army Hospital in Denver, Colorado, early in 1966, and went home to Iowa and the family farm. He was judged seventy percent disabled due to wounds suffered in LZ X-Ray. Poley, a bachelor, lives alone on his farm outside Ackley, Iowa, and in a 1990 letter explained himself far better than we could: "Some might ask why haven't I forgotten about Vietnam after all these years. Every night I rub a towel over all my scars and see them in the mirror. I think of all those guys killed in action, wounded in action, and their friends, their relatives and all those altered lives. How could I forget? It's not so much what we went through as it is knowing what the other guys went through. They died dirty. They died hot, hungry and exhausted. They died thinking that their loved ones would never know how they died. I'm so proud to have been there and so proud of the guys who were there with me. I fought for this country and now I own and farm 120 acres of my country. To me that seems proper, and just, and so right."

PUJALS, Enrique, fifty, platoon leader, Alpha Company, 2nd Battalion, 7th Cavalry in the Ia Drang, woke up on an X-ray table first, then on a C-141 ambulance plane, and finally in Ward One at Walter Reed Army Hospital in Washington, D.C. He spent seven months there while his shattered thigh and legs were repaired. He returned to active duty in July 1966, and served a second tour in Vietnam as an adviser in Long Binh district. He left the Army in 1971 with the rank of captain, returned home to Puerto Rico, and earned a law degree. His injured right hip deteriorated, and on the Thursday before Thanksgiving, 1986, he found himself back on an operating table—the same place he had been on the Thursday before Thanksgiving, 1965. Pujals recently closed his law practice. "More than anything else in the world I would like to be back in the Green Machine," he says. "Since I can't have that, I would like a job working as closely with the Army as possible." He is married and the father of four children.

RACKSTRAW, Jim, forty-nine, recon-platoon leader, 1st Battalion, 7th Cavalry at X-Ray, served a second tour in Vietnam as a rifle-company commander in the 25th Infantry Division. In 1974 he transferred from the infantry to the military police. He is a colonel and the provost marshal of the U.S. Army Forces Command (Forscom) in Atlanta, Georgia.

RESCORLA, Cyril R. (Rick), fifty-three, platoon leader, Bravo Company, 2nd Battalion, 7th Cavalry in the Ia Drang, completed a full tour with Bravo Company in Vietnam and did another year teaching at Officer Candidate School in the States. He left active duty in 1967, but continued in the Army Reserves until his retirement in 1990 as a colonel. The British-born Rescorla earned a master's degree and a law degree at universities in Oklahoma and went into corporate-security work. Today he is vice president for group security at a major stock-brokerage house in New York City. He and his wife have two teenage children. Rescorla kept the battered French Army bugle he captured on the field at Albany; in 1991 he turned it over to the Ia Drang Alumni for use in memorial ceremonies.

RIDDLE, Bill, fifty-two, artillery forward observer with Bravo Company, 1st Battalion, 7th Cavalry, completed his Army service in the summer of 1966. He went home to Salinas, California, where he lives with his wife and three sons. For the last twenty-one years he has been in the tire business.

ROBINSON, Edward Charles, fifty-five, Huey pilot at LZ X-Ray, served a second combat tour in Vietnam. He retired a colonel in 1983. He holds two master's degrees, is employed in the defense industry, and lives in Alexandria, Virginia.

ROLAND, William, forty-nine, rifle-squad leader, Bravo Company, 1st Battalion, 7th Cavalry at X-Ray, returned to Vietnam for a second combat tour. He retired a command sergeant major and lives in Columbus, Georgia.

ROZANSKI, Gordon P. (Rosie), fifty-four, 1st Battalion, 7th Cavalry S-4 in the Ia Drang, was wounded in both arms, both legs, and the stomach in the Bong Son campaign in early 1966. He returned to serve two more tours in Vietnam— one with the Special Forces, one with an intelligence agency. Rozanski returned to the Ia Drang five times on various intelligence missions and described the place as "a cemetery." He was retired, disabled, as a major in the mid-1970s.

He lives in Golden, Colorado, where he owns a firm that deals worldwide in antiques.

RUDEL, Karen Metsker, twenty-eight, daughter of Captain Thomas Metsker, intelligence officer, 1st Battalion, 7th Cavalry in Landing Zone X-Ray, killed in action November 14, 1965, lives in the Boston suburbs with her husband, Scott. They have three children, daughters Abigail and Alison and a son, Thomas Alexander. Karen works part-time as a free-lance designer and helps with her husband's construction and contracting business.

SAVAGE, Ernie, forty-eight, the fourth man to inherit command of Lieutenant Henry Herrick's 2nd Platoon, the Lost Platoon of Bravo Company, 1st Battalion, 7th Cavalry at LZ X-Ray, retired a sergeant first class in 1982 after twenty years' active duty. He works at Fort Benning, Georgia, evaluating Army Reserve training.

SCOTT, James A., sixty-nine, the 2nd Battalion, 7th Cavalry's sergeant major, served a second Vietnam tour in 1970–71 as command sergeant major, USARV. Scott retired as a command sergeant major on May 1, 1973, after thirty years, ten months, and twenty days of service, wearing the Combat Infantryman's Badge with one star; six Bronze Stars; three Purple Hearts; a European Campaign ribbon with four battle stars and one invasion arrow; a Korean Service ribbon with two battle stars; a Vietnam Service ribbon with four battle stars; and the Presidential Unit Citation badge. He and his wife, Kornelia, live in Columbus, Georgia, where for several years Scott taught military subjects to Junior ROTC in the high schools. Scott and Basil Plumley meet most Fridays over breakfast at a local café for spirited discussions of the relative merits of their service, their two 7th Cavalry battalions, and other weighty issues. Scott says: "On the boat going to Vietnam I bet Plumley a case of beer I would be wounded first, and that I would be home for Christmas. He accepted, I won, but he only recently began paying off—one bottle at a time." Plumley says, "Scott is so tight with a dollar you'd think he came out of West Point."

SELLECK, Pat, fifty-one, radio operator, recon platoon, 1st Battalion, 7th Cavalry at X-Ray, was discharged from the Army on November 29, 1965, and returned to his old job at the telephone company. He retired in August 1990, and now lives in Peekskill, New York.

SETELIN, John, forty-eight, squad leader, Bravo Company, 2nd Battalion, 7th Cavalry, left Vietnam with three Purple Hearts and left the Army a sergeant. He is a master gunsmith and runs his own business repairing and selling weapons. He and his wife, Theresa, and their six-year-old daughter, Megan, live in Glen Allen, Virginia. Setelin is president of the Major General George W. Casey chapter of the 1st Cavalry Division Association and a member of the national association's board of trustees; he also helps Bill Kreischer run the Ia Drang Alumni organization.

SHADDEN, James Haskell, fifty, mortarman, Delta Company, 2nd Battalion, 7th Cavalry, survived half a dozen operations and one year in Army hospitals recovering from the wounds received at LZ Albany. In the last operation, his shattered left knee joint was removed and the leg bones fused, leaving his left leg frozen straight and two inches shorter than his right leg. A miserly, ungrateful Veterans Administration ruled that Shadden was only thirty percent disabled. He studied to be a tool-and-die machinist and worked at that job for several years until the strain of long hours standing on his bad leg severely affected his hip and back. He is married and has four children. Shadden lives on a seven-acre farm outside Tellico Plains, Tennessee, and works part-time at odd jobs.

SHUCART, William, M.D., surgeon, 2nd Battalion, 7th Cavalry in the Ia Drang, had nearly completed his tour in Vietnam in the summer of 1966, when he suffered a broken back in the crash of a Chinook helicopter. He was evacuated, via Clark Field, to Fitzsimmons Army Hospital in Denver. Shucart says, "It was interesting; they just figured I was another grunt and I didn't tell them different. They didn't discover I was a doctor until the day I was discharged—when I had a long talk with them about treating their patients like pieces of meat." He was discharged in November 1966, and wound up in Boston in 1981. Today, Doc Shucart of Landing Zone Albany is the chief of neurosurgery at Tufts University Medical School.

SMITH, Jack P., forty-seven, returned to Charlie Company, 2nd Battalion, 7th Cavalry after his wounds healed, and completed his tour. He was discharged a sergeant, completed his college education, and is now an on-air national news correspondent for ABC Television's *Weekend News*. He lives in Washington, D.C.

SPIRES, James W., operations officer, 2nd Battalion, 7th Cavalry in the Ia Drang, retired a lieutenant colonel in 1976 and owns and operates his own industrial representational firm. He and his wife live in Lake Forest, Illinois. They have two grown children and one still at home.

STALEY, Les, sixty-seven, staff sergeant, Alpha Company, 1st Battalion, 7th Cavalry, in LZ X-Ray, retired on April 1, 1967, with twenty years' service.

Married and the father of three sons, Staley now lives in Waldoboro, Maine, where he and family members run a gun shop.

STINNETT, Robert L., fifty-eight, Bravo Company, 229th Assault Helicopter Battalion in LZ X-Ray and LZ Albany, returned to Vietnam for a second combat tour. He single-handedly raised five young children and earned a doctorate, retiring a lieutenant colonel after twenty years' service. He is president of his own management-consulting firm and lives in Oklahoma City.

STOCKTON, John B., seventy, commander, 1st Squadron, 9th Cavalry in the Ia Drang, retired a colonel in 1967. His last known address was Miami, Florida.

SUGDINIS, Joel E., fifty-five, who had already served one tour in Vietnam as an adviser, completed his second tour with Alpha Company, 2nd Battalion, 7th Cavalry. He retired a major in 1980, after twenty years' service. He lives in Pleasant Valley, Connecticut, and works in real estate sales and development.

TADEMY, Dudley, 3rd Brigade fire-support coordinator in the Ia Drang, served a second tour in Vietnam with the 1st Cavalry and retired a colonel in January 1987, after thirty years' service. He works for a consulting firm in McLean, Virginia.

TANNER, Ray, forty-nine, radio operator, Alpha Company, 1st Battalion, 7th Cavalry, returned home to South Carolina in April 1966 and went to work for a utility company in Charleston.

THORPE, Henry, fifty-eight, commander, Delta Company, 2nd Battalion, 7th Cavalry in the Ia Drang, left the Army as a captain in September 1967, after eight years' service, and went home to his native North Carolina. After LZ Albany, Thorpe requested a transfer from his company command to the division public-information office and finished his tour as an escort officer for visiting press and VIPs. Today he is an orchestra leader and serves in the state militia.

TIFFT, Richard P., Pathfinder team leader in LZ X-Ray, later served as commander of the Golden Knights, the Army's parachute team. He retired as a lieutenant colonel in 1985; on November 26, 1987, he was killed in the crash of a private plane in Bakersfield, California. He was forty-five.

TOWLES, Robert, forty-seven, rifleman, Delta Company, 2nd Battalion, 7th Cavalry, spent five months in Valley Forge General Hospital in Pennsylvania, recovering from twenty-eight shrapnel wounds he received at LZ Albany. He left the Army in October 1966, and went home to his native Ohio, where he works as a carpenter. Towles received a master's degree in history from Kent State in 1989, and is currently working on his doctorate. His dissertation is on the LZ Albany battle. He is married and has two children.

TULLY, Robert (Bob), sixty-eight, commander, 2nd Battalion, 5th Cavalry in the Ia Drang, served a second tour in Vietnam in 1968 as a brigade commander in the Americal Division. Tully retired a colonel in 1976. He and his wife, Pat, live in Avon Park, Florida.

TULLY, Walter Busill (Buse) Jr., commander, Bravo Company, 1st Battalion, 5th Cavalry in the Ia Drang, returned to Vietnam on a second tour as a major in the Americal Division. On March 2, 1969, thirty-two-year-old Buse Tully was killed in action.

VIERA, Arthur Jr., forty-eight, an M-79 grenadier with Charlie Company, 1st Battalion, 7th Cavalry, survived the terrible wounds he suffered in X-Ray, and now lives in Slatersville, Rhode Island, where he is in the photo business.

WALLACE, Bruce M. Jr., sixty-one, Air Force A-1E Skyraider pilot over the Ia Drang, served two more tours in Vietnam and retired a colonel in 1976. He is now an attorney in San Diego, California.

WALLENIUS, Jon, forty-nine, mortar observer, Bravo Company, 2nd Battalion, 7th Cavalry in LZ X-Ray and LZ Albany, got out of the Army in August 1966. He teaches art at Venice High School, Los Angeles, California. He and his wife, Nancy, live in Lawndale, California. In his spare time Wallenius draws, paints, and does etchings and prints, sometimes of Vietnam War scenes. He is the perennial master of ceremonies at the Ia Drang dinners; he claims he is the only one of the brothers who can get through an entire sentence without using the f-word.

WASHBURN, Richard B., fifty-seven, platoon leader, 2/20th Aerial Rocket Artillery in the Ia Drang, returned to Vietnam for a second combat tour. He retired a lieutenant colonel in 1977, and lives with his wife in Arlington, Texas.

WHITESIDE, Jerry E., fifty-five, fire-support coordinator in LZ X-Ray, served a second tour in Vietnam as an adviser. He retired a colonel in 1982, with twenty-three years' service. He earned a doctorate in education and is personnel director for the Cooperative Extension Service at the University of Georgia in Athens.

WINKEL, Paul Patton Jr., sixty, Orange 1 flight leader, Bravo Company, 229th Helicopter Assault Battalion in the Ia Drang, served a second combat tour in

Vietnam. Returning home, he single-handedly raised his two young children while earning two master's degrees. Winkel retired a colonel in 1986, with over thirty-one years of Army service. He is a consultant to industries seeking defense business. He plays volleyball two nights a week to keep trim and has devoted much of his spare time over the past two years to a detailed study of the part played in the Ia Drang battles by his fellow aviators of the 229th Assault Helicopter Battalion, our beloved Huey "slick" drivers. His personalized license plate proclaims: LZ X-Ray. Winkel and his wife live in Springfield, Virginia.

WINTER, Pete, fifty-one, rifleman, Alpha Company, 1st Battalion, 7th Cavalry, was discharged in December 1965. Married and the father of three children, Winter works for the Long Island Railroad and lives in Howard Beach, Queens, New York.

YOUNG, James, fifty-one, rifleman, Alpha Company, 1st Battalion, 5th Cavalry in LZ Albany, made it home to the family farm outside Keysville, Missouri, on Christmas Eve, 1965, with an Army discharge in his pocket and a quarter-size hole in the side of his skull. He checked in with the nearest Veterans Administration hospital; they sent him home, telling him they would call him back for an operation to place a plate over the hole. They never did. Young went to work for the railroad in Steelville, Missouri. "I'm not supposed to chop wood or do anything that might cause a lick on that side of my head, but it healed up pretty well so I don't worry much about it," he says. Five years ago he attended a reunion of Alpha Company veterans of LZ Albany. "That headquarters type turned up and he returned my old helmet, bullet hole and all. I have it here with me today." He lives with his wife and family in Steelville.

ACKNOWLEDGMENTS

The authors owe so large a debt to so many friends who have provided so much help during the last ten years of research that there can be no easy beginning or ending to this list of thank-you's.

First and foremost, to our wives, Julie Moore and Theresa Galloway, whose patience and endurance were tested to the extreme by our obsession with and pursuit of a long-ago and faraway story that kept circling back to interfere with all the things they had planned. They answered a thousand ringing telephones and played hostess to a hundred surprise guests. They typed and took notes and delivered messages and kept things running while we traveled to Vietnam and crisscrossed America and camped out in each other's homes. Julie and Theresa, this one's for you.

Our children came in for their share of alternately being neglected and dragooned into service, and put up with it all more or less cheerfully. So our gratitude to Steve Moore, Greg Moore, David Moore, Cecile Moore Jacobs, and Julie Moore Thompson; and to Lee Galloway and Joshua Galloway.

This project could never have been undertaken, or completed, without the encouragement, support, cooperation, and love of our comrades in arms who stood beside us in the Ia Drang Valley and stand with us today. Our questionnaires, telephone calls, interviews, and meetings took many of them back to a time and place they had tried hard to forget. They shared everything they had: their memories; their boxes of old treasures; the half-remembered hometowns of friends they hadn't seen in twenty-five years. Every man we found helped us find one or two other veterans of the valley. They read our notes and transcripts, and then our draft chapters, and lost almost as much sleep over them as we did. And in the end they *thanked us* for having helped restore a sense of pride and accomplishment in what they had endured. No one has ever had better or more constant friends. The glory of this book is theirs; the mistakes and omissions are ours.

To the strong and remarkable people who loved some of the men who died in the Ia Drang—Barbara Geoghegan Johns, Catherine Metsker McCray, Karen Metsker Rudel, Betty Jivens Mapson and Edward D. Monsewicz—the authors are forever indebted. Theirs is a dimension always present but too seldom explored in the telling of the history of a battle, a campaign, or a war. Each readily agreed to write his or her story of a life and a death, in the belief that these words would comfort others who have endured the same pain, if only by assuring them that they are not alone. To the list of medals for valor, bravery, and sacrifice that are awarded to soldiers on America's battlefields, the authors propose adding one for courage, to be bestowed on those citizens who have lost a son, a husband, a father, a brother—or, in these days, a daughter, a sister, a wife, a mother—in the service of a nation that too easily forgets the true cost of war.

We are most grateful to Brigadier General Douglas Kinnard (U.S. Army, ret.), former Army chief of military history. In May 1984, General Kinnard provided us with complete access to the Army historians and their files on the Vietnam War. That access, and the enthusiastic assistance of Lieutenant Colonel Alexander S. Cochran, Jr., put our hands on a treasure trove of documents, letters, photographs, military reports, and interview records on the Ia Drang battles that were amassed in the late 1960s by then–Major John Cash for his section of the book *Seven Firefights in Vietnam.* Colonel Cash, an Ia Drang veteran who remained on active duty until 1992, did everything in his power to assist in this project.

We have been equally blessed in our other associations. The editors at *U.S. News & World Report*—Michael Ruby, Merrill McLoughlin, and John Walcott—gambled on a long shot when they first sent us back to Vietnam to pursue an old story. Then they had the courage to put that story of a forgotten twenty-five-year-old battle on the cover of a weekly newsmagazine. They and every staff member at *U.S. News* involved in putting together that October 29, 1990, Ia Drang cover came to share our obsession. Harold Evans, president and publisher of Random House, read the story and *knew* there was a book hidden in it. Harry gave us the gift of Robert Loomis as the editor of this book. At the right times, Bob was patient, encouraging, helpful, and demanding—and at all times a true gentleman. Our agent, Robert Barnett of the law firm of Williams & Connolly in Washington, D.C., is of the same school. Graphic artist Matt Zang created the area maps and battle maps that contribute so much to understanding two difficult battles. A special thanks to our copy editor, Jolanta Benal, and production editor, Carsten Fries, who helped us make this a better book.

A monumental research chore was made easier by the willing assistance of David C. Humphrey and Regina Greenwell, archivists at the Lyndon Baines Johnson Library; Lieutenant Colonel J. D. Coleman (U.S. Army, ret.), historian and author; Colonel Clinton L. Williams, another Ia Drang scholar; Lieutenant Colonel Robert Cook (ret.) late of the Army Staff; Colonel Paul Patton Winkel (U.S. Army, ret.) of Springfield, Virginia; U.S. Air Force Lieutenant Colonel Mike Worden, fighter pilot, scholar, and historian, who delved into Air Force archives on our behalf and took time away from his own doctoral research to read our manuscript; Michael (M-60) Kelley, Vietnam War artist, historian, and veterans' networker; Lieutenant Colonel Richard S. Johnson (U.S. Army, ret.), author of *How to Find Anyone Who Is or Has Been in the Military;* David W. Schill, who is building the definitive computer data base on Vietnam War casualties; and Douglas Pike, curator of the Indochina Archives at the University of California–Berkeley.

Others who lent invaluable assistance and encouragement include Robert S. McNamara; General William C. Westmoreland (ret.);

General H. Norman Schwarzkopf (ret.); Lieutenant General Harry W. O. Kinnard (ret.); Lieutenant General Stanley R. Larsen (ret.); Will Bundy; and General Gordon R. Sullivan, Army Chief of Staff;

On two research trips to Hanoi we were taken in hand by photographer Tim Page, an old friend, an old Indochina hand, and a Zen master at the art of not only surviving but enjoying modern-day Vietnam. Our gracious official host in Vietnam was Nguyen Cong Quang, director of the Foreign Press Service in Hanoi, who worked hard to break down the walls for us. Mr. Quang believed that old enemies could become friends, and he was right. He also provided us the best and brightest of guide-interpreters: Duong Quang Thang and Tran Le Tien. They arranged our interviews with Senior General Vo Nguyen Giap, Senior General Chu Huy Man, Lieutenant General Nguyen Huu An, and Major General Hoang Phuong. Special thanks go to General Phuong, chief of the Hanoi Institute of Military History, who is so dedicated a professional historian that he left a hospital bed for our first meeting. Our base of operations for the Vietnam trips was Bangkok, and we would be remiss if we did not thank Nguyen Quang Dy, first secretary of the Embassy of Vietnam, for his help with visas and travel arrangements; Raymond Eaton, chairman of the Export Development Trading Corporation, for sharing his considerable knowledge of wind directions in Vietnam; Alan Dawson, another expert on the political meteorology of Indochina; and Jack Corman, genial host and message center for exhausted passersby.

We could not have done it without all of them, and to all of them we are deeply grateful.

HAL MOORE
JOE GALLOWAY
February 4, 1992

INTERVIEWS AND
STATEMENTS

The first draft of all history is written in the memories of the participants in and witnesses to any event. We have sought, through the
interviews for this book, to tap that resource on the Ia Drang battles
before it is forever lost. Joe Galloway began the process on the
battlefield itself, for the stories he wrote then. And although I was
not aware of it at the time, my work on this book began only a few
days later, when I sat down to write my after-action report.

The authors remained in close personal touch during the years
after 1965; in March of 1983, we began our research. That month,
our written questions were mailed to a scattering of Ia Drang veterans, and the first replies came back. In May 1983 I conducted my
first taped interviews, with Bob Edwards and Ray Lefebvre.

We agreed from the beginning that we would make every effort
to return to Vietnam to revisit the battlefield and interview the
North Vietnamese commanders who had fought against us. That
goal was realized, in part, during two trips to Hanoi—in August–
September of 1990, and again in October–November of 1991. We
were granted interviews with Senior General Vo Nguyen Giap and
Major General Hoang Phuong, chief of the Institute of Military
History, on the first trip; and with Senior General Chu Huy Man

and Lieutenant General Nguyen Huu An and again with General Phuong on the 1991 visit.

We talked for more than two hours with General Giap; for four hours each with General Man and General An; for six hours with General Phuong. All were tape-recorded. The discussions in every case were cordial and professional, and General Phuong was remarkably generous in sharing with us his 1965 Ia Drang diaries and sketch maps.

The men who fought in X-Ray and Albany have told their stories in hundreds of statements, written and taped, and in hundreds of hours of personal and telephone interviews. Many of those who were interviewed or provided written accounts are not mentioned by name in the text because the events described are the summation and essence of the research to which they contributed time and substance. We are no less grateful to them for their invaluable help. The names of all who contributed to this research are listed below.

American Military and Ex-Military

Dick Ackerman, Russell Adams, Warren E. Adams, Hank Ainsworth, J. L. (Bud) Alley, Jr., Roger K. Bean, Bill Beck, Larry Bennett, William Bercaw, Charlie Black, Clarence W. Blount, Toby Braveboy, David Bray, Ervin L. Brown, Thomas W. Brown, Galen Bungum, Vincent Cantu, Robert S. Carrara, John A. Cash, James P. Castleberry, John F. Clark, J. D. Coleman, Kenneth A. Cone, Bruce Crandall, Ronald W. Crooks, Dennis Deal, Myron F. Diduryk, Gregory P. Dillon, Kenneth Duncan, John H. Dutram, Robert E. Edwards, Jim Epperson, John A. Fesmire, George Forrest, Ed Freeman, Larry M. Gilreath, James T. Godfrey, Ewing P. Goff, Melvin Gregory, S. Lawrence Gwin, James F. Hackett, Bobby J. Hadaway, James Hall, Harold Hamilton, Ernest B. Hamm, Steven Hansen, Dallas Harper, Charlie W. Hastings, Robert Hazen, John A. Hemphill, John D. Herren, Sam Hollman, Jr., John Howard, Hans Hundsberger, Otis Hull, Joseph H. Ibach, Jimmie Jakes, Robert J. Jeanette, Alex S. Jekel, Robert Jemison, George W. Jennings, Thomas L. Keeton, George H. Kelling, Glenn F. Kennedy, Douglas Kinnard, Harry W. O. Kinnard, Fred J. Kluge, Richard T. Knowles, Ted C. Kolbusz, Leland Komich, William A. Kreischer, Stanley R. Larsen, David A. Lavender, L. R. (Ray) Lefebvre, Andrew Le Valli, James L. Litton, Riccardo Lombardo, Nick Lorris, Charles R. Lose, William Lund, Henri Mallet, Walter J. Marm, John C. Martin, George McCulley, Robert A. McDade, George J. McDonald, Jr., Robert

McMahon, Richard Merchant, E. C. Meyer, Carmen Miceli, Troy Miller, Jon Mills, Frank Moreno, Ramon A. (Tony) Nadal, Lorenzo Nathan, Jr., Arthur J. Newton, Walter A. Niemeyer, George J. Nye, Larry Owen, Ernest E. Paolone, William F. Parish, D. P. (Pat) Payne, Basil L. Plumley, Clinton S. Poley, John S. Pritchard, Enrique V. Pujals, Robert L. Read, Cyril R. (Rick) Rescorla, Dan Robinson, Edward C. Robinson, George Rogers, William N. Roland, Stanley Rothstein, Gordon P. Rozanski, C. Ernie Savage, H. Norman Schwarzkopf, James Scott, Pat Selleck, John R. Setelin, James H. Shadden, William Shucart, Benjamin E. Silver, Jack P. Smith, Ron Sleeis, Donald J. Slovak, James W. Spires, Robert Stinnett, John Stoner, Joel E. Sugdinis, Dudley Tademy, Ray E. Tanner, Henry Thorpe, Robert L. Towles, Robert B. Tully, Walter B. (Buse) Tully, Arthur Viera, Jr., Bruce M. Wallace, Jon Wallenius, Richard B. Washburn, William C. Westmoreland, Paul Patton Winkel, Jr., Peter J. Winter, Herman L. Wirth, James Young, Jerald D. Zallen, Jack Zent

Family Members

Mrs. Sara Elliott, Mrs. Barbara Geoghegan Johns, Mrs. Betty Jivens Mapson, Mrs. Catherine Metsker McCray, Edward Dennis Monsewicz, Mrs. Karen Metsker Rudel, Mrs. Delores Diduryk, Mrs. Frank Henry, Miss Camille Geoghegan

Former Government Officials

Robert S. McNamara, Will Bundy, Harry McPherson, Walt Whitman Rostow, Leonard Unger, Barry Zorthian

Other Americans

Wayne F. Hyde, Julia C. Moore, Kornelia Scott, Malcolm McConnell, Neil Sheehan, Peter Arnett, Robert Poos

Vietnamese Military

Senior General Vo Nguyen Giap, Senior General Chu Huy Man, Lieutenant General Nguyen Huu An, Major General Hoang Phuong

CHAPTER NOTES

Sources cited here are listed in order of appearance of an individual quoted, or the authors' statement of a fact, in a given chapter; each note is numbered for ease of subsequent reference.

Prologue

1. Army pay information: was taken from *U.S. Army Register* (U.S. Government Printing Office), January 1, 1965, vol. 1, pp. 785–86.

2. Information on the numbers of Americans killed in the Pleiku campaign was compiled from the March 4, 1966, after-action report of the 1st Cavalry Division, covering operations from October 23 to November 26, 1965, and the subsequent change of status from "missing in action" to "killed in action" of four men of the 2nd Battalion, 7th Cav and one man of Alpha Company, 1st Battalion, 5th Cav. In addition to the 1st Cavalry Division personnel, one U.S. Air Force A-1E Skyraider pilot was killed in action in the campaign.

3. *Regimental Strengths and Losses at Gettysburg,* by Busey and Martin, was used for the Gettysburg comparison. *Triumph Without Victory: The Unreported History of the Persian Gulf War,* by the staff of *U.S. News & World Report,* was used for the Persian Gulf War comparison.

1. Heat of Battle

1. All quotations and information from Robert H. Edwards in this and all subsequent chapters are from one or more of the following sources: unpublished 42-page U.S. Army Infantry School monograph, dated February 6, 1967, by then–Captain Edwards covering his personal experiences in LZ X-Ray.

Transcript of August 28, 1967, interview of Edwards by Major John A. Cash of the Office, Chief of Military History (OCMH). Letter, May 5, 1983, from Edwards to Galloway, with completed questionnaire and personal recollections. Taped discussion of X-Ray battle on May 21, 1983, between Edwards, Lt. Col. L. R. (Ray) Lefebvre (ret.) and Moore. Edwards letters to Moore dated June 12, 1988, and August 22, 1988. Taped discussion between Edwards and Moore at Ia Drang reunion, Fort Benning, August 1990. Telephone interview, Moore/Edwards, August 28, 1991. Edwards letters to Moore, August 19, 1991; December 1, 1991; December 11, 1991. Telephone interview with Moore, January 30, 1992.

2. Recorded interview/discussion, Moore/Ernest E. Paolone at Ia Drang reunions, July 1988 and November 1989.

3. Undated written statements, from about late November–early December 1965, by Platoon Sgt. Glenn A. Kennedy, Sgt. James P. Castleberry, and PFC Ervin L. Brown, Jr., in support of a recommendation for an award of valor for then–Captain Edwards.

4. 1965 Terrain/Topo Map Sheet #6536 III Series L 7014, PL. YA BO, Vietnam; Cambodia. Scale 1:50,000. Army Map Service, U.S. Army Corps of Engineers. "Map Information as of 1965."

5. Unless otherwise noted, all quotations and information in this and subsequent chapters, from Senior General Vo Nguyen Giap, Senior General Chu Huy Man, Lt. Gen. Nguyen Huu An, and Maj. Gen. Hoang Phuong are from the authors' recorded interviews with Giap and Phuong in September 1990, and the authors' recorded interviews and discussions with Man, An, and Phuong in November 1991, in Hanoi.

6. All quotations and information from Arthur Viera, Jr., in this and subsequent chapters are from one or more of the following sources: Telephone interview, August 28, 1991, Moore/Viera. Undated (1966 or 1967) feature article on Viera from the Providence (R.I.) *Journal-Bulletin.*

It is clear from Viera's statements that Lieutenant Neil Kroger died heroically. Unfortunately, Viera is the only survivor of the 1st Platoon of Charlie Company whom the authors have been able to locate; thus we have no other details of Kroger's death.

7. All quotations from Clinton S. Poley in this and subsequent chapters are from: Poley letters to Moore dated February 10, 1969; July 7, 1988; and September 1990, with details of the X-Ray battle. Interviews of Poley at the July 1988, summer 1989, November 1989, and July 1991 Ia Drang reunions. Sketch by Poley and Moore of locations of fighting positions of Poley and other 2nd Platoon, Charlie Company personnel. Article, "A Band of Brothers" by Joseph L. Galloway in *BRAVO Veterans Outlook,* December/January 1990. Multiple telephone discussions by Moore and Galloway with Poley, 1988–1992.

8. All quotations and information from retired SFC Robert Jemison, Jr., in

this and subsequent chapters are from the following sources: Undated 1984 response by Jemison to our questionnaire with statement on battle. Moore interview of Jemison, summer 1984. Galloway telephone interviews with Jemison, October 1990. Moore telephone interview with Jemison, August 28, 1991.

9. All quotations and comments from Air Force Col. Charlie W. Hastings (ret.) in this and subsequent chapters are from the following sources: Hastings letter to Moore, April 21, 1988. Telephone interview, Moore/Hastings, fall 1988, on air support at X-Ray. Telephone interviews, Galloway/Hastings, October 1990, December 1991, and May 1992.

2. The Roots of Conflict

1. On the birth of battlefield airmobility and the 11th Air Assault Division (Test): chapter 1 of Gen. John Tolson's monograph *Vietnam Studies: Airmobility 1961–71;* Moore's memories of his service in the Airmobility Division of Army Staff in the Pentagon in 1958–1959. *Airmobile: The Helicopter War in Vietnam,* by Jim Meskos, contains little-known information on the early days of the helicopter.

2. For the 11th Air Assault tests and subsequent formation of the 1st Cavalry Division (Airmobile), Tolson's monograph and Moore's personal records and recollections.

3. On the temper of the times and the situation in Vietnam: The authors' memories of those days; generally, see Bernard Fall's *The Two Viet-Nams* and *Street Without Joy;* Neil Sheehan's *A Bright Shining Lie;* David Halberstam's *The Best and the Brightest* and *The Making of a Quagmire;* Stanley Karnow's *Vietnam: A History;* Lt. Gen. Philip B. Davidson's *Vietnam at War: The History 1946–1975;* and Dave R. Palmer's *Summons of the Trumpet.*

4. For political-military decisions in Washington and Hanoi, and actions on troop buildups in South Vietnam in 1964–1965: Karnow, Palmer, and Davidson books.

5. On the February 6, 1965, sapper attack at Pleiku, and President Johnson's bombing decisions: Karnow, pp. 412–415. Chapter 2 of Mark Clodfelter's *The Limits of Air Power* contains more detailed information.

6. The Marine and logistics buildup in March and April and the President's Mekong River development speech: *The World Almanac of the Vietnam War,* edited by John S. Bowman. Also see Karnow, pp. 415–19.

7. Westmoreland's spring 1965 requests for U.S. reinforcements and 173rd Airborne Brigade operations: Karnow, p. 422. An excellent description of the 173rd deployment and ground operations from May 5 through November 9, 1965, can be found in Shelby L. Stanton's *The Rise and Fall of an American Army,* pp. 45–48.

8. President Johnson's guns-and-butter decisions on the conduct of the Viet-

nam War are extensively covered in the books cited in n. 3 for this ch.; Maj. Gen. John K. Singlaub's *Hazardous Duty,* pp. 277–83, describes the impact on the Army of the Johnson refusal to declare an emergency and extend enlistments.

9. The June 1965 Hanoi decision to change the plan of attack in the Central Highlands, and General Man's comments, are from the authors' November 4, 1991, interview with Man in Hanoi.

10. Activities at Fort Benning, Georgia, the summer of 1965: written records; Army documents; and Moore's personal recollections. Moore and his battalion officers and NCOs watched the President's televised address ordering the 1st Cavalry Division to Vietnam on a small TV set at battalion headquarters.

11. General H. K. Johnson's aborted trip to the White House to resign as Army Chief of Staff in protest: Singlaub's *Hazardous Duty,* p. 283. Also "The Parameters of Military Ethics: Introduction," by Col. Harry Summers, Jr., p. 27. Transcript Galloway interview with Lt. Gen. Stanley Larsen, August 19, 1990, and Galloway discussions with Summers and Singlaub, May 5–6, 1992.

12. Details of the North Vietnamese troop movement south and the Ia Drang sanctuary: From "The Lure and the Ambush," an unpublished article-length monograph, dated December 1965, by Majors William P. Boyle and Robert Samabria. On file at the Office of the Chief of Military History, U.S. Army, Washington, D.C.

13. Biographical data concerning the officers and NCOs are from division and battalion records; the West Point Register of Graduates; questionnaire responses and written biographies provided at our request; and (as in the case of Sgt. Maj. Plumley), personal interviews.

14. Data on organization and equipment of an airmobile infantry battalion from Army Tables of Organization and Equipment (T/O&Es) of the period. Available from Headquarters, Department of the Army, Deputy Chief of Staff for Operations, Washington, D.C.

15. Remarks by Vietnamese generals Giap, Man, An, and Phuong, here and elsewhere in this book, are from their taped interviews with the authors in Hanoi in 1990 and 1991.

16. In an interview with Galloway at his U.S. Central Command headquarters in Riyadh, Saudi Arabia, in late January 1991, General H. Norman Schwarzkopf detailed his participation with the South Vietnamese Airborne Task Force as a blocking force along the Cambodian border in the final days of the Ia Drang campaign.

17. Notes on the rapidly dwindling strength of the 1st Battalion, 7th Cavalry and activities at An Khe base camp in the fall of 1965 are from two of Moore's personal notebooks.

18. Descriptions of the attack on Plei Me, the hospital fight, and the Novem-

ber 3 ambush are based on the division after-action report, as well as a report dated November 6, 1965, which Lt. Col. Stockton wrote to division headquarters. Despite his troubles with Brig. Gen. Knowles and division headquarters, Stockton was on the colonel's promotion list and got his eagles in late November. He was then transferred out of the 1st Cavalry Division at Knowles's insistence. Knowles discussion with Galloway at the August 1990 Ia Drang reunion at Fort Benning, and in a telephone discussion with Galloway in April 1992.

3. Boots and Saddles

1. In a June 20, 1983, letter to Moore, Knowles detailed his discussion with Lt. Gen. Larsen which resulted in Moore's battalion being ordered into the Ia Drang Valley.

2. Viet Cong attack on 3rd Brigade command post: from division after-action report.

3. Catecka Tea Plantation and manager's villa: Galloway's observations and notes during his twenty-four-hour stay at 3rd Brigade headquarters, November 13–14, 1965.

4. ARA attack on Nadal's Alpha Company troops: Nadal letter to Moore.

5. All quotations and information from Lt. Col. Bruce Crandall (ret.) in this and subsequent chapters are from: Questionnaire, letter, and written statement, Crandall to Galloway, June 4, 1984. Copy of a Crandall letter dated November 20, 1965, addressed to himself at his home address, with a notation that it was not to be opened until his return from Vietnam. Crandall wrote his observations on the Ia Drang campaign while they were fresh. Moore/Crandall interviews, taped, in 1984 and 1985 in Colorado. Tape of Crandall's speech at Ia Drang reunion, Fort Benning, Georgia, August 1990. Telephone interviews, Galloway/Crandall, October 1990. Crandall statement to authors, January 1992.

6. Winkel's quotes on aviator training are extracted from a lengthy written description to Moore in November 1988 and from his completed questionnaire plus a detailed written statement to authors, summer 1983.

7. Information on manpower shortages came from 1st Battalion, 7th Cav headquarters records of November 1965, plus Moore notebooks of that time, and are included in Moore's December 9, 1965, after-action report. When a battalion is as understrength as this, the captains and lieutenants try to do the jobs of the missing officers and NCOs, and the remaining NCOs also try to do the jobs of missing NCOs and missing troopers in the ranks. The result is additional degradation of unit integrity and effectiveness, and higher officer and NCO casualties: exactly what happened in LZ X-Ray.

4. The Land and the Enemy

1. The description of the Central Highlands is from map studies and from personal observations of the authors. On the Montagnards: Personal observations of the authors. An especially good source is the book *Special Forces of the United States Army 1952/1982,* by Lt. Col. Ian D. W. Sutherland (ret.), pp. 113, 114, 259, 272. Also, Norman Lewis's *A Dragon Apparent* is a good source.

2. For information on North Vietnamese troop training and travel down the Ho Chi Minh Trail: "The Training, Infiltration and Operations of a North Vietnamese Soldier from 12 April 1963 to 11 June 1966 in North and South Vietnam and Laos (Based on a Personal Interview by a Battalion Civil Affairs Officer)," a monograph by Captain Jerry P. Laird, Advance Course Class 68-1, Roster Number 91, Advisory Group Number 9 of the Army Infantry School, Fort Benning, January 4, 1968. The People's Army soldier was a Sgt. Chien from the village of Hanan on the coast southeast of Hanoi. He entered South Vietnam in January 1966 and surrendered in June 1966. Laird interviewed Chien for fourteen hours.

3. For the travels of the 320th, 33rd, and 66th PAVN regiments down the trail and into South Vietnam, the Boyle and Samabria monograph (n. 12, ch. 2) was a valuable reference. The authors used captured diaries, interrogation reports, and Knowledgeability Briefs of 35 People's Army POWs.

4. For all quotations from Giap, Man, An, and Phuong in this chapter, see n. 5, ch. 1.

5. On the results of the Plei Me attack as it affected Man's forces: Boyle and Samabria monograph (see n. 12, ch. 2); Man, An, and Phuong, recorded statements (n. 5, ch. 1).

6. Information on the organization and strengths of the People's Army B-3 Front: Man, An, Phuong interviews (n. 5, ch. 1); and an undated, declassified U.S. Army Intelligence Document in the files of the OCMH, Army, which details the history, organization, and strengths of all units of the B-3 Front.

5. Into the Valley

1. Dillon's report of a Mandarin-language radio intercept: Dillon letter to Galloway, summer 1983. Undated 1987 letter Dillon to Moore commenting on the intercept and other matters. The frag order is "Copy #9 dated 131500 Nov 65, Frag 0 65-12," in Moore's possession.

2. It was Moore's personal practice always to land with the first wave of assault helicopters, and to put out operations orders verbally and personally. Listeners could thus discern the emphasis he placed on various elements of the concept.

3. Both Dillon and Moore recall Brown's remarks and his obvious concern.

4. The news back home on Saturday, November 13, 1965, is excerpted from *The New York Times*.

5. Dillon's quote on an air assault: letter to Galloway (n. 1, above).

6. Crandall's quotes: letter to Galloway, June 4, 1984.

7. The precise time of the landing is from the Battalion Operations Journal of November 14, 1965.

8. General An's quotes: n. 5, ch. 1.

9. All quotations and information for Master Sgt. Larry M. Gilreath (ret.) in this and subsequent chapters are from: taped interview, Gilreath/Moore, May 1985. Tape recording and letter, undated, from Gilreath to Moore, late 1985. Letter and annotated photographs and sketches, from Gilreath to Moore, August 28, 1988.

10. Hastings's comment: letter to Moore, April 21, 1988.

6. The Battle Begins

1. A treasure trove of research material was opened to the authors in 1988 when former Alpha Company, 1st Battalion, 7th Cav rifleman William Kreischer organized the first Ia Drang reunion in July in Orlando, Florida. All participants were urged to bring their photos, their letters, their newspaper and magazine clippings, their Army orders—and their memories. Moore did a slide show and talk on the battle at X-Ray, then threw the floor open to comments, questions, and remembrances of the audience. The entire proceeding was recorded and videotaped. Moore followed up with a number of taped interviews with individuals. There have been seven reunions of Ia Drang veterans since the first in July 1988. Those gatherings and the October 29, 1990, *U.S. News & World Report* cover article on the twenty-fifth anniversary of Ia Drang, written by Galloway, brought in literally scores more veterans of X-Ray and Albany— as well as the families of a number of Ia Drang casualties—who have contributed to the historical record.

2. All quotations and information from Colonel John D. Herren (ret.) in this and subsequent chapters are from: transcript of Major John Cash's interview of Herren, August 21, 1967; Herren's undated (1967) letter to Major John Cash; Herren interview with Major Cash, March 19, 1968; long, detailed battle narrative, complete with several map sketches, from Herren to Galloway, April 29, 1983; written response from Herren, undated (1987), to Moore, detailing answers to 12 specific questions, including notations on three aerial photos of the battlefield; letter, Herren to Moore, July 25, 1988; letter and sketch maps, Herren to Moore, November 10, 1988; telephone interview, Herren/Galloway, October 1990; letter and chapter revisions, Herren to Moore, December 1991.

3. All quotations and information from Galen F. Bungum for this chapter

and subsequent ones are from: letter to Moore entitled "My Ia Drang Valley Story," April 20, 1988; letter answering specific Moore questions, September 9, 1988; interview with authors at the August 1990 Ia Drang reunion at Fort Benning; telephone interviews, Bungum/Galloway, October 1990.

4. Platoon Sgt. Gilreath's letter/maps/photos/sketches to Moore, August 28, 1988.

5. All quotations and recollections in this and subsequent chapters from Dennis J. Deal are from: three hours of taped statements to the authors in 1983; sketches and manuscript he provided Moore at the 1986 1st Cavalry Division Association reunion; interview, Deal/Moore, at 1988 Ia Drang reunion; multiple telephone and personal interviews with both authors, 1989–1991; letter to Moore, December 1, 1991.

6. For Sgt. Jimmie Jakes's comments: his 1983 response to authors' questionnaire; telephone discussion with Moore, December 31, 1988; and Jakes letter to Moore, January 3, 1989.

7. Retired CSM William Roland's quote is from his completed questionnaire, April 1983.

8. All quotations, comments, and information from SFC Ernie Savage in this and subsequent chapters are from: undated (1967) transcript of an interview of Savage by Major John Cash; two recorded interviews, Savage/Moore, May 1983 and June 13, 1986; recordings and notes taken at the 1988 Ia Drang reunion. At the 1988 session, Savage and others of Lieutenant Herrick's platoon used a screened slide aerial photo to pinpoint the precise location of the Lost Platoon during its ordeal.

9. Information on the North Vietnamese battalion facing Herren is from an intelligence analysis cited in the March 1966 division after-action report. Also, General Phuong's statement that the air assault into X-Ray landed right in the 9th Battalion, 66th People's Army Regiment assembly area. Bill Beck, the Alpha Company machine gunner, says: "We landed right on top of 'em!"

10. All quotations and information from Medical Platoon Sergeant Keeton in this and subsequent chapters are from a recorded interview, Moore/Keeton, May 5, 1984; interview at Ia Drang reunion, August 1990; telephone interviews, June 8, 1991; January 1992; February 1992.

11. A declassified cable dated 28 Nov 65 from 2nd Air Div Tansonnhut, RVN, to Chief of Staff, U.S. Air Force, states: "From 1315 H [1:15 P.M.] on 14 Nov to 0600 H [6 A.M.] 15 Nov, 67 strike sorties expended GP [General Purpose bombs], Napalm, WP [white phosphorus bombs], Frag [bombs], .50 caliber machine gun and 20mm [cannon]. 28 F4B, 12 F-100, 10 A-1E, Six F4C, Six B-57, 4 A-4 and one FC-47 [Puff the Magic Dragon] saturated areas of reported concentrations." Note that the B-57 Canberra carried a typical load of 6,000 pounds of bombs in the bomb bay plus 2,000 pounds in wing racks. For details on the Canberra, see Chris Ellis, *A History of Combat Aircraft,* p. 234.

12. All quotations and comments from Sgt. George Nye in this and subsequent chapters are from: his completed questionnaire; a detailed early May 1983 telephone discussion with Galloway and a tape-recorded statement from Nye, transcribed on May 15, 1983; telephone interview, Moore/Nye, spring 1991. Also notes of literally dozens of telephone conversations between Nye and both authors, plus personal discussions at five different Ia Drang reunion gatherings over the years.

7. Closing with the Enemy

1. Account of Taft's death: recorded interview with Master Sgt. Robert Hazen (ret.) at the 1988 Orlando reunion, plus telephone interviews, Moore/Hazen, March 7 and 8, 1992.

2. All quotations and information from Colonel Ramon A. (Tony) Nadal in this and subsequent chapters are from the following sources: letter, Nadal to Major John Cash, October 2, 1967; undated (summer 1983) Nadal response to authors' questionnaire; Nadal letters to his wife and son, November 17, 19, 22, and 23, 1965; undated (summer 1983) letter, Nadal to Galloway; Nadal, taped statement to Galloway, late 1983; letter, Nadal to Moore, April 10, 1984; discussions, Moore/Nadal/Herren, at Nadal's home, May 1985; letter, Nadal to Moore, answering specific questions, July 13, 1988; discussions with Moore at July 1988 reunion; letter to Moore, July 31, 1988, with map sketches, annotated aerial photos; telephone interview, Moore/Nadal, August 1991; letter to Moore, comments on chapter drafts, December 1991.

3. Deal: See n. 5, ch. 6.

4. Nadal was a combat veteran of an earlier tour with the Special Forces and had fought the Viet Cong. Those within hearing, and those monitoring the battalion radio net, will never forget him yelling, as he first saw the khaki-clad North Vietnamese regulars swarming down the dry creekbed: "They're PAVN! They're PAVN!"

5. Quotations from Carmen Miceli are from the recorded discussion of X-Ray at the first Ia Drang reunion in 1988, plus a separate Moore/Miceli recorded interview at that same gathering.

6. Steven Hansen's statements in this and subsequent chapters: from recorded interview at the July 1988 reunion; letters, Hansen to Moore, June 22, 1988, and fall 1988.

7. On Taft's death: See n. 1 above.

8. On Hazen being shot: See n. 1 above.

9. Platoon Sgt. Troy Miller's statements on the enemy attack on 3rd Platoon: from telephone interview notes, Miller/Cash, December 26, 1967.

10. Kreischer's quotations and statements, here and subsequently: from an undated statement, Kreischer/Moore, received late August 1991.

11. The remarkable saga of Specialist Bill Beck detailed in this and subsequent chapters draws on a thick file of letters from Beck to Moore, beginning with the first, dated November 10, 1969, and including others dated April 11, 1983; May 16, 1983; June 14, 1985; September 3, 1986; February 24, 1988; and two from August 1989. The Beck story emerges from those letters and scores of telephone conversations and personal interviews with both authors. Beck is a trained professional graphic artist—which has much to do with the clarity and detail of his statements, his maps, and his sketches, and with his vivid memory. It was Beck who drew the map sketches for Moore's original December 9, 1965, after-action report. Notes from an April 6, 1989, telephone conversation, Beck/Moore, are important. Also extremely valuable are Beck's comments recorded during the 1988 Ia Drang reunion discussions. Also, Beck shipped home every scrap of official paper the Army handed him—and his mother preserved it all. He was thus able to provide the authors original company rosters, movement orders, and awards lists, with names and serial numbers, that were priceless.

12. Staley's quote is from the Cash research file at the OCMH, Army.

13. Miller: See n. 9 above.

14. Nadal: See n. 2 above.

15. Beck: See n. 11 above.

16. Russell Adams's statement, "Nobody told me to stop . . .": from a conversation with Moore at the 1990 Ia Drang reunion.

17. Description of the A-1E aircraft and their capabilities and support at X-Ray, and then–Captain Bruce Wallace's quotes and remarks: from a letter to Moore, dated August 8, 1983.

18. Dillon on calling ARA on the crash site: n. 1, ch. 5.

19. McClellan's death in the November 14 crash is reported in Wallace's letter; by the A-1 Skyraider Association; and the Vietnam Memorial Directory of Names. McClellan's body was recovered. The 2nd Air Div cable to Chief of Staff, USAF of 28 Nov 65 (n. 11, ch. 6) states: "One A1E was hit by ground fire at 1404 H [2:04 P.M.], Acft caught fire, exploded and crashed. No chute was observed and pilot's body was recovered 1720 H [5:20 P.M.]."

20. The identity of the enemy POW's parent regiment, and other nearby North Vietnamese units: from a 1967 undated letter to Major Cash from then–Captain John S. Prichard, former assistant intelligence officer, 3rd Brigade; and also letter, Prichard to Cash, April 4, 1968. Also, notes of a Cash telephone interview with Prichard, August 22, 1967: Prichard told Cash that the 66th Regiment prisoners pointed out on a map the location of the regimental supply point. A later napalm strike on that location resulted in five secondary explosions and an estimated 80 enemy killed.

21. Brig. Gen. Knowles's tense moments at the briefing for Maj. Gen. Kin-

nard at 1st Cav Div forward command post: described in letter, Knowles to Moore, June 20, 1983.

22. Information on Sgt. Hurdle's machine guns: from Sgt. Ernie Savage (n. 8, ch. 6). For the progress of the battle of Herrick's 2nd Platoon, including the actions of Hill, Hurdle, Anderson, and Zallen: Sgt. Zallen's interview at July 1989 Ia Drang reunion and Galen Bungum's submissions, n. 3, ch. 6.

23. Details of those wounded and types of wounds suffered by personnel of 2nd Platoon B/1/7: from a letter from then–Specialist 5 Charles Lose, the platoon medic, to Major John Cash, February 11, 1968.

24. Bungum's remarks: n. 3, ch. 6.

25. Dorman's statement was made to Galloway on November 16, 1965, on the battlefield.

26. All quotations and information provided by then–Specialist 4 Vincent Cantu in this chapter and subsequent ones: from Cantu's detailed recollections of X-Ray contained in a ten-page letter delivered to Galloway at the August 1990 Ia Drang reunion at Fort Benning.

27. Information on redistribution of ammunition, collecting maps and signal data: from Savage (n. 8, ch. 6).

8. The Storm of Battle

1. All quotations and information from Lt. Col. L. R. (Ray) Lefebvre (ret.) in this and subsequent chapters are from: taped discussion May 21, 1983, Moore with Edwards and Lefebvre; letter, then–Major Lefebvre to Major Cash, January 12, 1968; undated (summer 1984) questionnaire and written submission to authors; taped discussion at the 1988 Orlando Ia Drang reunion; multiple telephone discussions with Moore and Galloway, 1989–1992.

2. Quotations and personal accounts from Army Aviators Lombardo and Jekel derive from their written submissions and letters and completed questionnaires received in the summer of 1983; telephone interviews, Galloway/Jekel, October 1990; telephone interview, Moore/Lombardo, March 6, 1992. Jekel letters to Moore and Galloway of December 27, 1992, and January 24, 1993.

3. Letter from then–Brig. Gen. Roger Bean to Moore, July 7, 1989, described his experiences in the Ia Drang. Pilot Jon Mills's written account, provided in the summer of 1983, corroborates.

4. For General An's comment: n. 5, ch. 1.

5. For Edwards: n. 1, ch. 1.

6. For Herren: n. 2, ch. 6.

7. For Hansen: n. 6, ch. 7.

8. Beck's recollections: n. 11, ch. 7.

9. McDonald: from questionnaire and statement enclosed with letter to Moore, December 18, 1989.

10. Information on Edwards's platoon leaders and NCOs: from battalion records; Edwards material, n. 1, ch. 1; Vietnam Memorial Directory of Names; personal recollections.

11. Wallace material: n. 17, ch. 7.

12. Washburn account: his written notes, December 3, 1991, provided by Paul P. Winkel.

13. Barker comment about "five straight hours": from a personal conversation with Moore at An Khe base camp after the battle.

14. Winkel's observations: from an undated letter to Moore, received in late 1991.

9. Brave Aviators

1. Captain Metsker: Sgt. Maj. Plumley witnessed Metsker, down on one knee and firing his M-16 at the enemy on full automatic, when Metsker was struck in the shoulder by a bullet. Plumley said he last saw Metsker being bandaged by First Sergeant Arthur Newton of Alpha Company.

2. Crandall: See n. 5, ch. 3.

3. The detailed and invaluable recollections of Col. Paul Patton Winkel (ret.): from his letters, statements, and studies since 1983 of the helicopter operations and Army Aviator actions during the Ia Drang campaign. Winkel's completed questionnaire and accompanying written account to Galloway and Moore, May 27, 1983, was the reference most used. Titled "The First Team and Landing Zone X-Ray, November 1965: A Helicopter Pilot's View," it is a compelling and forceful account of Winkel's view of terror, death, and horribly wounded men in a vicious battle. He candidly writes about how he came to grips with and conquered his own fear in his first combat action. Other Winkel references: letters to authors, September 1, 1988; October 9, 1988; March 18, 1991; October 6, 1991; November 3, 1991; November 5, 1991; January 23, 1992; January 30, 1992; February 28, 1992; March 6, 1992; and countless telephone discussions with both authors over the years.

4. Winkel mentions battalion supply officer Rozanski personally bringing ammunition into X-Ray. The other side of this story took place at the ammo-supply point at Camp Holloway and is a good example of how our NCOs and troopers were trained to act on their own, in the absence of orders or instructions. Staff Sgt. James T. Godfrey, thirty, was battalion ammo sergeant. From a January 20, 1988, letter to Moore: "We had to use our own knowledge of what the units needed because the officers didn't have time to request it item-by-item. I used my knowledge of what type ammo they needed in a defense, and what they could carry if ordered to attack or move out. Everyone had to think. There was no time to wait for someone to tell [you]."

5. Then–Col. Thomas W. Brown's August 8, 1967, letter to Major Cash, and an August 25, 1967, letter to Cash from then–Major Henri S. Mallet, Brigade S-3, are very revealing on Brown's decisions on reinforcement of X-Ray. The letters clearly show that, on the basis of information from Dillon in the chopper overhead and 3rd Brigade's monitoring of our battalion command radio net, Brown was way ahead of the requirement.

6. Quotations and information from Joe Marm in this and subsequent chapters: from then–Captain Marm's January 10, 1968, letter to Major Cash and from the authors' personal and telephone discussions with Colonel Marm.

7. In a February 1992 telephone discussion with Moore, former Medical Platoon Sgt. Keeton said, "There was a hole as big as your fist in Bouknight's back."

8. Savage's terse description of his cheery greeting to the three NVA soldiers he then killed: *Time*, November 26, 1965, p. 32, headlined THE VALLEYS OF DEATH.

9. Dorman's remarks were made to Galloway, November 16, 1965.

10. Fix Bayonets!

1. Biographical information on then–Captain Diduryk: from a letter to Moore from Mrs. Delores Diduryk, June 10, 1984.

2. Quotes and information in this and subsequent chapters from Jon Wallenius are from: the 1983 questionnaire; Wallenius letter to Moore, August 29, 1986; 1988 Orlando reunion taped discussions; written statement, October 15, 1988, in which Wallenius recounts his experiences at X-Ray; letter to Moore, September 20, 1988; Wallenius discussion with Galloway at Ia Drang reunion in Washington, D.C., November 1989; recorded speech by Wallenius at July 1991 Ia Drang reunion lunch, Fort Hood, Texas; and numerous telephone discussions with both authors.

3. Nadal information: n. 2, ch. 7. Miller: n. 9, ch. 7. Deal: n. 5, ch. 6. Kreischer and Beck: n. 10, n. 11, ch. 7. Gell's last words: recounted by Sgt. Sam Hollman, Jr., to Bill Beck, August 1989.

4. Marm's charge against the machine-gun bunker was recounted by several witnesses. See Gilreath, n. 9, ch. 5, and Deal, n. 5, ch. 6. Also Marm's letter to Major Cash, January 10, 1968.

5. Wallenius landing: n. 2 above, and Paul Winkel's helicopter support study n. 3, ch. 9. Setelin quotes in this chapter and subsequent ones: from a tape-recorded statement by Setelin, December 1988; Setelin's completed questionnaire, December 1988; tapes of the Orlando 1988 reunion discussions; a second statement Setelin recorded in 1991; transcript of a recorded interview by Galloway, December 1991.

6. The DASPO film-crew mission was Project No. DCS 200-13B65. "Date

shot: 14–15 Nov" is on the caption forms. Also, Galloway interview of Sgt. Jack Yamaguchi (ret.), one of the two Army cameramen present in X-Ray, September 1990.

7. Nadal's request for permission to fall back and the WP smoke mission: n. 2, ch. 7. Gilreath's comment to Herren: n. 9, ch. 5.

8. Tanner on the noise and bright light: undated (early 1990) letter to Moore.

9. Edwards: n. 1, ch. 1. Herren: n. 2, ch. 6.

10. Setelin's anguish over the wounding of Willard: n. 5 above.

11. Tally of the day's killed and wounded: battalion records; Moore's personal records and notebooks.

12. Adams and the field antenna: Delta Company was designated the backup battalion CP; thus Adams carried the RC-292.

13. A North Vietnamese map sketch captured in 1966 and studied for this book shows three separate attacks on 1st Battalion, 7th Cav at X-Ray on November 14. That is corroborated by the statements of Generals An and Phuong (n. 5, ch. 1). There was one attack from the northwest by elements of the 33rd Regiment; one from the west-southwest by the 9th Battalion, 66th Regiment; and a third from the south and southeast by the 7th Battalion, 66th Regiment.

11. Night Falls

1. Rescorla's quotes and information: Col. USAR (ret.) Cyril R. (Rick) Rescorla's detailed memories of the Ia Drang campaign are drawn from a twenty-six-page written account, with map sketches, September 19, 1991, accompanying his completed questionnaire. Also multiple telephone discussions with Moore and Galloway, beginning in September 1991.

2. Dillon on the lights on the mountain: letter to Major Cash, August 18, 1967.

3. Night landing in X-Ray: Crandall, n. 5, ch. 3.

4. Crandall's return to the Turkey Farm: n. 5, ch. 3.

5. Medical treatment and evacuation: letter from Lt. Col. George H. Kelling (ret.), November 21, 1983; undated (spring 1984) letter and questionnaire; undated (summer 1984) letter with lengthy description of medical support activities.

6. Edwards on the probes: n. 1, ch. 1.

7. The foxholes: Platoon Sgt. Robert Jemison's questionnaire and written description, undated (summer 1983); Moore interview at Jemison's home in 1984; multiple telephone discussions with both authors, most recently August 1991.

8. Setelin's account of the sniper in the trees: n. 5, ch. 10.

9. Warren Adams's quotes and information: from two cassettes he recorded

in 1988; recorded discussions at the 1988 Orlando reunion and subsequent reunions; numerous telephone discussions, the last on January 30, 1992.

10. Cantu on his first-class foxhole: n. 26, ch. 7.

11. Quotations and information from then–Captain Diduryk in this and subsequent chapters: from an undated eight-page Diduryk paper with three sketch maps describing his and his company's actions at X-Ray provided by Delores Diduryk. Also a November 27, 1965, seven-page letter and sketch maps provided by Diduryk to a classmate for use in teaching ROTC students at Diduryk's alma mater. A copy was sent to the authors in November 1990.

12. Herren in the dry creekbed: n. 2, ch. 6.

13. Nadal on Herren's left: n. 2, ch. 7.

14. Tanner: n. 8, ch. 10.

15. Beck: n. 11, ch. 7.

16. Dillon to Nadal on the M-79 H&I fires: Moore recollection.

17. Bungum: n. 3, ch. 6.

18. Gilreath: n. 9, ch. 5.

19. Quotes from Lt. Dick Merchant in this and subsequent chapters: from his completed questionnaire and accompanying statement, April 24, 1983.

20. Information from Col. Wirth (ret.) are from his letters to the authors, August and September 1984.

21. Herren on Savage's report on possible attack: n. 2, ch. 6.

12. A Dawn Attack

1. Edwards on the patrols: n. 1, ch. 1.

2. Jemison's memory of how he and Lt. Geoghegan shared the last of the water was relayed to Moore by Geoghegan's parents during a visit in the summer of 1967. They had exchanged letters with Sgt. Jemison. Also see n. 8, ch. 1.

3. Phuong: n. 5, ch. 1.

4. Edwards, Jemison, Viera: n. 1, n. 6, and n. 8, ch. 1.

5. Setelin: n. 5, ch. 10.

6. Hastings uses the "Broken Arrow" code word for an American unit in trouble: n. 10, ch. 5. Hastings/Galloway telephone conversation, April 28, 1992. Also, 2nd Air Div cable to Chief of Staff USAF 28 Nov 65 (n. 11, ch. 6): "From 0600H 15 Nov until 0600H 16 Nov there were 48 fighter-bomber sorties by A1Es, F-100s, B-57s and F4Cs." Authors' note: Most of this firepower exploded forward of Charlie Company.

7. Adams and his RTO clean up the termite hill: n. 9, ch. 11.

8. McDonald uses the M-79 and grenades: from his letter of December 18, 1989.

9. McCulley shot in throat: from Nadal's award recommendation for Sgt. McCulley, late November 1965.

10. Wallenius and Sgt. Alvarez-Buzo and the pop-up targets: n. 2, ch. 10.

11. Parish's actions: his recorded 1987 statement to Moore and the citation accompanying his Silver Star award.

12. Not only did those nine machine guns create a wall of steel, but the terrain to their front was flat, and tree growth was sparse in the beaten zone. The maximum effective range of an M-60 is 1,100 meters (Infantry Leader's Reference Card, GTA 7-1-27, September 1975, Fort Benning). If an M-60 round did not hit a tree or termite hill, it could still kill a man three-quarters of a mile downrange from Adams's firing positions.

13. Cantu on the jets, artillery, De La Paz, and meeting his old friend Galloway: n. 26, ch. 7.

13. Friendly Fire

1. Viera and Jemison: n. 6 and n. 8, ch. 1. From what Viera says (and Edwards also) it is clear that had the NVA troops been better led and disciplined, and not diverted to killing our wounded and stripping them of loot, they would have had a fleeting opportunity to take Captain Edwards's command post. That, in turn, would have opened a path to the battalion CP. That brief opportunity was eliminated by the rain of air and artillery fire support.

2. Poley on getting hit: n. 7, ch. 1.

3. Edwards and Herren on fire support: n. 1, ch. 1; n. 2, ch. 6.

4. Edwards on the enemy sniper and Sgt. Kennedy: n. 1, ch. 1; Jemison on Byrd and Foxe: n. 8, ch. 1.

5. Keeton: n. 10, ch. 6.

6. Dillon on the napalm: n. 1, ch. 5; Nye on the napalm and Nakayama: n. 12, ch. 6.

7. Burlile's death: n. 1, ch. 11.

8. Hastings on the second F-100: n. 10, ch. 5.

9. Moore well remembers the black-uniformed enemy soldier stumbling, weaponless, into the clearing—the only enemy to break through the lines.

10. Setelin on the WP: n. 5, ch. 10.

11. Sugdinis and Sisson landing at X-Ray: from battalion after-action report, December 9, 1965.

12. On Gwin's quotations and information in this and subsequent chapters: transcript of Galloway telephone interview with Gwin, August 27, 1991; also "Narrative by Lt. Gwin," 1983; Gwin letter to Moore, October 18, 1991, with twenty-six-page transcript "A Day at Albany" and four map sketches; Gwin letter to Moore dated June 1, 1984, enclosing a draft chapter on LZ X-Ray

from "Some Came Home," a work in progress on the Ia Drang. Also multiple Galloway/Gwin telephone discussions.

13. Maruhnich's recollections: undated autobiography by SFC Maruhnich and ten-page handwritten attachment; Maruhnich statement and sketch, May 12, 1984; letter to Moore, March 19, 1991.

14. Jemison on why his platoon held: n. 8, ch. 1.

15. Tally of friendly casualties: battalion records and Moore notebooks.

16. Diduryk: n. 11, ch. 11. Rescorla: n. 1, ch. 11.

17. Robert Tully quotations and information in this and subsequent chapters: from Tully letter to Major Cash, September 5, 1967; Galloway telephone interview with Tully, September 1991.

18. Bennett on enemy resistance: from a letter from Bennett to Major Cash, September 20, 1967.

19. Pop Jekel waits in the landing zone: n. 2, ch. 8.

20. Edwards: n. 1, ch. 1. Dillon: n. 1, ch. 5. Wirth: n. 20, ch. 11.

21. Tully reaches X-Ray: Rescorla (n. 1, ch. 11); Adams (n. 9, ch. 11); Cantu (n. 26, ch. 7).

22. Selleck's information in this chapter and subsequent ones are from his undated questionnaire, received late in 1985, and his undated (1986) tape-recorded statement.

23. The artillery at LZ Falcon: letter to Moore from Gen. Bill Becker, formerly 1st Cav Div assistant division commander for support, June 25, 1984; completed questionnaire from James W. Green, formerly communications chief 1/21 Artillery, summer 1983; statement from Harold M. Hamilton, former 1/21 Artillery supply officer, 1983. Keeping the tubes supplied with 105mm ammo was critical. At Camp Holloway every man in reach was dragooned into service loading the shells aboard CH-47 Chinook helicopters. When the Chinooks reached Falcon, the pilots lowered the tail ramps while hovering, tilted the chopper rear-down, and let the round canisters roll out the back, ready for use.

14. Rescuing the Lost Platoon

1. On Tully's formation and use of Herren: Moore notes and n. 17, ch. 13.

2. Bennett quote: n. 18, ch. 13. Location of Boyt's company: letter, Capt. Edward A. Boyt to Major Cash, November 20, 1967. Time of attack: after-action report.

3. Herren and Deal quotes: n. 2, ch. 6, and n. 5, ch. 6, respectively.

4. Crooks quotations in this and subsequent chapters: letter, Crooks to Major Cash, September 19, 1967.

5. In July 1991, at the 1st Cav Div Reunion at Fort Hood, Moore taped an hour-long interview with three of Captain Bennett's men that was most helpful

in understanding the move out to Savage's perimeter; the physical appearance of the perimeter and the surrounding area; the linkup and brief firefight on arrival; the gathering-up of Savage's men and equipment; and the return to X-Ray. Those men are Melvin Gregory of Jefferson City, Mo.; Stanley Rothstein of Waco, Tex.; and Ted C. Kolbusz of Chicago, Ill. On April 3, 1966, the 1st Battalion, 7th Cav returned to X-Ray. With a platoon as security, Plumley and Moore retraced the attack route Bravo 1/7 had used on November 15, 1965, and walked the ground around Savage's perimeter on the knoll.

6. Setelin on McManus's death: n. 5, ch. 10.

7. Wallenius and the seven dead enemy: n. 2, ch. 10.

8. On the evacuation of the dead: Moore recollection and Cantu (n. 26, ch. 7).

9. Brown's visit and Merchant's quote: n. 19, ch. 11. Also recollection of Moore and others in CP. Also, Moore telephone discussions with Tademy and Plumley, June 1992.

10. Brown alerting us that 1/7 would pull out of X-Ray on November 16: Dillon (n. 1, ch. 5); Moore/Dillon telephone discussion, fall 1991.

11. The B-52 strike: an April 1983 chance meeting between Moore and Lt. Col. Ewing P. Goff, USAF Reserve, who flew on that mission. Goff said it was "the one meaningful memory from all my Vietnam missions to know that we helped your battalion when you were in a very tight situation. We'd been told you were in trouble and accuracy was paramount." From declassified Volume IV of 3rd Air Div and 3960th Strategic Wing records of July–December 1965: Goff was commander of B-52 Tail No. 170 on the "Ivory Tusk" Mission; his radio call sign was White 7. Goff says there were 18 B-52s on that mission in a trail formation, groups of three aircraft in a tight V, with each aircraft carrying 48 500-pound bombs. Each group of three dropped 36 tons of bombs in an area ¼ by ¾ of a mile. Total bombs dropped by all 18 aircraft: 216 tons.

12. General An: n. 5, ch. 1.

13. Herren, Savage, and Tully quotes from previously cited sources: Herren, n. 2, ch. 6; Savage, n. 8, ch. 6; Tully, n. 17, ch. 13.

14. Platoon casualty figures: Herren (n. 2, ch. 6).

15. Deal: n. 5, ch. 6.

16. Translation of NVA soldier's handwritten diary: provided 1987 by the Department of Defense Language Institute, Presidio of Monterey, Calif.

17. Tully: n. 17, ch. 13.

18. Gilreath: n. 9, ch. 5.

19. Stoner on smoking shrapnel and Knowles's visit: n. 21, ch. 7. Also, Moore telephone interviews with Plumley, Knudson, and Dillon in June 1992. See pp. 239–40 in Coleman: *Pleiku.*

20. Tally of casualties: battalion records; Moore notebooks and records.

15. Night Fighters

1. All quotations and information from Diduryk and Rescorla: n. 1, ch. 11; n. 11, ch. 11.

2. Martin: his undated 1988 written statement and completed questionnaire.

3. Lund quotes and information in this and later chapters are from his undated (January 1992) letter to Moore.

4. Both Dillon and Moore have a clear memory of the radio message that 1st Battalion, 7th Cav would be pulled out of X-Ray on November 16. It was logged in the battalion journal and reviewed by Moore during the writing of the after-action report, late November 1965. The journals of 3rd Brigade and the 1st and 2nd battalions, 7th Cav for the period of the Ia Drang campaign have never been located, according to the Office of the Chief of Military History and the Suitland Branch of the National Archives. It has never been adequately explained why those particular records are missing. The loss of those journals has been keenly felt by the authors and other historians interested in reconstructing the events of November 1965 in the Ia Drang.

5. Moore's memory of the radio message from then–Lt. Col. Meyer alerting him to leave the battlefield and brief the MACV staff in Saigon and the amazement and anger he felt is strong and clear, as is his memory of registering his objections in a radio conversation with Meyer two hours later. The Moore/Meyer radio conversations of that night are also covered in Major Cash's memo of a phone interview with Moore, August 8, 1967.

6. Plumley actions: from his Silver Star citation.

7. Setelin quotations: n. 5, ch. 10.

8. Selleck quotations: n. 22, ch. 13.

9. Results of the Mad Minute: 1/7 Battalion after-action report, December 9, 1965, p. 12.

16. Policing the Battlefield

1. Times of sweeps: after-action report, December 9, 1965.

2. Rescorla: n. 1, ch. 11.

3. Wallace quotes: n. 17, ch. 7.

4. The 2nd Battalion, 7th Cavalry march overland from Columbus to X-Ray: from 3rd Brigade and 2nd Battalion after-action reports.

5. Ackerman quote: from his November 25, 1990, letter to Galloway.

6. Selleck: n. 22, ch. 13.

7. The order at 10:40 A.M.: 1/7 Battalion after-action report.

8. Kluge finding the dead American sergeant: telephone conversation, Kluge/Galloway, December 21, 1991.

9. McCulloch recollection: notes from McCulloch/Galloway telephone conversation in November 1990.

10. Enemy weapons count: 1/7 Battalion after-action report.

11. Cantu: n. 26, ch. 7.

12. Parish: from previously cited recorded statement to Moore, 1987 (n. 11, ch. 12).

13. Julie Moore quote: tape-recorded statement made for the authors, December 1991.

14. On Dickey Chapelle's death: personal memory of Galloway. Also, *U.S. Marines in Vietnam: The Landing and the Buildup 1965,* book by Jack Shulimson and Maj. Charles M. Johnson, p. 94. Chapelle was killed on November 4, 1965, while on patrol with U.S. Marines on Operation Black Ferret ten miles south of Chu Lai. A Marine walking in front of her triggered a booby-trapped 81mm mortar shell and an M26 hand grenade, and a tiny piece of shrapnel severed an artery in Chapelle's throat. Chapelle was only the first of the war correspondents to die in combat; in the ten years that followed a total of 63 lost their lives covering the war in Indochina.

17. It Ain't Over Till It's Over

1. Adams: n. 9, ch. 11.

2. Blount: letter to authors, April 24, 1983.

3. Beck: n. 11, ch. 7.

4. Tanner: n. 8, ch. 10.

5. Wallenius: n. 2, ch. 10.

6. Hansen: n. 6, ch. 7.

7. The standoff at the Camp Holloway bar: J. D. Coleman, *Pleiku: The Dawn of Helicopter Warfare in Vietnam,* pp. 227–28; Galloway interview with Mills, November 1991; Moore's memory.

8. Rescorla: n. 1, ch. 11.

9. Staff Sgt. Robert Brown went on to become a sergeant major in the prestigious 3rd Infantry Regiment at Fort Myer, Virginia. Now retired, he supervises a veterans' cemetery in the Washington, D.C., area.

10. Information on the night of November 16 at X-Ray and the November 17 march out of X-Ray: from the after-action reports of 3rd Brigade, 2nd Battalion, 7th Cavalry and 2nd Battalion, 5th Cavalry.

11. Biographical information on Tully: West Point Register of Graduates. On McDade: Coleman, *Pleiku,* pp. 231–32. Transcript of Galloway telephone interview with McDade, October 1990.

12. Information and quotations from Col. Brown on the 2nd Battalion, 7th Cavalry in this and subsequent chapters: transcript of an interview of Brig. Gen. Brown (ret.) by Galloway, August 21, 1991.

13. Sgt. Maj. Scott on the 2nd Battalion: All Scott quotations and information in this and subsequent chapters are from: *Time,* December 31, 1965, "The

Year in Review: The War"; transcript of Galloway's interview with Scott, September 1991; letters and enclosures from Scott to Galloway, October–December 1991; telephone conversation, Scott/Galloway, January 1992.

14. Alley on the 2nd Battalion; Alley's biography: All quotations and information from J. L. (Bud) Alley in this and subsequent chapters are from the transcript of an interview of Alley by Galloway, November 20, 1991, and a letter from Alley to Galloway, November 25, 1991.

15. Quotations and information by then–Lt. Col. Edward C. (Shy) Meyer in this and subsequent chapters: transcript of an interview of Meyer by Galloway, August 28, 1991.

16. Biographical information on Gwin, and his comments on McDade and the battalion officers: n. 12, ch. 13.

17. Epperson on McDade: This and other quotations from Epperson in this and subsequent chapters are from the transcript of an interview of Epperson by Galloway, August 24, 1991.

18. All quotations, comments, and information attributed to then–Lt. Col. McDade in this and subsequent chapters: transcript of telephone interviews by Galloway, October 19, 1990, and November 15, 1991; interview by Galloway; notes of phone conversation Galloway/McDade, January 17, 1992; and letter, from McDade to Moore and Galloway, January 18, 1992.

19. All quotations and comments from Rescorla on the rest at Holloway, B Company 2/7 saddling up for more combat, and his subsequent accounts of what he saw in LZ Albany: from his nineteen-page written statement on the fight at Albany, provided the authors in late 1991; three hand-drawn sketches of the Albany battlefield; four-page "Postmortem" on Albany; and two memos with comments on draft chapters, December 1991–January 1992.

20. The nine A.M. departure time from X-Ray is from the 2nd Battalion, 5th Cavalry after-action report, December 5, 1965, p. 2.

18. A Walk in the Sun

1. All information and comments attributed to then–Lt. Col. Bob Tully in this and later chapters: from transcript of Galloway telephone interview with Tully, August 1991.

2. Brown at X-Ray, November 17: n. 12, ch. 17.

3. All quotations and comments by CWO Ainsworth in this and later chapters: April 1983 questionnaire; Ainsworth letters to Moore, June 2, 1983, and May 11, 1991; notes of phone conversation, Moore/Ainsworth, October 1991; transcript of Galloway interview of Ainsworth, November 1991.

4. Comments on the 2/7 Cav's mission: Brown, n. 12, ch. 17; Meyer, n. 15, ch. 17; McDade, n. 18, ch. 17.

4.1 On the journals: September 8, 1967, letter to OCMH from Army Records Center stating they had not been received; Moore/Galloway 1984 discussion with Chief of Military History Douglas Kinnard. Also, Moore's May 4, 1992, discussion with Richard Boylan, National Archives.

5. All quotations and information attributed to then–Captain Jim Spires in this and subsequent chapters: transcript of Galloway interview of Spires, June 4, 1991. Multiple telephone discussions, Galloway/Spires, fall 1991.

6. All quotations and information from then–Captain Dudley Tademy in this and later chapters: transcript of interview by Galloway, August 15, 1991.

7. Description of beginning of march by Scott, n. 13, ch. 17, and Gwin, n. 12, ch. 13.

8. All quotations and information from then–Captain Joel Sugdinis in this and later chapters are from a detailed thirty-page memoir of X-Ray and Albany by Sugdinis, November 20, 1991. Biographical information on Sugdinis is from the West Point Register of Graduates. Notes of multiple telephone discussions, Galloway/Sugdinis, summer and fall 1991.

9. All quotations and information from then–Captain Henry Thorpe in this and later chapters: transcript of a recorded interview of Thorpe by Galloway, August 9, 1991, Washington, D.C.

10. All quotations and information from then–Captain Skip Fesmire in this and subsequent chapters: detailed statement written by Fesmire at the request of Moore, October 21, 1991; letter, Fesmire to Moore, January 1992.

11. Pujals: All comments, information, and quotations from then–Lt. Enrique Pujals in this and later chapters: letter, Pujals to Moore, March 20, 1991; letter, Pujals to Galloway, March 22, 1991; and a most valuable, detailed twenty-page letter, Pujals to Moore, April 4, 1991.

12. Specialist Smith on the rotting bodies: Smith's article, "Death in the Ia Drang Valley," *Saturday Evening Post,* January 28, 1967, p. 81.

13. All comments and information from John Howard in this and later chapters: Howard's written statement, with maps, to Galloway, November 19, 1990; notes of multiple telephone conversations, Galloway/Howard, August–December 1991.

14. All quotations and information from then–Captain Shucart in this and subsequent chapters: transcript of an interview of Shucart by Galloway, November 1991.

15. All quotes, comments, and information from then–Captain George Forrest in this and later chapters: transcript of an interview of Forrest by Galloway, August 24, 1991.

16. All quotes from the Vietnamese generals: n. 5, ch. 1.

17. Slovak on the tracks and arrows: undated (December 1991) written statement from Donald J. Slovak to the authors.

18. All quotes, comments, and information from then–PFC James H. Shadden: letter to Moore, October 7, 1988; detailed seven-page letter to Moore,

November 17, 1988; Galloway discussion with Shadden at the August 1990 Ia Drang reunion; telephone conversations, Shadden/Moore/Galloway, fall 1991.

19. Then–Specialist 4 Bob Towles provided the authors with a detailed twenty-page account of his actions at LZ Albany, March 9, 1991; letter to Moore, March 21, 1991; multiple telephone discussions with Galloway, 1990–1991. All comments and information from Towles in this and subsequent chapters are from those sources.

20. Payne and the captured prisoners: With a cover letter of November 20, 1991, Pat Payne transmitted a detailed thirty-page account, with five sketch maps, of his recollections of the Albany battle. All quotes and comments in this and subsequent chapters attributed to Lt. Payne are from that account.

21. Captain Cash's recollections in this and subsequent chapters from transcript of taped discussion with Galloway on August 16, 1991, and multiple telephone discussions with Galloway, 1990–1992.

22. Casualty figures compiled and crosschecked from after-action reports of 2nd Battalion, 7th Cavalry, and 1st Cavalry Division. Also, Sergeant Cumberland's book of the dead, Army Adjutant-General's list of Vietnam dead.

19. Hell in a Very Small Place

1. All quotes and comments attributed to Specialist 4 Ackerman in this and later chapters: letters to *U.S. News & World Report,* November 25, 1990, and a December 27, 1990, letter to Galloway.

2. All attributions to Gooden in this and subsequent chapters: transcript of a Galloway interview of Gooden, August 17, 1991; multiple telephone discussions, Galloway/Gooden, in the latter part of 1991.

3. Then–PFC Jack Smith's account of the beginning of the fight at Albany and seeing his friends shot down: transcript of a speech by Smith, given at the Ia Drang reunion in Washington, D.C., November 1991. Material on Thorpe from n. 9, ch. 18, and a February 10, 1966, citation awarding Thorpe an Army Commendation Medal.

4. All quotes and information from David A. (Purp) Lavender in this and later chapters: letter to Moore, December 7, 1983; his completed questionnaire and the transcript of a statement recorded for Moore, spring 1984; transcript of Galloway's interview of Lavender, September 4, 1991.

5. All quotes and comments by James Young in this and subsequent chapters: transcript of a telephone interview of Young by Galloway, December 1991, during which time Young referred back to the pocket diary he kept after he was wounded for times and dates.

6. Tademy on himself and Brown at LZ Columbus and overflying Albany; also on Bartholomew and Price: n. 6, ch. 18.

7. Colonel Brown on his radio talks with McDade, the Westmoreland briefing, and reinforcements: n. 12, ch. 17.

8. Tademy and Cash on the radio conversations: n. 6, ch. 18 and n. 21, ch. 18, respectively.

9. McDade's view of the situation and his actions: n. 18, ch. 17.

10. Hemphill quotes in this and subsequent chapters: from transcript of August 21, 1991, telephone discussion with Galloway.

11. Knowles flies to Albany, talks to McDade: Moore telephone interviews of Knowles on May 5 and 6, 1992. Warrant officer reports 14 KIA to Knowles: corroborated by his letter to Moore cited in n. 21, ch. 7.

12. On the dispositions of the 2nd Battalion, 7th Cavalry at Albany and across the valley to the southeast; how the battle began and developed; and the resulting mêlée: These are the conclusions of the authors based on detailed study of all the accounts of the battle.

20. Death in the Tall Grass

1. Smith on what he saw all around him: n. 3, ch. 19.

2. Howard, Alley, Shucart, Shadden, Towles, Young, McDade, and Ackerman quotes and comments: See notes to in chapters 17, 18, and 19.

3. On the alerting of Myron Diduryk's company: Dillon, Moore, and three men of the 1/7 Battalion operations section had been listening to McDade's 2nd Battalion command frequency during the late morning and early afternoon of November 17 at Camp Holloway. Suddenly that radio went wild with the sound of explosions, small arms, and men shouting. We knew immediately that the 2nd Battalion, 7th Cav was in deep shit. The word for us to alert Diduryk's Bravo Company came at around four P.M. and was instantly relayed to him.

4. Wallenius's birthday: n. 2, ch. 10.

5. Rescorla: n. 19, ch. 17.

6. Although the 1st Cav Division after-action report and the 2nd Battalion, 5th Cav after-action report specify 6:25 P.M. as the time the reinforcements began landing, study of other reports and of comments by the aviators and the officers and men of Bravo 2/7 lead the authors to be more comfortable with the 6:45 P.M. time that we use here.

21. Escape and Evade

1. Howard: n. 13, ch. 18.

2. Alley: n. 14, ch. 17.

3. The story of James Young: See n. 5, ch. 19.

4. The saga of Toby Braveboy is covered briefly here from the following sources: article by Charlie Black in the *Columbus* (Ga.) *Ledger-Enquirer,* early

462 / Chapter Notes

December 1965; account in J. D. Coleman's *Pleiku;* letter to Moore, August 9, 1983, from Bob McMahon, who was in 2nd Brigade Headquarters when Braveboy was brought in; undated (December 1965) report of the 1st Squadron, 9th Cavalry on the rescue and its aftermath (this report states that within an hour of Braveboy's rescue, the North Vietnamese attempted unsuccessfully to lure another H-13 scout helicopter into an ambush by emulating the Braveboy circumstances; the scouts killed two North Vietnamese, and the rest ran for it). A letter dated July 12, 1991, from Dave Bray, former 1/9 pilot, to Moore provided details of the first sighting of Braveboy and how near he came to being shot by the H-13 observer; also, Joel Sugdinis, Braveboy's company commander (n. 8, ch. 18), details how he changed the Alpha Company 2/7 radio call sign to "Braveboy" after visiting Toby Braveboy in the hospital. Also, Galloway telephone discussions with members of the Braveboy family (his father and a sister-in-law) who still reside in Coward, S.C.

22. Night Without End

1. Lombardo and Jekel lose the chin bubble on their Huey: n. 2, ch. 8.
2. Stinnett: from Paul P. Winkel's "Table 11 and Enclosures" in his aviation studies of the exhaustively researched 257-page report compiled 1990–1991 to support Winkel's recommendation that 5 aviators of the 229th Assault Helicopter Battalion—Bruce P. Crandall, Ed W. Freeman, Jon R. Mills, Frank Moreno, and Leland Komich—be awarded, belatedly, the Medal of Honor for their heroic actions in the Ia Drang Valley, November 14–16, 1965. The authors and Winkel have copies. Also, Galloway's telephone interview of Stinnett, December 1991.
3. Diduryk: n. 11, ch. 11.
4. Rescorla: n. 19, ch. 17.
5. Gwin, Shadden, Payne: See Gwin, n. 12, ch. 13; Shadden, n. 18, ch. 18; Payne, n. 20, ch. 18.
6. Jack Smith lights a cigarette, even if it may get him killed: Smith's 1991 Veterans Day speech in Washington.
7. Shucart, n. 14, ch. 18; Pujals, n. 11, ch. 18; Forrest, n. 15, ch. 18; and Lavender: n. 4, ch. 19.
8. Sgt. Ibach isolated and eventually links up with battalion perimeter: undated written statement, Ibach to Galloway, December 1991.
9. Ainsworth: n. 3, ch. 18.
10. Stinnett and the landing under fire: n. 2, above.
11. Sugdinis, n. 8, ch. 18; Scott, n. 13, ch. 17; Gwin, n. 12, ch. 13; Ackerman, n. 1, ch. 19; Shucart, n. 14, ch. 18; Payne, n. 20, ch. 18; and Fesmire, n. 10, ch. 18.
12. Captured bugle: The inscription was taken by the authors directly from the bugle itself.

13. Tademy, n. 6, ch. 18; Tully, n. 1, ch. 18; Brown, n. 12, ch. 17; An, n. 5, ch. 1.

14. Wallenius and the dead: n. 2, ch. 10.

15. Shadden's ordeal ends: n. 18, ch. 18.

23. The Sergeant and the Ghost

1. Transcript of Galloway's interview of Fred J. Kluge, December 17, 1991.

2. Transcript of Galloway's interview of Robert J. Jeannette, December 18, 1991.

24. Mentioned in Dispatches

1. Knowles and the news conference: J. D. Coleman's *Pleiku;* Galloway, who was present at the conference. Also, Moore's telephone interviews with Knowles on May 5–6, 1992.

2. Entries from General Westmoreland's daily journal: "Memoirs, Gen. Westmoreland's History Notes 11/14–11/20/65 pp. 7–12 only" from Collection: "Papers of William C. Westmoreland." Folder Title: #2 History File 25 Oct–20 Dec 65, Lyndon B. Johnson Library. Also, daily schedule of events, November 14–20, 1965 (5 pages), "Papers of William C. Westmoreland," Box Seven: #2 History File, Document nos. 22 and 23, pp. 1–7. Lyndon B. Johnson Library.

3. Westmoreland visits the 1st Battalion at Holloway; the briefing; his talk to the troopers: Moore's personal recollections, verified by n. 2 above and by Galloway recollection. The matter of whether or not Chinese advisers were inside South Vietnam with the NVA regiments in late 1965 has never been answered to the satisfaction of Moore and Dillon.

4. General Johnson's message: quoted from a copy given Moore by Maj. Gen. Kinnard, and in Moore's collection.

5. Sugdinis, Rescorla: n. 8, ch. 18, and n. 19, ch. 17, respectively.

6. Move of 1st Battalion to Catecka: brigade and battalion after-action reports; Moore's personal recollection.

7. The 2nd Battalion, 7th Cavalry moves to LZ Crooks: 1st Cavalry Division and 2nd Battalion after-action reports.

8. Setelin: n. 5, ch. 10.

9. Friendly-fire tragedy at Catecka: Galen Bungum (n. 3, ch. 6); personal statements of Dillon, Herren, Plumley, and Whiteside, to Moore.

10. Some men leave Catecka—and the U.S. Army: Moore, Plumley, Warren Adams recollections.

11. Rescorla: n. 19, ch. 17.

12. The battalion leaves Catecka for An Khe: Moore and Plumley recollections and notes.

13. The 3rd Brigade turns over the Ia Drang operation to the 2nd Brigade, and the action of the ARVN Airborne Task Force: from 1st Cavalry Division after-action report; Samabria and Boyle, "The Lure and the Ambush."

14. General Schwarzkopf's recollection of the action along the Cambodian border: interview by Galloway in Riyadh, Saudi Arabia, January 1991.

15. Kinnard, Larsen, and Westmoreland on going into Cambodia: transcript of Galloway interview with Kinnard, September 19, 1990; transcript of Galloway interview with Larsen, September 19, 1990; transcript of Galloway interview with Westmoreland, September 1990.

16. Bundy's cable on ground rules for any cross-border actions in Cambodia: copy of four-page top-secret State Department cable from W. P. Bundy to the American embassy in Saigon, dated November 20, 1965, with copies to McNamara, Wheeler, McGeorge Bundy, and the secretary of state's office. Sanitized and declassified on September 17, 1991, at the authors' request. Approximately 1½ pages were blanked out in the "sanitization" process. National Security File, Country File Vietnam. Box 46. Lyndon B. Johnson Library, Austin, Tex.

17. Orders to cavalry commanders to keep quiet about NVA in Cambodia: Moore's personal recollection.

18. Rescorla, n. 19, ch. 17; Setelin, n. 5, ch. 10; Shucart, n. 14, ch. 18; Sugdinis, n. 8, ch. 18; Gwin, n. 12, ch. 13; McDade, n. 18, ch. 17; General An, n. 5, ch. 1.

19. Enemy weapons captured: 2nd Battalion, 7th Cavalry after-action report.

20. Setelin, n. 5, ch. 10; Tanner, n. 8, ch. 10; McDade, n. 18, ch. 17; Gwin, n. 12, ch. 13.

21. On Moore's promotion to colonel: He had been on the promotion list for over thirteen months. It was not a "battlefield promotion," as some media reports stated at the time.

22. The McNamara briefing: Moore's recollection, corroborated by Lt. Col. Ben Silver's history notes.

23. Charlie Hastings shot down: notes of conversation with Galloway in January 1992.

24. Forrest and his distress over the missing PFC Ackerman: n. 15, ch. 18.

25. Recovering the missing men's remains: Moore's recollection; also, page 6, 3rd Brigade after-action report on Operation Lincoln III, dated April 27, 1966.

25. "The Secretary of the Army regrets . . ."

1. Casualty totals: from battalion and division after-action reports.
2. Jemison, n. 8, ch. 1; Young, n. 5, ch. 19; Poley, n. 7, ch. 1.
3. Yellow Cab casualty notification: statements of surviving family members

who were thus notified. Drunk taxi driver: statement of Sara Elliott to Galloway at August 1990 Ia Drang reunion at Fort Benning.

4. Betty Jivens Mapson: letter to Galloway, November 28, 1990.

5. Julie Moore on the taxis and the funerals and on visiting the families: transcript of her tape-recorded statement of November 28, 1991.

6. Kornelia Scott: written statement provided to the authors, October 1991.

7. The remarkable story of Barbara Geoghegan Johns emerges in her own words in a series of typed single-spaced recollections to Galloway totaling more than ten pages, plus cover letters, dated between April 1991 and October 1991. Enclosures include the "before" and "after" copies of Lt. Geoghegan's death certificate; a copy of the elder Mrs. Geoghegan's September 24, 1965, letter to her son in Vietnam; a copy of the letter to the people of Pelham written by the elder Mrs. Geoghegan and published on January 13, 1966, in *The Pelham Sun;* and copies of Geoghegan's obituary in *The Dome* (the newspaper of Pennsylvania Military College), December 2, 1965, and in *The Catholic News* of New York, N.Y., December 9, 1965.

8. No less moving is the story told by Betty Jivens Mapson in two lengthy handwritten statements to Galloway dated November 28, 1990, and December 2, 1991. Also her enclosures of copies of letters September–October, 1965, from Sgt. Jerry Jivens, copies of newspaper clippings, and a telegram from the Army providing details of how Sgt. Jivens's body would be shipped home and details of how the family would be entitled to a burial allowance of between $75 and $200, depending on whether burial was in a national cemetery or a private one. Also multiple telephone discussions between Galloway and Mrs. Mapson between November 1990 and January 1992.

9. Catherine Metsker McCray: The story of her marriage to Captain Metsker and the impact of his death in combat is told in a handwritten statement to Galloway, November 16, 1991.

10. Karen Metsker Rudel: Her story of growing up without a father comes directly from a detailed typed, single-spaced statement provided at Galloway's request. Also, multiple telephone conversations with the authors, and a memorable personal meeting with Mrs. Rudel at the 1990 Ia Drang reunion in Washington, D.C.

11. Edward D. Monsewicz: His story of his father covers three typed pages, provided through the kind assistance of CSM James Scott (ret.).

26. Reflections and Perceptions

1. McNamara's "long war" prediction to the reporters in Saigon: Stanley Karnow, *Vietnam: A History,* p. 480.

2. McNamara's assessment of the Vietnam situation and recommendations to the President: from a declassified "Memorandum for the President," November 30, 1965. Collection National Security Country File, Vietnam. Con-

tainer No. 75. Folder Title 2EE. Lyndon B. Johnson Library, Austin, Tex. Declassified January 31, 1985.

3. The more detailed memo: "Memorandum for the President dated 6 December 1965, Subject: Military and Political actions recommended for South Vietnam." National Security Country File, Vietnam. 2E, Box 75. Lyndon B. Johnson Library, Austin, Tex. Declassified January 31, 1985.

4. The mid-December meeting: Karnow's coverage of this December 17–18, 1965, White House meeting is on pp. 481–82, and discusses McNamara's arguments and the concurrence of Rusk, Ball, and McGeorge Bundy. Will Bundy's comment on McNamara's option number one: transcript of telephone interview by Galloway, fall 1990. See also: ch. 33, pp. 7–14, Will Bundy's unpublished manuscript on the Vietnam decisions, in the Historical Office of the Department of State and the JFK and LBJ libraries for a more detailed discussion of the decision-making climate in December 1965, in the wake of the Ia Drang battles.

5. Kinnard on pursuit of the enemy into Cambodia: transcript of telephone interview by Galloway, September 19, 1990.

6. Will Bundy's comments on hot pursuit of enemy into Cambodia: See n. 16, ch. 24, also n. 4, above.

7. American casualties: 3rd Brigade after-action report. The Kys' visit: They were such a bizarre duo, in their matching black jump suits and purple silk scarves, that Moore never forget them. On the enemy return to the Bong Son within one week: intelligence reports of that time. The 3rd Brigade was ordered back in April for a "show of force" dubbed Operation Bee Bee. In early May, 3rd Brigade and ARVN units carried out Operation Davy Crockett in the Bong Son, destroying the 9th Battalion of the People's Army's Quyet Tam Regiment. This is when SFC Glenn Kennedy, a Charlie Company veteran of LZ X-Ray, lost his life in combat. Also of interest: When the 1st Cav Div left Bong Son in early 1968, the 173rd Airborne moved in, and remained there until at least early in 1969.

SELECTED BIBLIOGRAPHY

The most useful and most used historical documents in our research were:

1. The December 9, 1965, after-action report of the 1st Battalion, 7th Cavalry's battle at LZ X-Ray, November 14–16, 1965.

2. The March 4, 1966, after-action report of the 1st Cavalry Division (Airmobile) operations in the Pleiku campaign, October 23–November 26, 1965.

3. The November 24, 1965, after-action report of the 2nd Battalion, 7th Cavalry operations of November 12–21, 1965.

4. The December 4, 1965, after-action report of the 3rd Brigade, 1st Cavalry Division operations in Pleiku province, November 1965.

5. The operations journals of the 1st Cavalry Division (Airmobile) Tactical Operations Center at An Khe, covering the period from 12:01 A.M., November 14, 1965, through 12 P.M., November 18, 1965.

Why Plei Me?, published in Pleiku, August 1966, by the South Vietnamese II Corps Commander, Major General Vinh Loc, contains a wealth of information, derived from captured enemy documents and prisoner interrogations, on the People's Army units in the Plei Me–Ia Drang campaign. It also includes the translation of "Characteristics of the 1st U.S. Air Cavalry Division," the North Vietnamese after-action report written by then–Colonel Hoang Phuong. The Vinh Loc book also reprints a People's Army map, captured in August 1966, which shows in great detail the locations of North Vietnamese units in Cambodia.

William P. Boyle and Robert Samabria's "The Lure and the Ambush" is an unpublished article-length U.S. military monograph written in Vietnam and dated December 1965. It covers the departures of the People's Army's major units of the B-3 Front from North Vietnam and their arrival in South Vietnam, details the strengths of various units and their casualties, and emphasizes the enemy actions. What makes the document a treasure trove for the researcher is extensive quotation from intelligence documents and captured enemy documents and diaries. It also focuses on interrogation reports and "knowledgeability briefs" concerning 35 North Vietnamese prisoners—officers, NCOs, and line soldiers—most of whom were captured by the 1st Cavalry Division (Airmobile) during October and November 1965.

In the matter of dates of death, homes of record, birthdates, and, in some cases, places of death, three books, one document, and eyewitness accounts were all utilized. The basic reference was the Casualty Information System, 1961–1981 (machine-readable record), Records of the Adjutant General's Office, Record Group 407, National Archives Building. Next, the book *Vietnam Veterans Memorial: Directory of Names,* published by the Vietnam Veterans Memorial Fund, Inc., Washington, D.C. (May 1991), was most helpful in cross-checking ranks, birth and death dates, and homes of record. The second book was constructed over several years as a labor of love by the late Sergeant First Class James D. Cumberland, a veteran of the Pleiku campaign. This three-ring, 1¼-inch-thick book of names of 1st Cavalry Division troops killed in Vietnam from August 1965 to March 1967 breaks the casualties down by company and battalion and includes place and date of death, date of birth, home of record, and location of the name on the Wall. The third book, Edward Hymoff's *The First Air Cavalry Division,* (New York: M. W. Lads Publishing Co., 1967) covers the creation, deployment, and operations of the division through 1966. It provides lists of both killed and wounded by unit and date, as well as lists of awards of valor.

Other Books and Articles

Albright, John, John A. Cash, and Allan W. Sandstrum. *Seven Firefights in Vietnam.* Washington, D.C.: U.S. Army Office of the Chief of Military History, 1970.

Beckwith, Col. Charlie A. (ret.), and Donald Knox. *Delta Force.* New York: Harcourt Brace Jovanovich, 1983. Includes a section on the siege at Plei Me camp, October 1965.

Bowman, John S., ed. *The World Almanac of the Vietnam War.* New York: Bison Books, 1985.

Brelis, Dean, and Jill Krementz. *The Face of South Vietnam.* Boston: Houghton Mifflin, 1968.

Brennan, Matthew. *Headhunters: Stories from the 1st Squadron, 9th Cavalry, in Vietnam 1965–1971.* Novato, Calif.: Presidio Press, 1987.

Busey, John W., and David G. Martin. *Regimental Strengths and Losses at Gettysburg.* Hightstown, N.J.: Longstreet House, 1986.

"Cincinnatus." *Self-Destruction: The Disintegration and Decay of the U.S.*

Army During the Vietnam Era. Toronto: George J. McLeod Ltd., 1981.

Clodfelter, Mark. *The Limits of Air Power: The American Bombing of North Vietnam*. New York: The Free Press, 1989.

Cochran, Alexander S., Jr. "First Strike at River Drang." In *Military History*, October 1984.

Coleman, J. D. *Pleiku: The Dawn of Helicopter Warfare in Vietnam*. New York: St. Martin's Press, 1988. Coleman wrote the 1st Cavalry Division after-action report on Pleiku province. His book is based on that report, personal memories, and other sources.

————, ed. *The First Air Cavalry Division, Vietnam. Volume 1: 1965–1969*. Tokyo: Dai Nippon Printing Company, 1970.

Davidson, Phillip B. *Vietnam at War: The History 1946–1975*. Novato, Calif.: Presidio Press, 1988.

Dunn, Si. *The 1st Cavalry Division: A Historical Overview: 1921–1983*. Dallas: Taylor Publishing Co., 1984.

Edwards, Robert H. "Battle at LZ-X-Ray: Personal Experience of a Company Commander." This unpublished monograph of forty-two pages plus seven sketch maps, dated February 6, 1967, covers Edwards's memories of the battle and was written as a course requirement for the Infantry Officer Career Course No. 1-67, Infantry School, Fort Benning, Georgia. It was helpful for quotations and establishing accuracy, and for an appendix that details the organization and unit strength of an infantry battalion of the 1st Cavalry Division in 1965.

Ellis, Chris. *A History of Combat Aircraft*. London: Hamlyn Publishing Group, 1979.

Fall, Bernard B. *Street Without Joy*. New York: Schocken Books, 1961.

————. *The Two Viet-Nams*. New York: Praeger, 1963.

"Field Manual 100-5. Operations." Department of the Army. May 1986. U.S. Government Printing Office, Washington, D.C. Referred to for accuracy of military definitions.

Giap, Vo Nguyen. *Big Victory, Great Task*. New York: Praeger, 1968.

Griffith, Samuel B. *Sun Tzu: The Art of War*. London: Oxford University Press, 1963.

Hackworth, Colonel David H. (ret.), and Julie Sherman. *About Face: The Odyssey of an American Warrior*. New York: Simon & Schuster, 1989.

Halberstam, David. *The Best and the Brightest*. New York: Random House, 1969.

————. *The Making of a Quagmire*. New York: Random House, 1965.

Headquarters 2nd Battalion, 5th Cavalry After-Action Report Operation Silver Bayonet, November 11–26, 1965, dated December 5, 1965.

Headquarters 1st Battalion, 7th Cavalry After-Action Report Operations Lincoln and Mosby, March 31–April 16, 1966, dated April 19, 1966.

Headquarters 2nd Battalion, 7th Cavalry After-Action Report Operation Lincoln III Search and Destroy, March 30–April 8, 1966, dated April 22, 1966.

Headquarters 3rd Brigade, 1st Cavalry Division After-Action Report, March 31–April 15, 1966, dated April 27, 1966.

Heller, Charles E., and William A. Stofft, eds. *America's First Battles: 1776–1965.* Lawrence, Ks.: University of Kansas Press, 1986. Includes an article by George C. Herring on the Ia Drang battles.

Hilsman, Roger. *To Make a Nation.* New York: Doubleday, 1967.

Johnson, Lt. Col. Richard S. *How to Locate Anyone Who Is or Has Been in the Military.* Fort Sam Houston, Tex.: Military Information Enterprises, 1991.

Karnow, Stanley. *Vietnam: A History: The First Complete Account of the Vietnam War.* New York: Viking, 1983.

Kinnard, Douglas. *The War Managers.* Hanover, N.H.: University Press of New England, 1977.

Kinnard, Harry W. O. "Triumph of a Concept." *Army* magazine, October 1967.

———. "Airmobility Revisited." *U.S. Army Aviation Digest* (two-part series), June 1980, pp. 1–5, 26, 27; July 1980, pp. 8–14.

———. "Army Helicopters: Why?" *Armed Forces Journal,* May 1982, pp. 58–61, 98.

Knightley, Phillip. *The First Casualty.* New York: Harvest Books, 1975.

Krepinevich, Andrew F., Jr. *The Army and Vietnam.* Baltimore: Johns Hopkins University Press, 1986.

Laird, Jerry P. "The Training, Infiltration and Operations of a North Vietnamese Soldier from 12 April 1963–11 June 1966 in North Vietnam, South Vietnam and Laos (Based on a Personal Interview by a Battalion Civil Affairs Officer)." Unpublished monograph, 1968. Written for Advance Course Class 1968-1, on file in the Infantry School Library, Fort Benning, Ga.

Lewis, Norman. *A Dragon Apparent: Travels in Cambodia, Laos and Vietnam.* London: Jonathan Cape, 1951.

Mesko, Jim. *Airmobile: The Helicopter War in Vietnam.* Carrollton, Tex.: Squadron/Signal Publications, Inc., 1984.

Palmer, Dave Richard. *Summons of the Trumpet: U.S.-Vietnam in Perspective.* Novato, Calif.: Presidio Press, 1978.

Patti, Archimedes L. *Why Viet Nam? Prelude to America's Albatross.* Berkeley: University of California Press, 1980.

Pike, Douglas. *PAVN: People's Army of Vietnam.* Novato, Calif.: Presidio Press, 1986.

Pimlott, John. *Vietnam: The Decisive Battles.* New York: Macmillan, 1990.

Porter, Captain Melvin F. "PROJECT CHECO REPORT 'SILVER BAYO-

NET.' " Simpson Library, Air War College, Maxwell Air Base, Alabama. A declassified U.S. Air Force report, dated February 28, 1966, which covers air support activities in the Ia Drang Valley battles through 5:10 P.M., November 28, 1965.

Prashker, Ivan. *Duty, Honor, Vietnam: Twelve Men of West Point Tell Their Stories.* New York: William Morrow and Company, 1988. Includes a section on Ramon A. (Tony) Nadal, class of 1958.

Register of Graduates and Former Cadets 1802–1990 U.S. Military Academy. West Point, N.Y.: Association of Graduates, U.S.M.A., 1990.

Sheehan, Neil. *A Bright Shining Lie: John Paul Vann and America in Vietnam.* New York: Random House, 1988.

Shulimson, Jack, and Maj. Charles M. Johnson. *U.S. Marines in Vietnam: The Landing and the Buildup, 1965.* Washington, D.C.: History and Museums Division, Headquarters USMC, 1979.

Smith, Jack P. "Death in the Ia Drang Valley." *Saturday Evening Post,* January 28, 1967.

Spector, Ronald H. *Advice and Support: The Early Years: The U.S. Army in Vietnam.* Washington, D.C.: U.S. Government Printing Office, 1983.

Stanton, Shelby L. *Anatomy of a Division: 1st Cav in Vietnam.* Novato, Calif.: Presidio Press, 1987.

———. *The Rise and Fall of an American Army: U.S. Ground Forces in Vietnam, 1965–1973.* Novato, Calif.: Presidio Press, 1985.

Summers, Col. Harry. *A Critical Analysis of the Vietnam War.* Novato, Calif.: Presidio Press, 1982.

———. "The Bitter Triumph of Ia Drang." *American Heritage,* February/March 1984, pp. 51–58.

Sutherland, Lt. Col. Ian D. W. (ret.). *Special Forces of the United States Army 1952/1982.* San Jose, Calif.: R. James Bender Publishing Company, 1990.

Tolson, John J. "Vietnam Studies: Airmobility 1961–1971." Washington, D.C.: U.S. Government Printing Office, 1973.

Triplett, William. "Chaos in the Ia Drang." *Veteran* magazine, vol. 6, no. 10 (October 1986).

Tully, Major Walter B., Jr. "Company B." *Armor* magazine, September–October 1967. Tully, a veteran of the fight at Albany and the attack on LZ Columbus, sets forth his account of the battles.

Westmoreland, General William C. *A Soldier Reports.* Garden City, N.Y.: Doubleday, 1976.

Williams, Colonel Clinton L. "The Ia Drang Valley Campaign: The Army's First Battle in Vietnam." A thirty-nine-page paper submitted to the Naval War College, Newport, Rhode Island, on June 16, 1989, as part of course requirements.

ABOUT THE AUTHORS

HAROLD G. MOORE was born in Kentucky and is a West Point graduate, a master parachutist, and an Army aviator. He commanded two infantry companies in the Korean War and was a battalion and brigade commander in Vietnam. He retired from the Army in 1977 with thirty-two years' service and then was executive vice president of a Colorado ski resort for four years before founding a computer software company. An avid outdoorsman, Moore and his wife, Julie, divide their time between homes in Auburn, Alabama, and Crested Butte, Colorado.

JOSEPH L. GALLOWAY is a native Texan. At seventeen he was a reporter on a daily newspaper, at nineteen a bureau chief for United Press International. He spent fifteen years as a foreign and war correspondent based in Japan, Vietnam, Indonesia, India, Singapore, and the Soviet Union. Now a senior writer with *U.S. News & World Report*, he covered the Gulf War and coauthored *Triumph Without Victory: The Unreported History of the Persian Gulf War*. Galloway lives with his wife, Theresa, and sons, Lee and Joshua, on a farm in northern Virginia.